H

ır

# BEWARE the DRAGON

*For Maxime Alexandre William*
*without dragons*

First published in Great Britain in 2008 by

André Deutsch
an imprint of the
Carlton Publishing Group
20 Mortimer Street
London W1T 3JW

2 4 6 8 10 9 7 5 3 1

ISBN 978-0-233-00231-6

Typeset by e-type, Liverpool
Printed and bound in Great Britain by Mackays

*If you have never done anything evil, you should not be worrying about devils knocking at your door.*

Attributed to Kung Fu-tse (Confucius) (551–479 BC)

WE, BY THE GRACE AND DECREE OF HEAVEN, EMPEROR OF GREAT CHINA, KING OF THE CENTRE OF THE UNIVERSE, have pondered that from ancient time even the princes of small states have striven to cultivate friendly intercourse with those of adjoining territories. The princes, and their people, feeling grateful toward US, have visited OUR country, and while the relationship between US and them is that of Lord and vassal, its nature is as felicitous as that of a parent and child. Of this, no doubt, you are well aware. WE beg that thereafter you will establish friendly relations with US. Is it reasonable to refuse intercourse with each other? If not, it will lead to war, and who is there who likes such a state of things?

This threatening message from 1280, dispatched by the Chinese court to the Emperor of Japan, who failed to bend to the will of the greatest ruler of the Golden Age of China, Kublai Khan, was recorded for history by the first war correspondent of modern times, the Venetian explorer Marco Polo.

In ancient archives death takes on a meaning it often lacks in everyday life. With China down the centuries, the reason is obvious: death is on a scale massive beyond belief and is not mythology. The good and evil deeds of conquerors, the words uttered by kings, have been recorded by scribes for eternity and lie buried in archives, covered by centuries of dust. Those pages speak to us of war and conflict, in tones morally unambiguous and ultimately ennobling. I simply try to make others see what the ancients saw, and tell what they spoke. In this drama of the gigantic and mysterious Dragon, the result of years of research, omissions and mistakes are mine. But the voice is theirs.

The publishers would like to thank the following sources for their kind permission to reproduce the pictures in this book:

Page 1: Felice Beato/Getty Images

Page 2: *top* Underwood & Underwood/Corbis; *bottom* Michael Nicholson/Corbis

Page 3: *top* Ullstein Bild/Photo12.com; *bottom* Ullstein Bild/Photo12.com

Page 4: *top* Corbis; *bottom* Hulton Archive/Getty Images

Page 5: *top* Bettmann/Corbis; *bottom* Keystone/Getty Images

Page 6: *top* AP/PA Photos; *bottom* AP/PA Photos

Page 7: AP/PA Photos

Page 8: *top* Baldwin H. Ward & Kathryn C. Ward/Corbis; *bottom* AFP/Getty Images

Page 9: *top* Bibliothèque Nationale, Paris/Archives Charmet/The Bridgeman Art Library; *bottom* Xinhua/Photo12.com

Page 10: *top* Keystone/Getty Images; *bottom* Bettmann/Corbis

Page 11: *top* Hulton-Deutsch Collection/Corbis; *bottom* The Image Works/Topfoto.co.uk

Page 12: *top* private collection/The Bridgeman Art Library; *bottom* from the author's collection

Page 13: *top* private collection/Archives Charmet/The Bridgeman Art Library; *bottom* AFP/Getty Images

Page 14: Bettmann/Corbis

Page 15: *top* AP/PA Photo; *bottom* CNN/Getty Images

Page 16: *top* Eric Draper/AP/PA Photo; *bottom left* DOD/Newsmakers/Getty Images; *bottom right* Xinhua/AP/PA Photos

Every effort has been made to acknowledge correctly and contact the source and/or copyright-holder of each picture, and Carlton Books Limited apologizes for any unintentional errors or omissions, which will be corrected in future editions of this book.

# CONTENTS

# TIMELINE

1215 Genghis Khan's horde captures Peking (Beijing) and destroys Chin Empire.

1218 Otrar massacre of Tartar traders. Mongols cross China's border and invade Khwarezmian Empire.

1222 Pursuit of deposed Emperor Muhammad Shah leads Djepe's Mongols into Russia.

1223 Voivod of Kiev orders murder of Mongol ambassadors. Subotai defeats Russians at River Kalka.

1241 Battles of Liegnitz and River Sajo: Mongols annihilate knights' armies.

1242 Death of *Khakhan* Ogedei. Mongol hordes abandon advance and return to Karakorum.

1256 Hulagu Khan invades Mesopotamia and exterminates the Assassins (*Hachchâchin*) Sect.

1258 Hulagu Khan captures Baghdad; bloodbath ends five-hundred-year Abbasid Islamic Caliphate.

1260 Mameluke military leader Baibars defeats Hulagu Khan's horde under Kitboga near Nazareth, Palestine.

1281 Emperor Kublai Khan's invasion fleet struck by typhoon off Japan.

1347 Great Plague, imported from southern China, decimates Europe.

1405 Ming Admiral Cheng-ho sets out with Dragon Fleet on maritime explorations.

1517 Portuguese open way around Cape of Good Hope, make landfall in China and settle in Macao.

1552 Roman Catholic missionary St Francis Xavier dies on Xiang-gang island (Hong Kong).

1603 Spanish expel Chinese from the Philippines.

1637 First English vessel, the East India Company's *Macclesfield*, enters Guangzhou (Canton).

1839 Lin Zexu, Imperial Commissioner of Guangzhou, orders destruction of imported opium chests.

1841 First Opium War: Royal Navy smashes Chuengpee Fort and enters Guangzhou.

1842 Battle of Ningbo: British artillery crushes Chinese army of General I-ching.

1843 Hung Hsiu-chuan has religious vision and launches Taiping Movement.

1853 Taiping forces move along Yangtze Valley, capture Nanjing and establish dual empire.

1864 Major Charles Gordon ("Chinese Gordon") leads Ever-Victorious Army and fall of Nanjing ends Taiping Rebellion.

1885 Siege of Tuyen-Quang, French Foreign Legion's epic stand in Tonkin.

1894 Battle of River Yalu: Japanese navy sinks Chinese fleet and defeat leads to Chinese Empire's collapse.

1898 The Unequal Treaties and Great Land Grab. Great Britain obtains Hong Kong on 99-year lease.

1900 Boxer Rebellion: 55-day siege of foreign legations in Beijing.

1911 Chinese Revolution: troops riot in Wuhan and rebellion spreads throughout China.

1912 Sun Yat-sen proclaims First Republic of China.

1927 Chiang Kai-shek, leader of the Guomindang (Kuomintang), the National People's Party, establishes his capital in Nanjing.

1934 Mao Zedong's Long March begins. Battle of Luding Bridge.

1937 Marco Polo Bridge Incident. Japanese invade China. Rape of Nanjing.

1937 American gunboat USS *Panay* sunk by Japanese planes and war narrowly avoided.

1942 Second World War in Pacific. US General Joseph Stilwell's Battle for Burma Road.

1946 Civil War between Chiang Kai-shek's Nationalists and Mao's Communists.

1947 Battle of Harbin. US General George Marshall's failed China Mission.

1949 Mao's Communists victorious and Nationalists flee to Taiwan. Battle of Quemoy.

1950 Chinese invade Tibet, carrying out genocide and repression.

1950 Stalin defaults on promised support. Chinese cross River Yalu and enter Korean War.

1958 Mao's Great Leap Forward. Second Battle of Quemoy. US plans nuclear strikes on Chinese cities.

1964 China explodes its first nuclear device.

1969 Amur–Ussuri border clash; Soviet Union threatens to destroy China's nuclear facilities.

1972 Kissinger coup opens way for President Nixon's groundbreaking tour to China.

1989 Tiananmen Square student protest is crushed by Chinese troops and an unknown number of protesters are killed.

1997 Britain returns Hong Kong to Chinese rule.

2001 Mid-air collision between Chinese jet fighter and American spy plane.

2003 China launches its first astronaut into orbit.

Note: Geographic locations and proper names are mainly given in their modern Chinese spelling: e.g. Beijing for Peking, Guangzhou for Canton, Guomindang for Kuomintang, Mao Zedong for Mao Tse-tung, Nanjing for Nanking. Italicized emphasis in quoted material is the author's.

# PROLOGUE

# HEAVEN'S CHOICE

*Never has it been the lot of man, nor ever will it be, to avoid disaster.*
*Only Heaven is enthroned, ever steadfast, above all earthly strivings.*[1]

Throughout history, cause and effect are hard to separate and the occasions of sheer coincidence have vague boundaries. It is often a trivial hinge that turns history; one that is banal, unexpected and yet crucial. When fortune turns her giddy wheel ... The Chinese call it "Heaven's Choice".

On 18 August 1969 our world was 4.5 million years old and we had had the atomic bomb for exactly 24 years. The world was at the dawn of an era in which an extreme socialist order, undeterred by calculations of prudence, was wielding the big nuclear stick. It forecast a future of destruction on a scale never seen before. That day, in a secret meeting, a top-ranking Soviet intelligence officer demanded of his American counterpart: "How would the US react if the Soviet Union destroyed China's nuclear installations?"

What makes this incident so different from any other confrontation in the eight-hundred-year history of bloody strife between East and West is a permanent presence of the unimaginable – nuclear holocaust. Our world would never find out how close it came to ruin. Because, with one blood-curdling phrase, China's Mao Zedong had left no doubt about the heritage he was willing to bequeath to humanity:[2] "For the sake of the achievement of a specific political goal, it is possible to sacrifice half mankind."

A Red Emperor was ready to execute Heaven's Choice: Sacrifice Mankind!

"Oh, East is East, and West is West, and never the twain shall meet," wrote Rudyard Kipling in *The Ballad of East and West*. Not only *did* the twain meet, but much blood was spilled.

On the morning of 9 April 1241 a horde of riders came thundering from the East and shattered the steely might of German knights on the edges of western Europe. In the early hours of 24 November 1950 a mass of Chinese soldiers smashed into the army of the United Nations along a river line in Korea. Between these two events lie 709 years of near-uninter-rupted bloodshed.

The collisions between the "Kingdom of the Middle" and the rest of the world are among the most vexing challenges of time – a story of massive confrontations involving thousands and often millions. This is a saga of mayhem and confusion, blunders and mistakes that brought credit to none of the belligerents; a series of incredibly brutal and sanguinary conflicts, carpeted with millions of victims. China fascinates, as it frightens. At war China frightens even more – the never-ending tale of a man-devouring dragon feeding on the blood of treacheries and massacres. Everything about China is outsized. From its towering mountain peaks, megalithic cities and immense populations, to its famines, epidemics and conflicts, conducted with callousness, bloodlust and barbarism which produced casualty figures bordering on the unimaginable. We speak of our World Wars as "the greatest wars ever" and talk of deaths in the millions; histori-cally, the Chinese have multiplied such numbers by tens of times.

The rise of China, from its origins as the huge landmass of dispersed villages and nomadic tribes to an empire which unified the Asian world and a great deal beside it, is the story of a great and powerful people. China always was – as it still is today – the Kingdom of the Middle, ruled by a mighty emperor on the Dragon Throne. Emperors changed, but the system endured. To keep it that way, the first Chinese emperor put up the world's most monumental bulwark to isolation: the Great Wall, a gigantic undertaking which took them a mere 10 years to build and shows what this industrious giant is capable of. [3] The world's first Iron Curtain – made of bricks and cemented with the bones of its million workers – served to keep out foreign intruders and their alien and debilitating cultural influence.

China was not always closed in on itself, and when it campaigned beyond its borders it proved exceptional in aggressiveness and aptitude for combat. The memory of this might, which kept periodically colliding with other civilizations, has haunted nations around the globe. It was only during periods when China's internal safeguards broke down, and could no longer restrain venal mandarins from looting the lands, that invader armies marched into China in pursuit of their own aggrandizement – only to become swallowed up by the country's vastness and assimilated to its culture.

Ancient China remains the greatest civilization in the history of mankind, an empire that lasted longer than Rome and produced more philosophers than Greece. Every Chinese carries in him the pride of his cultural heritage. "My ancestors interpreted the celestial universe while yours were still living in caves," a Chinese once told me.

China shows us many façades; it speaks to us in a thousand dialects, sings of a thousand cultures and has a thousand enigmas to decipher. It has left us myths that call up the mighty dead – and what an amazing wealth of heroes and villains from which to choose, all with the power of decision over a vast human arsenal. But which have had the greater impact on world history – the heroes or the villains? Those that provided lasting inspiration or those that conquered and destroyed? It is the action by an individual which will lead a nation to greatness, or to disaster. In war it is as much an individual's skill as the kind of a chancy incident, unimportant in isolation, but disastrous when in collision with other forces, which determines the outcome and decides history. A man's upbringing, his social environment, a personal trauma, is all it takes that sets a nation's fate, and often that of all of mankind. China's rulers, from tribal chieftain to revolutionary dictator, are a case in point. Long before the West's epic poem of valour, the *Iliad*, many written tales of bravery and sacrifice marred by cruelty and horror were common fare on the "other side of the world". And just as the victory by a few Greeks changed the course of Western history, so did a fire-breathing Chinese dragon write pages in blood in the world's chronicle.

Nations, empires, civilizations and cultures – all have their glorious season in history. Nothing is permanent; what once was great is small today. Each civilization held, if for a short time, its dominant position. Only China held it longer.

We are directly, sometimes painfully, concerned about events that took place long before we were born. Amid today's silence the distant roar draws ever closer, like the mighty horde that once came thundering out of the East.

# ACT ONE

---

## 1218–1348

## Thunder from the East

*Behold a pale horse: And his name that*
*sat on him was Death*

—Jude 6:8

# 1

# A WOLF'S RAGE

"War!" swore the man they respectfully called the Great Wolf.
"War! War! War!" echoed the countless thousands, gathered on their horses around him. "Vengeance! We shall ride for you, Great Khan, and blood will flow to cleanse us of this shame."

The course for a collision between East and West was set by one of history's relatively minor incidents, and by a man who defeated more armies than Caesar or Napoleon, conquered more territory than Hannibal or Alexander and caused more people to die than Attila and Hitler combined, in a thunder that came roaring from the East.

A mighty horde was set to conquer the world. No warrior had ever set in motion forces more powerful and destructive, sweeping across Asia, the Middle East and Europe, as the apocalyptic horsemen of Temujin, or, under the name by which he became known and which still evokes demoniacal destruction and brutal terror, Genghis Khan.[1]

History amply demonstrates that a handful of individuals with strong ideas and the determination to carry them out have an outsized impact on the rest of us. These are the men and women who give hope and direction to the world – or who turn it upside down. From the region where the icy wind sweeps from Siberia across Lake Baikal, whipping the arid plateau of the Orkhon and Khangaï, came such a man destined to rewrite the history of the world. He was a Mongol, and Mongols are not Chinese. But neither were the Manchus, nor any of the strongmen of many races who emerged from the four corners of this landmass to shape its destiny.

This boy killed his first man at the age of 12 and established a world empire at 30. He left his name to history as the symbol of callousness and atrocity, as merciless conqueror and "Scourge of God", a despot who used devastation as the basis to carve out his cosmic empire. He used carnage to rid himself of tribes, then eliminated entire nations that had the ill fortune to stand in his way. With the wave of his hand he condemned thousands to instant death. Driven as he was by an insatiable will for domination, the mere mention of his name brought terror. He never spared an enemy, never took a prisoner and left bleached pyramids of skulls as his lasting monument. Millions died in vain trying to stop him. His senior commanders outshone anyone that East or West could put against them. In a series of brilliantly executed campaigns his taste for conquest shook the world to its foundations and led to the subjugation of civilizations. A byword for callousness and atrocity, this merciless conqueror and despot used carnage and devastation to carve out his massive kingdom.

In 35 years he, along with his sons and grandsons, founded an empire that extended from the Pacific Ocean to the Danube, and decided the fate of a major portion of the world's population.[2] When he died he bequeathed the biggest, most cruel empire that ever spanned the globe to his equally pitiless descendants.

It is not rare for men of strong personality, destined to leave their mark on history, to lead an unhappy childhood, and young Temujin was no exception. When the boy was nine – he was born in 1162 or 1167 near Dolumboldag on the River Onon, which formed the border between Mongolia and Russia – his father Yesugei, clan chief of the Qiyat of the nomadic Bordjijin tribe, died in his wife's arms, poisoned by a clansman from his Tartar tribe. Never would Temujin forget this traumatic experience, watching his father's body bend like a bow, with foam bubbling from his mouth, to expire in great agony. This vile deed by a murderous gang profoundly shaped the boy's outlook on life and provided him with the justification for pitiless terror.

Hoelun, Temujin's mother, was expelled from the clan to suffer the fate of an outcast. For years she and her teenage sons wandered the steppes. Lacking a yurt for shelter, they suffered the cold nights of the high plateau, and in caves sought refuge from the icy wind blasting Inner Asia, sleeping huddled up against the bellies of their two horses. Temujin, as first-born, became the provider; the family subsisted on field mice, roots, berries, their mare's milk and the occasional bird shot by the boy with his arrows. It was around this time that Temujin began to show signs of a ferocious temper. He was 12 when he got into a fight with his half-brother over a grouse, and Temujin shot Bekter as one shoots at a target, and then walked off.

Then followed the incident which changed not only the boy's life, but those of millions. One night after dark three men rode up to the family's campfire; one, with his left eye torn away by a sword cut, stared at Temujin with his good eye and then struck him hard with his horsewhip. Temujin fell with his face to the earth; when he regained consciousness he found his mother shamefully exposed, her eyes burning with pain and shame. The robbers made three mistakes: they shamed the family; stole their two horses; and left Temujin alive.

The boy had no time for tears, only for vengeance. It steeled his heart; from a boy hunter he grew into an adult avenger. For him the prospect of death held no fears. For months he practised with his father's bow to strengthen his shoulder muscles, until he could strike a moving target at three hundred paces. One day Temujin was gone; months later he came back, riding on the family's two horses – and in a bag he carried three heads.

He was now 15, short, stocky, his face stern, with lips tight, and across his right cheek a deep scar, but most noticeable were his eyes – cold and without pity. There was one more blood deed that called for revenge: his father's murder. When the sun stood high he galloped into the camp of his father's clan. Hanging sideways on his horse, he let fly an arrow which pierced the throat of his father's assassin. Before others had time to recover from their shock, he whipped around, and on the next passage struck down two more of the murderous gang. The killing was over in seconds. Three men lay in the dust, two dead and one groaning; the avenger jumped from his horse and cut the man's throat. He felt no pleasure, only a realization that this was but the beginning. There would be more, many more.

The dispatch of those three brutal men came as a relief to the clan, and Temujin's prowess so impressed the elders that they voted him their new chieftain. By taking a girl from another clan as his wife – Börte would present him with four sons, Djudji, Jagatai, Ogedei and Tului – he united two clans. That was only the beginning. The rest is the recorded legend of Genghis Khan.

He began by building the most fearsome war machine the world had known since the times of the Roman Empire. His rapid ascendancy surprised no one who knew him well. His boldness resonated with disaffected tribes, prompting them to join his ranks. Keeping the clans training together was hard work; every tribe had its individuality and there were only two things they had in common: they were born on horses and from their earliest youth hunted with the bow. Genghis used death as discipline and looting as reward. Nature, too, was a harsh master: only the toughest survived the pitiless climate and the harsh conditions.

Those selected by the Khan to join his Great Horde were tough and relentless, always a step ahead of their enemies. Their reconnaissance was supreme: a rapid system of intelligence about the enemy's moves that allowed the instantaneous change in the direction of a *tuman* (a Mongol unit of ten thousand riders plus wagon support, equivalent in number to a modern army division). Their horses were small, sturdy animals with nostrils that were flared for drinking in the desert wind. A Mongolian pony could travel two hundred kilometres in a day. A rider was armed with a bow made of laminated wood and horn, and carried 60 light (long-distance) or heavy (close-combat), metal-tipped arrows.

Genghis Khan also made use of a new, revolutionary weapon invented by two Chinese, Yu Yifang and Feng Ji-sheng: the powder-propelled rocket, the principal function of which was to make a frightening noise. Metal-studded leather jerkins, cut from thick yak hides and with heavy shoulder pads, and a metal peaked cap trimmed with fur, protected the riders in battle. The warriors also wore a long coat cut from two wolf skins, one fur turned inside for warmth, the other outside to repel rain and snow. They never washed, for water was much too precious. On their long rides they subsisted on mare's milk.

Most vital in any kind of warfare are strategy and tactic. And here Genghis Khan proved himself the great master. He discarded the traditional "in line" attack in favour of a combination of manoeuvre, deception and speed, in order to disorient a more heavily armed enemy. By using stripped-down units of riders he gave his commanders valuable freedom to exploit instantly an enemy's weakness. His standing order to his men was never to engage in heroic yet utterly futile single combat; instead they attacked in packs like the wolves of the steppes. Every unit was presented with its own flag, which its members were to guard with their lives. Loss of its colours brought about the execution of the entire unit.

Everyone knew Genghis Khan, and everyone feared him. As *Khakhan*, or Supreme Khan, he wore no crown, just a fur-trimmed leather cap. A greatcoat of wolf hide, a belt holding a dagger and a finely inlaid quiver of arrows completed his dress. His symbol was a nine-tailed flag bearing the head of a timber wolf, with open jaws and vicious fangs, ready to devour its neighbours. Soon Genghis Khan was seen outside his native Mongolia as the embodiment of menace. Later, during the long years of the Mongolian yoke, there were those who preached that it was God's will and that the Lord had sent the Mongol scourge to teach all His sinners a lesson that fulfilled the biblical prophesy "He makes nations great, and He destroys them. He enlarges nations, and leads them away" (Job 12: 23–4).

In the winter of 1214, with seventy-five thousand Mongol riders,

Genghis Khan broke through the barrier that no force had ever breached in its fifteen-century existence: the Great Wall. With his destruction of the Chin and Hsia dynasties, a new ruling house rose from the ashes and China became a Mongol empire. The *Khakhan's* taste for conquest, fed by the success of his brilliant military campaigns, led to the subjugation of many other advanced civilizations besides the Chinese. "Pay us tribute – or perish!"

And millions did perish – all because of a single incident.

"The longest journey must begin with the first step" is an ancient Chinese proverb. For three thousand years this vast land had lived on its own, the "Empire in Isolation". Then occurred an event that caused the Earth to wobble in its course. The world would never be the same again after one senseless, unprovoked bloodbath: the foolish murder of 450 Tartar traders, ordered by a megalomaniac Turcoman sultan. This act signalled the start of a drama that was to end with the death of millions. And as the Khan's horde rode west, crossing the Jaxartes, they took the first step in the Mongol invasion of the West.

The 14th day of October in the year of Our Lord 1218 is one of the key dates in history. That day Turcoman soldiers waylaid a caravan of 450 Mongol and Tartar traders to rob them of their precious cargo on the Silk Road near the Turcoman city of Samarkand. The soldiers dragged the hapless merchants before a cruel and greedy despot, Shah Alaud-Din Muhammad II, the Seljuk Turk Sultan of Khwarezm, Choresm, Transoxania and Afghanistan. Believing in his own unchallengeable power, the Shah ordered the beheading of the traders. There they lay, dead eyes staring into a burned-out sky. But one Tartar was spared, to carry an insulting message back to Genghis Khan. This survivor retraced his route with a basketful of heads and a note from the Seljuk Turk:

"This is OUR last warning to the slit-eyed ejection from a donkey ... should your dogs of non-believers ever dare to threaten us with combat, then WE, Overlord of all faithful, shall declare a Holy War and smash you with all the forces at OUR disposal, gathered together from OUR empire, which extends from the peaks of the High Pamir to the blue seas of Arabia and the lands beyond ..."

"Vengeance," promised the outraged Mongol Khan. "Vengeance, until the rocks are awash with the scoundrel's and all of his nation's blood ..."

Genghis Khan was not a man of words. He knew that the quality of a leader lay not in lengthy speeches but in personal example and the ability to execute a pledge with fury and might.

Ten years earlier the Great Wolf would have hesitated. Then he was assembling the tribes to create his mighty war machine and conquer northern China.[3] But now he commanded powerful forces, superbly trained and ably led, to give answer to insult. A wolf was not worried about a threat from a hyena – but dare he provoke the wrath of the wind and the sun and go against the prophecy of the shamans?

This was no mere caravan of five hundred camels carrying silk and spices, vulnerable to attack, but a Great Horde of one hundred and twenty thousand skilled and armed riders, crossing the forbidding Sea of Sand that lay to the west of the Khan's immense territory. Beyond the waterless waste of the Gobi Desert lay the five-mile-high peaks of the Hindu Kush and Pamir, with the only viable route being through the bottleneck of the Syr-Dariya (Jaxartes) gorges, which an enemy could easily block. Then the route crossed high mountain passes to Samarkand and Bokhara on the Amu Darja (Oxus), and from there led to Otrar,[4] capital city of the Seljuk Turk Shah's empire.

No Chinese monarch had ever hazarded such a gigantic venture. But a challenge so contemptuous must be avenged, cost what it may. After praying on the Mongols' holy mountain Burhan Chaldun, Genghis Khan abandoned his conquest of the Xia Xing Empire and rode at the head of his columns as they thundered west. Split up in several prongs, his "Dogs of War" – his sons Ogedei, Djudji and Jagatai and Jagatai's friend Djepe, assisted by Djepe's brother, Subotai Bahadur – crossed the "impassable" desert and mountains in fierce heat and with water in short supply in an incredible two months, surprising the Khwarezmian Shah.

In the spring of 1219 Djepe and Subotai led three *tuman*, thirty thousand riders, along the ancient caravan route into the Fergana Valley. Near the Khudjund Pass they met a mixed force of two hundred thousand Persians and Turks. In a gorge too narrow to deploy his overwhelming numerical superiority, the Turcoman emperor pushed his army *en masse* into a funnel. Jammed so tight, they were robbed of all freedom of action. Like a cork in a bottle, they were wedged, as Mongol arrows with iron-tipped shafts the length of a man's arm rained down on them. The Turks never thought that arrows could be fired so far, so fast, so accurately. Mongol bowmen could speed a death-dealing flight on its way every eight seconds. As one flight struck, another was already in the air. Djepe's archers buried the enemy under a long-range hail of winged shafts.

Demoralized, the Shah fled the field, leaving behind heaps of corpses. He had insulted the Khan, rousing his rage, and now the butcher's bill had to be paid. The Shah ran for his life, leaving behind a leaderless army, his rubies, his pearls and his harem – a hunted animal on his own soil. Otrar fell, then Bokhara. Next came Samarkand, defended by one hundred thousand Turks. The Mongols drove before them a wave of Persians, their human shield of flesh and blood, piling up the corpses of their enemies as a ramp to breach the wall. Samarkand, the great centre of Islamic culture, became rubble. The slaughter there and in Bokhara, Perwan, Kabul and all the way across Afghanistan and eastern Iran was so colossal that centuries would pass before the devastated country was repopulated.

When an internal rebellion forced Genghis Khan's return to China, he ordered Djepe and Subotai to continue the hunt for the elusive Shah. "Bring me the scoundrel's head!" – words that would engender a momentous collision between East and West.

As the two *tuman* rode west they devastated Herat, Nishapur and Hamadan. The pursuit of a fugitive brought twenty thousand Mongols to the shores of a large body of water, the Caspian Sea. Here word reached Djepe that the Shah had died of a broken heart. In fact, his followers had murdered him, hoping they could thus bring to an end the Mongols' relentless harrying. It might have, but the hunt had now led Djepe's warriors into the realms of a Russian noble, the Prince of Polovitsia in Georgia. In 1222, in skirmishes along the banks of the River Volga, the Mongols pushed aside the Georgian army, then pillaged and burned his capital, Astrakhan. The prince escaped to the court of his cousin Mstislav, the mighty Voivod, or prince, of Kievan Rus,[5] bringing tales of a Mongol horror, of Tartars raping and murdering Russian subjects.

Dark clouds gathered over eastern Europe. Yet the Great Horde's own future was uncertain. Djepe had overstretched his line of communications; he could not replace his losses; and now a Russian host barred his way. He had accomplished the mission the Great Khan had ordered. Djepe called a council, at which his subordinates urged him to turn back. But by now heavy snowfalls had closed the passes across the Caucasus Mountains and his only option was to march farther west and pass the winter months in the soft climate of the Crimea, then a part of the empire of Trebizond. There Djepe's army pushed its way past a force of Kipchak (Cuman) nomads under Prince Kolian. When the beaten Kipchak prince reached the court of Mstislav of Kievan Rus, he delivered a dark warning to the Voivod: "Beware, my prince. Today they have slaughtered my people and tomorrow they will come for you."

A basketful of Tartar heads had been enough to bring Genghis Khan's raging horde to the borders of Europe in pursuit of a despot. There winter conditions stopped them from returning home, but one certainty remained: if they headed north-west in the spring, history would change. And north-west they did ride, following the River Dnieper until they reached the borders of Kievan Rus. There they halted and set up camp.

Djepe dispatched 10 peace emissaries to Prince Mstislav's court. Subotai, his brother's military strategist who had taken over from Djepe when the latter returned east to take control of the Khwarezmian sultanate, instructed them: "When you meet the Voivod, stand your ground. Show no agitation and do not threaten him. Just make him see things as they are."

The Mongol ambassadors arrived in Kiev on 12 March 1223, carrying the Great Khan's personal wolf banner. Nobles all, they were attired in costly stuffs of deep and warm colours, as befitted the envoys of a mighty Khan, their embroidered greatcoats held together with clips of solid gold and their shaven heads covered by caps trimmed with precious furs. They had come to reassure the Russian of their leader's benign intent. Court functionaries ushered the ambassadors into a crown hall hung with flags and trophies of past Russian victories. The Khan's retainers placed a chest of gold before the Voivod, who was seated on a carpet-covered dais. The Mongol delegation bowed deeply before Prince Mstislav, who waved his hand to acknowledge their submissive gesture. A young Chinese, who spoke halting Russian, interpreted the opening remark of his Mongol delegation leader.

"We come as the representatives of the mightiest force under the sun, and..."

The Voivod cut him off: "Could it be you have never heard of us?" These were no facetious Greeks, cunning Egyptians, wily Jews or boisterous red-bearded Germans. These bow-legged midgets, slit-eyed outpourings of the devil, stinking of rancid milk and horse manure, were the sum of a Voivod's revulsion.

"We have come ..."

A shadow of irritation passed across Mstislav's eyes. "Hear me, Tartar, no man steps across my country's borders without my word," he growled ominously. Scouts had informed him that the Mongol horde, camped at his border, was only twenty thousand strong, a number he could outmatch fourfold.

The Mongol ambassadors realized that a single phrase pronounced too harshly or misunderstood could well be their last. "Great and noble prince, it is but a small favour we have come to ask. Our noble master, Khan of the Universe and Beyond, wishes to be at peace with you."

"Why offer us peace? Are we at war? Or does your Khan march against us?"

"My gracious lord, the Supreme Khan, Ruler over all the Oceans, wishes to assure you that he never intends to call out his mighty host to enter a step into your domains."

The Voivod drew the edge of his hand across his throat. "So it is that kind of peace you offer?" he laughed. "And what do you tender us in return?"

The chief delegate, speaking through his interpreter, had reason to worry. He could sense that things were not going well. He and the Voivod had no common language, and he was unable to make use of the finesse which diplomatic dialogue allows. He had to rely on an intermediary of dubious accuracy, whose misinterpretation of a word could lead to disaster. Perhaps the nervous Chinese had spoken in haste, perhaps he had chosen the wrong order of words – whatever the explanation, Mstislav gazed aghast at the translation of the ambassador's words.

"Magnificent Prince, our message is that all the many and varied princes of this world look in gratitude toward Our Great Khan, as a child to his father. We ask that you will establish friendly intercourse with us. Our Great Khan, Master of the Universe, offers his recognition to all his faithful vassals ..."

At the words "faithful vassals" the Voivod's heavy lips trembled; his face grew red with ire as he listened to such outrage from a Tartar who dared to address him as the "faithful vassal" of some slit-eyed Mongol Khan. Mstislav's rages were monumental. But this time it was not his anger that caused consternation among his attending barons, but his blasphemy.

"Who does that misshapen outpouring of a bitch's belly think he is, ordering *us* what to do?" he bellowed, having never learned to control his temper. "Curse that yellow dog to eternal hellfire!"

At the prince's outburst, the fists of his knights knotted white around the pommels of their swords. The Khan's 10 ambassadors stared in shock at the Voivod's livid features and knew they were looking into the face of death. The Voivod crashed his throne against the wall, kicked over the chest of Mongol gold and stormed from the hall.

"Kill them all!" he screamed.

On that day in March 1223 the Russian barons drew their swords – and the Occident skipped a heartbeat. For to touch Genghis Khan's messenger was to touch the person of the Khan himself. Ten severed heads lay next to the blooded bodies in gold-embroidered greatcoats. Mstislav, in a show of utter contempt, ordered the corpses of the envoys to be tied backward on to their horses and whipped across the stream into the camp of the Mongols. Murdering the Great Khan's envoys, and adding the insult of headless corpses mounted backward, failed to have the desired effect, for Subotai did not know fear. He abandoned plans to take his outnumbered horde back to Mongolia.

"We shall heap terror upon those who have sullied our Great Khan's name," he vowed. Two months later he kept his promise.

If "boldness, directed by an overruling intelligence, is the stamp of a hero", Subotai, grand master of improvisation, was a prime example. This outstanding military strategist, never more dangerous than when facing a numerically overwhelming foe, had won 60 campaigns against vastly greater forces. He was a bold leader who staked his life, his army and even the fortunes of his Khan's empire on a single thrust against a better-armed, more numerous force. Speed, finesse and deception were his principal arms, which he used like the hunter who strikes from a distance. His tactical skill put him alongside those greatest exponents of mobile warfare Hannibal and Attila.

In early May 1223 Subotai's men captured a dozen Russian riders; one was told to carry Genghis Khan's message, as brief as it was menacing: "Let it be known to all that you have killed the Great Khan's emissaries. As you wish for war, so be it. But we have not attacked you. May the Great Spirit be judge of all men."

Then, with sixteen thousand highly disciplined Mongol elite riders, Subotai crossed into Kievan Rus territory. Filled with cold fury, he struck out in a relentless drive against the Russians, who could not withstand the waves of destruction which came crashing down upon them. But Mstislav had not been idle. Around himself he had assembled a formidable body of some seventy to eighty thousand men. Soldiers joined his ranks from the lands that owed him allegiance, among them Smolensk and Kursk, which sent forces that were bolstered by Cuman horsemen from the Russian steppes.

On 31 May the two forces came face to face across the River Kalka, near the Sea of Azov.[6] That day Subotai earned fame with the enveloping tactic that other Mongol chieftains were to repeat successfully in years to come. He relied on his lightning-fast cavalry to inflict frightful punishment on a Western army, with its sluggish formations of foot soldiers and mounted knights. With four times as many men, the Voivod was confident that he had Subotai and his "Tartar rabble" at his mercy. He showed an arrogant self-assurance, announcing to his foe that he would grant neither terms nor pardon. Victory seemed a foregone conclusion, but the impatience of two of Mstislav's barons precipitated disaster: depressed by their holding role, they disobeyed his strict battle orders and forded the Kalka with their men. The Mongols concentrated a massive barrage of arrows on the group as they were jammed in the narrow river crossing. The result was a massacre: the two barons and their best knights paid for their folly.

Now a gaping hole had opened at one of the three fords. Before Mstislav knew of this dangerous gap in his line, Subotai had taken the initiative. Here was the opportunity to sweep down from the rear on the Russians.

Subotai sent two major formations splashing across the river and fanning out behind Mstislav's flank. As the combined force of Russians began their leisurely advance, two Mongol formations broke from the cover of a wood and attacked the open rear of the army now moving forward in a ragged line. A shower of iron-tipped arrows struck down Russians by the thousands. With the Voivod still commanding a crushing numerical superiority, an order from him to turn about might well have saved Europe from the "Mongol Peril" of the future. Yet, instead of turning and dealing with the danger to their rear, the Russians and their allies pressed forward stubbornly, instinctively edging away from the threat of Mongol archers at their back and front. This opened a highway for an attack by light Mongol cavalry.

Turning on his horse, Subotai shouted orders at his dispatch riders. Before their enemy could react, a full *tuman* swung into co-ordinated action. Subotai's *tuman*, lightly armoured, on horses much faster than the Russians', favoured relentless cavalry attack. Their lance charge drove the enemy foot soldiers into swarming clusters of confused men who stumbled over one another, turning them into massed targets for volleys from the circling swarms of Mongol archers.

With ten thousand Russians already dead and dying, Mstislav launched his final reserves into the fray. The Russians made an inroad, roaring a premature cry of victory as they got within arm's length of the Mongols and hacked away with sword and battle-axe, forcing the enemy's centre to give. But the Mongols' flanks were still holding and, like Hannibal at Cannae, the wily Subotai was counting on his centre's retreat. By sacrificing a fraction of his warriors, he managed to pull the mass of Russian knights toward a hidden force of dismounted archers. A devastating hail of arrows met the Russians' onslaught, felling horses and dismounting their steel-clad riders, who found themselves helplessly writhing on the ground, immobilized by the sheer weight of their armour. Mstislav's might was crumbling in a tangled mass of seething men and beasts. The Russians' courage withered as they broke and stumbled toward the relative security of their fortified camp, hotly pursued by Mongol horsemen. But they found the morale of those inside the camp was lamentable; the will to fight had deserted them.

His voice almost drowned out by the groans all around him, Prince Mstislav raised his arms. "Men of Rus, you have fought most valiantly. No Mongol shall ever boast he caused the men of Russia to fall." For a moment there was quiet, before a great cry burst from thousands of throats. At the head of his remaining knights, the Voivod broke through the ring of Mongol riders and made a dash for freedom. The Mongols showed their contempt for their foe by refusing to pursue the humiliated rabble.

Subotai, after his astounding victory against near-impossible odds, dispatched a report to Karakorum: "Oh Great Khan, your will has been done. We have destroyed your enemy."

For Russia, the Kalka was an unmitigated disaster. Of the eighty thousand Russians and their allies who had done battle, fifty thousand lay slain or wounded. But their sacrifice was not in vain, for it had blunted the Mongol invasion. The victorious, all-conquering Mongols had suffered grievous losses themselves, and their remaining force was not nearly strong enough to risk encounters with the armies of the dukes of Vladimir and Novgorod, or the ferocious Bulgar and Kipchak tribes along the Volga. That, and his loot of gold, horses and slaves – in great part the sacred share of his Great Khan – made Subotai decide to head for home.

But this merely delayed the final cataclysm by 15 years. At the Kalka ended the first Mongol foray into Europe. For the Occident the battle was a lesson it refused to learn. The consequences were dramatic.

With the beheading of 10 Mongol ambassadors the clash of civilizations became a reality. For two and a half centuries the price of this senseless murder would change not only the history of China, but also that of the Occident. On the day that a vast army from the Centre of the Universe spilled over its own western frontiers, the Kingdom of the Middle stopped being the Empire in Isolation.

# 2

## THE SAVAGE CHEVAUCHÉE

### 6 DECEMBER 1240, KIEV, KIEVAN RUS (UKRAINE)

"God, the most merciful and most excellent, angered by the manifold sins of the Poles, inflicts upon them not the plague, nor famine, nor the enmity of their Catholic neighbours as in previous years, but the savagery and fury of the heathen. Batu Khan, third of the Tatar khans since the foundation of their state, having conquered many eastern kingdoms and overthrown their kings and rulers, and grown enormously in power and beyond all belief in riches, thanks to the number and wealth of the peoples beneath his yoke, now, as if their abodes in the East were too cramped for the Tatar people, sends his armies into the West and North, hoping to conquer them as he has the East."

*The Annals of Friar Jan Dlugosz*, c. 1247

The spring of 1241 brought upon central and western Europe one of its most dangerous crises of the Middle Ages. European royalty had provoked war with the Mongols, but then showed itself quite incompetent to wage it. The monarchs lacked confidence and resolve; peoples of the continent were disunited, an amalgam of quarrelling kingdoms, conniving bishoprics and feuding principalities. In the west, the Christian King of Aragon, already at war with Catholic Castile, expelled the Moors from Valencia, while England continuously warred with France, Scotland and Castile, singly or with all three at the same time. The richest, most populated region of Europe, Lombardy, was caught in permanent war between Germanic emperors and Roman popes. In the north, Danes fought Swedes, while the Teutonic Knights and settlers from Saxony invaded the Polish and Lithuanian plains in search of *Lebensraum*. Down from the mountains came Bavarians to push out the Magyars. The Bohemian king fought the Austrian archduke for control of the Danube Valley.

Farther to the east, beyond Slavonic Poland, lay the territories of Kievan Rus, the Dukedom of Novgorod and another half-dozen half-barbaric

Russian principalities of Orthodox Christianity, none at peace with the others. The better part of the Occident's steel-clad "flower of chivalry", charged with the protection of Christendom, had embarked on yet another Holy Crusade, in which they kept themselves busy stripping Orthodox Constantinople of its treasures before carrying booty and leprosy back to Italy and France. Beyond Frankish Palestine lay the Abbasid Caliphate of Baghdad; beyond that only the dark rim of an unknown world over the horizon. Few travelled there save an occasional monk eager for martyrdom. And then, like a thunderclap, from that darkness swept a plague of horsemen. The Golden Horde of Batu Khan, grandson of Genghis Khan.

From the descendants of Genghis Khan there had emerged a new breed of warrior. No nation on Earth, east or west, could compete with the military skill, discipline and organization of the Mongols. Yet the only legacy the Mongols have left for history is the image of a horde charging through a sea of bloody destruction and leaving nothing positive in its wake – only ruin and death. There are mythic numbers of the overall human cost to eastern and central Europe of this "Great Mongol Terror"; the only source is a contemporary account of the number of sacks filled with enemy ears, diligently collected by the Mongols after each battle. Taking into account the brutal punishment meted out on the vanquished populations, for which there are no records, and adding civilian casualties to those of the military, the overall death toll in eastern and central Europe is well over two million – which, projected into today's population density, is a staggering 35–45 million, a figure exceeding the number of deaths in all wars from Napoleon to Hitler.

It is a historical untruth that the Mongols completed their conquest of Europe by virtue of overwhelming numbers. On the contrary, they fought most battles with numbers decidedly inferior to those of their adversary. The idea of knightly and civilized combat taught noblemen how to die bravely; frontal attack and single combat idealized Christian chivalry. Against a wild horde relying on ruse and treachery, this approach made no sense. A ban by the Church added a further handicap;[1] it outlawed the use of missile weapons, such as the crossbow, as "a weapon hateful to God and unfit for Christians"; contemporary accounts deemed long-distance massacre as removing the heroism of an honourable head-on charge with sword and lance. Rulers feared that the rabble on foot, armed with long-distance weapons, would "proletariarize" combat. And thus it came about that, in the rapidly approaching confrontation, Mongols archers with their iron-tipped arrows would dramatically reduce the number of knights long before the two sides engaged in hand-to-hand conflict.[2]

In the spring of 1236 Khan Ogedei, who had followed his father Genghis Khan as *Khakhan*, dispatched a host of one hundred and twenty thousand toward the West. Ogedei put Batu Khan, prince of the blood, in nominal command of the second Mongol invasion of eastern and central Europe of 1236–42. To ensure military success, Ogedei appointed Subotai, the grand master of strategy and ruse, as Batu's strategic adviser. With genius Subotai planned all strategy on the basis of detailed information from his advance scouts. He knew that any push beyond Russia's big rivers must inevitably lead to open conflict with the monarchs of Bohemia, Hungary, France, the Germanic Empire and the Pope, and through him, all of the rest of Christendom. Subotai astutely counted on the disunity of European princes to enable him to overcome each opponent separately. The "enlightened" Europeans despised the Mongol horde as less than human dogs, as blood-sucking vermin, and no prince considered that this heathen rabble could ever present a danger to his own army of steel-clad knights. European royalty had forgotten – or ignored – the lesson taught them 15 years earlier at the Kalka.

In the autumn of 1236 Subotai's three hordes "came together in the territory of the Bulghar. The earth echoed and reverberated from the multitude of their armies, and at the size and tumult of their forces the very beasts stood amazed."[3] A three-pronged Mongol horde crossed the ice-covered Volga and broke into eastern Europe. What took place over the next five years defies description. The Mongol invaders acted like cannibals holding a blood feast. They ravaged the land, plundered, burned, raped and slaughtered the people as one bleeds pigs, before leaving rotting bodies and piles of skulls to mark their passage. One of the principal reasons for the insane bloodshed was the deep mutual loathing felt by nomads and sedentary civilizations. Nomads could not understand how people could lock themselves inside walled cities, just as sedentary civilizations considered nomads to be thieves, out to rob them of their property, which indeed the Mongols did very thoroughly. What Batu Khan's hordes did not eat or rape, they killed or burned.

The Russian town of Rajzan, under its teenage prince, resisted for seven heroic weeks. When the town fell the Mongols torched it and butchered its citizens. Likewise they obliterated the army of the Voivod of Suzdal and took no captives. Next to stand up to the rampaging horde was Jurij II, Voivod of Vladimir. On 4 February 1238 Mongols stormed Vladimir and killed the city's prince, and Batu Khan ordered a drinking cup to be made from the Voivod's skull. They burned Moscow to the ground and impaled its citizens. From there the horde headed for Novgorod. Providentially a sudden spring thaw flooded the fields and turned the surrounding countryside into a quagmire; only a fluke of the weather saved the city. Then it was the turn of Kozelsk, where the population was slain to the last man and child. The Mongols spent a harsh winter stripping the countryside bare, thereby condemning many hundreds of thousands to death by starvation. As winter came to an end, Batu Khan crossed the frozen Dnieper. Before his horde lay "Kiev the Golden", or "Mother of all Russia".

Voivod Mikhail was not made of the same stern stuff as his predecessor, Mstislav. Mikhail fled and ordered the local governor to defend the city. Fever and famine reduced its defenders, and in the end Kiev could offer little resistance, save for a small band who defended its fortified cathedral. On 6 December 1240 Kiev fell. Batu Khan's men slaughtered most of its citizens and razed its churches and sanctuaries. The wooden statues of saints were used to kindle giant bonfires that melted the gold relics. Of Kiev's magnificent gilt cupolas, only that of the Cathedral of St Sophia survived the inferno. Heavenly intervention seemed to produce this miracle: as the flames were kindling the roof beams, a torrential shower doused the fire.

The Polish monk Jan Dlugosz left the only record of the Mongols' wrath:

> … Victory goes to the Tatars, who then go on the rampage. The priests, monks and other servants of the Church come out in procession with their holy relics in an attempt to mitigate the fury of the Tatars, only to be slaughtered and have their churches plundered and their sacred relics flung to the ground. Many thousands of captives, men and women are taken back to their camp, where the Tatar women deal cruelly with any woman or girl whom they consider pretty or beautiful, cutting off her nose, cheeks or lips, lest their men be attracted and prefer her to themselves. The Tatar boys are encouraged by their mothers to bully the boy prisoners; indeed if any of them can kill one with a single blow, he receives great acclaim.[4]

With Kiev smouldering ashes, Batu had achieved his aim of destroying Russian resistance. His Khanate of the Golden Horde now stretched seven thousand miles from Lake Baikal in Siberia to the eastern border of Poland.

Then followed an incident insignificant in size but huge in consequences. Tagtei, Batu's second son, 15 years old and especially close to the Khan's heart, had been groomed to become a great leader. This youngster was as wily as he was hot-tempered and ambitious, and to entrust him with a mission that required mature judgement was asking for trouble. None the less Batu did just that when he put Tagtei in charge of a scouting party of four hundred riders. He gave strict orders not to engage in combat against a superior force. After several days' ride, scouring the countryside and laying several villages to waste, Tagtei rode ahead with a small outrider group and happened upon a band of Cuman hunters. Words were exchanged and a brief scuffle fought with arrows left one Mongol and most of the hunters dead, but then, to gain glory for himself, Tagtei foolishly gave chase to the dozen survivors.

The youth and 30 of his men charged into the hostile camp, where they found themselves at the mercy of thousands of Cumans. The tribesmen cut off the Mongols' retreat and hacked them from their horses. As Tagtei tried to escape, his horse stumbled over a tent rope and a Cuman speared his shoulder through his leather jacket. One of the Mongols pulled Tagtei on to his horse and made good their escape, but he could do nothing to stop the boy's bleeding. During the ride the badly wounded Tagtei paid for his rashness with his life. Dreading the wrath of the Khan, the warrior who rescued Tagtei told Batu a story not of his son's reckless charge but of an unprovoked ambush by Cuman riders.

What might have been is not. History is concrete, and fate is cynical. If Kiev had been the Mongols' ultimate target in their drive west, now this "unprovoked ambush" which had taken his beloved son from him blinded Batu Khan into pursuing a reprisal. It pushed the Golden Horde into a direct confrontation with the forces of Western Christianity. History pivoted on the grief of a khan.

The challenge came in the form of a message sent from Batu Khan to the Magyar (Hungarian) King Béla IV as he held court in his fortress in the city of Pest. "I know that you are a rich and powerful king," said Batu, "and that you have many soldiers under you, and that you govern alone a great kingdom. Therefore it is difficult for you to submit to me voluntarily. Further, I have been informed that you have taken the Cumans, who are our slaves, under your protection. Cease harbouring them, or you will make of me an enemy."

In fact, fearing the Mongol onslaught, thousands of Cumans had fled across the High Carpathians to seek refuge in Hungary. King Béla offered them refuge once they pledged to convert to Christianity, a decision which was calculated to enhance his standing with the Holy See. Besides, the Cumans could muster forty thousand warriors, boosting the king's army. The numerical superiority these reinforcements gave him convinced Béla that he could stop the "Mongol Terror" and save Christianity. With this act he would become the much-venerated St Béla.

The Archduke of Austria warned Béla not to offer the Mongols a reason to attack. But the king ignored the sage advice that to welcome the Cumans would give the Mongols the excuse they needed to make Hungary their next target. And the die was cast when Béla rejected Batu Khan's threat, though he refrained from cutting off the heads of the Mongol emissaries. When he learned of Béla's refusal to submit, Batu wanted to strike immediately. Subotai prevented this, knowing that to invade Hungary they first needed to secure their northern flank. Scouts had brought disturbing news: not one, but two powerful armies of knights were assembling: a Hungarian force of fifty to sixty thousand and a Bohemian army of roughly equal strength.

The invasion of western Europe is a classic example of Subotai's long-term strategic planning, executed with meticulous care on a scale until then unseen. Against Hungary Subotai envisaged an attack with his main force in the centre, guarding his flanks with a right and a left wing. Following his proven strategy, he would divide the enemy and fight each separately before they had a chance to unite. He could ignore Poland, then divided into four dukedoms, each ruled by a branch of the Piastow family, who hated one another as only relatives can. King Boleslav V of Krakow was king of the Poles in name only, for the country's dukes did not recognize him as their suzerain. Instead of according one prince power over all the others, they had handed the regency to a German prince, *Fürst* Heinrich II von Schlesien (Silesia), a pious man and valiant warrior.

Subotai laid out his plans. In the centre, five *tuman* under Batu Khan would cross the Carpathians into Hungary. Kadan Khan, with one *tuman*, would hold off any possible intervention by Bulgars from the south. And two *tuman*, one each under Ogedei's sons Kaidu and Baidar, would deploy into south-west Poland to protect Subotai's northern flank, for an attack on this flank presented the greatest danger to his army. He had to prevent the Bohemians from joining forces with the Hungarians to form an army of at least one hundred thousand. To accomplish this, Kaidu and Baidar would menace the Bohemian host with forays into their northerly domains, the idea being that this potent threat should suffice to keep the attention of the Bohemian king, Wenceslas I, fixed on his northern border. But, unknown to Subotai, a third army was gathering, made up of Polish and Teutonic Knights. This force was destined to bring his two northern *tuman* into collision with a formidable host: the combined might of western Europe.

Kaidu and Baidar's northern column sacked and burned the town of Sandomir. Then, on 3 March 1241, they thrashed a hastily assembled force of Poles under King Boleslav outside the fortress of Krakow. Two weeks later, on 18 March, they rode over another Polish force, barring their way at Chmielnik. Within a week the Mongols were back in Krakow, which they torched on 24 March. Their only setback came during Baidar's attempt to storm the walled Church of St Andrew, where a small force put up a furious defence. Here Baidar had to abandon his offensive when Kaidu sent a message to join him immediately on the River Oder, strengthening a Mongol siege of the border fortress of Wroclaw (Breslau), *Fürst* Heinrich's capital. After raging fires levelled most of the city, the Mongol drive on Wroclaw's castle stalled in the face of unyielding resistance by its valiant citizens. At a critical juncture Prince Meshko (Mieczyslaw) of Opole attacked a Mongol unit that found itself stranded on the wrong side of the Oder, and smashed it, saving the city. Kaidu Khan now had to face the new danger to his rear; he abandoned the siege of Wroclaw to confront Meshko. But, before the Mongols could attack, the Pole slipped the trap and joined forces with his cousin, *Fürst* Heinrich, whose army was quartered in the nearby town of Liegnitz.

The Silesian prince's call to join him there had already been answered by fifteen thousand steel-clad knights, their retainers and sundry foot folk, numbering altogether thirty thousand. This should be sufficient to stop the Mongols, he believed. But an operational plan must be based on accurate intelligence, not only to reduce the risk of surprise but also to greatly improve a commander's chances. While this shuffling of large bodies of men was going on, uncertainty reigned in the camps of the Western allies, who knew little of the enemy's strength or moves.

Meanwhile Kaidu's scouts raced over the countryside gathering information. Good news came with the intelligence that King Wenceslas's men were huddled in their bivouacs and showing no sign of movement in any direction. More disturbing was the report that straight to the west of them, at Liegnitz, was gathering a mighty force of Christian knights, as daily more knights and foot folk arrived. Now the critical issue became how the Mongols might tie down the Bohemians. Military logic called for Wenceslas's fifty thousand to move south to assist his Magyar cousin with a strike into the exposed flank of Batu Khan's principal attack column. On the other hand, if the Bohemian turned north, Kaidu and Baidar's two *tuman* would find themselves crushed between twin masses of knightly steel.

Wenceslas I possessed none of the hallmarks of the heroic age of knighthood. His decision was supreme, yet he was bereft of both the will and the energy for a successful campaign. False rumours paralysed the king's mind; his sole sources of information were the excited tales of terrified refugees who arrived with fearful reports of Mongols in "hordes in the hundreds of thousands". These exaggerated numbers would have had less effect if the king had decided not to believe them. Now there was news of not one but two Mongol hordes: one (Kaidu and Baidar in Polish Silesia) threatening from the north and the other (Batu and Subotai in Slovakia-Hungary) endangering his southern border. Panicked, Wenceslas temporized, grew indecisive and committed one monumental blunder after another. At one of medieval history's critical junctures, this king who allowed fear to dominate his thinking was transfixed, his timidity the Occident's undoing. Wenceslas moved his army neither south, toward Béla's forces in Hungary, nor north, in support of Heinrich's knights.

The result of this hesitancy was two decisive battles. Heinrich von Schlesien, with an army of over thirty thousand men at Liegnitz in the north, faced Kaidu and Baidar with their twenty thousand. In Hungary King Béla's seventy to eighty thousand men stood ready against sixty thousand Mongols under Subotai. Between the two Mongol hordes was another great host, Wenceslas's fifty thousand men. For a crucial week the Bohemian king kept his army immobile, acting only when it was much too late.

On the day that Kaidu Khan finally received the news that Wenceslas's army was on the move – north – heading straight for his and Baidar's two *tuman* and closing in, the two khans had to decide whether to stand and fight or slip away in a tactical withdrawal. The Bohemians, joined with Heinrich's Poles and Germans, were too great a force to take on with two *tuman*. While twenty thousand Mongols versus Heinrich's thirty thousand men represented decent odds, twenty thousand against eighty or ninety thousand did not.

The situation changed again when a scout on a sweat-soaked horse dashed into Kaidu's camp with further news of the Bohemians. Because of his sluggish advance, Wenceslas was at least six days away. This vital information, added to the disparity in numbers, left the Mongols with no option – they had to strike at once against one of the two enemy hosts. So fate rather than any coherent strategy fixed the date of battle. Subotai's specific orders were to immobilize the Bohemian host, but the presence of a newly constituted Polish–German army at Liegnitz changed that situation. Unless Kaidu and Baidar could prevent the massing of German and Poles with the Bohemians, Batu Khan's main horde would be lost.

Their two *tuman* were headed for a single decisive encounter. The two leaders decided to take on Heinrich's Poles and Teutons, still in camp at Liegnitz. They drove their *tuman* at breakneck speed, so fast that they left behind the ponderous wagons with their crucial reserves of arrows. On 6 April, only two days after receiving news of the Bohemian advance, the Mongols crossed the Oder and late the next day reached the Weidelach creek. They needed to lure the Silesian prince out of his fortified lair and defeat his army before the Bohemians arrived to lengthen the odds. They allowed a captured knight to escape and carry the news of the impending danger to Liegnitz, thus pushing Heinrich into premature action on their terms.

Heinrich, with a face whose frown would not frighten nor whose smile would hearten, summoned his closest advisers. All were men of proven valour who were protective of their knightly reputation. The escaped knight had brought them the first firm news about the Mongol moves but had no crucial intelligence of their strength. Many, he said – but how many? Tens of thousands or hundreds of thousands? It was information that could make all the difference in battle. Everyone voiced an opinion.

"Our steel tide will crush them," said one voice. But, in truth, Heinrich's knights had no idea but to use their prowess as a shock force in a head-on charge across a battlefield. The time when steel-clad horsemen could prevail on a battlefield dominated by arrow fire was already in the past. Ruses such as using hidden reserves or attacking from the flank were considered not chivalresque and a betrayal of the knightly code of honour. Head-on slaughter was the only proper manner for a knight to earn immortal fame.

"I've heard of the Mongols in action. They are fast, and they are many," said another, even though nobody had a notion of their overall numbers.

"We must await the arrival of reinforcements."

"We shall meet King Wenceslas on the way. He is near."

"How near?"

"A day, two at most." In fact, it was closer to five.

"My noble Prince, can we count on the Bohemian's support?"

"Wenceslas is greedier than the Pope. From the Hohenstaufen emperor he has demanded Moravia for his services."

"Where does that leave the Austrian, Friedrich von Babenberg?"

"He is a vassal of the Hohenstaufen and must obey his emperor. No, the Hohenstaufen can hardly refuse Wenceslas. And since Boleslav's Polish army is gone, we and the Bohemians are all that is left to hold the border."

"And the Magyar?"

"He is too far to be of help." Heinrich looked up at a crucifix. "We must stop the horde, or they will ravage the German countryside and our people will suffer greatly."

If the warriors of Kaidu and Baidar thought that it was madness for twenty thousand mounted archers to pit themselves against thirty thousand armoured knights, they knew better than to complain. They had trust in their leaders, grandsons of the Great Wolf. As the last glimmer of daylight faded they reached the side of a creek. There they set up camp without fires and sent out scouts. Tomorrow they would move toward

Liegnitz. The two khans rode across the creek to reconnoitre. If it came to a battle, this place seemed ideal, with soft ground, not too soggy for the light Mongol ponies, but a deadly trap for the huge horses bearing knights in armour.

With the timely arrival of nearly a thousand Teutonic Knights under their *Heermeister*, Poppo von Ostern, and five hundred French Knights Templars, the Christian forces had excellent prospects of victory. Furthermore, Heinrich could count on Meshko of Opole and his survivors from Boleslav's army, who all had vengeance on their mind. From the German town of Goldberg came a large band of tough miners armed with pointed staves and clubs, eager to cash in on the reward for going into battle and the chance to plunder; they boosted the numbers of civilian auxiliaries from neighbouring farms and settlements. Undisciplined, untrained and badly armed, auxiliary foot troops often prove more of a hindrance than assistance. Heinrich would have done better with an army half the size but of higher quality.

However, that was not his only handicap, for he knew nothing of the other side. While Kaidu's spies kept him informed every hour of the Bohemian army's progress, Heinrich was operating blind. He still had no idea of his enemy's strength or even his Bohemian ally's precise location. The latter he thought were much nearer than they actually were. In such circumstances the prudent strategy would have been to remain behind the walls of Liegnitz to gather intelligence and await the arrival of his powerful ally. But local barons, fearful of the ravage that the Mongols would inflict on their property, convinced their *Fürst* to march toward the Bohemians and await their arrival in a camp on the Weidelach creek. But, by moving out into the boggy Oder Marshes, he would be fighting the Mongols on ground that favoured the enemy rather than himself.

On the morning of 7 April the church bells rang, the drawbridge of Liegnitz came down and Heinrich, resplendent in a white battle coat with an embroidered red cross worn over steel armour, rode out at the head of his knights to do battle with the Mongol horde. As he passed the Church of the Blessed Virgin an incident portended bad fortune: a chunk of masonry fell from the tower and narrowly missed the prince. He shrugged off the divine warning; he was not superstitious and nothing would deter him from crushing the Mongols at a place of his choosing – the field along-side the Weidelach creek. Since the German word for "choice" is *Wahl* and for "place" *Statt*, the plain he selected on which to engage in knightly battle he named Wahlstatt, the name under which the epic battle would enter the book of history.

To his utter surprise, when Heinrich reached his chosen battlefield he discovered a plain already occupied by the horde. Even so, his barons nurtured the illusion that their steel armour and long swords would inevitably crush the enemy. And tomorrow, with the Good Lord by their side, when their Bohemian ally arrived, they would crush the Mongol rabble. For the rest of the afternoon the two armies kept their distance across the flat field, which was limited by the creek on one side and terrain that rose slightly toward a wooded round hilltop on the other. Baidar had hidden most of his heavy cavalry behind the wooded rise. They were to deliver the death stroke or, in the event of a forced retreat, be used as final reserve. The field in front of the Mongol khans was filled with armour in motion, gleaming in the low evening sun, as hundreds of standards fluttered lazily in the soft breeze.

"There are too many. They will trample over us," said Baidar.

"Only if the German manages to hold his men's reins. And that is impossible with warriors who cannot converse in the same tongue."

"And the Bohemians?"

"Nowhere near."

One of their sub-commanders had joined them on the rise, and dared to express his concern. "My Khan, it is an open field. There is no place to hide. We will have no chance to launch an ambush."

Kaidu's eyes narrowed into a slit, his mouth showing a wicked grin. "It is good if not even you can see what I have planned."

Brave is the knight who meets a foe head-on in chivalresque joust. But only a fool will engage in mortal combat without knowledge of the whereabouts of his nearest ally,[5] or the size and tactics of his enemies. None the less, a Silesian prince was about to do precisely that – ride blindly into a battle that would decide the fate of Christendom. As for the King of Bohemia, he neither supported his Hungarian cousin's call to smash Batu Khan's main horde, nor reached the Poles and Germans in time. It shows how little it takes to determine the course of history – two days of fruitless dawdling by an irresolute monarch were to decide the outcome of a huge military clash.

# 3

# THE BATTLE OF NATIONS
# AT LIEGNITZ

### April 1241, Liegnitz, Silesia

"*Gott mit uns!* God be with us!" they prayed on the morning of 9 April 1241.

But God was far, and the Mongols so near.

It takes little to alter the run of events and change the course of history. In the middle of the thirteenth century three men achieved just that. A procrastinating king, a prince with a fool's courage and a knight who cried out in panic.

Dense fog crept up from the Oder Marshes. The camp of Heinrich's foot soldiery was deathly quiet – not the silence of professionals, confident in their abilities, but that of conscripted farmers and coal miners who had never before faced a mortal foe. They were on their knees praying, seeking guidance from the Good Lord. *Gott mit uns!*

*Fürst* Heinrich was a big man, well over six feet tall. His blond hair was shoulder length and his full beard neatly trimmed. His eyes were blue and his nose was slightly bent, the result of a jousting accident. He looked the image of a Germanic ruler. Striding back and forth outside his tent, he was filled with the spirit of the hour. The fate of Christendom rested on his shoulders as he stood before his knights, a barrier between a horde of Mongols and the heart of Europe. With dawn would come the decisive battle. Heinrich mounted his huge white charger and rode to the top of a rise. His view to the east was a ghostly grey obscured by low-lying fog; even so, he could make out many thousands of lances sticking up through the ground mist. It was a Mongol ruse. Counting on morning fog to hide his numerical weakness, Kaidu Khan had ordered his men to cut saplings to spear length. Viewed from a distance, they resembled a forest of lances; each man carried several shafts, and all that Heinrich could see was numberless lances held up by mist-shrouded ghosts.

In Christianity's holy quest to "teach the heathen Tartar a lesson", the boldest and most experienced warriors had joined *Fürst* Heinrich's banner. His army boasted an amalgamation of the chivalry of central Europe, as Polish and French knights added their weight to the German contingent. Each army spoke in their own tongue, each obeyed only their barons, making it an impossible task to impose any kind of order in battle formations. Heinrich was annoyed by the barons' irksome mood and their eagerness to do battle, while he still counted on the arrival of Wenceslas's fifty thousand. He squinted toward the sunrise. "Where are the Bohemians?"

"They'll be here soon enough, *messire*," the *Heermeister* of the Teutonic Knights assured him. In fact, they were still three days off. "But, my Prince, we dare not wait. Our men are in harness and the horses tire. We must attack – now!"

By contrast, Meshko of Opole, who had tangled with the Mongols before, counselled caution; he tried to persuade the *Fürst* to wait in camp for the arrival of the Bohemians. The German *Heermeister* showed contempt for his Polish ally equal to that he felt toward the Mongol adversary. He taunted Meshko. "*Messire*, you and your *chevaliers* may stay behind. For us to wait is to dishonour the pledge to our Order, and every minute's delay exposes us to the derision of that heathen rabble over there." Earlier he had stared from afar at the enemy's position and liked what he saw. Not too many: eight, perhaps ten, thousand, lacking adequate body armour. His prejudiced observation encouraged the Germans to underestimate the fighting qualities of their opponents. It would be a walkover for his Teutonic Knights, whose pride did not allow sharing victory with the King of Bohemia.

There comes a moment in every commander's life when a decision must be made. Heinrich's moment was now. The impatience of the Teutonic Knights, intensely proud and very arrogant, forced his hand. With it, the scene was set for the *Völkerschlacht*, or "Battle of Nations". "Take your men and post them strongly," ordered Heinrich. "Wait for my signal for your advance. Then take to the steel and keep to the steel, and promise your foot folk rich spoil. With the Lord's help, if we move concerted we shall make the heathen pay a heavy toll."

Heinrich arrayed his forces into five battles. The first battle was the Polish knights under Boleslav, son of the Margrave of Moravia, backed by advancing foot squares. Sulislav, brother of the killed Palatine of Krakow, formed the second battle. Next in line was the contingent of Meshko of Opole, holding the left wing to keep the Mongols from encircling the knights' army, followed by the Teutonic Knights under *Heermeister* Poppo von Ostern. The killing thrust would be given by Heinrich and his Silesian barons, together with the experienced French Knights Templars. It was a solid plan.

Battle horns sounded, calling pike men to their weapons. Retainers helped armoured knights on to their massive chargers; an armoured noble was a heavy burden, even for a sturdy charger, and the longer they were in the saddle and standing idle, the slower their horses would move during a charge. A forest of pikes from his foot ranks rose in front of Heinrich. These inexperienced soldiers-for-a-day formed into self-protecting rectangles with pikes and boar spears sticking out like the needles on a porcupine. Knights jostled for the front rank, counts before barons and barons in front of yeomen.

Kaidu Khan reviewed the accelerating situation from across the field. The Mongols had worked out tactics to deal with most challenges, but this was a difficult one. Kaidu's *tuman* would have to go up against five massive blocks of steel-clad knights protected by foot squares of pike men. Yet the Mongol leader held one advantage: deception. Knightly hosts would always launch into a broad, frontal attack; a ruse was not only unknightly, but unimaginable. That chivalresque battle code of Europe did not apply to an Asian Tartar, whose main weapon was cunning. To flee before the advancing enemy was not dishonourable; Sun Tzu, the Chinese sage of war, had even deemed it preferable to giving battle.

Standard Mongol practice was to allow the enemy into extreme bow range of dismounted archers and gall rider and horse with arrows, then strike into the confusion with a lightning rider charge. But here Kaidu had a problem. With all of his heavy Mongol cavalry in ambush position, he was left with only a thin, vulnerable screen of archers to slow the enemy's attack. He would have to lure the knights into a pocket before sending a force around their line of attack to pounce on them from their vulnerable rear. The effect on the enemy's morale of a sudden strike complemented by a surprise from the rear should prove decisive. Even so, Kaidu suspected that, contrary to earlier encounters, these solid blocks of Polish and German professionals might not be shaken by it. He put a thin screen of riders ahead of his dismounted archers, his long-distance weapon with the biggest stopping power. Next to them he placed his "rocket battery", a new invention out of the East, which produced great noise to frighten the enemy's horses. His heavy cavalry, hidden away in reserve, would be his shock unit once he enticed the knights into a trap. But danger was inherent in the plan: if the enemy's five blocks attacked at the same time, and the armoured knights got among his dismounted archers to mêlée in hand-to-hand fighting, the battle would be over.

Heinrich rode a hundred paces ahead of the battle formations to survey the good order of his army. It was a splendid sight: close to forty thousand men aligned on a front, extending nearly a kilometre from flank to flank.

The sun broke through the morning mist. As far as the eye could see, the sun's rays were reflected from plumed steel helmets, steel cuirasses and steel spear points – thousands upon thousands of steel statues glistening on the plain. Only these statues were living beings, breathing men nerved and ready to do bloody battle, prepared to commit slaughter most horrid. Silence fell over the plain; priests carried the canopy-covered statue of the Black Virgin of Czestochowa along the line of Polish knights. Farther down the line, Teutonic Knights knelt around a field altar, a thousand in white battle coats, emblazoned with the Holy Cross, draped over their chain mail, chanting and raising their swords by the blades to form a thousand crosses held high, and in a single voice asked for the Lord's blessing: "*So Du den Gott bist, hilf Deinem Prinzen und seinem christliches Heer.* You, that You are God, give assistance to Your Prince and his Christian host." They embraced and forgave one another their sins of the past and absolved them of those they were about to commit in the forthcoming murderous clash.

The hour of decision had arrived. Heinrich issued the order: "Sound the battle horns." His standard bearer raised the banner. To the blare of horns and the roll of drums, the line of thousands began its advance, welded together into one solid battering ram. Though it would be better for the morale of the troop to see their *Fürst* in front, for once he could not afford courageous gestures. More than one battle had been lost because the commander did not stay aware of what was happening to all his forces; later warriors would call it "situation awareness". Heinrich rode up a hillock and watched his first battle. Knights held high their many thousand pennants, trotted forward in a solid wave of steel and lances, horse to horse and knee to knee, their polished armour like mirrors in the rising sun. They spurred their steeds to a canter, and their lances came down in unison. On they came, two ranks deep. Their hard charge would carry them into the centre of the Mongol horde. A shout rose from many thousand throats: "*Gott mit uns!*"

Kaidu Khan had been watching his enemy's preparations; he heard the trumpets and then saw movement. A mounted steel tide broke into a walk, then a trot. Kaidu could almost feel the effect of the deadly long spears, soon to be levelled to make their fearsome impact against his lightly protected riders. Before that happened, his archers had to halt the steel tide. The Polish and Teutonic nobles, archetypes of tactical conservatism, were about to receive a rude shock. Kaidu's archers had marked out the distance with stakes. They lifted their bows and drew back. Ten thousand shafts flocked upward in a single volley, and arced high out over the heads of their rider screen. The charging knights could see this curtain of death descending on them like numberless raindrops from the sky. Before the knights could build up momentum they were struck by a shower of arrows. And then a second shower, and a third; with the battlefield already strewn with corpses of men and writhing horses, momentum carried the next battle of knights straight into the maelstrom. That line also dissolved in death cries and chaos as the attackers felt the bite of the iron-tipped shafts. Men were thrown over the heads of their collapsing steeds and broke their limbs in the fall. Wounded and riderless horses galloped into one another's way, dashing chaotically around the battlefield.

In less than a minute Heinrich's initial offensive had been wasted, showing no significant results. Until now a charge by armoured knights, if carried out with courage and force, had always proved decisive. Heinrich had expected the Tartars to break and run. His second battle moved forward, but before they could make bodily contact with the Mongols they too were hit by a rainbow of shafts. Their accompanying foot soldiers had never faced anything like it; as might have been expected, they panicked. While they were trying to escape, the next line of knights rode over them.

Kaidu pushed his own counter-attack into the confusion. But his light cavalry charge was no match for the knights' steel and shattered against their lances. More horns sounded. Through a cold mist now rising from the Weidelach marshes pressed forward the next wave of armoured knights on their great war-horses, without waiting for their foot soldiers to deploy to protect their flank. The mass of plunging knights built their own momentum; this attack came so suddenly that the Mongols were caught with their light cavalry worn out from battling the first wave, while their archer screen had exhausted their supply of arrows. Kaidu dashed out in front of his mauled light cavalry, trying to cheer them on, when he was spotted and chased by some knights. His horse, being much the faster, carried him from danger. He pushed a new group of light cavalry in to plug the hole with whatever arrows they had collected from the field. But already the next wave of knights came on ponderously; when they reached the line of the archers they bowled them over. The valour of individual Mongols was beyond question, but their short blades were no match for heavy broadswords. The knights cut through them like bears going through an anthill.

With events turning his way, Heinrich allowed his knights an instant to catch their breath, unaware that the enemy's main cavalry force was still hiding in ambush.

A third wave of knights, the Poles under Prince Meshko, entered the fury of battle. For the first time the Mongol cavalry found themselves in dire straits; they were confronted by a fresh mass of steel and, their heavier shafts now expended, their light arrows bounced off the armour. Hundreds of

Mongols were thrown from their ponies and, after some ineffective skirmishing, Kaidu's light cavalry fell back in confusion. The dismounted and unhorsed Mongols turned their bodies toward enemies who were now within a sword's length. It took only moments before they were hacked down with such force that few survived. Those left standing now faced an assault by massed ranks of foot soldiery who advanced on them in solid blocks.

Heinrich looked upon the spectacle of an enemy horde beginning to disintegrate from the rear instead of from the front, since the forces were so entangled that it could not disengage. Pressed beyond the limit of human endurance, Kaidu abandoned his dismounted archers to their fate. His attention now focused on Heinrich's next attack, for he knew that it would determine the day.

Split into individual combats, and disregarding those who asked for time so that the knights could form a solid battle array, Meshko ordered his knights to charge the enemy flank of Baidar Khan. The Mongolian spears proved no obstacle for steel-clad chargers, and then knights were among the enemy, slashing and killing. The Mongols cracked. Meshko and his men pressed the assault upon the reeling enemy. With lances levelled, they churned like a moving wall into the horde, driving the enemy before them, hacking them to pieces with such a grisly din that it could be heard in far-off Liegnitz. Speared bodies fell backward; slashed bodies toppled from horses. A great cheer of victory rose. The Mongol was on the run! The brief but bloody fight had left Meshko's foot soldiers exhausted. Confident of their victory, they dropped to their knees, sucking laboured breath in gasps, staring vacantly. At that critical moment the incredible happened.

With victory in their grasp, a single rider without helmet, his armour splashed with blood, dashed out of nowhere and rode across the knights' successful advance, screaming at the top of his voice: "*Byegaycze! Byegaycze!* Run! Run! The Mongol is upon you!"

Jan Dlugosz tells us that "then someone from the Tatar ranks starts running hither and thither between the two armies shouting 'Run, run!' to the Poles". But he doesn't tell us who that solitary rider was. Was it a knight who had lost his mind after wading in rivers of blood? Or was it a Mongol ruse – a renegade Pole, the single most important element in Kaidu Khan's battle plan? An enigma, but a most decisive one in history. Nobody knows his name, nor where he had come from. We are told only that it happened. Whoever he was, there can be no doubt of the effect of his panicked cry. Even above the cacophony of blaring trumpets, the cries of the commanders, the explosion of firecrackers, the din of steel on steel and the faltering moans of those dying, his shriek of panic was deafening to their ears.

The shock was instantaneous. Polish knights and Prince Meshko's civilian soldiers looked around in confusion. Like a shuddering wave, first a murmur, then a cry moved from the front to the rear ranks. Stiff with cold and fear, and taken unawares by the scream, the front ranks of the foot soldiery stopped, fearful, confused and undecided, their concentration irrevocably broken by the shout of a single knight. Some stood with mouths ajar, others yelled, with arms raised and weapons brandished. Foot soldiers are always weakest at the rear of the battle, those who have not as yet joined combat; they freeze in fear and panic, while only those engaged in the front remain capable of action. The rear ranks faltered, pulling the rest with them, until the entire mass flooded back, meeting more oncoming blocks of footmen in the middle of the field.

For Mongol archers, newly supplied with arrows, the compressed mob was a target impossible to miss. Flights of arrows wreaked havoc; formations were broken up and stumbled blindly over the corpses of their comrades. Amid screams, across the field more ranks broke and joined in headless flight. Like an ancient plague, panic infected thousands upon thousands.

Alerted by the distant clamour, Heinrich looked at Meshko's front. The Polish prince's rigid battle formation had become a thing scattered beyond recognition, the ground littered with the crushed. What moments before had been a victorious, forward-moving phalanx of pikes was now a disorderly rabble running for its life. Mounted Mongols hunted down those who somehow managed to get across a growing wall of corpses, slicing them up and spreading their entrails across the field. Meshko was staring at the carnage, when his charger reared up and threw him off. He was flung to the ground, where instants later he died, his neck broken by the hooves of his own knights. Their prince dead, and before his barons could gather their men, Meshko's attack crumbled like a sand castle pounded by the ocean's waves.

One side of the field was thrown into confused retreat, while a great roar of "*Gott mit uns!*" rose from the other flank, where another block of knights was still advancing. An interlocking chaos resulted in midfield between Heinrich's disintegrating left wing and his advancing right wing. Within minutes the face of battle had changed. As soon as Heinrich saw the debacle engulfing a portion of his forces, he could only pray that Kaidu would fail to react quickly enough to exploit the situation. Seconds counted. He sent a rider to the German *Heermeister* to launch his Teutonic Knights immediately against the right wing of the Mongols. The *Heermeister* flipped shut his helmet guard and pointed with his spear. "*Vorwärts!* Advance!"

One final, concentrated attack and they would push the Mongols into the river. The German monastic knights would decide the battle, saving Christendom from the horror of the heathen Tartar! To the quickening beat of heavy drums, the Order of Teutonic Knights advanced toward the flank, impressive in their solid formation yet entirely unaware of the disaster on their now vulnerable wing.

"*Gott mit uns ... Gott mit uns ... Gott mit uns...*" they cried out, and advanced into a hail of arrows. Heinrich had moved to the head of his own column, all young Silesian nobles. With his standard raised high, he led his battle formation into combat; the line could not easily manoeuvre and could do little but advance in a straight line. The knights, still unaware that Meshko's battle was in chaos, charged after their *Fürst*. Eager for glory, they rode so fast[1] that the pike men could not keep up with them and were soon left behind. With the gap between the foot and horse widening, a Mongol horde surrounded the lightly armed farmers and miners, and in minutes cut them to pieces with iron-tipped shafts fired from point-blank range. Heinrich now lacked any protection for the naked flanks of his mounted knights.

"*Sieg ist unser!* Victory is ours!" he yelled, brandishing his sword for all to see.

The great host roared their answer: "*Sieg ist unser!* Victory is ours!"

A mass of shining steel erupted in that peculiar disorder which precedes even a co-ordinated attack. They trusted their *Fürst's* instinct and, in doing so, were following a man who gave no thought to tactics. All they saw was great victory and eternal glory. The initial contact was awesome: Mongol ponies were no match for the powerful warhorses of attacking knights. The charge of steel pushed the Mongols into flight. Kaidu's standard was seen among the riders in panicky retreat. Heinrich now committed a fatal blunder: he assumed that the escaping horde was the best the Mongol khans could offer. "*Sieg ist unser!*" At the head of his knights, he charged after the enemy. His knights, driven on by their own lust for glory, pressed on with their sentence of steel upon the fleeing Mongols. No force on earth could stop them now. Even the rawest, untrained eye should have been able to read the field like a book. Heinrich and his men had ridden into the oldest trick: the feigned retreat.

At the approach of the steel tide, Kaidu Khan threw his horse about and, with his standard bearer at his heels, fled from the field. In an instant his horde was racing after him. His ruse was to be crowned with brilliant success. On the heels of the retreating Mongols, Heinrich drove with his mounted knights in a straight line for the boggy marshes, the one place where the earth itself would destroy them. The farther they advanced into the bog, the more their heavily laden horses were dragged down by the soft ground. The moment of decision that Kaidu had planned had arrived – there had been no point in committing his heavy cavalry into the mêlée until now – and now was the moment to launch his hordes held in reserve. The sly Mongol was deftly preparing the death stroke. He knew that a knights' army in a line charge were fated to keep moving forward; they could not wheel about. His Mongols could change direction in a heartbeat, and at his signal, they did.

Screams and shouts were heard from Heinrich's rear ranks. The knights looked over their shoulders, bewildered. From behind came the thundering mass of a new Mongol horde. Baidar Khan had timed his death stroke to perfection. He launched his hordes into a bogged-down enemy, discharging their heavier, steel-penetrating arrows into the flanks of the knights' horses. Shafts ripped with murderous velocity into Heinrich's formation. The air was filled with whistling arrows, screams and sharp bangs as arrow tips caromed off armour, or more often, the dull whack of dead-on shots as they penetrated steel and flesh and gristle. The struck horses thrashed about, with arrows sticking from their unprotected flanks, adding to the mayhem.

From the swampy ground came the roar of orders, mixed with shrieks of pain and cries of death. Men fell quicker than stems of wheat cut by a sickle. The wounded were smothered beneath the bellies of their pained steeds. The carnage spread across the battlefield as the churned-up field became a slippery slime of mud, blood and gore. Amid the chaos of falling knights and terror-stricken horses, a new force entered the battle. Before the knights had time to fathom the number of their assailants, shouts of a new onslaught sounded from the other side of the field; it was the horde that had finished slaughtering the fleeing foot soldiers. A tightening ring of Mongols forced Heinrich's knights inexorably farther into the swamp, where their armour was a fatal hindrance. Suddenly the prince's problem was how to save his knights trapped in the bog. That decision was taken out of his hands with an attack by a new Mongol horde.

That wave of Tartars showed no mercy. Knights cried out to their God, their saints, their mothers, as if they could be of help in this moment of desperate need. Barons tried to rally their knights into defensive stands, with the result that they became wedged into tight clusters, unable to move in any direction. Inside the various pockets, the carnage reached its most savage concentration. Mortally wounded, transpierced by arrow or spear, knights and Mongols alike fought on valiantly until their lifeblood ran out.

It had ceased to be a battle and had become a feast of slaughter. Baidar's hordes killed the unhorsed knights, made helpless by the weight of their armour as they sprawled on the ground. The Mongols' spiked shafts skewered the bellies of the enemy. Dead knights spread like a carpet of bloody corpses on the fiercely chewed turf. Inside the cauldron, where groups of warriors made their final stand against a huge horde of blood-crazed, gore-splattered horsemen, the knights were massed so closely that their long swords became useless. Heavy broadswords and protective steel came at a high physical price; their muscles knotted up and they were tiring. Suddenly Heinrich was aware of a great trumpeting and drumming from the other side of the field. At last, the Bohemians! But it was not to be – only a great charge by thousands of Mongol lances.

"Don't give in – by all the holy martyrs fight on!" Heinrich tried in vain to encourage his men, but his cry of desperation marked the beginning of the end. The Mongols continued to ride around their foes, reaping carnage. Arrow-pierced bodies toppled from horses, limbless corpses fell rearward. It was plain that the finest of Europe's knights were teetering on the brink of disaster. A relentless enemy in front and the bogs of the Oder Marshes behind them equally deadly. There were so many dead that the very few who did manage to get away did so by crossing the soggy marsh on the carpet of corpses of their fallen comrades.

The battle reached its climax with the wreckage of the Order of Teutonic Knights as they counter-charged with suicidal courage. A hail of arrows from the deadly range of less than a hundred yards hit the first wave as they advanced in a straight line. The second wave could do nothing but carry on, even as they saw their fate before them. Their magnificent gallantry showed no results. Against steel-piercing arrows, shot from short bows of horn and sinew, the valiant knights had no chance. Their casualties were numberless and total. A cluster of Teutonic Knights had formed around their unhorsed *Heermeister*, swinging his mighty battle-axe, parrying, thrusting, while trying to keep his balance in the mud. It left the Christian knights with but one choice: emerge victorious or die. The *Heermeister's* entourage tried to hustle their master through the hacking mob to safety, but he just shook his head and stood his ground to meet his doom. The chaos swirled around him and, one by one, his companions died, their blood soaking the earth. He received a cut but felt no pain and, before his foe could regain balance, the *Heermeister* struck him with his axe. Without let-up, he faced his next enemy.

Anguished, Heinrich saw his knights moving slowly, then more slowly still as in an endless nightmare. Finally, time stopped for them. His brave knights, frozen in their movement, lay still, except for two or three here and there. He did not know who was alive, who was dead or who was injured; he dared not break his concentration to look. What his mind was seeing and what his eyes were watching began to blend together. Pressed beyond the limit of endurance, the French Templars, covered in layers of mud and blood that dripped from their steel armour, and with mangled corpses of friend and foe piling up around them, made a final determined stand around Heinrich. Their attempt to save their leader was noble but futile, and they fell one by one in a sea of murder.

The ground was a mass of sliced, bent pieces of bleeding armour and parts of butchered torsos, of wounded writhing against dead, crying out for a final deliverance from pain, others blindly groping for a way out. No pity was asked, nor given. Five hundred Templars died to a man. Heinrich, with his great horse stabbed from under him, a giant among a pack of snapping wolves, his visor lowered and his sword raised high, fended off a mass of attackers with his reach of arm and the length of his great two-handed sword. His huge blade flashed and descended, cutting deep into his assailants. Steel clanged upon steel, blade cut through leather into flesh. Again and again the valiant prince slashed out with his sword. Up went his sword a last time, and before he could strike again, a lance pierced him through his unprotected armpit. With a roar of agony and the steel deep in his side, he collapsed mortally wounded.

"… the Tatars pounce on the Prince and, dragging him two bowshots clear, cut off his head with a sword, tear off all his badges and leave his corpse naked. In this great battle a number of the Polish nobility and gentry find honourable martyrdom in defence of their Faith," recorded Jan Dlugosz.

A great Mongol war cry rose from thousands of triumphant voices and rolled up into heaven. A Mongol impaled Heinrich's head on his spear, and rode along the line, to the cheer of his warriors, and the horror of the handful of remaining knights. A Christian host had been shattered, its leaders dead or dying.

"*Der Fürst ist gefallen* … The prince is dead…" The moan rose to the heavens and the last of the fighting ended.[2]

The Great Battle of Wahlstatt was over. But there was no quiet; the screams of pain from horse and man mingled with the shouts of triumph and joy from the victors. The Mongols jumped from their horses; a divine wolf had shown himself in all his glory. The ferocious beast of war showed no signs of favour, for even among the victors he had chosen the most valiant to be slain. The battlefield displayed only scenes of horror. Arrows and swords, battle-axes and lances had inflicted most frightful damage. The badly wounded could hope only for a quick death. Those with broken bones and gashes in their sides knew that death would come at its own speed, slowly and painfully. Survivors stumbled across the field to search for a friend in need. It is recorded that those who tried to still their thirst with water from the Weidelach creek scooped up blood instead.

Night dropped its dark mantle over a field of carnage. Only then did the murdering stop. For hours after darkness the battlefield of Wahlstatt resounded with the groans of the dying. But nobody fought any longer, not even the ghosts of the thousands lying still. A few torches sent out pools of light – they were looking for what? For survivors? Or to slaughter the wounded enemy? Who could tell? The following day the Mongols lowered their dead into a mass grave; they stripped the enemy dead of armour and sword and left them for the scavengers.

The drama of Liegnitz, the obliteration of the Great Knights' Army, is a story of incomprehensible suffering, and the stunning fact remains that no one will ever know how many men were killed during the battle, or died later of wounds or exhaustion. There is no reliable record of the number of casualties; only that it was massive. One source, however, gives a good indication, for Jan Dlugosz wrote that "... having collected their booty, the Tatars, wishing to know the exact number of the enemy dead, cut one ear off each corpse, filling nine huge sacks to the brim".[3]

Nine bags of ears! No fewer than twenty-five thousand knights and foot folk died for what German historians termed for many centuries "the legendary defence of Europe against the Mongol horde".

Certain events have a moral effect that transcends their physical import-ance. Liegnitz was one of these. If the panicked cry of a Polish knight – most likely a Mongol ruse – played a decisive role, the real key to the calamity was the Mongols' superior weapon, the bow, and their use of tactical, non-chivalresque surprise, while on the other side, a knight's courage[4] was regarded as valid replacement for tactical planning.

For by that lethal process whereby one mistaken decision leads irresist-ibly to another, a most fearsome struggle was waged on this fateful ground. The knights' pride and vanity cost a terrible price. Hopelessly unaware of the Mongols' tactics, they dismissed the valour of their opponents and fought a battle according to their own preconceptions and prejudices. The noble barons were unwilling to accept that a "socially inferior rabble" with metal-tipped shafts had begun to dominate the battlefield.[5] In their fight against superior tactics and a brilliant tactical manoeuvre by their enemy, what may have been the best army of knights ever put in the field was destroyed. They fought the Mongols in conditions that suited the enemy rather than themselves, and so lost the day through their pride.

The only epitaph for the valiant *Fürst* Heinrich is: too much courage, too little sense. One can never be a substitute for the other on the field of battle, even today.

# 4

# LAST EXIT TO HELL

## 10 APRIL 1241, RIVER SAJO, HUNGARY

"Lighten our darkness, we beseech thee, O Lord."[1] Inside the Hungarian fortress of Pest, the men kneeling in prayer around their king were all members of the Magyar high aristocracy – and proud of it. A young nobleman, his face drawn and haggard, giving him an appearance of wisdom beyond his tender years, dared to say aloud what all thought.

"Noble King, the heathen is using your generosity to the Cumans as his excuse."

Standing a few feet apart from his knights, King Béla IV, ruler of the Magyar Kingdom and supreme lord of its vassal dominions, snorted. "As if the Mongol needs an excuse to be treacherous!"

"Majesty, you must call for support."

"Call on the tender pride of my fellow princes? They have abandoned us quickly enough. The German emperor is warring with the Pope in Lombardy, the French king is in Jerusalem, my Bohemian cousin is an arrogant ass and the Austrian archduke is an opportunist. No, *messires*, we are on our own."

Subotai had read it correctly: Europe was as divided as ever. With Kaidu's horde moving through Poland and Mongol danger to Scandinavia removed, King Waldemar IV of Denmark marched against the Swedes. Pope Gregory IX put a church ban on Germany's Emperor Friedrich II over his annexation of Tuscan church lands, while Friedrich kept himself busy fighting the Lombard League, the only viable force in northern Italy capable of holding the mountain passes against a possible Mongol invasion. When King Wenceslas of Bohemia was informed about Liegnitz, instead of countermarching his fifty thousand to bolster the army of his Hungarian cousin, he moved into position – against his Austrian neighbour! And as for the Austrian archduke, he counted on the Mongolians to tie down the Bohemians and Hungarians, so that he might grab the disputed provinces of Burgenland and Slovakia by coming to a deal with the Emperor. It left King Béla all on his own.

In late March of 1241 the Magyar king rode out of his fortress of Pest to confront a mounting Mongolian danger. It was on the march that he received a severe shock. Batu Khan and Subotai, with their sixty thousand men, had already crossed the Carpathian Mountains by the ancient "Gateway to Russia", the Verecki Pass. Worse was to follow: in this moment of great danger Béla's Cuman allies abandoned him. He had counted on using them as shock cavalry. During their flight, the Cumans stripped Hungary bare and devastated its flatlands.

But Béla could still count on some seventy to eighty thousand fighting men. His soldiers were not quite as bold as the men who had fought at Liegnitz, yet still outnumbered the horde of Batu Khan and Subotai. For once a Western king knew all about his enemy's real fighting strength. Béla marched his army along the River Theiss until he reached the River Sajo, then turned upstream toward the Plain of Mohi, a valley of fertile fields[2] leading up to the Carpathian passes. He established camp at the only bridge over the white-water torrent, intended for ox carts but not an army of knights. This narrow wooden bridge was to become the key in a drama.

On the day Kaidu and Baidar had engaged in battle against the Polish and German host, 9 April 1241, Batu and Subotai had force-marched their horde into the woods bordering this plain. Their scouts had encountered no Hungarian pickets. Subotai was certain that Béla's numerical superiority would make him careless and overconfident. By late evening Subotai was in an ideal position to carry out an ambush, but still lacked news from Kaidu and Baidar. Had their two northern *tuman* managed to delay the Bohemians? Late that night a courier came dashing up to Batu's column, bringing a message that Kaidu was about to engage the Poles in a precipitated battle because the Bohemian army was marching north. This confirmation told Subotai that his own flank was secure.

On 10 April, when Batu's advance party saw Béla's host, they withdrew. Later that afternoon, while the Hungarians rested or played dice in the security of their camp, Subotai sent scouts in search of a ford. The scouts discovered a shallow crossing six kilometres downstream. They brought another piece of good news: Béla had split his forces and encamped his army on both sides of the Sajo, with only a narrow bridge to mass his force. The Hungarian host was oblivious to any danger threatening them. Subotai, with thirty thousand of his best riders, crossed the Sajo in the dead of night and hid out in a dense forest.

Before dawn on 11 April, Subotai climbed to the crest of a hill and saw nothing but a tranquil and unwarlike countryside. On the blue horizon were mountain peaks, and on the plain, in between peaks and forest, something sparkled like hundreds of flickering stars: the campfires of the Hungarians. Subotai was alone; he needed to be, for it was best to think in solitude, taking his own counsel. Had he made a mistake, overlooked a detail? The trees hid his thirty thousand men; no campfires disclosed their presence. They squatted next to their horses, waiting for his signal to rush out of cover and slay the enemy.

It had been a chilly night, cold and damp. It took a while for the Hungarian camp to wake up; breakfast was cooked and Béla's soldiery sat around the fires pumping warmth into their bones when, like a thunder-clap, a great clamour arose on the opposite bank of the river. Batu had launched an advance attack, surprising the Hungarians. Three thousand Mongolian horsemen dashed for the bridge. For the detachment of Hungarians camping on the east bank of the Sajo, it came so suddenly that few were able even to don their armour. The fighting was brief but bloody. In spite of an heroic defence of the bridgehead, the Hungarians were bowled over.

As Batu expected, his surprise attack had set off a rush by Béla's men from both sides for the key bridge, leaving their rear undefended. With Béla leading the van, a thousand of his knights drove headlong for the bridge. They finally cleared the bridge; the knights dismounted to lead their horses to the water and ordered their retainers to cross back over and fetch replacements for their broken lances. Béla, now on the far bank, called for reinforcements, and many answered the call. With this two-way traffic, servants carrying wounded one way and knights riding the other, the narrow span across the raging water turned into a place of utter confusion. Half of the army was on one side, the other half near the camp on the opposite bank.

While this commotion was going on, nobody thought of sending out scouts and to keep a sharp eye for the rest of the enemy's forces. Just as the Hungarians and their allies thought that the Mongols had given up, and that they had somehow won a victory, a massive horde of thirty thousand Mongols appeared on the Plain of Mohi, racing headlong into the unpro-tected rear of Béla's divided forces. Subotai himself led the charge of light cavalry. The surprise to the now dismounted Hungarians and their allies was shattering. Sensing an imminent collapse of his forces on the opposite bank, Béla ordered the bulk of his army to re-cross the bridge and fend off the riders' attack. For this the bridge funnelled them into a narrow column. Chaos erupted as too many struggled to get across at the same time. Arrows struck mounted knights; they crashed in the middle of the span, and their wounded, kicking horses had to be heaved over the side to clear the bridge.

The brief, bloody encounter took only a few minutes. Batu's men succeeded in scattering Béla's formations. Almost before battle was joined, the fickle wheel of fortune turned. The Hungarian foot folk broke, and fled into the safety of their laager of wagons, abandoning their knights and leaving behind their wounded and dying.

There now followed a brief standoff. Though the dead were piled up outside Béla's camp, the situation inside began to settle down. The Magyar king prayed that order would soon emerge from chaos. His losses had been substantial, but not excessive in view of the magnitude of the battle, and he could still count on a numerical superiority from which to form new units. He began organizing the forces that would drive home another assault. Then he would hold out behind a strong defensive position until the Bohemian relief army showed up to attack the Mongols from the rear.

But this situation changed yet again when what looked like a flight of flickering yellow birds took wing; pots of burning pitch trailing threads of flame sailed over the wagon rampart, spreading flame when they shattered. Subotai was using captured Hungarian siege catapults to pound the camp with boulder and pitch. Massive casualties and great confusion resulted among the crowded Hungarians, who were trapped, pounded and roasted alive. This bombardment cracked their morale. Their only option – not good but all that was left – lay in a massive breakout, whatever the cost.

Then, when they seemed to be hopelessly trapped, a knight on a foaming horse dashed into Béla's camp, turned halfway in his saddle and pointed in the direction from which he had come. He had slipped past the encircling Mongols, he said, on a small, unguarded forest trail.

News spread from mouth to mouth: "There's a way out of hell."

Desperate men will grab at any hope to save their lives, however slight it might appear, and it was no different here. Pounded to flaming bits, the nobles became victims of the elementary error of trusting blindly in a questionable hope. Especially when that hope lay in a knight they did not know. As with that yelling Polish rider at Liegnitz, history does not reveal the identity of this man. It was another Mongol subterfuge, opening a tempting road to safety. It lured the knights from their strong defensive position. The Hungarians wasted no time – after all, there was little time to lose. The first knights shouldered past overturned carts in their dash from the camp. Taking to the forest trail, they managed to slip unharmed past the Mongols, and then waved to their beleaguered comrades from a distant rise. It was the signal that all was well; they would live to see tomorrow.

Soon the rest of Béla's army followed. They did so in a ragged, strung-out column with not the slightest chance of presenting a united battlefront. A man is never so vulnerable as when he flees; like a wounded animal to a pursuer, he gets the hunter's bloodlust up. And that is precisely what now happened. The Hungarians had reached the middle of the forest when massed hordes of Mongols flooded the forest trail. The result was devastating. A cry of anguish erupted; the slaughter surpassed the mind's capacity. Those who climbed trees to hide from the horror were plucked like pigeons from the branches.

"No survivors!" Batu Khan's order was based on revenge. The remnants of a broken army were followed wherever they fled, into marshes and forests, villages and churches, and there butchered. In a few hours of carnage the hordes cut down any man they found, knight or peasant. The dead and wounded lay crowded together in fields and forests, in villages and churches. Not counting local peasantry, their wives and children, it was estimated that sixty to seventy thousand Hungarians warriors had been put to death.

As at Liegnitz, Mongol deception had done its work. Béla's army, numerically still superior, but with its morale low, had been offered a tempting exit – only to discover that it was their last ride into hell. In just two days in April 1241 the Mongols annihilated two Christian armies three times their own strength. The Battle of the River Sajo, in its own way more dramatic than Liegnitz, marks no period in history. While the slaughter at Liegnitz carried on in fable, that of the Sajo faded into embarrassed silence. The folly of underestimating the skill and fortitude of the Mongols ended in disaster because the Hungarians failed to take their adversaries seriously. No doubt the knights had hoped that earnest combat would not interfere with what was essentially a battle to gain knightly honour. It had never been that way.

Liegnitz demolished in a single blow all the military achievements from Charlemagne to the Holy Crusades. Sajo merely set the seal on a Mongol predominance that was already absolute. A Hungarian victory would not have made the survival of Europe more than the forlorn hope it had always been ever since the murder of the Great Khan's 10 ambassadors.

# 5

# THE DIVINE MIRACLE

"*Vom Schrecken des Mongolen, befrei uns, Oh Herr!* Liberate us from the terror of the Mongol, O Lord!"

The news of the defeat of the Magyars reached Vienna, barely beating the terrified fugitives who fled before the Mongol advance like a flock of birds before a storm. All across Hungary and Austria, Lombardy, Germany and Bohemia people fell to their knees and prayed. Hope was gone. With the annihilation of the last *Ritterheer*, or knights' army, the gate to Europe was thrown open to the spectre of the rampaging Tartar. No one knew what horrors the Mongol tide would inflict. The terror had first put a nation, then half a continent, on the run. Villagers lit their houses and slaughtered their cattle, leaving nothing behind. Jan Dlugosz wrote that he had never experienced such frantic, unreasoning fear as he saw now. The *Grand Maître des Templiers* had to inform his monarch, King Louis IX: "The Tartars have destroyed the army of *le noble Duc* Henry de Pologne, with five hundred of our knights slain. Then they overran the army of *le Roi des Magyars*. There now stands nothing between us and the barbarous horde. *Sire*, it is the Hun all over again."

This was no exaggeration. With the flower of Europe's knightly class rotting in the Oder Marshes and on the Plains of Mohi, what was there to stop the Mongols from reaching the Rhine, Reims and Orléans, as Attila had done eight hundred years before? Europe trembled. King Louis of France swore to his mother, Queen Blanche: "We shall send the Tartars to hell,[1] or they shall send us to paradise."

Louis recalled his crusaders from Cyprus, Malta and the Holy Land; he dispatched ambassadors to the Pope and the German emperor, pleading with them to settle their personal grievances and unite behind the Holy Cross. To achieve that union would have been a divine wonder.

On the evening of the Battle of the Sajo, a wounded King Béla, weak from loss of blood, had managed to drag himself on to a horse. With two of his devoted barons, he finally reached Vienna with news that Batu Khan was rearming his hordes. This could only mean Bohemia, Austria or Lombardy was next. A Bohemian king and an Austrian archduke regretted their decision to deny assistance to their neighbour. Wenceslas's army could have found much better use farther north with Heinrich, or farther south with Béla. But then of course one doesn't rerun a battle a second time. As for the Austrian Friedrich von Babenberg, with five thousand armed townsmen he could hardly achieve what Heinrich's forty thousand, or Béla's eighty thousand, knights had failed to do.

All became clear when a delegate from Subotai Khan arrived at the archducal castle inside walled Vienna. His message was full of flowery phrases and elaborate compliments, but the meaning was clear enough: "Surrender, open the way along the Danube, or ..." In company of his lords, the Austrian *Erzherzog* (archduke) heard him out, then had the Mongol delegation led from the hall. The archduke looked down the long wooden table.

"Well, *messires*, Subotai Khan makes us an offer. Have you advice?"

A baron with a hard look in his eyes snapped: "An offer from a cursed Mongol who wades to the ankles in hot blood? I count my body cheaper in an hour of glory. This is our battle and here we make our stand, I say."

"Gallant spirit. But mark my word, noble baron, the worst is yet to come."

From the little they had learned about Liegnitz and the Sajo, knights knew that on their own they could never face lightning-fast mounted archers and lances. Noble knights had the silly notion of an obligation to fight for their honour – sprint out in front, and be slaughtered in the first three minutes of contact.

A knight spoke out: "Honour demands that we fight."

Graf Kuenring, who had recently returned from the Holy Land, chimed in: "I have never been one to fight for honour alone. I prefer to win. But we can do no good elsewhere, and we must hold Vienna. We sit astride the only way into the Holy Roman Empire."

The *Markgraf* of Enns rose; he was old, but his voice was steady enough when he said: "We cannot fight the Tartar in the open. If you mean to die here, I will stand with you. If we are caught outside these walls, we are finished."

"I agree, our city has stout walls, and its granaries are full. Until this town is taken, Subotai can take no great force up the Danube Valley. We can hold off until aid arrives."

"Aid? We've never been so thoroughly cut off from help." It was impossible to ignore the undercurrent of despair.

"Do you counsel surrender?" the *Markgraf* wanted to know.

"To take that choice is not only immoral, but dangerous. It's a forlorn fight all the same."

Two months passed. From the towers of the Austrian border fortress of Pressburg (Bratislava), the men guarding the ramparts saw great columns of smoke rising. The Great Horde was on its way! The fortress, built a century before on a rock which locals called "The Virgin", because it had defied all onslaughts, was strategically placed in a fork of the rivers March and Danube. Beyond, to the north, loomed the Low Carpathian Mountains, and to the south were the reed-covered bogs of Lake Neusiedl. It was easy to see why this fortress controlled access to the Upper Danube Valley, and its capital, Vienna.

The first of Subotai's advance reached the walls of the fortress. While they waited for their siege train to catch up, wildly whirling Mongol horsemen trampled the surrounding fields into mud. It did not impress the two thousand defenders on the outer ramparts, standing to their ranks.

"Make your posts good and strong," ordered Pressburg's commander, the valiant *Ritter* Marko von Marchegg. Mongol trebuchets discharged, their stones bouncing off the solid walls. Time and again the Mongol archers advanced, their arrows falling thick and heavy. The savagery of the attackers and the heroism of the defenders were repeated day after endless day, until fields and barricades were heaped with the dead. Holding a small outer bastion which protected the boat landing had become impossible. *Ritter* von Marchegg rode out to the relief of this besieged garrison. Fighting as they retreated step by step, wielding their long swords and leaving the ground covered with Mongol bodies, he and his hard-pressed warriors retired behind the safety of the solid walls around "The Virgin's" mighty *donjon* and their holy Church of the Ascension. The fortress commander was everywhere, encouraging his men's valour by word and deed, until he too was struck by an arrow. Another knight took over. "… and fearful noise and slaughter began, lances and swords … the ringing of bells, the clashing of arms, the cries of fighting men, the shrieks of women and the wailing of children, produced such a noise that it seemed as if the earth trembled. Clouds of rancid smoke fell over the town, until the combatants could no longer see each other…"[2]

But the fortress held, one week, two, then a third. Praise went to those who stood and fought, at a high cost, but they bought precious time for readying Vienna's defences. Out of the two thousand defenders, vigilant in their watchfulness and courage, not a hundred were finally left who could still stand to arms. But the fortress of Pressburg held. Day after interminable day the stench of death from bloated bodies and burned houses drifted across the walls; and day after day the knights beat back savage rushes: sometimes with "thick clouds of quarrels they shot"; sometimes on top of the stone rampart "with lance's tip and sword's cut moved to fury because they were desperate".

Then, as the noble knights of Pressburg were beginning to think that everything was over for them, a miracle took place. On the morning of 22 March 1242 the exhausted defenders woke to the quiet stirrings of a dawning day. Fat grey gulls squawked and launched sweeping attacks on the fire-blackened stone walls, their wings beating against the breeze as they landed. There was no other sound. Sleep-drugged defenders rushed to the top of the ramparts, taking in the scene. From up high they stared with incredulity at broken lances and heaps of dead. But there were no more trebuchets, no archers and no madly circling riders. The battle-weary defenders stumbled from the fortress to fetch water from the Danube; there was not one of them who was not wounded after the long siege.

Fortunately for Pressburg and Europe, Subotai's main column never even reached the fortress on the Danube. Suddenly the fierce horsemen from the East were gone, man and horse and wagon. Nobody could tell why or where the enemy had stolen away. Gone was the spectre of the murderous Mongol. A brutal horde, set to obliterate Europe, had vanished, never again to be seen in the heart of the continent.

"*Halleluiah ...*", rejoiced the citizens of Vienna, who burned candles and flocked into their churches.

"We've stopped them," claimed barons who had never been involved in combat.

And Pope Gregory IX praised the Lord. "His divine providence has saved Christianity."

What was this divine providence, this miracle, which saved central Europe?

On 11 December 1241 *Khakhan* Ogedei passed away in the Mongol capital. His father, Genghis Khan, had laid down a binding law of succession that decided the issue: "Following the death of a Supreme Khan any offspring of the House of Genghis Khan, wherever he might be, must return to Mongolia to take part in the election of a new *Khakhan*."

From the Mongol capital, Karakorum, a relay of dispatch riders had set out in the middle of that month. Changing horse and rider hourly allowed a never-ending chain of messengers to dash across the arid sands, climb mountains and ford raging streams; in a few months they rode eight thousand miles to deliver a recall to all princes of royal blood. By the middle of the spring of 1242 they reached Batu Khan, to whom they gave the electrifying news: "The Khan of All Khans is dead!" In the scramble for Ogedei's succession, the conquest of Europe counted for naught. The khans reversed their hordes and disappeared to whence they had come.

The death of a single man was all it took to deliver Western civilization from annihilation. Miracle – or divine providence?

In face of mortal danger, Europe's monarchs had failed wretchedly in their duty to protect their societies by uniting into a single front. For that to happen it would have taken intelligence, co-ordination and will. The European monarchs lacked all three. At the decisive point in the struggle to stem the Mongol tide, the Occident was plagued by a Bohemian king who was afraid of his responsibility and allowed fear to dominate his thinking. The result was two disastrous defeats. United, the three knightly armies of Heinrich II von Schlesien, Béla of Hungary and Wenceslas of Bohemia would have undoubtedly achieved a great victory. With the peril of the Mongol gone, the memory of bloodthirsty hordes from the East became the bogeyman of a forgotten past, and the disunity of monarchical Europe flourished anew.

King Béla IV of Hungary managed to escape to Austria, where Archduke Friedrich von Babenberg put him in irons,[3] before grabbing the Magyar king's Burgenland province.

King Wenceslas of Bohemia used the same opportunity to incorporate the Magyar's lands north of the Danube (today's Slovakia) into his domain.

Emperor Friedrich II of Germany led his army into Italy and annexed Tuscany, which earned him papal excommunication.

The Plantagenet King Henry III of England invaded France in 1242, where King Louis IX defeated him at Saintes. The French recovered Aquitaine and Toulouse.

Alexander Nevski, Prince of Novgorod, defeated a Teutonic host on frozen Lake Peipus and became a heroic symbol for Russia.

Pope Innocent IV fled to France, where Louis IX encouraged him to renew his church ban on the German emperor. Pope Innocent died and Clemens IV took the Holy See. Under his guidance, and in a historic reversal, the Church tried a novel approach with the Mongols. In 1247 the pope's nuncio Gianni di Plano Carpini delivered a message to Mangu Khan at the court at Karakorum: "We, Clemens IV, Shepherd of all Christendom, extend our greetings to the Great Khan ..."

At stake was the Mongols' conversion to Christianity, as well as the formation of a two-front alliance against Islam. To get the Mongol interested, the papal nuncios talked of the golden riches in Islam's holy centres. The newly elected *Khakhan* Mangu listened carefully to Rome's proposal – and it gave him an idea. Why ally himself with the earthly representative of some strange god? Instead he decided to dispatch a horde to conquer the Caliphate of Islam and grab its fabled riches. From there he would move west, into Europe, continuing what Subotai and Batu had left unfinished.

For this it took a leader. That man was Hulagu and his name spelled terror.

# 6

# THE CULT OF BLIND TERROR

## SPRING 1256, FORTRESS OF ALAMUT, ELBORZ MOUNTAINS, PERSIA

Hulagu, a man known for his cruel eyes, glared with approval on the extermination of a villainous sect. With their bodies flung from the battlements into the dark abyss died the terror they had spread. Vultures spiralled over the site that had, for all too long, dispatched fear and death. In the rocky upthrusts of the Elborz Mountains lived a sect so diligently ruthless that from their name derives the expression for fanatical murder: the Assassins. In the long roll call of blind villainous acts which stain the pages of history, there is nothing quite like the Cult of the Assassins. In their quest for a global demonization they applied appalling terror and destroyed what others held dear.

The day that the newly elected *Khakhan* Mangu ordered his brother Hulagu Khan to continue the Mongol conquest of the "lands beyond the Sea of Sand",[1] Hulagu Khan trampled over every force that dared to stand in his way. Finally he came upon a foe, unseen but no less dangerous: a sect of religious fanatics who boasted a burning desire for self-sacrifice as the bringer of death in a sacred cause. Terrorists there had been before, but never this type of robotic killer, the creation of an evil genius, practitioner of psychological warfare and brainwashing. Hassan al-Sabbah, "The Man of the Mountain", leader of the *Hachchâchin*. In 1090 this Islamic zealot preached his gospel of hate in the mountainous regions of Persia. He sermonized that every faithful man must prepare his path to messianic redemption by an act of subservient sacrifice. What better way to achieve eternal bliss than by turning into a suicidal terrorist? This bigoted Ismaili managed to stir such religious fervour that his *fidayeen* (devotees) gladly offered him their lives in self-destructive missions. His followers prostrated themselves before him and swore to obey his every command, however deranged, that would bring upheaval and chaos. "You do my will, and obey any of my orders. Never shall you question my wisdom, because I'm the enlightened of Allah."

With his overpowering charisma Hassan al-Sabbah mystified countless youngsters, who otherwise faced a bleak future in the abject poverty of their mountain villages. Susceptible to the Imam's promise of a martyr's place in paradise, complete with the affections of kohl-eyed virgins, they came to see this exceedingly dangerous man as the incarnation of God on Earth. During their initiation into the sect they were drugged with a potent brew of hashish. When they woke from their drug-induced sleep they felt that they had entered into an afterlife in paradise and that their life on this Earth was only a passage to bliss thereafter. To their drugged senses, myth, fantasy and reality converged, creating violent imagery. So Hassan al-Sabbah converted his embryonic monsters into fanatically religious terrorists. All came from the radical Shia Muslims, who considered anyone outside their faction to be without faith; and Allah decreed that faithlessness must be punished by unprecedented severity. Before he dispatched them to do his evil command, Hassan al-Sabbah explained the nobility of their act of sacrificing themselves in the pursuit of holy revenge: "Nothing can stop him who chooses a martyr's glory, from his sacred mission."

From their fortress of Alamut ("The Eagle's Nest"), located in the lunar landscape of the Elborz Mountains, the sect's members roamed their region, refining the use of murder as a political weapon by "assassinating" kings and potentates. They struck out blindly, with no apparent reason; their ultimate goal was to spread terror. They lived by hatred and perished with their fanaticism intact. Hassan al-Sabbah flashed his daggers without selecting sides; he established an entirely new kind of warfare: fear by terrorism. A devilish sect was born. At its leader's death, the sect morphed from a hierarchical organization into a multi-headed hydra, with independently operating cells spreading terror throughout Persia, Anatolia and Mesopotamia. Whenever a new force moved into the region, it wisely allied itself with the sect of killers in order to overthrow the existing political structure by assassination. This persuaded the Mongol Hulagu Khan to enter into a loose alliance with the Assassins. He allowed them to do his dirty work, and then stepped in to fill the vacuum.

Such a coalition could not last with someone as ruthless and ambitious as Hulagu. After several successful "assignments", Kurshah, successor to the notorious Hassan al-Sabbah, staked his demand. Hulagu saw no place in his future plans for a religious zealot. The bond between two equally ruthless characters was broken. Within the month Kurshah dispatched a killer to demonstrate his power to strike whomever he selected for terminal punishment. The man in ragged clothes uttered a stifled scream when a

Mongol grabbed him by the hair and twisted his head. He stared at a number of leathery faces. Soon he admitted that he was not who he pretended to be, an outcast, but a man with a sacred mission; his life had no more meaning, since he could no longer fulfil his mission, which was to kill the Khan of the Mongols. Hulagu had the assassin slow-roasted over an open fire. The devotee died screaming; with his last breath he praised the name of Allah and asked his master's forgiveness for having failed him. To Hulagu this attempt on his life signalled a need to eliminate the danger, according to the ancient wisdom: "Kill him before he kills you." But first he had to reach the Assassins' fortress. Not an easy task.

The wind blew thick snow clouds over the land, swept great stretches bare and drove huge billows of white before it. Animal and man sank deep into the powdered snow on narrow valley paths, marked by poles which were often barely visible. Nothing would stop a Mongol horseman. Foam froze on the horses' mouths as the riders trotted on, until the land rose to a number of high ridges, where leafless trees raised their naked arms to the sky to warn the uninvited not to penetrate into this kingdom of evil. Porters and non-combatants kept hanging back, showing fear that would give the mightiest warrior pause. They were terrified by this land of demons, with its craggy peaks and deep valleys, where the temperature seemed to remain for ever below zero. Rocks were honeycombed with fissures housing deadly snakes. Trees twined their roots about the crags which rose from narrow defiles. Paths were strewn with rocks, chafing the legs of horses. To the shouts of drivers, animals strained on the harnesses of wagons laden with heavy siege catapults. On both sides of the track lay the snow-covered corpses of slave porters, cut down by frost and famine. Then suddenly the narrow chasm gave out and before them lay a fairytale sight: mountainous crags reaching into the sky, snow glistening in the sun and, clinging precariously to a cliff like a swallow's nest, a mighty fortress: the Alamut of the Assassins.

Kurshah's lookouts had informed him of the approach of "a great column of horsemen". Despite the warning he ignored the alternatives open to him. The Assassins' Grand Master decided to demonstrate the magic powers which had been bestowed on him by the Almighty and show his deep contempt for the Mongol horde. "Stand fast, and with Allah by your side, we shall meet in Paradise."

Fanatical and suicidal, his disciples pledged to honour their promise to lay down their lives for the glory of their master. Within a week the situation inside the beleaguered fortress was desperate. Winter was harsh, with temperatures so low that the wounded froze to death within minutes. Food was severely rationed. The ill or weak were pushed out and left to freeze, to keep their provisions for those who could fight. Days went by with nothing to eat; sometimes there was a handful of uncooked rye, which the men cupped in their hands and, after blowing away the dust, chewed on. Despite the hardship, a sacred fire consumed them, their eyes shining in ecstasy. They were eager to die for something that was worth much more than their lives: the prospect of earthly sacrifice in exchange for heavenly salvation. "All men must die," they repeatedly reassured one another, "and tomorrow is Paradise."

Hulagu's catapults did no damage to the rocky precipice, and the defenders seemed to have provisions to survive a lengthy blockade. Alamut's ramparts were so cleverly interlocked that a frontal assault was impossible. That is, until a local herder told the Mongol Khan about a weak point in the fortifications – a spur extending from a precipice so steep and distant that it was thought invulnerable and need not be included in the castle's breastwork. Hulagu selected a hundred men from his personal guard and ordered them to use grappling hooks to scale the cliff leading up to the spur, while he drew the Assassins' attention by bombarding the fortress with flaming pitch.

That night one hundred of Hulagu's men climbed the precipice in total darkness; they searched for finger holds and pulled themselves upward by wedging shoulders and feet into cracks. Since much of the rock was covered with a thin layer of ice, their fingers were numbed with cold. Many could not hold on and crashed to their death; but a few made it to the top and lowered ropes to others. A strong breeze blew away the clouds and the fortress was bathed in moonlight, outlining individual targets. Perched like dark vultures on the spur, the Mongols began burying part of the defences under a hail of feathered missiles. Confusion broke out among the *fidayeen*, allowing a group of attackers to slip past them and grope their way along the walls toward the main gate, where they quickly dealt with the group guarding the entrance. Then they cut the tie ropes of the drawbridge, which dropped with an ear-shattering bang. Masses of Mongols swarmed through the open gate.

Hulagu Khan sat on his horse and watched, his face a mask of scorn; his visible presence fired his men. With the final breastwork overcome, the fighting was over, but not the killing. The surviving defenders leapt to their deaths or were tossed over the side from the top of the ramparts, twisting and screaming as their bodies spun off into the darkness below. An eyewitness wrote: "The world has been cleansed of the evil that polluted it. A wind seemed to have died."[2]

The Assassins subscribed to an extreme suicidal model, based on a twisted interpretation of Muslim law, and the mistaken, if deeply held, belief in a never-ending *jihad*. With the Mongols their luck came to an end. The evil spread by a callous master of terrorism was outmatched when he met up with an even greater master of brutality. No prisoners were taken, no leaders were tried and no one was left to tell a story. A handful managed to slip through the ring of attackers, but the Mongols hunted them down and killed them brutally.

An evil sect died, but its legacy carried on, and its ghost has haunted the world ever since. A primeval outcrop from a dark period of the human mind, motivated by an extreme, religious terrorism and cursed by a violent past, had perished. Hulagu Khan himself, conqueror of Persia and Turkistan, Mesopotamia and Transcaucasia, Anatolia and Syria, watched the destruction of Alamut, Fortress of the Assassins. But as an old terror disappeared, so a new terror arose from it, for terror never dies.

# 7

# THE FLAMING END OF 1,001 NIGHTS

## 7TH OF SAFAR 656 (13 FEBRUARY 1258), BAGHDAD, ABBASID CALIPHATE

From the entrance of his campaign yurt, Hulagu Khan stared out across the central plain of Mesopotamia. Millions had died on these fertile plains since Abraham's flocks roamed the rich fields. Hittites, Egyptians, Assyrians, Babylonians, Persians, Greeks, Romans, Huns and Turks had ravaged it; the Prophet's armies drove out the non-believers; Frankish crusaders clashed over it against the forces of Islam. And now Hulagu's rapidly advancing Mongol horde whipped up dense clouds of swirling dust on the plains where civilization was born, between the two great rivers Euphrates and Tigris; prisoners, slaves and carts laden with plunder followed them. The pillage had been pathetic; there was no gold to be found in the hovels of peasants. There was no loot worth carrying, unless it was taken in memory of the carnage which had obtained it. For a measly earthen jar or a wooden bedstead, they had spent hours torturing the natives in an attempt to find hidden treasures that never existed.

By contrast, great plunder could be expected in the capital of the Caliphate; women wrapped in silks and pearls, men with turbans studded with rubies and emeralds. Cool interior courtyards with fountains, streets paved with marble and a thousand mosques covered with precious carpets. "Baghdad the Golden". That was where Hulagu's horde was headed. Peace was about to be shattered in the Caliphate of the Prophet. A new breed was entering the World of Islam – the pagan lords of the steppes. It was no longer Allah who would hold court on a heavenly throne; the Mongol Beast had replaced God the Almighty.

Men are best at what they love, and Hulagu Khan loved conquering; at that he would not be beaten. His message to the Abbasid Caliph al-Mustassim was brief and to the point: "Bow before the mighty Khan and the lives of your faithful may be spared. Fight us and they will assuredly perish. There will be no further warning. We will not negotiate."

The Caliph received the note with consternation; no mortal had ever dared threaten the sacrosanct figure of the Prophet's representative on Earth. Whoever defied the Caliph would heap the wrath of the World of Islam upon his head. Caliph al-Mustassim felt sure in his belief that he could rely on every Muslim rushing to his assistance. To buy time for such an army to be assembled and to ensure the protection of the Faith, he ordered his general, Abu Omar, "to ride forth under the green banner of the Prophet, and, with his mighty fist, bar the route to the pagan horde".

Hulagu Khan was not worried about the wrath of the Prophet. He could handle wrath, and any one army at a time. But his scouts had warned him of the existence of a relief force in Egypt. To prevent the two armies from joining he would precipitate a battle on the banks of the Tigris.

Abu Omar's army was packed into rectangles, with a soldier every three feet. A Shia foot force of several thousand formed up as the centre of the line, their eight-foot lances glistening in the desert sun. For Hulagu's forces, if danger existed, it would come from the desert tribes on their lightning-fast Arabian horses in a contest where better weapons training and discipline would make the difference.

The Caliph's cavalry was five hundred yards away and accelerating. While the bulk of Islam's army headed straight for the line of dismounted Mongol archers, its cavalry divided into two flanking movements. The Mongol archers released their arrows at three hundred yards; the flight brought down the first row of desert horsemen. Despite the incredible punishment inflicted, the next wave of riders hurtled over the fallen and continued at a tremendous clip. The suicidal cavalry charge was decisive. The Muslim riders were among the Mongols and slaughtered them like cattle. In despair over the unforeseen disaster, Hulagu tried to rally his men. Leading a *tuman* himself, he launched another attack, but it broke on the wall of Islam's levelled lances.

The Caliph's general watched the massacre, until a piece of shattering news reached him. In one of history's decisive acts of treachery, the contingent of Muslim warriors, anchoring his centre – not Sunni, but the fanatical Shia – had gone over to the enemy! Without hesitation Hulagu led his heavy rider units in a new assault on the gap that had formed in the line. With a thousand paces to build momentum, they struck into the open flank of Abu Omar's foot force, driving their enemy back toward the riverbank and into a hail of Mongol arrows. Seized by terror, the Arabs and Turks took flight. The Caliph's army crumbled. The Mongols chased after the fugitives and hacked down thousands. Above the field of slaughter rose a lance with a silver crescent, the symbolic tombstone of a last stand. For the Caliph the battle was lost and so was his capital, into which the human flotsam of a routed army drifted, as bloodied and depressed as the broken Caliphate itself.

After his surprise victory Hulagu Khan repaid the Shia betrayal in kind. His Mongols rounded up the renegade Shia soldiers and sent them to work in the Persian silver mines. Their chieftains were done to death because "A man who betrays once and lives to talk of it, will betray again". On that, Hulagu had learned to take no chances.

Abu Omar never believed that any of the faithful would ever betray the most sacred representative of his Prophet. And yet, at the height of a decisive battle, the century-old religious strife between the two main branches of Islam, Sunni and Shia, led to a monumental brotherly betrayal – one of the most significant in history. Without the Shia pullout, the forces of Islam would surely have won a crushing victory. Instead it was a thoroughly humiliating defeat. The outcome of one battle was to bring about the fall of five and a half centuries of the glorious Islamic Caliphate.

The desert sun rose in a blood-red ball over Baghdad, the magnificent capital of Islam, a city of fabulous wealth and priceless treasures, on the 4th of Safar in the Year of the Prophet 656 (10 February 1258). Caliph al-Mustassim, a white-bearded man old beyond his years, stared from the window of his palace at the smoke that smouldered from many parts of his tortured city. The face of this most holy man of Islam showed only an image of despair. His defiance was gone. "In a few days the horde will scale the walls; whatever we may do, the people will suffer when a place is taken by storm. What choice is there?" he asked his closest advisers, no hope in his voice.

After a heated discussion of possible new strategies, there seemed only two courses open to the Caliph: hope for a miracle, resist with his paltry force and risk the sacking that would follow; or throw himself on a Mongol's never tender mercy. Caliph al-Mustassim chose to take the softer course; he thus revealed an extraordinary lack of knowledge of his enemy's character, and a misplaced trust in a Mongol's capacity for chivalry.

Over five centuries Baghdad had developed into the most important trade centre of the medieval world. Through its gates passed diamonds and slaves from Africa and spice and silk from the Orient. Craftsmen designed intricate enamelled lamps for the mosques, goldsmiths fashioned elaborate jewellery and weavers transformed silk threads into the finest cloth. The centre of the city, around the Caliph's splendid palace, was reserved for parks with an abundance of citrus trees, with exotic animals roaming freely on its lawns and birdcages full of chirping of birds from Africa. Regiments of slaves tended to the needs of the palace. The harems held the most beautiful slaves of any colour; pale European women and exotic black Nubians fetched the highest prices. Each patrician house displayed its foremost treasure: water, gurgling from intricate fountains.

And then there was the gold, uncountable gold, and precious stones. Such treasures had to be well protected and an earlier Caliph had thought it prudent to build two lines of ramparts; an outer wall to protect the town and an inner wall to protect the wealth at its heart. But walls can serve a double function: if they are meant to keep out an enemy, they can also lock in contagious diseases. Leaning against the outer wall was a jumble of slums swept by hot desert winds, shantytowns of misery and choking dust. These parts of the city had suffered a recent cholera epidemic which had spread across the walls. The fear of a renewed outbreak was to play heavily in the weeks to come.

Once the defeat of Abu Omar's army became known, the Caliph sent out messages soliciting compassion and assistance in fighting the Mongol Peril. There was no immediate danger. Baghdad's battlements were strong, the supply of corn would last a month – or longer if tightly rationed – and there was water aplenty from the Tigris. So assured, the Caliph awaited the arrival of a relief army of a hundred and twenty thousand tough desert fighters from the Sultanate of Egypt.

There was another powerful force, closer than the Egyptians, which could have made all the difference, if only by threatening the Mongols' open flank. A mighty host of Frankish knights was based in the great fortresses of the Holy Land. They saw little to choose between fighting infidels or pagans. Despite the obvious danger that a Mongol victory would bring to Christian possessions, neither Antioch nor Constantinople made its move. Their loathing of anything Muslim was too inbred. And so, with the venerable head of all Islam threatened with extinction, the opportunity for an accommodation between Christian and Muslim was sadly missed. Then the moment was gone.

In a ritual perfected on other towns at other times in other lands, Hulagu Khan's move was predictable. He never allowed an enemy time to prepare defences; only five days after the Tigris battle, on 22 January 1258, his siege train appeared before the walls of Baghdad, the most challenging siege he had ever carried out. In only three days his Mongols, assisted by thousands of forced labourers, constructed battlements and aligned their catapults and ballistas. Hulagu had no time to waste; his scouts had spotted the Egyptian relief force on the move. Should this reach Baghdad in time, his horde would find itself hopelessly squeezed between the ramparts and the huge relief army. To prevent news of the approaching Egyptians from reaching the Caliph, he sealed off the city.

Hulagu's attack began simultaneously on each of the five main gates. Siege towers rolled forward; hundreds of muscled slaves strained to push the wooden monsters. Leaders shouted the rhythm, boys poured melted fat on the axles. The defenders fired flaming arrows at the siege machines; to counter them, the Mongols pushed a great number of hostages into baskets, pulled these to the top of the siege towers and watched the defenders pour volleys of flaming arrows into the baskets. The first assaults were successfully halted.

The Mongols then began bombarding the city with dozens of ballistas and catapults; but not just a routine bombardment of boulder and pitch. Instead, Hulagu had had thousands of battle casualties piled up on wagons and he used them now – as ammunition. His catapults lobbed decapitated bodies and baskets full of heads into the city. The horror of corpses raining down from the sky and the spectre of an epidemic from the fetid bodies achieved in a short time what the ruthless Mongol Khan could not achieve by frontal attack: a collapse of morale and a general panic among the citizens passed on to the defenders manning the ramparts. A city's defence is only as solid as a defender's will to resist, and that will was gone.

A final, desperate attempt to break through Hulagu's siege ring ended in disaster. Those manning the walls had to look on helplessly as the Mongols fell upon their retreating friends until the pale sand outside the ramparts became soaked with their blood. But still Baghdad held out. The Mongols tried again and again, each effort failing to breach the high ramparts. After all else failed they began firing flaming arrows. They set the canvas-covered soukh on fire, robbing themselves of rich plunder as the flames turned the city into an immense brazier. The heat ignited furniture in homes and carpets in mosques. Survivors ran blindly through the nauseating smoke, wrapped in water-soaked rags as feeble protection against the searing flames; they stumbled over the grossly swollen carcasses of man and beast, while inside mosques the great heat welded them together into a sputtering, smoking black mass. Those who escaped the inferno had their hair singed off so the sexes resembled each other.

Four weeks of horror. With no news from the outside, and no relief army in sight, the Prophet's representative on Earth was chagrined by what he considered a betrayal by the faithful. On the morning of 10 February 1258, after all defences had failed, with tens of thousands of dead or dying and much of the city destroyed by fire, the Caliph capitulated. He ordered Abu Omar to ride out and meet with Hulagu Khan to "make a good bargain for my people". Hulagu received the Caliph's emissary with diplomatic courtesy. He studied the Caliph's commander, a head bloodied but unbowed, a proud man aware that he had lost. Hulagu promised to spare the city and its inhabitants on condition that it opened its doors and surrendered all the Caliph's men.

"You can prevent great slaughter," the Khan said, "we've come not for bloodlust but for loot. Now that we've beaten your army, you are powerless to stop us from sacking the city. That will be a lot of trouble – I'd rather not do that. If you arrange for all the wealth of Baghdad to be loaded on wagons and delivered to me, I will spare the town. If you do not, we will take Baghdad by storm – then there will be no controlling my warriors."

Abu Omar's eyes narrowed. "You ask for tribute from Islam's most holy man?"

"I make no request, I only demand what is already mine. The sole uncertainty is whether the city will survive. Tell him that he is a lucky man. His fate is for him to decide."

Hulagu Khan presented the general with a rich purse and sent him back to deliver his offer of clemency to his Caliph. With the promise of safe conduct, the Caliph ordered the surrender of his battered defenders. As the meaning of his words sank into their addled brains, they knew their fate was sealed. They – more than their Caliph – knew how a Mongol kept his promise. But they obeyed, laid down their arms and left the town by its five gates. Outside the city walls the Mongols rounded them up and butchered them like cattle.

Knowing nothing of the Khan's predictable betrayal, Caliph al-Mustassim rode out of town to parley with the Mongol leader. Accompanied by his sons and wearing the full regalia of the representative of the Prophet on Earth, with the magnificent Ruby of the Caliph on his turban, the Caliph approached Hulagu's yurt. On the way he had to pass through a line of warriors whose eyes greedily assessed him. When they saw the old man's sons still bearing their arms, tension rippled among them and they raised their weapons. Hulagu barked a command and led the Caliph into his tent. Slaves served the visitors scented tea and Hulagu enquired about the state of his "honoured visitor's" health, when suddenly Mongol warriors threw open the flaps of the yurt and the Khan's guards dragged Abu Omar in. His tunic was torn and there was blood on his face. Caliph al-Mustassim suddenly realized the trap into which he had stumbled.

"Is this how Hulagu Khan keeps his promises?" he demanded. "You gave your word that my officers would be treated with respect. You are villainous traitors."

"Traitors do not die easily, as you will learn," replied Hulagu Khan, then motioned to Abu Omar's guards. "Take that carrion out of my presence and cut his throat with the rest. Then bring me his head."

The guards took firm hold of the Caliph and his sons. The old man's face twisted with inner pain over the immensity of the betrayal, and his lips turned blue.

"You will not dare touch a holy man." Never had a representative of the Prophet been reduced to such deprivation, no Caliph of Baghdad so humiliated.

"Get this worthless old crow out of my sight," Hulagu Khan barked. "But first I want him do me proper homage."

Hulagu's guards forced the Abbasid to his knees, a man representing an unbroken line of Caliphs stretching back five centuries. The Khan ripped off the Caliph's *rubis regalis*, and with it, stripped the Caliph of his power. They dragged the old man outside, muddying his white robe. Then there was nothing. As Juvaini wrote:

> After a Siege of Twenty days, accompanied with a Thousand Difficulties, Sicknesses, Want of Provisions, and great Effusion of Blood, after a Million of Catapult Shot, and Headless Bodies of the Faithful raining down, and all sorts of Fire Works, which has changed the Face of the fairest and most flourishing City in the World, disfigured and ruined most part of the best Palaces of the same, and chiefly those of the Caliph; and damaged in many places the Beautiful Minarets, with many Sumptuous Buildings. After a Resistance so vigorous, and the Loss of so many brave Faithful Defenders, whose Valour and Bravery deserve Immortal Glory. After so many Toils endured, so many Watchings and so many Orders so prudently distributed by Our Most Venerated Holy Caliph, and so punctually executed by the other Officers. After so many new Retrenchments, Bastions, Courtins, and principal Streets and Houses in the Town: Finally, after a Vigorous Defence and a Resistance without parallel, The One and Only in Heaven did not hear the Prayers and Tears of His Cast-down and Mournful People and drove him the Fearful Horde from the Walls of Baghdad. And then having so Vigorously attacked the Splendid City with a Hundred Thousand Men; and by endless Workings, Trenchings, and Minings, reduced it to its last gasp.

Three days later, on the 7th of Safar 656 (13 February 1258), Hulagu's Mongols sacked Baghdad. Through the open gates came thundering a cyclone of horsemen in pursuit of plunder, rape and murder. Citizens to whom their venerated Caliph had promised their lives were ridden down at the point of the lance. That they had been denied the promise of easy plunder when they burned the city pushed the wild riders into berserk madness. Corpses littered the streets, while Mongol gangs hurried from house to house, pillaging, raping and stabbing. From every quarter came the sounds of violence and outrage: thundering blows of war maces on barricaded doors, miserable shrieks of women suffering brutal rape, the death rattles of the fatally wounded.

The Mongols enjoyed flinging people from battlements. Inside holy places which had somehow survived the firestorm, and where thousands had gathered seeking salvation, they rode their ponies through the doors and hacked down worshippers still kneeling in prayer. Reprisals were beyond description. Whenever any Mongol was hurt in a trivial act of defiance, or a man tried to protect his wife from rape, a hundred hostages were buried alive. Worst off were "terrorists": citizens who dared to stand up against the Mongols or even kill a few of them; they had their bellies slashed and were hung upside down beside their family. For seven days this city of legend, with its slender minarets, its beautiful manicured gardens and its women known for their grace and exquisite beauty, was sacked in an orgy of blood, looting and rape.

As Juvaini recounted, "Hulagu Khan decamped from Baghdad on the 14th of Safar 656 [20 February 1258] on account of the foul air."

Seven days of blood-dripping horror made Hulagu Khan go down in history as the "Butcher of Baghdad", a sad record only matched a century later by another Tartar Khan, Tamerlane. No scholar has ever arrived at an exact number of victims, but certainly it exceeded half a million souls. Numbers were only details, insignificant to contemporary scribes; they wrote history to flatter their master, exaggerating or diminishing, glorifying or accusing. And statistics written up years after the event from hearsay are unreliable. One thing is, however, sure: Baghdad suffered beyond imagination.

The earthly representative of the Prophet, the Abbasid Caliph, and his three sons would meet the perfidious Hulagu Khan one final time. It happened on the day of their death, the 14th of Safar 656.

"I want the blood of this mullah to make the soil at my feet a crimson carpet!" Hulagu Khan wished the Caliph dead, but shrank from the odium of killing himself a holy man. A learned Chinese had warned his Khan of an ancient prophecy: the blood of a Caliph was never to touch the ground; spilling it would bring wrath upon the assassin's head. The Mongols knew a simple method to avoid this fate. Hulagu ordered the Caliph and his sons to be sewn into carpets, placed on the ground and trampled under the hooves of horses. No blood was spilled. With the death of the Abbasid al-Mustassim ended the line of Islamic Caliphs which had lasted more than half a millennium.

History belongs to victors, even those morally ambiguous. Their deeds belong to that category of crimes which abound in world history and add so much to its sinister character; crimes that are effortlessly committed and often completely wanton. A Caliph's ill-placed trust in a Mongol's promise was the deciding mistake. In less than a month a brutal Khan achieved what all the Pope's men had not accomplished through five and a half centuries: put an end to the Caliphate of Islam. Hulagu Khan destroyed it, inadvertently aiding the Crusaders and the papacy by temporarily stemming the spread of Islam.

# 8

# THE TURN OF THE TIDE

## 8 SEPTEMBER 1260, THE WELLS OF GOLIATH (AIN JALUT), NEAR NAZARETH, PALESTINE

With the Caliphate destroyed, there was nothing to slow Hulagu Khan's westward progress. In 1260 the city of Damascus was the first to fall to his horde. Next on his list was Constantinople, and from there he planned to attain the goal denied to Batu Khan: the conquest of Europe.

To attain this ambition he had to overcome not one but two obstacles: Muslim Egypt and its powerful army of the Mameluke Sultan; and the string of hulking Crusader fortresses in the Frankish Kingdom of Jerusalem. As so often, several disparate events changed the run of history. Hulagu Khan dispatched an ambassador to the court of the Mameluke Sultan Saif ad-Din Kotuz with a message to surrender or face battle: "God the great has elevated Genghis Khan and his progeny and given us the realms of the face of the Earth altogether."

Sultan Kotuz ordered Hulagu's ambassador to be killed, and the war was on. Hulagu sent his emissaries to the King of Antioch, Bohemund VI, offering him an alliance against the Mameluke. Pope Alexander IV forbade the Crusader knights to enter into an alliance with "the pagan Tartar". It was an astute ploy to let the Muslims of Egypt and the Tartars from China grind each other to dust.

The other portentous event occurred in China. While Hulagu's preparations for war with Egypt were under way, his brother the *Khakhan* Mangu died, and Hulagu rushed to Karakorum to press his own claim to succeed him. He appointed his lieutenant Kitboga (Ket-boka) as temporary ruler, but then left him only a fraction of the strength needed to defend a big khanate. With half of Hulagu's forces *en route* to Mongolia, the Seljuk Turks barring the exit from Syria, with both the huge and hostile Crusader fortresses on his flank and a Mameluke army on its way to Palestine,

Kitboga was faced with a serious problem. He was brave, but he was no Subotai. Instead of taking on each enemy in their turn, he moved against all of them simultaneously.

Sultan Kotuz, on the advice of his brilliant young general Baibars,[1] split his force. It would prove a masterstroke. Kitboga dispatched one *tuman* to prevent the Mameluke from crossing the River Orontes. Baibars was lying in ambush. He caught the Mongols between heights on one side and the river on the other. His warriors poured down the hillsides and drove the surprised Mongols over the edge and into the river, annihilating the *tuman*. To forestall news of the debacle reaching Kitboga's main force, Baibars set up a cavalry screen. It proved highly efficient and, for the first time, a Mongol general stumbled blindly into a trap.

On 8 September 1260 Kitboga bumped into Sultan Kotuz's main force at the Wells of Goliath, near Nazareth. By the standards of its time it was not a big battle, perhaps fifteen thousand fighters on each side. None the less it was a battle that would destroy the myth of Mongol invincibility. While Kitboga was counting on the arrival of his advance *tuman*, it was the timely appearance of Baibars that decided the issue. Beset from both sides, Kitboga's horde was overrun and massacred. His lieutenants tried to induce their Khan to ride for safety, but he shook his head. "Death is inevitable. It is better to die with a good name than to flee in disgrace."

Bleeding from deep cuts, his sword arm hanging useless by his side, he was dragged before Baibars and beheaded. It is said that when Hulagu Khan learned of the crushing defeat, he wept.

At the height of its glory, Hulagu's khanate extended from Turkistan to Syria, and from Mesopotamia to Transcaucasia. By withdrawing a major portion of his army from Mesopotamia, Hulagu Khan wrote *finis* to his own achievements and conquests. On 8 February 1265, worn out by a life of intrigue and battle, he died. Hulagu Khan's lasting epitaph in the great tome of history remains the butchery at Baghdad. Never has there been a more senseless and bloody act.

Just as the battle at Liegnitz had thrown open the door to Europe, a decisive battle at the gates of Nazareth wrote an end to the Mongol advance into the Occident. And though the Mongol yoke would continue for another two centuries in Oriental Russia, the Mongols abandoned all further attempts to enter southern and central Europe. In a few short years they had brought Western and Islamic civilization to the brink of disintegration. Terror and more terror with no positive result would remain the ultimate achievement for which the Great Mongol Invasion will be remembered. As a monument to eternity they left behind ghastly pyramids of millions of bleached skulls.

The thirteenth century was that of the Mongols. They ruled the world. The overwhelming military strength of a Mongol–Chinese Empire was much too solidly based to be challenged. A series of brilliant Mongol khans set new rules of engagement. Their unparalleled mastery of cavalry and archery tactics[2] defeated one enemy after another. They exploited the potential of new inventions with spectacular results, such as the use of gunpowder and a new type of siege catapult developed by Chinese scientists. Of course, the tactical innovations did not spring merely from the application of exceptionally intelligent minds unhampered by preconceived military ideas. They evolved partly from circumstances, but mostly from the numerical limitations, and were designed around the high quality of the human material from which Genghis Khan built his Great Horde. Secondly, and the most important contribution by far, there was the Mongols' unquestioned acceptance of the very limits of strategic safety. Rigid though they were in matters of efficiency of their troop, they never allowed their strategic conceptions to become rigid or to dominate.

Nothing is eternal. Genghis Khan's very success contained the seeds of future dangers; after his death there erupted quarrels over succession in his world-spanning empire. Where Genghis Khan had ruled over Asia, the Middle East and eastern Europe with a combination of military superiority, cunning intrigue and wise diplomacy, his heirs parcelled out the world's greatest realm, in order to assemble their own khanates. Disunited, they quarrelled, fought and fell.

Even the greatest of all Mongol emperors experienced disaster. In 1281 Kublai Khan dispatched a fleet of some three thousand vessels to invade Japan. The Japanese Bakufu *Shogun* of Kamakura, Hojo Tokimune, knew that he had to stop the invader on the beaches. In that holy task he was willing to sacrifice his samurai knights. It finally came down to six hundred samurai versus one hundred thousand Tartars. Help of a different kind was already on its way. The super-heated air over the China Sea sucked up millions of tons of water vapour and now a water-laden hot air mass forced its way upward until it collided with the icy air currents of the upper troposphere. This formed a giant dome of ferociously turbulent air, creating a dangerous vacuum. It forced the surface air to rush into this vacuum at high speed. The forces of the Earth's rotation turned the inrushing air mass into a rapidly accelerated rotation and a *taifun* (typhoon) was born, spiralling ever faster upon itself at unbelievable velocities until it reached the Korean Strait, on a collision course with Kyushu, where Kublai Khan's mighty fleet was bottled up inside a bay.

Like a berserk monster, nature's unleashed fury whipped across the congested waters of Akasaka Bay, its winds ripping out and overturning everything that stood in its path. Panic and confusion reigned among the units that had already been landed. They were helpless in the face of the power of nature. God had taken sides, trapping them between cliffs and a wild sea. A few ships tried to make a run through the narrows into the open sea, only to be lifted up and smashed into one another like toys. The admiral's ship turned turtle, with only her keel above the waves, until the next wave sent her stern-first to the bottom. Caught in the cauldron of a *taifun*, an army of one hundred thousand disappeared without trace beneath the ocean.

"*Kamikaze! Kamikaze!*" shouted the thin line of defenders at sunrise, and raised their arms toward the heavens. The entire Mongol fleet had disappeared, and likewise its army, sucked into fathomless depths. The shore was littered with a frothy mattress of jetsam, algae-covered planking and horribly mangled carcasses. A khan's mighty invasion fleet, ground to pieces by nature's unbridled forces.[3] Indeed, *Kamikaze*, the "Divine Wind", had saved Japan.

"When wind and wave to wrath are stirred, the mightiest of emperors must bend to a superior will" was even then an ancient Chinese proverb. Kublai Khan was the mightiest of all Chinese emperors, and yet his powers proved naught when challenged by nature's fury. For when even the mightiest of mortals collides with the gigantic forces of nature, a stench of death is in the wind.

Kublai Khan, the greatest of all Mongol emperors, died in 1294. It signalled the beginning of the end of Mongol-ruled China.

# CHRONICLE: 1348:
## THE YELLOW SCOURGE

The world of medieval Europe was far more harsh and cruel than ours, although some cruelties familiar to us were unknown to it. If the Great Mongol Invasion killed millions, God had already prepared an even more terrible punishment, and this time for all of Europe. A century after the terrible Mongol came another killer; this stealthy assassin slayed a third of Europe's people.

Death arrived in baskets and bales along the Great Silk Road, the only viable trade passage overland from the Orient. Silk, tea and spice had long proved invaluable commodities in the Occident. With Kublai Khan opening China's door to international trade, Chinese, but also Venetian, Genoese, Levantine and Arab, merchants quickly grasped the opportunity. Indeed, the Great Trade Route was paved with gold, but this wealth was linked with great risk. While Edward III's English were laying siege to Calais – five thousand kilometres off – a caravan arrived in the city of Antioch. A few days after its arrival an epidemic struck, known in the port only as "*muerto*": death. And though Levantine merchants and ship captains must have been aware of the mortal danger of propagation, they looked only as far as their purse strings. Cargo from Antioch was loaded on to vessels bound for European ports, and in a matter of a few weeks, *muerto* was carried to all the harbours along the Mediterranean coastline.

The bubonic plague had its origin in the putrefaction of unburied corpses after an earthquake that struck southern China in the summer of 1336. At the height of a heat wave many thousands perished in the quake and their unburied corpses became the prey of rodents. The bacillus *Pasteurella pestis* evolved a symbiotic relationship with rodents infested with fleas. In Europe medieval sanitary conditions were appalling; everyone dumped human waste into open sewers; no one thought of bathing; and people accepted lice and fleas as something natural and unavoidable. It was the fleas, nesting on rats, and infesting every ship and every cellar, that took the bacillus to humans, infecting others through droplets in a cough or sneeze, or by simple touch.

The symptoms of plague were an almost immediate gangrenous inflammation of the lungs, vomiting and the spitting of blood. Within a couple of days hard, black buboes formed in the armpits and groin, heralding imminent death. Pallor, sudden shivering and retching, dreaded scarlet botches and black boils were followed by a fast slide into delirium and the accompanying agony that came unexpectedly and carried victims to eternity in a few hours. Walled cities locked their gates; it did not stop the infection from creeping in, killing first one, then a family, then the clan, then the neighbourhood, and finally the entire citizenry. Piles of corpses accumulated before every church, in hovels and in ditches, or wherever else the doomed had collapsed to die. Only a few wealthy could afford a Christian burial; men with hoods collected their corpses, tinkling bells warning others not to come anywhere near them and crying: "Corpses ... corpses." They threw the dead on to their carts, dumping baron and merchant into a common lime pit. The poor were left to rot wherever they had perished.

No human power could slow the spread of the plague. Once it entered Europe, it spared neither bishop nor beggar. By the spring of 1348 Italy had fallen victim to the pestilence; Venice and Genoa became cities of the dead, with a stench of the sick and the reckless drinking and wenching in taverns. It was the same everywhere: Siena, Parma, Vienna, Nuremberg, Frankfurt, Strasbourg, Marseilles, Lyon, Paris, Calais. By the autumn of 1348 the Black Death had jumped the English Channel. A country that had been spared the Mongol Peril was now strangling in the clutches of a fatal killer, silent and unseen.

The plague reached London around the beginning of November and took many lives every day. Flagellants, naked from the waist and wearing tall, peaked caps emblazoned with a red cross, marched through London past corpses, singing and whipping one another, to atone for man's sins and drive out the evil they thought was God's punishment for their fellow men's sins. Plague struck down the Archbishop of Canterbury, Thomas of Bradwardine, on Christmas Eve.

The Scottish lairds, having been given notice of the "terribilous plight that striketh down Engelond", considered it an Act of God righteously punishing the thrice-cursed English. It was a heaven-sent opportunity. A large host of Scots assembled in Selkirk Forest to invade their stricken neighbour, but the Black Death struck and all five thousand of them fell down dead.

Still the disease raged on, leaving rotting corpses unburied, torn apart by carrion birds. Farms, villages and entire towns were annihilated, abandoned and left as ruins. Mobs, fearing for their lives, put houses of plague victims to the torch and started fires that devoured entire towns. Those seeking salvation from their God in churches pressed together and doomed one another. Preachers prophesied the end of the world. "Hear me all ye sinners, Our Lord punishes your sinful ways, your hour has come…"

Without defence, life such as it was became a dance on a volcano, a collapse of morals and a boisterous abandonment to every kind of vice and villainy. "Let us live now, because tomorrow we shall all be dead." Brother cared not for brother, and wife not for husband; women gave their bodies to all; and bandits cut throats with no fear of retribution. "… the plague's victims ate lunch with their friends, and had dinner with their ancestors in paradise," wrote Giovanni Boccaccio in 1348.[1] The cataclysm carried off one in every three in Europe – man, woman and child – in less than a year. Its effect was chaos. "The people for the greater part ever became more depraved, more prone to every vice and more inclined than before to evil and wickedness, not thinking of death nor of the past plague nor of their own salvation …" wrote the monk William Dene, of Rochester, England, in 1349.

By the time the Great Plague petered out, it had claimed 25 million victims throughout Europe. In England alone well over two million souls were scythed down by the "Chinese curse".

After every disaster a plausible culprit must be found. With the Mongol Peril still fresh on their minds, and believing that everything wicked had its origin in the unknown East, a contemporary German quack described the Great Plague as "the Yellow Scourge". That explanation stuck. Death was triumphant – and, like all unexplainable evil, it had originated in China.

Seven centuries have passed since that silent killer struck. Today another epidemic scare looms, and once again it originates in China. This plague does not travel by camel, but comes on the flight of unstoppable wings: bird flu. Aside from the potentially monumental human cost, history has amply demonstrated the destabilizing social consequences of a widespread killer virus once it mutates. A densely populated China cannot let a menace hang over it, and neither can the rest of the world. This is one war we all must fight together, side by side.

# ACT TWO

## 1554–1911:
# Gunboat Diplomacy

*Cannon, n., instrument employed in the rectification
of national boundaries.*

—Ambrose Bierce, *The Devil's Dictionary*

# 1

# A FLEET OF MONSTROUS DRAGONS

SEPTEMBER 1405, IMPERIAL DRAGON BAY SHIPYARD,
NANJING, MING EMPIRE OF CHINA

On a bright day in 1411, while looking after his family's four goats on the meagre pastures upon the craggy rocks which formed the headland of the Arabian Peninsula, a boy was staring out to sea at a flock of distant white birds perched on the waves, when he jumped up, stunned. These were not seagulls floating on the swell, but ships with bright sails! First a few … then some more … and then one so huge that its sails filled the horizon. All coming his way. He touched the blue bead on a thong around his neck to ward off the evil eye, before he ran screaming to the hut, fully knowing that his father would never believe the story of a ship so huge that it blocked out the sky – and with a frightful fire-spitting dragon on its bow.

For days the gulls had circled tirelessly and noisily. Below them the massive flagship shouldered aside the swell with a beautiful easy motion – a gigantic man-of-war with nine masts so tall they touched the clouds, and a thousand men on board, a force of immense destructive power. It was the largest warship the world had ever seen, surrounded by many other vessels, every one substantial, though in comparison with the admiral's *Treasure Ship*, they seemed a flock of ducklings. This was the pride of Middle Earth, an armada in search of the unknown, not to conquer but to spread the fame of their Celestial Emperor, Yong-le the Magnificent, Ming ruler of the Universe. An adventurous seafarer had answered the call of his monarch to take possession of half the known world. He journeyed the world's seas not in search of gold and riches, nor of conquest of land, but in pursuit of glory – and the eternal dream: to discover what nobody before him had found.

And so it was that, years before Bartolomeu Dias rounded the Cape of Good Hope, Vasco da Gama entered the Indian Ocean and Magellan circumnavigated the world, a Chinese fleet of monstrous size sailed the globe. (A recently discovered eighteenth-century copy of a Chinese map of the world, purportedly from 1418, and showing the outlines of the American continent, suggests that Cheng-ho had indeed reached America almost a hundred years before Columbus. However, there are serious doubts about this map, since it marks oceans and passages with names that were not in use before the end of the seventeenth century.)

In 1933, children playing in China's Fukian province discovered a stone stele hidden behind thick vines. This pillar had been placed in the Temple of the Celestial Spouse, a Taoist goddess, five hundred years earlier. Wars had laid waste to the temple, but the central pillar remained untouched. It told the story of a mighty Ming emperor who wanted all the world to know of his greatness and therefore ordered his admiral to sail to the countries beyond the horizon and dispatch his message into the four corners of the world.

"Journey along the rainbow to the end of the earth, visit the barbarians beyond the seas, and impress on them the power of the Ming. Collect their tribute, and conduct their ambassadors to do us homage at our Celestial Court." In such words the stele tells an amazing tale of a seafarer, one that is lent substance by an Arab tale about a Muslim adventurer, Sinbad the Sailor. Only this Sinbad might well have been a Chinese admiral called by his contemporaries San-bao, or, as he is known to history, Cheng-ho, "the Seafarer".

"We have beheld in the ocean huge waves like mountains rising sky-high, and we have set eyes on barbarian regions far away hidden in a blue transparency of light vapours, while our sails, loftily unfurled like clouds, day and night continued their course rapid like that of a star, transversing the savage waves as if we were treading a public thoroughfare."

The inscription names most of the countries this intrepid seafarer and his ships visited, from Asia to Africa, from Arabia to the South Seas. It speaks of great adventures, journeys into the world of new discoveries. Judging by the vast distances his fleet travelled – more than a thousand *li* (over 50,000 kilometres) – this is hardly surprising. Incredible, however, is the size of Cheng-ho's fleet. Where Columbus had three nutshells to sail into the unknown, Cheng-ho commanded 317 ships with 27,870 men. Whatever the underlying reason for his voyages – conquest or commerce – this admiral's achievement cannot be measured by modern standards. In seven momentous journeys the Admiral of the "Dragon Fleet" made nations tremble wherever his armada appeared. One thing is certain: Cheng-ho stands among the greatest, if he is not *the* greatest, seafaring explorers in history.

*

"Men should worry about fame just as pigs about being fat" is an ancient Chinese proverb. The Emperor Yong-le (or Ch'eng Tsu, 1403–24), a supreme megalomaniac yet brilliant in his vision and determined that his reign must surpass in splendour that of any previous dynasty, had the Great Wall repaired, constructed a Forbidden City in the capital of the north, Beijing, and ordered that his fame and glory be spread to all the lands on the horizon, and beyond. That called for a fleet.

Since Kublai Khan's "Divine Wind" debacle in 1281, China's position on the high seas had gone into decline. To regain its commanding position called for a man of exceptional imagination and navigational skills, one familiar with the disparate cultures and religions he would visit, and who could approach foreign monarchs with both firmness and diplomatic finesse. What better man to design and oversee the fleet's construction, and then carry the imperial banner way beyond the Centre of the Universe, than Yong-le's enlightened court eunuch and naval officer, Cheng-ho?

For this young admiral grasped the fact that control over maritime routes must rely on a great battle fleet, whose initial function it was to win command of the sea by destroying the enemy's forces. The imperative was to gain control over the sea lanes and then exploit this commanding position to impose China's will on other countries and civilizations. This required the embarkation of massive land forces for amphibious operations, the blockade of enemy seaports and the protection of merchant shipping. Cheng-ho outlined to the Emperor that any nation possessing the largest number of virtually unsinkable battle monsters was unassailable. In a Ming fleet nothing was to be small, nothing too perfect. A mighty armada, bigger than anything the world had ever seen (and would see before the arrival of the dreadnoughts of the early twentieth century), was to give China a matchless superiority over its neighbours, as well as lead to imperial expansion, profit and personal glory. In fact, it was a "parade fleet" to boost an emperor's "politics of prestige". Kingdoms, near or far, would rather make concessions than risk war after a "friendly call" by a Ming armada.

The war galley, powered by oars, with auxiliary sail power, had for over a thousand years dominated naval warfare. A galley was manoeuvrable and held her own as long as naval battles were personal-contact encounters between seagoing infantry. First it rammed an enemy vessel, then soldiers invaded the decks and decided the battle by sheer physical butchery. Ships of sail were used only for coastal transport of merchandise. Then a revolutionary change in ship construction took place, because Emperor Yong-le had grandiose plans: his ships would be big, with many masts and many sails. To gather the necessary funds for his massive plan, he put all foreign trade under the seal of an imperial monopoly, trampling the wish of the merchant class to safeguard the amenities of their deals according to commercial opportunism. In Cheng-ho he had found the man to complete the gigantic challenge.

Captured and castrated as a boy, then sold into a royal household, Cheng-ho was a Muslim convert to Buddhism. His emperor's ambition inflamed the imagination of the 32-year-old admiral. Working from the Imperial Dragon Bay Shipyard at Nanjing, Cheng-ho produced initial designs that were overpowering and magnificent, the largest and most complicated wind-powered fighting machines ever built. The central portion of this incredible fleet was four massive vessels. When Cheng-ho presented his drawings to the expert shipbuilders they said it could not be done. He overrode their objections: "Build me these ships, or your life is forfeited." Work began. Thousands of oaks and teaks went into each of the monsters. His designs were so outsized, and the need for timber so great, that Chinese armies had to raid neighbouring Annam's teak forests just to supply the beams and planking needed for the armada. This led to a war with the King of Annam, which the Chinese won, and they then annexed his kingdom.

Meanwhile Cheng-ho studied all available information and soon there was little he did not know that we, with our satellites and computers, know today. The South China Sea encompasses some 1.25 million square kilometres; some areas are extremely deep, others shallow and studded with hidden coral reefs. Sudden changes in weather, and the seasonal monsoon, make navigation hazardous and have caused many disasters.

Cheng-ho was a strong executive. Using the limitless resources of manual labour and material put at his disposal, as well as the combined efforts of all the sail weavers of South China, it took him only two years to make his designs a reality. The sheer size of his four central-command vessels boggles the mind; every one was 10 times the size of Columbus's caravels and three times that of Nelson's 74-gun ship *Victory*. No other wooden sailing ships have ever come anywhere near their size. Wind-powered by nine huge masts, each ship was 68 feet wide and 440 feet long, and bristling with armaments. The vessels, named *Treasure Ship*, *Horse Ship*, *Supply Ship* and *Combat Ship*, were clearly identified by their figureheads of dragons on their bowsprit, so all those who saw them approaching their coasts called them the Dragon Fleet.

These four dragon ships were accompanied by more than three hundred smaller vessels to accommodate a full complement of almost twenty-eight thousand – sailors, soldiers, scientists, mapmakers, tradesmen, diplomats and teachers, as well as the great number of hostages and slaves – and all these had to be fed and watered, as did the horses and a sundry collection of strange animals. All in all, it was a Noah's Ark of truly biblical proportions. The ships carried the latest technical improvements – a main-deck-operated stern-post rudder, fore and aft sails, navigational aids especially developed by the country's great mathematicians and astronomers. Yet perhaps their most significant contribution was an eleventh-century Chinese invention, the magnetic compass, a magnetized needle floating in a bowl of water; without this simple but indispensable nautical aid, the great voyages into an uncharted world, the discoveries of oceans and continents, could never have been realized.

Emperor Yong-le's purpose in pursuing this gigantic venture was not the establishment of far-flung colonies. Ming China needed nothing; was it not the only truly civilized society on Earth? The fleet's mission was to establish a number of trade ports and keep out foreign intruders. The Emperor was quite specific on this issue: crush all intruding ships to matchwood. China had developed its culture apart from lesser societies, so why should its heavenly emperor allow his people to become infected by ideas from outlandish and much inferior civilizations? Let other nations humbly kowtow before him, pay tribute to the glory of the Great Ming and pay a vassal's homage to the Celestial Kingdom. The Emperor had given detailed instructions for Cheng-ho's first voyage and designated the fleet's first port of call: Calicut on the west coast of India, an important trading centre which until then could only be reached overland, over the "Himalayan hump", because Sumatran and Thai pirates seized merchant vessels and never left survivors to tell their story. One of Cheng's objectives was to rid the China Sea of the scourge.

The great day had come. Swathed in yellow silks, the Emperor presented his admiral with the gold-embossed imperial dragon banner to be flown from the command vessel's tallest mast. To the sound of gongs and cymbals and cheers the fleet set sail, bound for the open sea. From the deck of his ship the Admiral of the Western Seas (Atlantic) looked with pride on his creation as the huge armada cast off and made for the centre of the majestic River Yangtze. Never had the world seen anything remotely like it, a fleet of many thousand sails, on the biggest ships ever built.

The ships that took to the Southern Sea were likened to huge temples or, when their sails were spread, to great clouds in the sky. Among the smaller vessels were weapon ships, ships with scientists, mathematicians, mapmakers and astrologers. There were merchant ships filled with tons of Chinese trade goods, anything from spices to porcelain, splendid presents for friendly potentates, and iron chains for the not so friendly – and all this to show the might of the Emperor of Middle Earth. To run such an inordinate undertaking called for order, discipline and a solid command structure. Navigators used the astrolabe to determine the fleet's position. Communications between the admiral and his vessels relied on an ingenious system of mirrors, flags, bells, gunpowder rockets of different colours and carrier pigeons. Incense sticks each lasting roughly two and a half hours were used to divide a day into 10 units.

The armada advanced steadily, its massive ships parting towering waves, their bows crowned in white spray, climbing heavily out of the water, cutting the combers and straddling the troughs. On the outward journey to India the pirates kept well out of harm's way. Once a great storm gathered on the horizon, flashes lit the sky. Mountainous rollers chased after the fleet, breaking in gigantic crests, frothing and foaming with unearthly roar. The outriders of the storm gave them a run at a fearsome clip through the treacherous Malacca Strait. The danger lay in the many submerged coral reefs. Whenever the uncharted ocean's depth was uncertain, Cheng-ho remained on deck and listened to the leadsman in the forecastle calling out the numbers.

They sailed into Calicut like a visitation from another planet and time. Never before had a fleet of this size anchored at its shore, and no Indian prince or trader was certain whether the visitors came in peace. Teeming with both those who fled from the city to escape the "invading dragons" and those who came rushing to the shore to stare in awe at the dragon ships, the town resembled a nervous ant hive. Many fled in panic when the Chinese fleet, to announce their friendly visit and salute their hosts, set off a barrage of fireworks. Cheng-ho debarked with presents and was received with honours worthy of a conqueror. His ride through town turned into triumph after his retainers showered the seething masses with copper coins. Cheng-ho delivered a message from his emperor with a velvet-covered iron fist. He displayed an outward calm that showed in no way his hard core.

Cheng-ho smiled when the ruler of Calicut spoke: "I recognize that the friendship of your suzerain is worth a lot."

"You will put yourself under his protection?"

"We shall."

Next came the hard part: "Of course, I will have to bring our gracious Emperor some sign of recognition on your part, great prince."

"Recognition? Must I kneel before you as the representative of your Emperor? Do you really think that I will accept such pressure?"

"Not pressure, great king. We ask only for a token of your appreciation for our freely extended protection of your realm. I ask that you will offer a sanctuary to a few of our traders and ensure their safety, and also ask that one of your noble line will accompany us on our return journey. I am sure, after you have given it a thought, you will see the benefit."

If the ruler of Calicut intended to retain his kingdom, he had no choice in the matter. He assigned his brother as "goodwill ambassador" and opened his seafront to Chinese traders. After several months in Calicut Cheng-ho began his return voyage, taking his dragon monsters to the kingdom of Ceylon, a noted treasure island, where pearls and precious stones were abundant. Cheng-ho obtained homage from the Ceylonese king, together with a suitable number of hostages, many of them female dancers.

It still left him to deal with the pirates of the China Sea. The problem was first to find them. Their base must lie along the main shipping channel, but where? With dozens of islands as hiding place, the Chinese admiral decided he had to lure them into the open. He dispatched three rapid decoys. The pirates took the bait and went after the harmless-looking traders. The three ships turned and pulled the pirate fleet into the midst of Cheng-ho's armada, which advanced on them like the claws of a gigantic lobster. Great shapes rose above the horizon and soon giant bows crested above the pirate ships. Frantically the pirates tried to steer away from the rapidly approaching hulls, as tall as cliffs. It was already too late to escape.

Cheng-ho's flagship rose slightly, canting up the bowsprit. There was a crunch of breaking timber as a pirate's dhow was pushed down beneath the keel of the monstrous *Treasure Ship*. It disappeared, crew and all. In an unequal contest Cheng's huge vessels cut a swath through the hapless pirates, crushing them into matchwood, riding their vessels into the deep. A fleet of villainous pirates were wiped from the sea; with a mile to sink, it took them a while before they touched their final, cold tomb. Pirates who had jumped overboard and managed to break surface, retching and coughing, were used by Tartar archers for target practice.

From Cheng-ho's smaller attack vessels, soldiers boarded the pirate ships and swarmed over their decks like ants dissecting a carcass. Pirates caught on deck were thrown overboard, the rest locked into the lower decks, and their ships set on fire. The vessels collapsed in a cataclysm of burning timber; masts came down and, with a dull boom, the hulls cracked. As the smoke cleared, the few pirate ships still afloat were decapitated hulks with only the ragged stumps of their lower yards sticking up. In the swirling waters floated masts, shredded sailcloth, planking and bodies. Like monumental islands, the Chinese ships loomed proudly out of the dense smoke.

Cheng-ho and his men returned to Nanjing in 1407 to a hero's welcome. Emperor Yong-le heaped great honours on his valiant admiral and ordered him to prepare for his next journey. While these preparations were in progress Cheng-ho fell ill with a tropical fever, which prevented him from leading the second voyage of the Imperial Treasure Fleet (1407–9). No sooner had the fleet once more returned to China than a message was received from Ceylon that its king had gone back on his promise to protect Chinese merchants and that a number of them had been murdered and their properties confiscated. For this third, punitive voyage, Cheng-ho took command of the fleet. He followed the same route he had carefully charted on his initial voyage and made landfall on the island's east coast. An overland campaign in appalling territory lay ahead; its outcome proved that Cheng-ho was not only a great admiral but also a brilliant general. He posted strong rearguards and led fifteen thousand picked men through a swampy inferno, alive with serpents and poisonous insects, then fought a brilliantly conceived battle, routing an army that greatly outnumbered him. The Ceylonese king was captured and put aboard a ship to be held for the Celestial Emperor's pleasure. The admiral and his fleet were back in Nanjing in late 1411.

For his next journey Cheng-ho's principal mission was to scout for a sea route to circumvent the lands of the terrible Tartar prince Tamerlane; in a series of ruthless conquests Tamerlane and his Jagatai Mongols had cut the ancient Silk Road and a new, safe trade route by sea had to be found. For weeks the Dragon Fleet crossed the Indian Ocean on a westerly course on its way to far-off Arabia. Having reached a headland (the Yemen Peninsula), a northerly course (into the Persian Gulf) seemed Cheng-ho's best bet. The mountainous cliffs (Hadramaut) were replaced by rolling dunes of golden sand (the Empty Quarter) with no creek, no harbour, only sand, and every day more of it.

The wind died and the heat became almost unbearable, making man and beast suffer. Cheng-ho decided to turn around. The ships rounded the same promontory (Yemen), and headed north along the coastline (into the Red Sea). Again the land became barren; the wind died on them, the sun perched in the centre of the sky and the sea shimmered white like a sheet of molten glass. The heat deepened and strange mirages teased the sailors' weary eyes, mirror images of great cities. With the wind freshening, the fleet continued sailing along the desolate tract of land. They were almost out of drinking water when, above a strip of sand, a slender minaret appeared on the horizon (probably Jeddah).

Cheng-ho signalled his ships to turn toward the shore; before them lay a beautiful sight: the deep azure of sea stretched to within a few hundred yards of the shore, before merging into pale, sparkling green as the waves swept over coral reefs and outlying shoals, then through a narrow passage into a natural harbour with a dozen dhows floating on the water: slavers, squat and ugly compared with the majestic Chinese ships. The sea broke in a narrow ribbon of white foam on a strip of silver sand, beyond which stood a row of low houses clustered around clumps of palm trees. Where there are people there is drinking water. A number of boats with people clad in billowing robes came out to meet them, indicating the safe passages between reefs and pearl banks. Other than to replenish their water supply, Cheng-ho had a valid reason to make for shore. Despite his conversion to Buddhism, in his heart he was still a Muslim. Could this be the magic gateway to the Holiest of Holies – Mecca? It was.

This was not the first encounter between China and the World of Islam. Two hundred years earlier Hulagu had burned Baghdad and, 25 years before, Tamerlane had done the same. The news of Cheng-ho's surprise visit preceded his caravan and people fled before him, thinking of yet another Chinese horror. Cheng-ho had not come to plunder, but to trade, bring presents and pay silent homage to Allah. Despite the crowds from around the Muslim world that thronged Mecca, Cheng-ho's arrival was widely remarked; 60 wagons strong, with an escort of a thousand cavalrymen. No one had ever seen splendour like these wagons carrying porcelain and silks. The ceremonial Arab guards flashed their sabres in salute before conducting the visitor to meet the Sheriff of Mecca, the highest religious dignitary of the city. The Sheriff appreciated the admiral's generous presents; soon a regular Arab-Chinese soukh had established itself on the outskirts of the city.

It turned out to be a profitable journey but one place the Chinese party did not visit was the legendary city of Baghdad. Pilgrims returning from Mecca told of the splendour of the mighty Chinese seafarer and it is likely that their stories were embellished with feats of conquest and great daring, and that the person of San-pao – Cheng-ho's Buddhist name – became the mythical Sinbad the Sailor. Before the great fleet set sail from the Arabian Sea, 19 local monarchs had dispatched their ambassadors to board Cheng-ho's vessels and pay homage to the Great Ming Emperor Yong-le.

Cheng-ho's fifth voyage, which started in 1417, could have led to a decisive page in history. This time his fleet headed straight into the uncharted waters of the Indian Ocean. He felt certain of avoiding the great storms which whipped the South China Sea during the height of the typhoon season. As he made his passage into the Indian Ocean through the Sunda Strait, the weather worsened. A storm was brewing somewhere to his north. By keeping his fleet on its present course, he gave it a chance to ride out the storm. It was a gamble because, if the southerlies blew from the open sea, he would be caught in crosswinds with almost no leeway; his fleet might be smashed against some unknown island or uncharted reef. Figures and angles came together in his head. His officers watched him, but he ignored their worried faces. The decision was his to take, and his alone. He was sailing into unknown territory. Throughout most of recorded history the oceans were barriers, watery deserts, and not highways. Even after the early discoveries by the Phoenicians, Greeks and Vikings, many coasts remained inaccessible and uncharted because of unfavourable winds and currents.

"Hold to this course." He studied the sails; the mains were drawing well for now. He would let them remain up, unless the wind began to veer. A squall was approaching from the north-west, the white line of its fury whipping up the already stiffening swell, while above the water the cloud bunched and darkened and came on, its underside flickering with lightning. In the space of an hour the sky grew black, rain swept down, the wind howled and lightning crackled around their heads. Before the deckhands were able to bring down the big sails, the first squall smote the *Treasure Ship* and knocked her several points off course. Four strong helmsmen fought the jerking of the double wheel, while Cheng-ho watched the compass needle spin wildly, until the bow pointed south-east and the ship was running before the wind. His crews stared at the galloping clouds, the flicker of the lightning and the shifting silver curtain of the rain, while the ship's stern rose and the waves soared up in white foam, only to come crashing over the high deck. Troops were thrown about and became seasick: thirty thousand souls with no means to help their suffering.

The storm had dispersed the fleet and thrown it off course. By the time Cheng-ho had managed to reassemble his ships, he opted for a new course straight into the unknown. He assumed that the world did not end somewhere over the horizon, that the Arabian Peninsula was part of a much greater landmass, as he had previously learned from the tales of Arab sailors. The vision of an imaginary chart floated into his mind. Where did this vast expanse of water end? What lay ahead of them? Would his ships tumble over the edge of the world? A darkening mood began to settle over the Dragon Fleet, and only the admiral's force of character kept a mutiny from exploding – when an incident took place that turned him into the nearest thing to a deity.

Above them was the eternal sky of the immense universe, with stars as brilliant pinpoints in that black vault and the moon as bright as a silver lantern. Cheng-ho was on deck, surrounded by his lieutenants, when something caught their attention. They looked up at the ink-black sky and saw a bright light moving among the mast tops. The light moved in weird patterns; as it came lower a bright ray stabbed down to illuminate the decks, outlining their admiral. A heavenly signal! Throughout the fleet the men forgot their doubts and suffering. "As soon as this miraculous light appeared, all danger was appeased," Cheng-ho was to write in a message to the Emperor. The miraculous light that appeared on the mast tops was certainly St Elmo's fire, nowadays a sight familiar to experienced sailors. But because the sailors had prayed to the Taoist goddess for deliverance from their uncertain fate, they believed it a clear sign that their great admiral stood under her divine protection. From that moment the ships' companies looked upon Cheng-ho as an emissary of the Taoist goddess – a fact that was to bear heavily on the jealousies of the next Ming emperor, since there could be only one divinity in the Celestial Empire, the imperial monarch.

It was one of those endless days of glaring sky and infinite ocean when Cheng-ho was shaken from his reverie by a voice from the topmast. "Land ahead!" Before him loomed rocky promontories like unconquerable ramparts of a fortress, stretching for many leagues in each direction (probably near the Horn of Africa). Land meant a release from the uncertainty as to whether the world beyond the sea ended in a sudden drop. The fleet turned south, where the mountains ended and dense vegetation covered the coastal regions. At one of the wide coves Cheng-ho anchored his fleet and began trekking across the country.

A snake of men and animals, with half the races of China marching in its ranks, entered the savannah with its abundance of animals, occasionally passing a tumbledown village with its inhabitants staring bewildered in dumbfounded panic at these beings descended from some strange heaven. But the Chinese too could not help gaping in wonder. The natives were of a black they had never seen before, and naked. The Africans offered Cheng-ho's men dragon saliva, incense, golden amber, ginger, cloves, cinnamon, frankincense, sandalwood, myrrh and ivory. The Chinese traded knives and other goods for an amazing panoply of African animals: gold-spotted leopards, ostriches, zebras and oryx. In fact, Cheng's flagship soon resembled Noah's Ark. To the Chinese way of thinking, these four-legged creatures possessed special powers and were portents of good fortune. The admiral's appetite was sharpened by the promise of an even bigger menagerie of strange and wonderful beasts for the Emperor, a great collector.

As the fleet sailed farther south, along the coast of a vast continent, wherever they made landfall the natives paddled out to the ships in canoes: only men, tall warriors, their black nudity set off with white plumes, gold ornaments and strings of coloured stones. Their attitude was one of curious suspicion. They had no use for wealth, but they did love playing games and dancing, and were miraculously free of any known disease.

Cheng-ho had by now discovered a large part of a distant coast and the holds of his ships could hardly take any more loads, overflowing with ivory, precious woods and a menagerie of animals. The days dragged on and things began to change; after many thousands of miles and great dangers the crews were exhausted and many had fallen victim to the recurrent high fever of malaria. Still Cheng-ho pushed on in a southerly direction, skimming the eastern coast of Africa, past Madagascar, past Zululand and the imposing Drakensberg mountain range, and, according to the scarce notes and native tales which have survived, he reached as far south as Algoa Bay (Port Elisabeth) or even Plettenbergs Bay near the tip of Africa. And that is where the mighty armada stopped. Its admiral had contracted the same disabling malaria. A mere one hundred nautical miles from the Cape of Good Hope, before the pivotal turn north into the open Atlantic and onward to Europe, with a likely naval confrontation on the Western Seas, the most powerful fleet of its era turned – and headed for home.

By the time the treasure fleet reached Nanjing, Cheng-ho had recovered enough to present a special gift to his emperor. The ruler of Malindi (a coastal state in Kenya) had provided the admiral with the mythical beast that had played a vital role in Confucius's birth, the very animal Cheng-ho had drawn in his youth, the celestial unicorn. The delighted Emperor broke with court ritual and travelled from his palace to welcome his "present from heaven". What kings and princes had never before achieved, to make a Ming Emperor kneel before them, a giraffe did, for that was what the creature was.

Little is known of Cheng-ho's sixth voyage (1421–3). He did sail south, and he certainly made landfall on the north coast of Australia or Queensland. In 1424 his mentor and protector Emperor Yong-le died suddenly, probably poisoned by his son, Zhu Gaozhi, who became the next emperor and then cancelled all further ventures of the Dragon Fleet. Cheng-ho was relieved of his sea command and for a while served as military commander of Nanjing, a land-bound job the seafarer thoroughly hated.

In 1426 Emperor Zhu Gaozhi was murdered by Yong-le's grandson, Zhu Zhanji, who became the new Ming emperor. Cheng-ho was brought back from his mothballed position, appointed Zhu Zhanji's admiral and ordered to launch a seventh voyage. However, the years of semi-retirement had been harsh on the brilliant seafarer; he was but a shadow of himself and gone was his entrepreneurial spirit. Even so, he obeyed his emperor's orders. In 1431 he sailed with a hundred ships in a westerly direction, stopping off in Siam, Malacca and the east coast of Africa. The main purpose of the earlier "exploratory endeavours" had changed into simple "treasure hunts", to enrich the court and establish profitable foreign trade. Furthermore, since Cheng-ho had rid the ocean of pirates and his chart makers had drawn up detailed maps of navigable sea lanes, with their depths, shallows and predominant wind directions, together with the coastlines of visited continents with points of landing, the seventh voyage (1431–3) turned into a routine sail with no more honours to be won.

Cheng-ho had already achieved the unimaginable. He had sailed a mighty ocean and charted it. He had flexed Chinese muscle and demonstrated China's role as the world's maritime and terrestrial superpower. Wherever his Dragon Fleet showed up, kings ran for cover; in an early version of nineteenth-century gunboat politics, he used gentle persuasion backed up by his terrible dragon ships.

A head-on clash with Western seafaring nations was now merely a question of time. One more voyage, this time with a turn around the Cape of Good Hope, before the mighty Dragon Fleet would collide with the merchant fleets of Venetians, Genoese or the Sultan of Istanbul, and the Turkish or European floating nutshells would face destruction as had the pirates of the South China Sea. It was not to be.

"Abandon all voyages on the sea." With a single stroke of the vermilion brush a young Chinese monarch altered China's policy for centuries to come. He listened to poor advice and was further swayed by his own jealousy over his admiral's achievements. To the inexperienced Emperor Zhu Zhanji, China was and always would be the Centre of the Universe; he closed off his country to further penetration from other cultures, religions and customs. He raised a bamboo curtain around China, prohibited foreign trade and the construction of ocean-going vessels – and therewith condemned China to almost total isolation. The Emperor had Cheng-ho's magnificent vessels run on to a sandbank. Four dragon ships lay in foul anchorage with their hulls eaten by teredo worms and reduced to giant ribcages. Beset by insane envy of his admiral's heavenly mission – confirmed by the appearance of a celestial halo, St Elmo's fire – and irked by the public admiration shown to China's greatest admiral, Zhu Zhanji ordered Cheng-ho's notes and diaries to be destroyed and his invaluable maps burned.

The Emperor's admiral was vilified by evil tongues at court and his name was sullied as the "eunuch of a former monarch".[1] His ideas carried on, and it is still the universally accepted doctrine that any seafaring nation, whether it is protecting its shores, policing its trade routes, hounding the enemy's merchant commerce off the seas or striving for territorial conquest, depends on a battle fleet. It was as indispensable in the fifteenth century as it would be in the days of Nelson. Given the overwhelming size of the dragon ships, for centuries no other nation of its time could challenge the might of the Chinese armada. Admirals of the Celestial Empire would have crushed the tiny caravels of emerging Western colonial powers as an elephant crushes an ant.

Sea power is world power. The great Emperor Yong-le fully understood this. His grandson did not; with none of the geo-political foresight of his grandfather, he decreed an end to China's supremacy on the high seas. But for an edict by a potentate blinded by jealousy, that would have been China's greatness. For a brief instant China had created the means, but not the deep-rooted rationale, for overseas expansion. A nation was deprived of its predominant place in the world.

With a giant like Cheng-ho, the dragon woke, and then it fell asleep again.

# 2

# DEVILS KNOCKING AT THE DOOR

## MID-JULY 1530, GUANGZHOU, MING DYNASTY, CHINA

Since time immemorial a succession of emperors had kept the gates to their country tightly shut. Only under Emperor Kublai Khan had China allowed a few foreigners, notably Marco Polo, a glimpse into this isolated empire. So it must have come as somewhat of a surprise to the good citizens of Guangzhou (Canton), on this summer day in 1530, to watch a procession of silk-covered palanquins, displaying the wealth of officials and merchants of the capital of southern China, heading for a European caravel lying at anchor in the harbour. Mandarins in heavily embroidered ceremonial robes alighted from portable chairs and mounted the gangplank to sit down at the richly ornamented dinner table that stood on the oak deck.

The master of the ship played his part superbly, never hinting at his real purpose. He treated his guests to roast capon with cabbage and water chestnuts. To accompany the meat, sailors kept refilling the guests' silver goblets with sweet, cooked wine, which the ship's captain had brought along in wooden caskets. Soon this wine, "from Porto", as the captain was quick to explain to his privileged guests, created an atmosphere of joyfulness. Quiet deals were struck, and it was decided to allow foreign goods to be bartered – against "a small token" of 10 per cent for the local governor, 5 per cent for the harbour commissioner and 15 per cent for His Celestial Majesty in far-away Beijing, who was left in total ignorance of the deals struck in his name. And that is how the Portuguese stuck their foot into the door of a huge country and a profitable future market.

It all began weeks before this memorable feast. Three ships had arrived unannounced outside the port of Guangzhou. This was a daring act, since foreign vessels were forbidden to enter the Pearl River (Yue Jiang) estuary. This time it was different. Everything had to do with the genial idea of a Portuguese adventurer, Leonel da Souza, who had sailed with his three caravels laden with goods from Goa, settled by the Portuguese twenty years earlier in 1510. On his approach to the shores of China's mainland, da Souza put his ships at anchor in a sheltered bay at an island off the Chinese coast, Xiang-gang,[1] where, protected from the elements, he waited for a storm. Within two weeks his wish was granted with a tropical gale that caused no damage to his ships. Da Souza had his crews fetch ripped sail from the sail locker and hoist them most artistically on the mast. With ripped sails, this resourceful captain made his way brazenly up the Pearl River. A chilly wind blew over this daring enterprise. It was not the crew's first sail into danger, and the easy forays had always produced much reward. But this time the bearded men were worried; with hundreds of war junks ready to pounce on an intruder, they feared that this journey could end only in disaster.

Nevertheless they arrived safely at Guangzhou, where da Souza dropped his anchor outside the harbour chain and had himself rowed ashore to parley with the port commissioner. The mandarin received him with cold courtesy, but allowed the Portuguese to present his problem through an interpreter. "The wares aboard my ships have been water-soaked during the recent storm, and I would most humbly ask Your Magnificence's permission to lay them out on shore to dry."

A lacquered box was passed across the table; it contained 20 pieces of gold. The commissioner, Wang Bo, did not open it but merely weighed it in his hand before he nodded. "I shall see that your problem is brought before our exalted civil governor." There was plenty of money to be made, and should he fail with the governor, he could always shift the responsibility on to his underlings. Da Souza felt relieved; at least he would never have to bargain with the military governor. Theoretically, the civil and military governors (*tsungtu* and *shiinwu*) were equal in rank, and although they had well-defined areas of authority, the word of the military governor overrode that of the civil governor. Furthermore, only the former could order an attack. Da Souza's thoughts were interrupted by the port commissioner: "It would be easier to arrange matters with a word spoken over a fine dinner table." And that is how Leonel de Souza came to invite the high mandarins and wealthy merchants of Guangzhou to dine aboard his caravel.

The rest was simple. In exchange for 10 per cent of "the spoiled goods", Commissioner Wang Bo, in connivance with the military, graciously allowed the Portuguese captain to unload his wares so that they might be "dried by the sun". Sailors brought the ship's stores ashore and laid them out. There was no need to explain how water could have seeped into sealed wooden casks of sweet wine, or why the many wax-wrapped bolts of cloth had to be dried. Within hours of this ostentatious display a crowd of merchants had gathered on shore, inspecting, touching and dealing. The rest is history.

Throughout the ages China's sole contact with the outside world was by terrestrial caravans, travelling a long and torturous road. Few Europeans had ever journeyed this overland route – it would take them years – and travellers faced bandits, desert storms, death by thirst and substantial bribes to buy their passage through sheikhdoms and principalities. This would change with the revolutionary European design for a new type of vessel, sturdy, seaworthy and fast: the caravel. A single ship could carry a bigger load than the biggest camel caravan; additionally, because water-borne transport was safe from highway robbers and covered great distances much faster than overland travel, the caravel signalled the dawn of European exploration.

Maritime supremacy was at stake. Europe came to the fore. It was a close call. A century before the Portuguese and Spanish explorers sailed forth to conquer the world, the great admiral Cheng-ho had flexed Chinese muscle and established his country's role as the world's first maritime superpower. Owing his sudden illness, a predicable collision with the Occident on the open sea never happened.

At the turn of the fifteenth century European seafarers took charge. Under King Manuel I the Great, Portugal reached the height of its maritime glory. Five years before Columbus sailed west the Portuguese Admiral Bartolomeu Dias rounded Africa by the Cape of Good Hope (1487). In 1498 Vasco da Gama discovered Mozambique and then retraced Cheng-ho's maritime route to reach Calicut in India. In 1510 one of the world-class admirals of history, Afonso de Albuquerque, forcibly took Goa from the Sultan of Bijapur and established a Portuguese maritime base. On a spring day in 1511 Albuquerque seized Malacca, the key fortress controlling access from the Indian Ocean into the South China Sea. This superb navigator was among the first to realize that sea power, anchored on land bases and supported by merchant shipping, is as vital as the fighting capabilities of an armada. Albuquerque established the oldest and most enduring European colonial system along the shores of the Indian Ocean. With it he opened the fastest and safest way for maritime trade to the Orient.[2] Self-sufficient China did not react. In fact, it could not. Ever since its maritime glory days under Cheng-ho, the once-mighty Ming fleet lay rotting on sand.

In 1513 the viceroy of Goa, Almeida, dispatched several caravels under Jorge Alvares into the Pearl River estuary, with orders to establish a trade interest with the local governor. This attempt ended in dismal failure, when an iron chain placed across the river barred their way. A year passed before the Portuguese viceroy sent Fernão Peres de Andrade to head another expedition into Chinese waters. Peres de Andrade made landfall in Tuen Mun and temporarily occupied it in 1517. When Ming emperor Zheng-de found out about the intrusion, which he considered more of a nuisance than a threat, he sent an army to deal with the Portuguese.

On Zheng-de's death, Jia-jing succeeded him as emperor. Both Portuguese and Chinese merchants saw the huge profits that could be made by bribing Guangdong's provincial authorities, who turned a blind eye to merchants doing trade with the foreign devils, just so long as it was not conducted under everyone's nose. Commercial transactions were sealed in bays on one of the many off-shore islands, transferring goods from caravel to junk. But to conduct serious business called for direct access to Guangzhou – Canton in Portuguese – the country's major port, located on the Pearl River.

Lin Fu, governor of Guangdong province, dared not act openly against the wishes of his Celestial Emperor in far-off Beijing; none the less Portuguese traders bribed the governor to give them permission to install themselves in a small enclave on the outlying coastline, at Hao-jing ("Oyster Mirror"), which the Portuguese renamed Macau. Trade was conducted on a minor scale and absolutely illegal. The Emperor had expressly forbidden foreign vessels sailing upriver, especially in view of the Tomé Pires fiasco at the Celestial court.

In 1516 a Portuguese ship arrived at the entrance to the Pearl River with an overbearing Tomé Pires, apothecary to King Manuel I of Portugal, carrying a personal message from his monarch.[3] He travelled overland to Guangzhou and, with the customary bag of gold, paved his way to the Emperor's court in Beijing. After an exhausting voyage lasting four years he reached Beijing in late 1520, where court officials kept him waiting in palace corridors. Since he felt far more important than his function, the long delay did nothing to calm his disposition toward "the uncouth pagans". While Pires was calling impatiently for an audience, an incident happened in the palace grounds. To cheer up their morose Celestial Emperor Cheng-te, a notorious alcoholic subsisting on a permanent binge, his eunuchs had arranged for a lantern festival. The great courtyard of the Imperial Palace was lit by thousands of lanterns. Stored in yurts near the wall was gunpowder for a mock battle. A gust of wind blew over one of the many lanterns, ignited the powder, blew up the wall and gutted the buildings. Thirty thousand skilled labourers worked for seven years to rebuild the palace.

As months turned into years, the Portuguese apothecary showed such demeaning contempt toward the palace eunuchs that they never permitted him an audience with the august presence. By order of the chief minister, Tomé Pires was exiled to Kiangsu province, where he died soon afterward.

An apothecary's lack of diplomatic skills blocked Portuguese trade with China – until Captain Leonel da Souza, with a will to crack the embargo, arrived armed with a brilliant scheme. And that came to pass in 1530. In what became the first demonstration of European might, da Souza was back at Guangzhou in 1554, this time heading a fleet of 17 heavily armed caravels, "to help the local governor getting rid of a plague of pirates and marauders, the *wokou*", but equally to ensure a more amenable stance by the haughty Guangdong official.

While da Souza dined in the governor's Guangzhou palace to deliver his king's forceful demand, Portuguese sailors broke into the ship's food locker and hauled out a cask of wine. Soon the crews were so drunk that a few dozen armed Chinese could have routed them and captured the invaders. The "polite Chinese" did nothing of the kind. In fact, this greedy horde of official harpies were utterly satisfied to prey upon the profits from trade with foreigners. Because of duties and squeezes levied by the governors and harbourmasters that far exceeded the actual cost of production, smuggling became one of the great trades of the Chinese empire, providing steady employment for a mass of boatmen, carriers, armed bandits and illicit retailers on the one hand, and barrier watchmen, river patrols, examiners and informers on the other.

"If you have never done anything evil, you should not be worrying about devils knocking at your door." The Chinese were not worried,[4] but they should have been, for the "barbarians from across the seas" proved tenacious. First came Bible-waving missionaries who lived – so they trusted – under the protection of their Lord. These were followed by an increasing number of foreign traders. Doing business was extremely lucrative, although always open to piracy or confiscation by greedy officials. Every year more Western sea captains arrived, armed with a new equalizer: the cannon.

A colonial enterprise precipitated the explosion. By 1565 Europe's greatest sea power was Spain. Jealous of the Portuguese successes in trading with China, Castile eyed the Far East and dispatched a naval expedition under Miguel López de Legaspi to lay claim to an island chain for the Spanish crown. It was the same string of islands which, at the height of the Ming period, in 1421, the great seafarer Cheng-ho had settled with Chinese officials and traders, with the long-term goal of encircling China's enemy Japan. López de Villalobos had named the islands the Philippines to honour the Infante Philip, later Philip II. It brought the Spaniards into direct conflict with the big Chinese community and relations between the two communities deteriorated. The Chinese merchants asked Beijing for help, but Emperor Wan-li was too preoccupied with arranging his afterlife to bother about an island chain of no consequence.

Though the Spanish king ruled out an invasion of the Chinese mainland, he did dispatch a fleet of ships to the Philippines to wave the flag. Its captains, not content with a strictly diplomatic mission, used their cannon. In 1603, having annihilated a Chinese relief flotilla under the pirate Lim-hong, the Spaniards, with cannon and employing Filipino auxiliaries, massacred twenty thousand Chinese. This war led to a temporary halt in commercial and diplomatic dealing between Europe and China. But nothing stops for long where profit – legal or not – is at stake.

Now an emerging seafaring nation of traders entered the scene: England. The age of gunboat diplomacy was dawning over China.

# 3

# THE LIN ZEXU MEMORANDUM

## 27 MARCH 1841, GUANGZHOU, MANCHU DYNASTY, CHINA

In the spring of 1637 the Honourable East India Company's ship *Macclesfield*, under the command of Captain Wedell, made landfall in Guangzhou (Canton) in order to establish a trading post for a newly prized commodity on Europe's markets: a green leaf that grew plentifully on mountain slopes in China, delicious and fragrant when boiled – tea. The European demand for tea became overwhelming overnight and the amount shipped from China doubled annually. Soon the tea trade became so important that His Majesty's Government discovered a new source of revenues from its American colonies by establishing its infamous stamp tax on boxes of the dried leaves.

Guangzhou, which had started out as a minor trading post, mushroomed into a hugely profitable business centre with factory buildings and harbour facilities. Chinese traders formed for themselves a monopolistic society, the *Cohong*, under a *Hoppo*, or maritime superintendent, who controlled the tea export and answered to the Chinese government for collection of custom duties. Everything went well until the late summer of 1784.

The *Lady Hughes*, an English merchant trader, arrived in the port of Guangzhou and fired the customary one-gun salute, which killed two Chinese customs officials. The Imperial Governor, already looking for an excuse to increase the duties, used the incident to close the harbour to all foreign shipping. A compromise was reached. The British concession manager handed over the English gunner, who was publicly put to death. Beheading a British subject did nothing to improve an already strained situation.

Over the past century sporadic rebellions and ever-increasing smuggling along the coastline of southern China had signalled a weakening of central control. Local mandarins were greedy, generals corrupt and salt merchants cheated on the salt tax. Weak emperors could not meet the many challenges and dynastic China entered a long downslide. Flexing its muscle, the British government used the *Lady Hughes* incident to appoint Lord Halliday Macartney as its envoy to the Beijing court, and deliver an unequivocal message from King George III to His Celestial Majesty, Emperor Quianlong, to demand port facilities adequate for British trade along China's coastline. Macartney's mission of 1792 was doomed from the start. The main discussion concerned not trade, but the delicate details of protocol. "When you enter into the attendance of the Celestial Emperor, be sure your head is always below that of His Celestial Presence," court mandarins insisted.

There was no way that a British lord, subject only to His Majesty King George, would kowtow before a heathen despot, especially since Lord Macartney already knew that the Emperor reclined on a low chair, which meant that an English lord would have to crawl on the floor. This silly haggling dragged on for months before a compromise was reached. The lord would make his court appearance without his ceremonial hat and his hairline would rest an inch below that of the Emperor. Macartney, annoyed by the wait, agreed, and the mandarins finally allowed him an audience with the celestial personality to present the letter from his king.

The Emperor's reply, when it came after months of waiting, was couched in diplomatic terms: "You, O King, live beyond the confines of many seas, nevertheless, impelled by your humble desire to partake of the benefits of OUR civilization … OUR Celestial Empire possesses all things in prolific abundance and within its own borders lacks no product …" And then it went on to refuse every single request, "as WE have no use for your country's manufactures".

With this phrase, which London considered an insult, the door to China's riches was slammed. The business of import and export had become so valuable and important for England that the refusal would lead inexorably to war. But not a war over tea.

Tea was not the only commodity the Honourable East India Company traded – even more important was opium. The illegal import into China of the addictive drug was big, and growing bigger. Despite a Chinese ban on the substance – in 1729 Emperor Yongzhen had outlawed all *use* of opium – English ships were bringing in great quantities from their factories in East India, where plantations grew and processed poppies for the China market. In 1796, pushed by the justified fear that his subjects were becoming ever more dependent on a foul paste that addled their brains, the Emperor issued an edict: it banned all *import* of opium into China, making it a crime punishable by death. With imports annually totalling four thousand chests, each containing 150 pounds of opium, this decree – if followed – would be a fatal blow to the profits of the not-so-Honourable East India Company.

Of course, this imperial decree alone could never stop opium from reaching China's addicts; where monumental profits are involved, nothing ever can. Bribed with bundles of cash, Guangzhou's government officials looked the other way, and the importing of opium became "a tolerated smuggling operation". In one case a well-known "tea merchant" agreed to co-operate with the central authorities by denouncing the use of official junks to smuggle in the drug. The local *tao* (magistrate) had to drop the case when his key witness was found floating in the river. And though the governor was clearly implicated in the murder, nothing could be gained by disgracing a high mandarin.

In 1816, thanks to research by an English pharmacist who invented a process producing Malwa opium[1] faster and more cheaply, the price of opium dropped drastically. Increased production called for expanded distribution networks. The use of opium had caught on (much as the cigarette in twentieth-century China, a country of 360 million smokers). China was *the* opium market, but a market that was officially closed. Criminal organizations, notably the Mafia-like Triads, created an efficient drug distribution network. These Chinese gangs controlled the harbours and their officials by bribe or murder; fortunes were made as each year more opium found its way up the main rivers. Opium divans sprung up in every major city, sinkholes of iniquity with no allowance for basic hygiene. Mandarins, merchants and sailors lay alongside one another on wooden cots, their staging place on the road to self-destruction. Drug addicts were not interested in sex; opium dulled their senses and created a feeling of dreamy lethargy. Their only interest was in the next pipe, the key to which was money.

But opium was not exclusively used by men; women were also hooked on the hallucinating poison, many of them at a tender age. To buy more forgetfulness these girls found themselves vulnerable to sexual exploitations. Addicted girls were reduced to serving the tastes of those who would pay a few coins to accommodate their favourite perversions. Opium and prostitution were bedfellows and many opium dens served a double function as drug parlours and bordellos.

Addicts hankered for more opium, but supply never matched demand. The cost of addiction rose; the price of opium reached new heights, and the value of silver rose commensurably and devalued the government's paper currency. Within a few years the cost of distribution, and the bribes to generals and local mandarins, became so high that the illegal purchase of opium began to drain China's silver hoard. Trading silver for opium resulted in huge fortunes for European traders. Zhu Zun, an imperial official, put it quite strongly for a "polite Chinese": "by introducing opium into this country, their [English] purpose has been to weaken and enfeeble the Central Empire. If not early aroused to a sense of our danger, we shall find ourselves, ere long, on the last step toward ruin ... "

The main obstacle was getting enough opium from the southern coast to the central China market. A mule could carry two boxes (150 kilograms) but a schooner carried two thousand boxes – in other words, one shipload equalled a thousand donkeys. In 1832 William Jardine and his partner James Matheson, tea traders with well-established contacts in Guangzhou, chartered fast and well-armed tea clippers, which could outrun imperial war junks, fight off pirates and deliver opium to covert landing places along the northern coastline of China. Being hanged from the masthead was the punishment for opium smuggling, regardless of a culprit's nationality, but such restrictions could never be enforced, and every opium ship was a law unto itself. There was even gunfire between lawless bands of smugglers whenever two opium ships disputed the right to a landing.

If there was precious little glamour in these men's lives, there was still less in the trade they followed. In London the honourable members of parliament could have done something about it; instead they were counting their firm's benefit from the illegal trade with China, and not likely to be moved by the news that two million Chinese were already hooked on a deadly drug. Smuggling opium was one thing, legal trade quite another. Ensuring uninterrupted commerce in manufactured goods and cloth became a major issue.

In 1836 the British government sent an official trade delegation of merchants and diplomats, presided over by Lord Napier, to China to promote trade in English products. When local officials refused the delegation permission to proceed upriver, the inept Napier commandeered two British frigates to bombard the Bogue forts at the entrance to the River Zhu, when the two frigates found themselves bottled up by a solid chain of Chinese war junks; Napier, besieged by his diplomats not to cause irreparable harm to British trade interests, had to beat a humiliating retreat. The "Napier Fizzle" instilled in the Chinese a false belief that their war junks were equal to European warships and could repulse any future maritime challenge.

With the successful outcome of the Napier Affair still fresh on his mind, the Celestial Emperor Daoguang decided to end the use of opium in China. Initial steps brought no noticeable results, until the Governor General of Hunan and Hubei, Lin Zexu, suggested that his emperor punish not only the providers and smugglers but the users, which would lead to a collapse of the drug trade by the red-haired, long-nosed devils. The way Lin Zexu outlined his plan before the court in Beijing, the "Ocean People" (Europeans) would most assuredly sacrifice their illegal drug trade to safeguard their highly profitable legal commerce. His suggestion so pleased the Celestial Emperor that he ordered the governor to "sever the trunk from its roots". With this imperial edict began the suppression of the opium bane.

With Imperial Commissioner Lin Zexu (Tse-hsü), a tough, incorruptible official emerged on the scene; his reputation of holding to strict morals gave him the sobriquet "Lin of the Clear Sky". He faced a formidable task: two million Chinese were then addicted to opium. From the beginning he made it clear that any Chinese caught trading in the drug faced instant execution without trial. Independent of the intrigues of Beijing's serpentine court, Lin Zexu retained the purity of a neutral outsider. Undoubtedly the single bright light on a darkening Chinese horizon, he said: "We are having both economic and political structure imposed on us from the outside colonial exploitation. The foreign presence on our shores is nothing more than a prescription for more structural enslavement, with the added problem that we do not even control the structure."

Lin Zexu's appointment as Imperial Commissioner was to have a decisive impact on future events in more than one way. He began his anti-smuggling campaign with a remarkable document in international diplomacy, the Lin Zexu Memorandum addressed to Queen Victoria:[2]

A communication: magnificently our Great Emperor soothes and pacifies China and foreign countries …

… After a long period of commercial intercourse, there appear among the crowd of barbarians both good persons and bad, unevenly. Consequently there are those who smuggle opium to seduce Chinese people and so cause the spread of poison to all provinces. Such persons, who only care to profit themselves, and disregard their harm to others, are not tolerated by the laws of heaven and are hated by human beings. All those people in China who sell opium or smoke opium should receive the death penalty …

… May you, O King [sic], check your wicked and sift your wicked people before they come to China in order to guarantee the peace of your nation, and to let the two countries enjoy together the blessings of peace.

This document, in a language easy to understand, explained the laws of a sovereign country and expressed the general feeling of China. It shocked Britain's Foreign Office into action, since it threatened reprisals against British trade interests. A diplomatic solution would have been the easy way out, but Britain's Foreign Secretary, Lord Palmerston, was not known for simple solutions. He opted for a hard choice: "Send in the Navy!"

The Lin Zexu Memorandum was intercepted before it even reached Queen Victoria. Left without the courtesy of a reply, Lin Zexu's next step was predictable. On 10 March 1839 he issued a proclamation – with a copy delivered to the head of the British concession in Guangzhou – that no import or trade in opium would be tolerated; the government would impose heavy fines, and if misconduct persisted the culprit would face execution by beheading. If Europeans had thought that Lin Zexu's anti-opium decree did not concern them, and that a Chinese commissioner had no jurisdiction over their lives, he left them in no doubt by adding that "this law applies to everyone, *whatever his nationality*". Lin Zexu's pressure increased. He expelled Chinese stevedores working for foreign shipping interests from the port. It left the foreign traders without the manual workers needed to unload incoming ships carrying legal merchandise. In the ships' holds bales of cotton turned green with mould. When the foreign traders still failed to react to the opium ban, a clash became unavoidable.

On 18 March 1839, a week after his edict went into effect, Lin Zexu cut off Guangzhou's foreign trade concessions with a *cordon sanitaire* of a thousand troops and ordered foreign merchants – on penalty of instant execution – to hand over every ounce of opium stored in their warehouses or aboard their ships in the harbour. The British trade commissioner Charles Elliot tried in vain to argue his way out of the dilemma. To make good on his ban, Lin Zexu ordered a number of wealthy, "untouchable" Chinese to be rounded up and publicly strangled. "Let this be a warning to everyone on our territories that we will persist on behalf of Our Celestial Emperor until the opium scourge has been eradicated."

On 27 March 1839 Lin Zexu took a fateful step when he ordered his troops to invade the foreign factory compound. They smashed the doors into the warehouses and rounded up some of the traders.

"You cannot accuse, arrest and judge Her Majesty's loyal subjects," foamed Commissioner Elliot.

"How dare you English threaten me with the laws of your nation in our lands?" responded Lin Zexu.

This reply, together with the execution of the Chinese merchants, left Elliot with no option but to ask his English traders to hand over their stores of twenty-one thousand chests of opium. Lin Zexu had ponds dug and filled with seawater and then forced the foreign traders to look on as he poured their opium into the giant vats and left it to dissolve. Then he had the Europeans escorted to his palace and made them all sign a firm promise never again – on pain of death – to deal in opium. The dejected foreign traders packed up and departed for the nearby Portuguese enclave of Macau.

Aboard one of the last ships to sail from Guangzhou to London, Charles

Elliot dispatched a letter to Lord Palmerston, asking the Foreign Secretary for a rapid intervention to protect England's interests in China. For Britain's foreign exchange, the future of its profitable opium trade was at stake. With a yearly turnover of $18 million, opium was outselling tea by far. Elliot explained that Lin Zexu's unjustifiable action translated an opium issue into one of transgression of territorial law, though he did not stress which territory he was referring to – in fact, China.

The British press accused the Chinese authorities of any and all evil, and war drums began to sound. Only a few warning voices were raised; underestimating their enemies on the basis of racial prejudice had played a part in a number of previous disasters in the colonial context. On 8 April 1840 William Gladstone stood up in the House of Commons and said:

> I do not know how it can be argued as a crime against the Chinese that they refused provisions to those who refused obedience to their laws whilst residing within their territory. I am not competent to judge how long this war may last. But this I can say, that a war more unjust in its origin, a war more calculated in its progress to cover this country with disgrace, I do not know and I have not read of.

His voice was not heard. A British fleet set sail. This step ushered in a half-century of enforced exploitation of China. Ever since, this has been China's primary emotional and symbolic reason for resenting trading with the West.

A series of diplomatic blunders led to a bloody confrontation. It was entirely unnecessary and could easily have been avoided. Officially, the belief that China felt itself superior to the rest of the world in its civilization, as expressed by the Lin Zexu Memorandum, was seen as a condescending attitude that proved unacceptable to the nation that had just bested Napoleon.[3] Neutral observers saw the truth otherwise. "The occasion of this outbreak of war has unquestionably been afforded by the English cannon forcing upon China that soporific drug called Opium," wrote Karl Marx in the *New York Daily Tribune* in 1853.

The Opium Wars were not so much a clash of two cultures as conflicts for Western trade. Opium was the underlying cause and profit its mover. The irony of it is that the sale of opium so absorbed China's purchasing capacity that it blocked the market for legal British imports.

In the mid-nineteenth century, however, England dictated the order of events.

# 4

# THE PEARL RIVER GROUSE SHOOT

## 7 JANUARY 1841, PEARL RIVER, GUANGDONG, CHINA

The first episode in the Opium Wars showed how little it took in the nineteenth century to set off a colonial war. During the first week of July 1839, with tensions already high, some British sailors on shore leave got drunk; on the way back to their ship, they ran into a Chinese farmer named Lin Weixi. What happened next is unclear, except that the farmer ended up with a bashed-in head and the Imperial Commissioner of Guangzhou, Lin Zexu, demanded that the ship's captain hand over the rowdy British crew. Recalling the humiliating public execution of the English gunner of the *Lady Hughes*, the British trade commissioner, Charles Elliot, refused.

With Guangzhou's British trade community already exiled to an unprofitable existence in Macao, which granted them temporary residence but prohibited trading activities, Lin Zexu now dispatched an ultimatum to the Portuguese governor ordering him to hand over the British subjects involved in the farmer's death. The Portuguese governor, hostile to the stiff competition from British merchants in the region, played the China card. Fearful of a confrontation with British warships, instead of handing over the culprits he expelled the British from his colony. Once again the British had to travel, but this time only across the bay. They settled in a fishing village on a sparsely inhabited island, Xiang-gang. Owing to the efforts of a trading company founded by two young English entrepreneurs, Jardine and Matheson, Xiang-gang blossomed into a metropolis – Hong Kong.

Imperial Commissioner Lin Zexu seethed over Charles Elliot's refusal to hand over the crew for judgement. He ordered the admiral of the imperial fleet to sail to Xiang-gang, board any one of the 50 foreign merchant traders lying at anchor and take hostages, whom he intended to put on public trial for the murder of the farmer Lin Weixi. The commander of the imperial naval forces at Guangzhou, Admiral Kwan, took a fleet of 29 war junks downriver. It so happened that two British men-of-war had come to call on Xiang-gang. Charles Elliot commandeered the two warships and sailed them upriver to confront Admiral Kwan's flotilla. The belligerents met near the Bogue forts. HMS *Volage* and *Hyacinth* opened fire and, in the spirit of Admiral Nelson, blasted three war junks out of the water, while the rest of Kwan's fleet skulked back to shore.

After the First Battle of the Bogue the Chinese admiral asked for a cease-fire, which Elliot granted. When the British realized that the Chinese were using this momentary calm to build up their forces, Elliot dispatched an urgent message for assistance to London. Forced by commercial pressures from manufacturers and traders in London and Manchester over losing the lucrative trade with China, British Foreign Secretary Lord Palmerston dispatched a naval force under Admiral George Elliot[1] "to place our intercourse with China on a real basis".

As England's admiral sailed for the China coast he had plenty of reason to be confident; after all, his squadron was made up of 20 battle-tested ships of the line, while the Chinese had nothing to challenge the technological superiority of the British armada. Beyond that, Elliot could count on the professionalism of his officers, seamen and Royal Marines.

At Hong Kong Admiral Elliot summoned his captains for a council of war aboard his flagship to acquaint them with the situation. While the British were relying on speed, manoeuvrability and the power of their long-range guns, the Chinese standard procedure was to ram the enemy before boarding his ships with an overwhelming force of soldiers. Shortly after Christmas 1840 Elliot's fleet hoisted sails and caught the wind up the Pearl River on their way to do battle for Britain. Before them, the mouth of the river gaped wide open as if to swallow them. Instead of smashing into the formidable river forts headlong, Elliot sent two fast corvettes to probe farther upriver.

Admiral Kwan's messages to the Emperor for reinforcements had been left unanswered. With his numerous but lightly armed war junks he lay in ambush behind a promontory, with the guns of the twin river forts covering his fleet from elevated firing positions on the high battlements. The dawn of 7 January 1841 brought the Chinese commander a nasty shock. Counting on yet another combat with only two outgunned English warships – the previous day his outposts had reported two enemy ships coming upriver, in fact Elliot's advance scouts – Kwan now saw 20 ships of the line, along with a few steamers, emerging from the morning mist. Confronted by such firepower, he could achieve little but an honourable death. The crews of Kwan's fleet of war junks joined in his despair long before the long-range British guns went into action. He signalled his vessels to link together as a chain blocking the narrows.

The first British salvo boomed out across the water and the Chinese suffered great damage but made no adequate response. The British ships stood off and pounded the junks into matchsticks. Swirling demons of yellow flame danced upon the wide river. Water rushed in through the junks' splintered holes and the ships turned turtle, spilling sailors into the floods. The next hour saw the "Pearl River Grouse Shoot", in which 72 junks were reduced to splinters. Blackened bodies came floating downriver; a few survivors clung to bits of smoking wood. In the final stage of the attack a British rocket scored a direct hit on the leading junk. The ship exploded in a shower of sparks, killing its brave commander, Admiral Kwan. Once the black cloud had dissipated, there was no more sign of the junk, reduced to flotsam like the rest of the fleet. For the British it was not really a battle but more like live shooting practice.

Meanwhile fourteen hundred Royal Marines under Major Pratt landed two miles south of Chuengpee Fort, supported by the guns of HMS *Calliope*, *Larne*, *Hyacinth*, *Queen* and *Nemesis*. It was in this encounter that one of the modern ships engaged showed its value. The *Nemesis*, a paddle steamer powered by a 120-horsepower engine, launched in November 1839, and then under the command of Captain William Hutcheon Hall, RN, used her two 32-pound muzzle-loaders to bring down the walls of Chuengpee Fort, through which a landing party of Marines rushed at bayonet point. The British suffered 38 wounded, while the Chinese left hundreds of corpses behind. The works at the Chuengpee Fort were dismantled and its 97 ancient guns dumped into the river, before buildings and stores were blown up. That still left the strongest defence of all, the Bogue Forts, some 30 miles downriver from Guangzhou, and the key to the city. The fort's massive walls gave it the aspect of a ferocious primeval beast sprawling astride the river. However fearsome the fort looked, its armaments were antiquated cast-iron cannon, more dangerous to the gunners than their targets.

At dawn on 26 February 1841 a British amphibious force swung into operation. These veterans had been blooded in colonial scraps in the years since the Napoleonic Wars. For them it was just another "Fix your bayonets – and go!" This time, however, the Chinese were ready for them; what they may have lacked in armour and training they made up in fervour by standing fast and putting up a fierce fight. Heavy British shells crashed into the ramparts with devastating results. Smoke billowing from exploding shells obscured the ships' view of the fort ahead. Captain Thomas Bourchier, commander of the naval brigade, could see nothing. He heard only the sounds of battle, the explosions and the shrieks of the wounded.

Then the artillery stopped and the Marines began their rush for the walls. It was not to be a repeat of their earlier conquests. Their boats were within 30 metres of the wall, when from the top of the ramparts Chinese cannon and muskets roared. The naval brigade suffered many casualties. The cast-iron Chinese cannon were firing too fast, their shells thundering every three minutes, a rate just short of reckless. The problem lay not with the gunners but with their guns; the barrels were quickly overheating. The inevitable occurred when an ear-shattering explosion shook the ground and glowing debris shot high in one spectacular shower after another. One of the guns had blown up and its blast had set off the fort's powder magazine.

By eight o'clock the Bogue Forts, reduced to smoking hulks, were in British hands. There was nothing to take. The blast had killed the defenders. The riverway to the greatest city in southern China had been forced open. With the arrival of a British fleet off Guangzhou, a new expression was born: "gunboat diplomacy".

To defuse the situation, the Emperor sacked the only honest official in China. Commissioner Lin Zexu was replaced by the immensely rich and corrupt Chi-shan, who had paid his way in silver to become Governor of Zhili. Instead of taking his garrison of thousands and fighting it out with the few hundred invaders, Chi-shan withdrew behind the walls of Guangzhou. The siege of the place will not be remembered for any great feat; there was, however, one incident, which has been emphasized in recent Chinese history books as the heroic stand by the country's peasants against the foreign intruder.

Sir Hugh Gough, commanding the British land force, had set up a blockade of Guangzhou with four thousand troops at his disposal, some regulars but the rest mercenaries in the pay of the East India Company. These mercenaries had engaged in looting and raping, as well as an act which the Chinese considered an unforgivable sacrilege, the desecration of tombs. To defend their ancestral tombs from grave robbers, members of the local gentry and their serfs formed into militias.

On 21 May 1841, on a night of pouring rain, a company of roving East India Company mercenaries became separated from the main force and ended up in San-yuan-li, a village a few miles north of beleaguered Guangzhou. As no enemy was nearby to spoil their fun, they enjoyed a night of drinking and carousing. Villagers ran to a nearby unit of Chinese militia for help. Quite correctly, its energetic commander figured that the foreigners' flintlocks would only sputter and fail to fire in the heavy downpour.[2] The militia caught the mercenaries with their pants down. In darkness and heavy rain in which nobody could tell friend from foe, a fracas ensued with fists, shovels, knives and sticks. The brawlers floundered around in the mud and fell over those on the ground. It left a single mercenary dead and 15 others with serious bumps, before a detachment from the regular British force came to their rescue. This brawl – it was nothing more than that – led to a surviving legend about an armed peasant uprising that annihilated a foreign invasion force.

The British planned a final attack on walled Guangzhou for Queen Victoria's birthday, 24 May 1841. The morning peace was shattered by a royal salute from the ship's mighty artillery. The city's ramparts of stone and brick were reduced to dust. Sir Hugh Gough landed his Royal Marines in two divisions, while the guns of the Royal Navy continued to blast away at the walls and houses. Under cover of the naval bombardment, some units made it to the battlements. As suddenly as it had begun, the firing ceased, and within minutes companies of Marines poured across the moat and occupied the abandoned wall.

Sir Hugh still faced the problem of a vast Chinese numerical superiority inside the city. Should Governor Chi-shan act vigorously now, a British victory could be endangered. But the cowardly Chi-shan was hiding out in the cellar of his palace. To make up for his shortage of manpower, Gough ordered 15 howitzers to be set up ashore and trained on the wealthy city centre. The British gunners had finished their preparations and awaited their admiral's order, when a group of high mandarins approached under a white flag. The political representative of Queen Victoria, Commissioner Charles Elliot, dictated the surrender terms:

1. Withdrawal of all remaining Imperial forces to a distance of 60 miles from Canton.
2. Payment, within one week, of $6,000,000, along with a complete indemnity for all damage done to British property.
3. Hong Kong to become a British possession.

Commissioner Elliot was satisfied. After all, he got Hong Kong for Britain in the bargain. While negotiations were in progress, a Chinese regiment west of the city attacked the British in such force that only the fortunate intervention of two companies of Royal Marines, who happened to be marching past with their cannon, averted a disaster for the British. It was the war's fiercest battle. British losses were 130 soldiers, while more than 10 times as many Chinese troops fell, mostly to grapeshot from British cannon.

Coming as it did in the midst of ongoing surrender talks, the British considered this assault an act of treachery. So when the Chinese failed to deliver the $6-million ransom – part of which was the pay for the East India Company's mercenaries – this rowdy pack looted the city; women suffered rape, while husbands or relatives rushing to their defence were bayoneted. The people of Guangzhou accused their local governor of having capitulated to the foreign devils only to save his own skin, yet still trying to profit from continuing trade with the despicable Ocean People. Beijing blamed the fearless Lin Zexu for his decision to execute the Emperor's orders to the letter, but Chi-shan's cowardly behaviour was the real cause of China's loss of face. In the end the truth came out; Chi-shan was tried on a charge of cowardice; his fortune was confiscated, and he was led in chains past a jeering crowd.

The fall of Guangzhou to British warships marked the end of phase one of the First Opium War. There is no doubt that the Chinese had the manpower to destroy the small British invasion force. They lacked, however, the two vital ingredients for victory: effective leadership and modern artillery. Otherwise Britain's prize of Hong Kong might never have been.

The Manchu dynasty had inherited an empire that stretched far and wide, and defending it required a large standing army spread over a huge territory. For centuries this system had worked, and stabilized the frontiers, though at the expense of concentrating power in a few hands. At the court in Beijing mandarins struggled to establish themselves in senior positions, giving rise to vicious rivalries and intrigues. With the British invasion a shift took place which should have united the aristocrats but instead divided the court anew into pro-war and anti-war factions. The hardliners argued that it was dishonourable and politically unacceptable to lose face, even if this meant a huge human sacrifice, while the others feared that any further defeat might finally lead to the collapse of the Manchu dynasty. One thing was clear: Britain's war was fought not for territorial gains, but for commercial benefits. Thus, the doves argued, was it not better to grant a few trade concessions than lose the empire?

While these arguments were mulled over in Beijing, anti-war voices began to surface in Europe. One attack came from the theologian of social equality, Karl Marx: "The representative of the antiquated world appears prompted by ethical motives, while the representative of overwhelming modern society fights for the privilege of buying in the cheapest and selling in the dearest markets – this, indeed, is a sort of tragic couplet stranger than any poet would ever have dared to fancy."

Marx went on to argue, quite rightly, that continuing the war in the antipodes was a vicious capitalist scheme to further the capacity for distributing ever more British-manufactured goods to a developing market.

London fully realized that every European power would soon be involved in the vigorous nineteenth-century colonial expansion known as imperialism. Therefore Britain shut its ears to all criticism. Its imperialist case involved one or more arguments – economic, missionary or strategic – wrapped in the most powerful appeal of all: national prestige and glory. The active agents of imperialism were businessmen, militarists and politicians, many of whom knew little about foreign countries and had even less intention of ever going there. But it was the nationalistic masses that applauded it, backed it and carried the vote at the ballot box.

It is hard to separate the tangible military fruits of a victory such as treaties for naval bases and strategic raw materials from the intangibles of national pride and world status. London's consensus was that China would rather make concessions than risk a war that would leave it too weak to face the many internal threats of popular risings. Conversely, dissenters argued that a big fleet would give Britain the naval power to concentrate her striking forces in the region.

There is a gentleman's agreement that other national governments will look the other way when any one of them abuses its own colonial population. Only when a strong national government attempts to overwhelm a weaker nation's government and compel the locals to do its will does the world community – sometimes – voice mild disapproval. However, despite all the high-minded advocacy for law and order, the world community still honours the law of conquest. And Great Britain was set on conquering the Chinese market. With this in mind, London named Sir Henry Pottinger as its new Chief Commissioner, to replace Charles Elliot, unjustly accused by Lord Palmerston of having given in too easily. A Royal Navy squadron from India joined the ships anchored in Hong Kong Bay, with a directive to proceed along the coast to Chushan and Ningbo.

The continuation of British gunboat diplomacy stirred the fire in Victorian poets with heroic epic and verse: "Nothing will stop a British fleet!"

Nothing and nobody did when a Royal Navy squadron sailed north.

# 5

# TIGER DAY, TIGER HOUR

## 10 MARCH 1842, NINGBO, ZHEJIANG PROVINCE, MANCHU DYNASTY, CHINA

"Fire at will!" bellowed an English voice. As the first human wave approached the forward positions, every firearm in the British Expeditionary Force, army and navy, was discharged in one long volley that seemed to echo for ever. The front ranks of the Chinese army shuddered under the impact of ball and shot; attackers were blown off their feet and flung through the air. Only a moment passed before the next wave of soldiers came hurtling out of the fog of black powder with blood-curdling shrieks. The next wave was stopped, and then the next. Once the smoke of the volleys cleared and drifted out to sea in ragged patches, it was possible to see the carnage that British cannon and muskets had wrought. Thousands of corpses littered the plain; in places there were mounds three and four deep. The grass was dark and slippery with blood.

The follow-up move in this dismal conflict over opium was as pathetic as it was tragic. With a British invasion force of 20 battleships, hundreds of heavy-calibre cannon, with nine thousand cold-faced Royal Marines on their way north to threaten Shanghai, the Manchu Emperor replied to the challenge by appointing a distant cousin to rally his army. For once, at Ningbo,[1] the Chinese held a definite advantage; the British contingent would find itself on land, drawn beyond the reach of its supportive naval guns and facing a crushing numerical superiority. One battle would decide the issue. For this it took a man of destiny to lead the men into combat, someone dogged and unbreakable, who demonstrated his personal valour by bravery under fire. The man picked for the task was the worst possible choice.

There are commanders who are so beset by fear and indecision that it leads to their defeat before the enemy has fired his first shot. Such a man was the High Mandarin I-ching, a figure of tragic grandeur, a prince of doubt and hesitation, a Hamlet without military brains, sadly offended by the whispering sneers of the Imperial courtiers about his poetry. His principal qualification to lead an army into battle was that he was the Emperor's cousin, and in charge of the imperial gardens. His talent lay in writing flowery poetry, but not planning military campaigns. History would blame him for the disaster, but the court intrigue that put him into this impossible position was really responsible. So when the Emperor presented I-ching with his appointment as head of a non-existent army, this gentle poet who never dared to say *no* obliged his sovereign, even though he felt incompetent to lead soldiers into battle. The pressure of military command imposes greater stress on an individual than almost any other activity. Psychological weaknesses which pass unnoticed in ordinary life emerge with catastrophic consequence in wartime.

Such was the case with the unfit I-ching, the opening act of whose military career was to organize a contest for the best-composed victory announcement. He followed this by consulting the oracle in the Hangzhou pagoda for the best day to do battle. The answer he received was: "Tiger day in tiger month at tiger hour."

Tiger day, tiger hour – an absurdity in military terms, since it coincided with the pre-dawn hours of 10 March 1842, when it would be too dark to launch an attack, and furthermore, happened to fall in the spring monsoon season, when the ground was too soggy to get an army and its supplies into its jump-off position. But the oracle had spoken, and General I-ching did not waver; a superior spirit had fixed the date and the hour. He composed a victory verse before he began to marshal an army by pulling serfs and peasants from the nearby provinces. The conscripts had to arm themselves with whatever was at hand: forks, sickles, knives and staves. In the face of British cannon, I-ching's artillery was hopelessly outclassed. His guns were of different calibre, cannon balls could not be interchanged and the powder had been left in the open and become damp.

A British Expeditionary Force of nine thousand Royal Marines, engineers and support, three thousand seamen, 18 men-of-war and nine paddle steamers, including the now famous *Nemesis*, was put under the command of Sir Hugh Gough. The commander was an impetuous officer, ably assisted by three hard-fighting generals, Saltoun, Schoedde and Bartley. The British ships had sailed north along the China coast and lay anchored offshore, in sight of the British land forces, which had set up camp in a field outside the city of Ningbo. It was an unfortunate choice for a military campsite, since a level plain fronted it, making it an ideal target for the massed human-wave attack for which the Chinese were known. To protect the camp from such an eventuality, the British commanders had placed 25 field pieces – guns, howitzers and mortars – behind defensive earthworks. Although the rifled, breech-loading cannon was the weapon of the future, British generals retained a preference for the smooth-bore muzzle-loaders, using them at close range, and preferred good, old-fashioned grapeshot over explosive shells.

*Tiger day!* General I-ching's army had been on the march for days; they were a ragged, tattered and dirty lot, exhausted and hungry, since their inept commander had made no provision for rations. The strength of I-ching's army is uncertain, but it was probably nearly one hundred thousand. He allocated a large portion of this force for the protection of his own headquarters. Next he failed to line up his units in a coherent attack formation, trusting them to find their own start-off position. And lastly, I-ching had no idea of the deployment of the enemy's defensive disposition; he knew only that the British were "in front of him". The British generals had interspersed musketry with field pieces, the best manner in which to provide mutual protection. In intricately laid-out redoubts, Gough's mustachioed veterans were preparing powder, shot and wads for the batteries. The only problem was visibility. It was still too dark for gunners to aim at specific targets.

*Tiger hour!* A war horn sounded, long and low. Then another, and another. Shortly before first light a cry arose from many thousands of human ants rushing forward. I-ching launched fifty thousand untrained natives, armed with knives and sticks, into a formidable array of British field guns.

"Here they come," General Gough remarked dryly. "He won't waste good troops in the first wave. He must know we've got the field ranged." Gough gave his counterpart I-ching too much credit. The fact was, the Chinese knew nothing. A kilometre away Gough could dimly make out that the attackers were moving in a ragged line. Their roar was deafening as they charged. Close behind the first wave followed a second, then another. They kept to no formation; some carried pikes and swords, others jogged along with ancient muskets resting on their shoulders.

Gough had ordered his gunnery officers to hold their fire until the enemy was well within killing range. He raised his hand and dropped it. A blinding flash split the darkness; a puff of smoke, followed a second later by the dull boom of the discharge. A blinding flash blossomed in the midst of the enemy formation, then a geyser of earth went up, flinging aside the ragged remains of men, ripping holes in the tight mass of figures. Every British gun opened up. The thunder of artillery of the opening salvo was felt through the whole body rather than just the ears. The first waves disintegrated in a maelstrom of explosions and shrapnel. The field erupted in fountains of stone and dirt. Waves of hot air and smoke billowed up from the gun redoubts. A massed scream mixed with the thunder of the guns. Unforgiving grapeshot tore the Chinese to pieces while they were still three hundred yards from Gough's mighty guns.

Hell had opened its jaws for the men of General I-ching. A great confused disorder that would not stop … thick, oily smoke … the fumes of bursting shells … fiery showers spurting into the air … the incessant crack from iron cannon mouths … flash and smoke … the echo returning. A horizontal hail of grapeshot and musket ball wiped out three successive waves. The follow-up waves could hear the screams of the wounded. The rout of his initial attack did not deter I-ching. He concluded that if he were to send in more attacks the British would soon be out of powder and ball and the end result would be favourable. Tiger Hour, the oracle had promised. I-ching summoned his sub-commanders and ordered another attack that met the same devastating result, as fire struck them down.

This absurd struggle continued well into daylight. I-ching could not cope with the enormity of the pressure he was under. Unfortunately, he was also not one to trouble himself greatly over casualties, and piled mistake on mistake. Not content with slaughtering thousands in the first waves, he ordered further human waves. He made no attempt to try anything but a frontal assault. Like a mindless herd, his untrained peasants went duly forward, stumbling over the bodies of those that had gone before them. The butchery could have been avoided had I-ching spread his units; but he let his fear of responsibility dominate his thinking, and in his panic he did just the opposite, allowing his troops to bunch together, creating such a compact mass of human flesh that British cannonballs could not miss, cutting highways through the attackers.

For the British gunners it became a question of how many of the enemy could be killed in how short a time. Even so, because of the sheer number of the Chinese, and the fact that the tubes of the British cannon were beginning to run hot, the subsequent waves did make some progress; they advanced, cumbersome but seemingly unstoppable. The noise of battle cries was added to the cracking of the cannon. At most places they were stopped by musket fire when they were still some distance from the British line, but some units eventually managed to break through to tackle the Royal Marines with their primitive weapons.

The battle's climax came under an early morning sun. A final offensive began after all the other attempts had ended in horror, and although it was the weakest push it almost succeeded. But I-ching did nothing to exploit a momentary weakness in the British flank; he was late in ordering in the last reserves, and his field commanders were slow to execute the order. Until this moment British cannon and troops, firing from behind breastwork, were invisible to the attacker. The few Chinese who did make it to the British defences and tried to clamber over the earthworks, sword in hand, were shot down at point-blank range or bayoneted. But there seemed to be no end to the howling, yelling Chinese, and the British gunners could not load fast enough. With the tubes overheating and the infantry running out of ammo, yet another bunched human wave came rushing at them.

In battle it never takes much to make the difference. In military terms this is known as the Hinge Factor. One instantaneous decision, one shift of formation, and history pivots.

"Swivel the guns!" yelled a young battery lieutenant, and when his gunners were not fast enough he roared once more: "Damn it, swivel the bloody guns." Grunting with exertion, the sweating, soot-covered gunners heaved and pushed on the spokes of the gun carriages to align the tubes. Before the Chinese wave managed to overrun the British front line, this junior officer in command of a battery in a flanking position had shifted his battery's lane of fire – hot tubes or not – and four cannon began pouring a devastating barrage into the enemy's open flank. The gunnery officer, young but well trained, knew how to maximize his guns' effectiveness. By using an enfilading angle of fire, he was taking full advantage of their maximum destructiveness. The gunners could not keep to that rate of fire indefinitely, of course, or their tubes would explode.

"Keep on firing," their lieutenant roared, willing to let his cannon fire long past the point of safety, a decision which was on the edge of reckless. "Let the blasted things melt!" There was no need to scream: the artillerymen knew that everything depended on them in the next few minutes, so they sweated and fired, and the air sang with the deadly whistle of their grapeshot, which bowled over the advancing waves. Even when all hope had gone the Chinese showed incredible bravery; again and again they rallied and ran into the withering cannon and musket fire. However, each successive charge began to wane, becoming a little feebler than the one before. The British gunners knew that in another dozen rounds their cannon would be useless. But Sheffield steel held, and then there was no need to fire another dozen rounds; the last Chinese hurrah, which made it to the British line, was stopped by a hail of musket balls from a range of just 10 yards. A few of the survivors surged back only to become absorbed in the next and final wave.

The last wave recoiled. Some got away, but not many. This final failed charge decided the outcome. What had begun as a slow retreat turned into a rout, until the Chinese streamed away in their thousands, trampling over their officers. There would be no survival even in retreat.

Another volley, and then another. The heavy bullets whined across the battlefield, scything down the Chinese in swaths. Disaster was complete. The sun shone on thousands upon thousands of dead men's faces with blue lips and eyes staring blindly into the open sky. Finally the guns went silent.

A planned assault by a still unengaged Chinese force failed because, at the critical moment, their promised reserves never showed up; their commanding general had passed out when he tried to gather courage in a haze of opium. And a seaborne operation by fifteen thousand Chinese, embarked on hundreds of junks and intended to fall into the rear of the British line, never materialized – their admiral was so fearful of the reputation of British naval guns that he did not even sail.

I-ching was a commander afraid of responsibility who allowed his personal fear to overmaster his thinking. He was physically and psychologically shattered. Ordered by the Emperor to win a decisive victory, he had failed. He had lost an army, and the campaign. He stared at his entourage with vacant eyes. "I've betrayed the honour of my Emperor." He calligraphed an apology to his Celestial Majesty and then swallowed a cup of poison. This pitiful figure had wasted the lives of his men on a massive scale. Because of the obstinate stupidity of their commander, the Chinese suffered seventy to eighty thousand casualties.

Sir Hugh Gough held his troops in line; he did not chase after a broken foe. It was a wise decision. The road into the interior of a big country was now wide open. After Ningbo the British crossed the river and walked into Shanghai without firing a shot.

The Battle of Ningbo remains the most futile, stupid and wasteful operation of the Opium Wars. "Tiger day" had turned into the death knell of a Chinese army, inadequately armed and incompetently led. Bronze swords were no match for cannon shot and musket ball. In the end, the great ranks of guns proved stronger than the great ranks of men who tried to take these guns. Sending badly armed men into the fire of cannon handled by professionals was a lesson that not only I-ching but also the Chinese in general had obstinately refused to learn over 30 years, and so they suffered the consequences. The fact that General I-ching was a bungling commander and committed the most horrid blunder is overshadowed by the fact that he was forced to fight a battle he had no chance of winning.

The cannonade by a single British battery highlighted one of the strange but frequent occurrences in battle. A young English gunnery lieutenant pivoted his guns and destroyed an army. "Even a chicken could not have survived before my cannon," he said afterward.

*

Still one more battle remained to decide the issue. On 6 July 1842 the British river flotilla left Shanghai to sail up the Yangtze. Just under two weeks later, on 19 July, Generals Saltoun, Schoedde and Bartley led their brigades in an attack on Chingkiang. This time the Chinese had put their best troops, the Manchu "Bannermen", under General Hai-ling to defend this strategic city, controlling the entrance from the Yangtze into the Grand Canal. Saltoun and Schoedde's men made good progress and both units advanced under an umbrella of naval artillery. Bartley's attack failed; in trying to take a gate located in an angle of the ramparts that the naval guns could not reach they suffered great loss. Bartley was about to order a withdrawal, when, to his surprise, the gate was thrown open and a vast column of Chinese spilled out. Staring down from the ramparts, General Hai-ling had noticed how thinly the English were spread on the ground. He decided to lead his men in a charge at their centre and roll up their line.

There was great confusion as a mass of Bannermen launched themselves like a wedge at the already severely depleted British force. Never before had the Royal Marines faced such homicidal maniacs, who attacked them with grim determination. With a triumphant roar the Chinese broke through the British line, their shouts echoing from the walls of Chingkiang and adding to the pandemonium. Before the entire British line collapsed, gunners hauled a number of field pieces into position to blast gaping holes into the attackers. Units of Royal Marines took the gate at the point of their bayonets, and Chingkiang was carried after fierce street fighting. With all hope gone, the Bannermen killed their wives to prevent their dishonour and then committed suicide. Their heroic commander, General Hai-ling, immolated himself by setting his house on fire.

The impact of the fall of Chingkiang was overpowering. For the Emperor the issue was a moral one: the wrongness of yielding to brute force or continuing the fight – he thought to choose between danger and safety, rather than between right and wrong. Why risk the loss of an empire for mere trading rights? asked his most influential counsellor, the highly polished Quiying. The Emperor accepted the high mandarin's view that the British would be satisfied with some concessions on trade exploitation and appointed him his imperial commissioner to negotiate a settlement.

News reached Commissioner Pottinger aboard his ship anchored off Nanjing that the Celestial Emperor was dispatching Quiying for a parley, in which the British dictated the terms. On 29 August 1842 the Treaty of Nanjing was signed in the cabin of Pottinger's flagship HMS *Cornwallis*.

The flowery discussion was conducted courteously, but the deal granted was humiliating. China was forced into paying war reparations of $21 million. But money was not all; there were additional indignities. Around a baize table, a foreign power decided that China would not be allowed to continue its traditional policy of self-sufficiency. The treaties required China to throw open its doors in order to serve Britain's imperialistic design. (In the end, a British Inspector General ran the Chinese Maritime Customs Service!) The High Mandarin Quiying had to agree to foreign residency in five treaty ports – Guangzhou, Amoy, Fuchou, Ningbo and Shanghai. Provisions included the stationing of British warships in these harbours. Placing European warships in the port of Shanghai would play a significant roll in the not-too-distant future. As the cherry on the poisoned cake, Hong Kong was ceded in perpetuity to Britain. The result of these harsh conditions became known as the Unequal Treaties.

"The grand cardinal point of the expedition was the future mode of conducting the foreign trade in China." With this statement James Matheson, of Jardine, Matheson & Co. of Hong Kong, the principal beneficiary of the war, summed up the overall British sentiment. In fact, trade with China was not only an integral part of Britain's economic ties with the Far East, but equally fundamental to the economic and industrial development of its dominions of India and Australia. Britain's victory held benefits only for a minority of merchants rather than the majority of its population.

"The confiscated and destroyed chests of opium are no more the cause of war than were the chests of tea thrown overboard in Boston, and which were said to be the cause of the American Revolution," declared former American president John Quincy Adams. Opium it certainly was not, and everyone agreed on that.

Could China have emerged victorious from this war? The answer was given with the booming roar of a naval gun. The triumphant powers were blinded by their easy success. The Unequal Treaties sowed the seeds of more dramatic conflict.

The First Opium War was over. At Ningbo an inept, hapless General I-ching had lost an army, but not the war. At Nanjing China lost its independence.

# 6

# THE HOUSE OF A
# THOUSAND BLOSSOMS

## 17 AUGUST 1860, ON THE ROAD TO BEIJING

"Anyone bringing us the head of an Englishman will receive 30 *taels* of silver." Thirty pieces of silver for the head of an Englishman! For days hysterical rumours had swept Guangzhou (Canton): the English fleet was coming. The British wanted to depose the much-beloved Governor Yeh, but the people would never surrender him. Yeh Mingchen had given them back their pride, and people raised their voice in his glory. During the conquest of Guangzhou, the British mercenaries had committed countless acts of rape and plunder, fanning the grudge which the city's people bore the British to a white flame. That was one year after the incident which set off the crisis which was to lead to another war.

On 14 October 1856 the *Arrow*, a merchant trader flying the British flag, arrived in Guangzhou harbour to unload British-manufactured goods. In doing so, the ship's captain disregarded a recent edict by the Governor General of Guangdong province, Yeh Mingchen, which had unleashed an outburst of violent nationalism against "the English invader". Shortly after the ship dropped anchor, a barge carrying the local harbour commissioner rowed out to the ship. The official waved a paper. "You must sign that your ship does not carry forbidden goods."

"What do you call forbidden goods?"

Probably all the harbour official had in mind was a bribe to allow the ship to unload. "You know what I mean. Forbidden goods."

"I bloody well will not sign anything. My country and your country have already signed a treaty, and it is valid."

The two men exchanged threats, followed by more threats, as neither seemed to realize where this was leading. Not only did both countries have a treaty – albeit an unequal one – but under its stipulation a number of ponderous black-hulled ships of the British Navy had been swinging on their anchor chains in the treaty harbours; they represented military power the Chinese could never match. This time the situation was different. Most of the much-feared warships had been called back to Europe to lend their support to the British and French armies battling Russians in the Crimea. That altered the balance in favour of China.

Governor Yeh Mingchen, a short, plump-faced man with a turned eye, a sallow complexion and betel-stained teeth, was not someone known for his restraint. When he spoke he did so with a rasping cough. There was nothing gentle about his words, accusing the captain of the *Arrow* of smuggling opium. Yeh Mingchen ordered his men to seize the ship, put its English captain and crew in chains and – the worst possible insult to Her Majesty Queen Victoria – a Chinaman ordered the Union Flag to be brought down. Rather than try to calm the situation with words or money, the British consul in Guangzhou, Harry Parks, even though he knew he held a bad hand in this game, threatened the Governor with reprisal.

In the absence of the British Naval Squadron, Yeh Mingchen professed outrage at this "barefaced interference into internal Chinese affairs" and took the entire foreign community hostage by engineering a riot in the foreign concessions. His agents provocateurs, dressed up as Chinese dockworkers, set fire to the warehouse along the waterfront. Things spiralled out of hand when the mob began looting. During the scuffle a number of foreigners got banged over the head. When news of the Guangzhou riots eventually reached London, the Prime Minister, Lord Palmerston, declared: "The time is fast coming when we shall be obliged to strike another blow in China. These half-civilized governments such as those of China, require a dressing down every eight or ten years to keep them in order."

*The Times*, in an editorial signed by its editor, John Delane, defended Palmerston's position: "… We express these feelings not as our own alone, but as those natural to all Englishmen. The result of an appeal to the country will prove we are not mistaken in this estimate of our national spirit …"[1]

And so the *Arrow* Incident brought about the Arrow War, more often known as the Second Opium War, between England and its French ally against Manchu China.

When Emperor Daoguang died in 1850, his son, Xianfeng (Hsien-feng), a xenophobic monarch, ascended to the throne. His first act was to accuse his father's chief adviser, the High Mandarin Quiying, of having appeased the foreigners by signing the Unequal Treaties. Then he replaced the reigning Guangdong governor with a pair of ferociously anti-British mandarins, Xu Guangjin and the impulsive Yeh Mingchen, who began by stirring up trouble in the foreign trade concessions, formed militias, organized dockers' strikes and issued an edict refusing foreigners entry into the walled city – all in violation of specific clauses in the Unequal Treaties. All non-Chinese living inside Guangzhou were evicted *manu militari*, and their possessions confiscated. Yeh Mingchen sensed victory and issued a series of warlike threats to the British trade representative, George Bonham, who had little choice but to accept the situation.

Britain and France, heavily engaged in the Crimean War, could not immediately react; and when that war was over, a bloody mutiny broke out in India. Therefore the response Lord Palmerston had promised was put on hold until December 1857 when a British naval squadron showed up outside Hong Kong.

The *Arrow* affair and Yeh Mingchen's sabre-rattling clearly rankled London, while Paris saw a golden opportunity to put in its own claim. Allied, they decided that China needed some tangible demonstration of the hopelessness of its position. The French dispatched a naval squadron, while the British government appointed Lord Elgin with full powers to act as he saw best. Elgin was not a suave diplomat; he decided to settle the problem with a whiff of gunpowder and ordered a reprisal bombardment of Guangzhou by an Anglo-French force under Admiral Sir Michael Seymour.

On 21 December 1857 a mighty British flotilla sailed up the Pearl River and, just before dawn, opened an artillery barrage with over a hundred cannon on the city's walls and the governor's residential compound. A landing by Royal Marines was bungled and Her British Majesty's land army might well have come to harm except that their inept enemy managed to match the British blundering. When the Marines marched into the city they were surprised to find that their reception was nowhere unfriendly. This encouraged their commander to issue permission to soldiers to walk around town. From the harbour section, which was poor and dilapidated, the new occupiers wandered into the secluded section, where the *hutons* (streets) were spotlessly clean, without the piles of rubbish in the not-so-clean canteens of the British trade concession.

The British soldiers discovered another world, the magic of the Extreme Orient; houses of glazed yellow brick with green-tiled roofs and delicate porcelain dragons decorating the cornices. This was the ostentatious atmosphere of wealth and comfort of a China the sailors had seen only in picture books. Women showed a great curiosity, throwing furtive glances through latticed windows at the "long-nosed devils" who had enlivened their secluded existence with great clamour and explosions.

The arrest of Governor Yeh Mingchen could have settled the issue. It

Havoc caused by British naval guns during the storming of the Dagu Fort, Tianjin, 17 June 1900.

The Empress Dowager Cixi.

Colonel Charles George "Chinese" Gordon, commander of the Ever-Victorious Army.

Above and below: The execution of Ambassador von Ketteler's assassin, En-hai, in Beijing on 23 September 1900, shortly after the Boxer Rebellion.

Above: The bloodbath of Shanghai: slain Communists during the Nationalists' brutal crackdown of 12 April 1927.

Below: Communists set off on Mao's Long March, 21 October 1934.

Above and below: The Rape of Nanjing – the December 1937 genocide by Japanese troops, in which some 250,000 Chinese died.

US Marines aboard the USS *Panay* (above) fire machine-guns at Japanese attack aircraft before the *Panay*'s sinking (below) in the Yangtze River off Nanjing, 12 December 1937.

Too little too late: a Chinese division on its way to defend the Burma Road, 30 April 1942.

The East Is Red:
the victory parade,
1 October 1949.

Mao Zedong proclaims the People's
Republic of China, 1 October 1949.

did not. The crisis only deepened once the new High Mandarin blithely advised his Emperor that the Western allies would never risk a major war against China's mighty manpower. Lord Elgin dispatched a naval force north to "make some noise close to Beijing". The battleships began their campaign by shelling the Dagu Fort at Tianjin (Tientsin) and put a landing party of Royal Marines ashore, while overhead the shells flew. Before many more rounds were fired, the ground rocked under the Marines' feet; a noise louder than a thousand gongs and then the top of the hill blew off, with bricks and bodies tumbling from the black cloud. "Dear God Almighty!" came the hoarse whisper from a naval gunner. With one lucky shot the Royal Navy had made its point. Further shelling was unnecessary. With the Allied fleet poised to move upriver to shell Beijing, a panicked Emperor recalled the man he had fired, his father's wise negotiator Quiying, to arrange for a truce in preparation for peace talks to be held in Beijing. To set up the parley, Lord Elgin appointed Harry Parks, the Guangzhou concession commissioner, as his special envoy. Commissioner Parks set out for Beijing under a flag of truce, accompanied by a group of advisers.

On the night of 17 August 1860 the British peace delegation had reached a hamlet within a day's ride of the capital and settled for the night in a rich landowner's residence, the House of a Thousand Blossoms. Their wealthy host did his utmost to entertain his honoured guests. Parks had felt great stress over the importance of his upcoming talks but had sipped enough alcohol to be able to relax, when suddenly a great number of armed men burst into the room. Behind them strutted the cousin of the Emperor, Prince Yi, a man devoid of conspicuous charm.

"What is the meaning of this?" barked Parks, his face scarlet and the veins swelling in his temples. They would not dare lay a hand on a representative of Her British Majesty, travelling under a flag of truce.

"Kneel down!" ordered the prince.

Parks was furious over the affront. "I kneel only before my Queen, not before a treacherous Chinese!"

The prince controlled his fury; his emperor's command must be obeyed, even at the price of his personal honour. He turned away, not wishing to watch; he only heard the shots and screams as the British negotiators were killed, one by one. He spared Parks and delivered him in chains to Beijing. When Lord Elgin was informed of the duplicity, he marched with his army on the Emperor's abandoned Palace of Summer Pleasure. British troops and Indian auxiliaries dug gun positions in the neatly tended flowerbeds and then used the Emperor's pagoda for target practice, before setting the palace on fire.

Elgin refused any further talks with the Celestial Court. With his British artillery trained on Beijing, the harassed Emperor called for the Russian ambassador, Count Ignatiev, and begged him to act as mediator. Ignatiev was willing, but for a price: in exchange for his country's intervention he demanded large tracts of land north of the Ussuri and Amur rivers, to be known as the Maritime Province. This territory would give Russia direct access to its recently opened, ice-free port of Vladivostok. A century later this Russian land grab would lead to a conflict which brought the world to the brink of nuclear war.

Diplomats arranged a compromise. Imperial Prince Gong, a brother of the Emperor, had the thankless task of calming the outraged Elgin. He did so by signing away the port of Tianjin (Tientsin), gateway to Beijing, as well as the territories on the mainland opposite Hong Kong, the Kowloon (Jiulong) Peninsula. In a series of annexed amendments to the existing Treaty of Nanjing, more harbours were forcibly thrown open to European trade; the original treaty covered Guangzhou, Shanghai, Xiamen, Fuzhou and Ningbo. This only helped whet the appetite of invading foreign powers. Next followed Shantou, Zhenjiang, Tianjin, Hankow, Jiujiang, Zhifu, Tainan and Danshui. Or, in the words of a British Foreign Office official, "a joint Sino-foreign administration of the government of China under a foreign dynasty".

With the signing of the Treaty of Tientsin, the Second Opium War was over.

If Elgin, as he was to claim, had been quite willing to stick to the existing articles in the Unequal Treaties without additional clauses, this changed with the massacre of his peace delegation. This breach of trust proved a costly blunder for China, and nobody could foresee the dire aftermath of this war. The British intervention stirred a Chinese dragon in the shape of a fire-breathing sect of God-worshippers, who called for a holy war against everything foreign.

Soon they swept across the lands, bringing blood-soaked terror.

# 7

# THE TAIPING MADNESS

7 SEPTEMBER 1853, SHANGHAI (ZHONG GUO)

"Throughout the empire all must praise the Heavenly Father, the Supreme Lord and Great God." With these words a young mystic of peasant background launched a popular revolution that resulted in the most destructive civil war of the nineteenth century, which slaughtered more people than the entire population of contemporary Victorian Great Britain. The familiar Chinese countryside had gone mad. Like a demonic thunderstorm, an orchestration of sound swept across its fields and forests. Guns boomed. Grenades cracked, muskets chattered, swords cut savagely. The vast scale of mayhem and death took this revolution beyond the frame of any human memory. Warfare had taken on a new countenance. Twenty million, thirty million victims? The horror of the Taiping Rebellion can only be captured in apocalyptic imagery. Everyday expressions fail to describe this carnage.

In January 1851 a certain Hung Hsiu-chuan launched the era of the Taiping, a word which, ironically, means "Great Peace". This fact did not prevent the horrors perpetrated by this army on the march; nothing ever does. Like an evil snake, a brown smear of dust-covered robes and gleaming spear tips advanced over paddies and meadows, through marshes and woods, with its advance "clearing" the countryside of elements, hostile or not. A juggernaut, crushing life under its wheels, left a long trail of devastated villages and gratuitous bloodshed. Those who survived this murderous roller stood dazed beside their burning huts, and an unending lament rose from the earth.

Back in January 1814, with corruption rife, warlords ravaging and tax collectors filling their pockets, a boy was born in a Hakka tribal village near Guangzhou in southern China. Huo-hsin ("Fireflash") grew up in the Taoist tradition, the Puritan reaction to a somewhat loose Confucianism.

One day a Manchu tax collector visited their village and took all of the family's possessions down to the last flock of geese. This injustice so upset the youngster that it sent him into a violent spasm. Delirious with fever, he had a vision in which he was borne on wings to the Thirty-Third Heaven where he found himself face to face with the Venerable-in-Years, who girded him with a sword and ordered him to exterminate the demon worshippers who had rebelled against God's rule on earth. The Venerable-in-Years gave him a new name, Hung Hsiu-chuan (or Hong Xiuquan), "Hung the Accomplished and Perfected". Then he ordered Hung to return to Earth to serve his cause and be of good courage, "for you are my son". Hung recovered from his fever, certain that he had been sent by the Heavenly Father on a mission "to slay the depraved, and to relieve the people's distress". He began his sacred quest with a bold and unheard of act: he wrote a proclamation – in vermilion, a colour reserved for the Emperor – in which he outlined "the noble principles", and signed it "The Heavenly King".

At this crucial point an event transformed Hung's life. One night in Guangzhou a stranger entered his room and handed him a scroll. This man was a Christian convert working for the London Missionary Society, trying to win over people of his own race to the "true faith". The scroll contained an annotated translation of the holy scriptures of the Bible. As Hung began to read the Book of Genesis he recalled the visitation during his feverish trance. From the pages of the Bible spoke a Christian God in words almost identical to those of the Venerable-in-Years: "In chains shall they come over and … they shall make supplication unto thee."

In Hung's interpretation of the words, he himself was the younger Son of God, destined "to wrestle against principalities, against powers, against the rulers of the darkness in this world, against spiritual wickedness in high places", and the man they called Christ was his elder brother. After taking lessons from a Southern Baptist missionary, Isaachar J. Roberts, who became instrumental in his future outlook, Hung began preaching a Gospel according to his own insight, his message a mixture of populism and Western Christianity. This able propagandist preached a kind of pre-Marxist Communism. In his sermon "The Great Awakening of the People" he thundered against the rich landowners and advocated division of land with equality for all, a daring challenge to the existing situation. It was a language that a simple serf understood.

But Hung knew that it took more than just words, so he forged a military alliance with the secret Heaven and Earth Society, the notorious Triad. He also raised a Heavenly Army of ten thousand, saying: "Each man throughout the empire who has a wife and sons, must give up one to become a Soldier of Heaven." In this Heavenly Army, with its peculiar mix of religion and terror, discipline was brutally enforced; looting was prohibited on pain of death, as were rape, prostitution, adultery, opium smoking and desertion. Hung parcelled out the corps commands to members of his own clan or others of unquestionable loyalty. These men became the nucleus of a powerful revolutionary army, which was divided into four columns. On each of his corps commander he bestowed the title of *wang* (prince).

Agitation erupted; China dissolved into civil war and anarchy. The starving serfs rose and avenged themselves on their landlords with massacre, torture and rape. They became part of Hung's Heavenly Revolution. The Doaguang Emperor showed little concern about the fermenting revolutionary movement; Beijing thought that they were dealing with yet another unorganized horde of religious fanatics incapable of banding into a coherent force. Imperial Army commanders continued in wilful ignorance until January 1853, when the Taiping *wang* Yang Hsiu-ch'ing crushed the Imperial forces at a cost of one hundred thousand casualties in the battle for the Triple Cities: Hanyang, Wuchang and Hankow. He then marched down the Upper Yangtze Valley until he reached the gates of Nanjing, pearl of central China.

With Hankow gone and Nanjing threatened, Empress Yehonala, a former palace concubine, prevailed on the young Emperor to appoint a man of destiny, Zeng Guofan (Tseng Kuo-fan), a squat, coarse-featured veteran with experience in mercenary warfare and brutal executions, as overall commander of the Imperial forces. This Confucian warlord had no use for the Christianity-inspired Taiping. Zeng Guofan's Braves set a new standard for bloodshed; with them came rape, murder and mayhem. Taiping responded in kind and killed anyone who had been remotely in contact with Zeng's men. As a result the ruling elite of Zeng's province – its officials, together with their servants and supporters, their wives and children – were all massacred. In his fury Zeng had every village set on fire and had murdered all inhabitants of townships which had supplied even just one man to his foe's Heavenly Army. The vengeance taken by Zeng and his unbridled troops shocked even the unsqueamish court at Beijing.

A great Taiping host laid siege to Nanjing, the mightiest fortress on the River Yangtze. In 1852 10-metre-high walls protected the town, and a well-armed and well-trained garrison manned its ramparts, though it was a garrison without the moral conviction of the crusading Heavenly Army. One night, as the city's Imperial Governor was having dinner in his residence, his palace's roof flew off in a whirlwind of splinters, tiles and bodies. A mine had been set off under the ramparts. Ghostly figures, lit by the raging fires, burst through the breach. Nothing could withstand the onslaught of the horde of religious zealots, who became a fire-breathing dragon that fanned out into the city streets. Most defenders died quickly, including the Governor, whose head was paraded on the point of a lance.

That same night hell's pocket burst and spilled over Nanjing. Taiping General Yang rewarded his valiant fighters by allowing them a few hours of free rein.[1] The frenzied warriors of the Heavenly Kingdom of Great Peace celebrated their triumph with a massacre of Nanjing's defenders on a scale so great that the corpses in the Yangtze blocked the passage of the ceremonial Dragon Boat bringing Hung to announce the birth of a new dynasty – the Taiping T'ien-kuo – and proclaim himself the Tien Wang, or Heavenly King. China had now two ruling dynasties: in the south the Heavenly Kingdom of Great Peace and in the north the Eternal Celestial Empire.

The new ruler's coronation speech foresaw a continuing clash with the foreign powers: "I dream of the day when OUR benevolent Chinese rule WE have introduced in OUR lands will extend to all of Asia. Having done away with the foreign devils, WE will unite this great country under one ruler, one language, spiritually guided by OUR Cult of Eternal Peace." He gave no thought to the millions of victims his revolution had already caused, or the millions more it would claim in the years to come.

On 12 May 1853 a Taiping army headed for Beijing. Their luck ran out two hundred kilometres south of Beijing, where, caught in a river crossing, they suffered horrendous losses, ending their drive north. When news of the disaster reached the Heavenly King he cast his eye on the Yangtze estuary, a move that would bring his Taiping forces uncomfortably close to the British trade concession of Shanghai. To calm the fears of European traders and residents in the region, the British Governor of Hong Kong, Sir George Bonham, travelled to Hung's campaign court to discuss the situation with the Messenger of God. As the nearest thing to divinity, the Heavenly King would not stoop to receive so lowly a person as a British ambassador. He poured oil on the fire by letting it be known that he had decided to add Shanghai to his list of conquests, "but WE will graciously spare the lives of foreigners, and will only hold Chinese merchants accountable for their treacherous ways". Then he added a phrase which made his ultimate aim quite clear: "The conquest of China is OUR moral and sacred duty. If we must, WE will achieve it by force of arms."

Ambition overtook the Taiping monarch and made him blind to diplomatic realities. He felt that he could afford his unbending posture. Bonham was handed by a courtier a royal decree which declared the existing Manchu treaty concessions open for revision. Should European powers resist, their local residents would face the consequences.

Hung's spokesman left Bonham in no doubt of the document's meaning. "Britain must achieve the merit of diligently serving Our Heavenly Sovereign."

To this the ambassador replied, sticking to the proven tradition of nineteenth-century gunboat diplomacy: "We English are already serving *our* Sovereign."

"Then we cannot vouch for the safety of foreign vessels in *our* port of Shanghai."

"Is that your personal interpretation of things?"

"No. This is the divine will of Our Heavenly King."

Peace missions from France and the United States proved equally unproductive. It should have warned the Heavenly King that he now faced three major Western powers. Hung was incensed over the European challenge and his anger clouded his vision. More than ever he now wanted Shanghai.

Prince Yang, his best strategist, tried to warn the ruler: "O Heavenly King, YOUR harbours are on the sea, and YOUR cities lie along the wide river. The Westerners have ships with big cannon. We do not. They can do YOU much harm, while YOUR armies cannot march on the open water."

The Heavenly King followed some of Prince Yang's advice. He did not involve his own Taiping forces, but deftly manoeuvred a particularly violent gang of Triad killers, the Small Swords Society (Xiao Dao Hu), into acting as his vanguard. In Shanghai, a sea terminus on the river route from the Yangtze Valley, the concession warehouses were crammed with tea, spices and silks, paid for in gold coin, which was piling up in the iron-bound coffers of Chinese merchants. Hung counted on the Triad's greed to make an attack on the wealthy port city an enticing and highly profitable proposition.

A hot and humid 7 September 1853 was to end in a river of blood. On that day Shanghai fell to the Triad hordes. Early that morning infiltrated gangs killed the gate guards, Triad members flooded into town and the garrison's will to resist had collapsed. A wealthy town lay at the invaders' mercy. Despite a king's promise, they looted European warehouses and went on a rampage, pillaging and ruthlessly slaughtering anyone who resisted. They released criminals from the town jail and let them have their will with those whom they regarded as oppressors – their social superiors – torturing men and women alike to reveal where their fortunes were concealed. Madly yelling gangs poured from the centre of town, dragging Chinese merchants by the hair to the quays, where they bludgeoned them with clubs and dumped their mutilated corpses into the water, while the victims' spouses were stripped to suffer collective rape. And all this in plain sight of a number of foreign vessels anchored in the harbour, as their European crews stared at a scene from the Inferno. Only supreme self-control and strong words from their captains stopped the ships' gunners from firing on the raging mob. Nobody wished for an international incident.

The rampage led to grave repercussions once foreign papers had reported it. The guiding hand behind the massacre, as stated in the foreign press, was the Heavenly King of Eternal Peace. Journalists in Europe made him out to be a bloodthirsty revolutionary, while in strait-laced Victorian England he was portrayed as a blasphemer. Yet nothing was done because a Taiping success could only lead to a further weakening of the Manchu dynasty. The West's best response was to sit it out and pick up the pieces once the killing stopped. They left the Chinese to their own devices – until a Chinese cannon threatened the French compound.

The Heavenly King had shown himself an oppressor, and a wholly irresponsible one; his mystical kingship engendered in him a belief that, as the Lord's anointed, he could impose his will on whoever opposed it. This was a crucial error. His very success at Shanghai was to prove his undoing. Beijing was finally forced to react by dispatching a huge force of troops under its new commander, Zeng Guofan, to lay siege to Shanghai. However, Zeng lacked just about everything, most of all the heavy guns it took to breach the walls, while the Triad-held garrison lacked the manpower for a breakout. This led to stalemate. Zeng fell back on the medieval strategy of sitting by and starving out the fortress; in doing so he managed to kill more civilians than Triad fighters. To keep his men from getting rusty, Zeng launched occasional feeble attempts to take the city, which the occupiers repeatedly repulsed – until an incident in the French concession set off the spark which finally brought the Europeans into the fray.

After the initial horror, things had settled down, though there was a severe shortage of food and water. Europeans who had fled into their compounds to seek the protection of their flag were treated as bargaining chips to stop Western powers from interfering in Taiping politics. For a while they went unharmed and their stockpiles of food remained relatively untouched. But a starving mob will act unpredictably, and that is precisely what happened. Pushed by hunger, a crowd began gathering outside the foreigners' compound. Hundreds of baton-wielding rioters overcame the few guards, and stripped one warehouse, then another. The violence left a few dozen people bleeding on the ground, three of them Europeans.

An American sloop reached Hong Kong with an urgent appeal from Shanghai's severely pressed foreign communities. The naval force nearest

Shanghai happened to be the French Far East Squadron, made up of several steam-powered battle cruisers. In the past, loaded flag-waving had always done the job. The squadron entered Shanghai harbour on a *visite de courtoisie*, as the French consul had not failed to advise the local Taiping commander. Courtesy or not, the fleet's heavy breech-loaders were trained on the garrison. In reprisal, the Taiping commander ordered one of his cannon wheeled into a position overlooking the French compound. The puny gun was more of a nuisance than a serious threat; even so, the French consul insisted on the immediate removal of the artillery piece. Words were thrown back and forth, and nothing was resolved. It was the Taiping's undoing, since now the mighty guns of the French armada were free to enter the action and blast the city into submission.

On the French admiral's order the squadron opened up. The ships shook and vibrated as every one of their guns joined in the chorus of destruction. The scream of heavy shells was followed by the roar of explosions. Each impacting shell punched the rampart like a steel fist, and every hit drove the French gunners into a cheering frenzy. The Triad had nothing to reply with, as their antiquated pieces could not even reach the fleet. One of their guns fired back, and the crews of the French warships watched with amusement as a ball skipped across the surface of the water and sank before reaching a vessel. A final salvo from the big naval guns, billowing dense black clouds into the air, brought down the wall, and Zeng's imperial battalions rushed through the breach. It was now the turn of the Triad to suffer strangulation or beheading.

His diplomatic blindness, his demand to others to bow before him and a cannon on the wall threatening European interests brought about the first military setback suffered by the Heavenly King – painful to his pride, yet strategically not crucial. China was big, and he still owned half of it.

Shanghai was the first crack in the Taiping's invincibility. The second act was not long in coming.

# 8

# THE EVER-VICTORIOUS ARMY

In the end it wasn't the reported scenes of the Shanghai massacre that shifted Western support from "Christian" Nanjing to "heathen" Beijing, but the Heavenly King's diplomatic arrogance, combined with his open threat to Western trade concessions. In February 1862, Sir Frederick Bruce confronted Hung's new overall commander, Li Xiuchen, known as the Faithful Prince, and told him without further niceties that any interference with Britain's trading interests would meet the combined fury of British and French naval guns. Upset by this, the Heavenly King ordered his commander to march on Shanghai. Only this time it proved a fatal error.

In the Treaty of Tientsin between the Manchu Emperor's representatives and Lord Elgin, which accorded England the right to trade all along the Yangtze Valley, Beijing had cleverly inserted a clause which stipulated "as soon as the peace presently disturbed by an outlaw army shall have been restored". This made the Taiping force, installed in Nanjing on the Yangtze, an outlaw army. With the stroke of a pen the Allied Naval Squadron switched from being an enemy of Beijing into its ally, because this served best Britain and France's future interests. Sir Frederick Bruce declared a neutral zone extending 30 miles inland from Shanghai. There was only one problem: the British envoy did not have the means to ensure an exclusion zone, and no ready terrestrial force to throw against the Taiping should they advance.

A new force entered the fray. The reconstituted Chinese community of Shanghai had provided funds for a mercenary army, led by European officers and trained by European professionals, armed with European cannon and paid for by Chinese merchants. This mercenary force under the overall command of Frederick Townsend Ward, an American soldier of fortune from Massachusetts, managed to clear the perimeter around Shanghai in 11 skirmishes against small Taiping units. This string of minor successes earned the force the undeserved sobriquet "The Ever-Victorious Army". On 20 August 1862 Ward was mortally wounded. For a brief period his deputy, a callous French-American named H. A. Burgevine, took command.

However, an article in the *Times of India* revealed that following the capture of Kahding on the perimeter of the 30-mile zone, Burgevine had stood by while his troops looted a friendly town, and looked on smiling as hacked-off body parts of the town's nobles were blown out of gun barrels. And when Burgevine refused to march on a numerically superior enemy force, Chinese merchants withheld the pay of his men. He and a few dozen of his rowdies marched into a bank, beat up the banker, blew open his safe and stripped it of cash. The bank robbery finished Burgevine.

Next a Captain Holland, as lazy as he was incompetent, took charge of the force. The looting, straggling and lack of discipline continued and harmed the mercenary army; but then it had never been an army. It became obvious that this force could be equally used to protect British mercantile interests. Commissioner Sir Frederick Bruce suggested to London that a British staff officer should be put in charge, someone determined and uncommonly clear-minded. None of the officers chosen for the task could control the rowdy body of men until one came along who was ideally suited for the post: Captain Charles George Gordon. Under the *nom de guerre* of "Chinese Gordon" he was to play a significant part in containing, and subsequently destroying, the Taiping Movement.

Taking command on 26 March 1863, Gordon set out to transform an undisciplined mercenary rabble into a motivated troop. It was not an easy task with 3,500 soldiers of fortune used to taking whatever plunder they could lay their hands on. They were "reliable in action, but troublesome in garrison and touchy to a degree about precedence", as he described them. "I consider the force even under a British officer a most dangerous collection of men, never to be depended on, and very expensive. In my opinion more would be done by a force of Chinese, who do not want for bravery when properly instructed by our officers."

Captain Gordon began by announcing to his troop that he wanted to hear no more about defensive positions and lines of retreat; an army that advanced and won battles did not need to worry about such things. He spelled out his policy toward non-combatants in a series of orders which clearly indicated a change in atmosphere; murderers were to be hanged, looters would lose a hand and rapists would forfeit their manhood. With the help of several no-nonsense British sergeant majors, he changed the look and morale of the Ever-Victorious Army. The men were required to wear uniforms of brown tunic and green turban and issued with the modern Enfield rifle. Their mobile field guns were vastly superior in accuracy and distance to anything that the Taiping could put against them. Rifled artillery shells reduced walls of brick to rubble. To increase his firepower, Gordon mounted nine- and 12-pounders into the forecastle of shallow-draught river gunboats; his *force de frappe* were American paddle steamers, equipped with 32-pounder naval breech-loaders plus rapid-fire 2.8-inch howitzers, and run by American riverboat captains who had learned their trade on the Mississippi.

With Britain now openly engaged on the side of Beijing, the Manchu Emperor signed a brevet which seconded the 3,500 men of the Ever-Victorious Army to the army of Imperial Governor Field Marshal Li Hung-chang, commanding a "Chinese-size force" of a hundred and twenty-five thousand. While Gordon was waiting for his combat orders the sacked Burgevine travelled to Beijing, where he contacted the American ambassador to help him be reinstated as commander of the mercenary force on the principle that "a foreigner who does his duty to *his* government shall not be thrown out at a moment's notice by *another* government without sufficient cause". Prince Kung, the High Mandarin, was determined to forge a diplomatic link with the United States, the rising power in the Pacific. It would serve to trump the overbearing British lion, and he listened favourably to Burgevine's request. But Field Marshal Li refused to replace the efficient Gordon with the discredited Burgevine.

In late November 1863, while a combined Franco-Chinese brigade cleared the area around Ningbo of Taiping infiltrators, Gordon, brevetted major, moved north, and with a few blasts from the *Hyson*'s 32-pounder, captured Chanzu. From there he pushed along the line of the Grand Canal toward the Taiping stronghold of Taitsan. Field Marshal Li's Imperial Chinese had been laying siege to the city without noticeable results. The Chinese commander showed his restlessness and asked Gordon to bring up his flotilla of 60 riverboats. Three thousand men of the Ever-Victorious Army debarked on a spit which had been inundated by the tide. They slogged stubbornly through deep mud toward the walls. Caught in the quagmire as they were, heavy fire from the fort's water batteries caused casualties among the troop and stopped them cold, until Gordon's river gunboats opened up at point-blank range. The *Hyson*'s fourth explosive shell blew a hole in the wall.

"Chinese" Gordon, armed as always with nothing more lethal than a rattan cane, bellowed: "Onward!" Of a garrison of fifteen thousand, a mere two hundred survived. In a letter to his mother Gordon admitted that it had been a tough battle and that his casualties amounted to 10 per cent of his force; but he also stressed the part that Marshal Li's Chinese had played:

"Their bravery is passive, they require to be led to the attack, when they will follow, but in some instances ... they will outdo even foreigners in bravery."

Gordon recovered his wounded and buried his dead, then loaded his men on his river flotilla and steamed upriver toward the fortress of Quinsan. There his military career very nearly came to an end.

It was a dreadful night, that 27 May 1864. Flashes of lightning illuminated hideous scenes – the dead lay everywhere, with the river's edge a ghastly tint from the blood of the wounded who had crawled down to drink and died with their faces in the water; a field carpeted with torn bodies and wounded men lying in the downpour chanting weak calls for help. Such were the scenes described by the headlines back in England.

On the direct order of Lord Elgin, Gordon had taken an extra passenger aboard the *Hyson*, a reporter from the *Times of India*, who happened to be a gentleman specializing in the paper's society column but had never been exposed to the cruelty of warfare. Until that time the horrors of battle were described mostly in soldiers' personal letters to their mothers, but never brought to the attention of a wider public. This changed when William Russell of *The Times* immortalized the Charge of the Light Brigade, and modern war reporting came into vogue. A favourable article in a major paper could make a man's career, just as it could break it. At the height of the Quinsan cannonade, and the ensuing horror of ripped flesh, this frazzled *Times of India* reporter rushed up to the commanding officer and screamed: "My God, Sir, I beseech you to stop it! *Stop it!*"

Major Gordon, whose business it was to win battles at the least cost to his own men, snapped: "Mind your business."

"But this is my business ..." the reporter replied, and his article reflected an outraged English gentleman's dismay at what he had been witness to. It was none of the highly romanticized "Theirs not to reason why ..." but rather "by direct order of a blood-thirsty English commander ...".

A few days before, arriving at the walled city of Quinsan, another Taiping stronghold on the Yangtze, Gordon had a run-in with a man who was nominally his superior in rank, General Ching, a Taiping turncoat and now a corps commander in the Manchu Imperial Forces. Ching, who never counted lives, wanted Gordon's brigade to launch a frontal assault on the ramparts. Gordon argued that the town's east gate was too heavily defended to waste his men on an action that could only lead to disaster, saying: "General, our main objective must be to trap the ten-thousand-strong Taiping garrison and prevent their breakout, so that they cannot join their Faithful Prince at Soochow." Ching accepted Gordon's plan to sail his river flotilla around a bend in the river to the western wall of the town and "lock the back exit", while Ching's masses would press the assault on the eastern wall.

With the sun below the horizon, and guns booming on the eastern side of the town, Gordon's flotilla were approaching the western jetty, when the gate was thrown open and the Taiping streamed out. Eight thousand yelling Taiping fighters made for the anchorage. Gordon ordered his gunnery mates to switch from shell to canister: metal cans filled with egg-sized shot. At the sound of the *Hyson's* whistle the slaughter commenced. At two hundred yards naval cannon blasted iron pellets by the thousands into the dense mass of Taiping. They never heard the thunder; they died, ripped to shreds by the fury of the point-blank cannonade. With cannon before them and to their flanks, they were caught in a cauldron with nowhere to go. They ran forward and died; they stumbled back and died; and those who stayed still died as well; all ending in a chorus of screams from the wounded and the wails of the dying. The whole action took a mere 10 minutes.

When the smoke cleared, fifteen hundred shredded Taiping lay before Gordon's force, which had not suffered a single casualty. The gentleman reporter aboard the *Hyson* witnessed the slaughter. His story in the *Times of India*, entitled "The Quinsan Massacre", created an outcry in London. How could an upright English officer and gentleman behave so foully, slaughtering thousands of men – even if they were Chinese? Questions were raised in the House of Commons, some members expressing their outrage that a colonial commander should participate on behalf of an idolatrous Manchu tyranny in the massacre of what was seen as a Christian Taiping movement. Gordon came in for severe criticism, which he took with soldierly silence. He could have argued that the use of his cannon at Quinsan was necessary in the face of the masses of panicked enemy, trying to storm his small flotilla as their only means to effect their escape. He offered no alibis. In a brief dispatch to London he justified his action:

"Matters were in too critical a state to hesitate, as the mass of the rebels would have swept our small force aside. We were forced to fire into them and pursue them toward Quinsan, firing however very rarely and only when the rebels looked as if they would make a stand ... and though humanity might have desired a smaller destruction, it was indispensably necessary to inflict such a blow on the garrison as would cause them not to risk another engagement."[1]

By a slim margin Gordon survived the parliamentary inquiry, but the stigma of the Quinsan Incident was to cling to him for the rest of his life. Had he been sacked, never would the world have witnessed the tragic-heroic figure of Gordon of Khartoum.

\*

The cracked walls of Soochow, decaying after centuries of standing guard along the mighty Yangtze, shimmered in the heat. Moh Wang, a ruthless Taiping commander, defended the town with thirty thousand Taiping warriors. His fellow *wangs*, wanting to rid themselves of this suicidal maniac, planned a fake sortie from town. Then they would return behind its walls, shut the gate and lock out Moh Wang; their scheme was betrayed. Before Moh Wang could take revenge, the princes surprised and killed him. They surrendered the town and announced themselves prisoners. By a fluke of destiny, Major Gordon, rather than an imperial general, accepted their surrender. He promised them an honourable and safe departure, but the vengeful General Ching ordered the beheading of the princely captives.

Gordon could not believe that such vile treachery had taken place, until a teenager led him to the place of execution situated on an island. Faith had not been kept, and for a man as straight as Gordon that was unforgivable. He asked Field Marshal Li for a personal apology and demanded General Ching's instant dismissal, saying: "In matters of morality or truth there can be no compromise. Compromising with assassins grants them moral equivalence where none can rightfully exist. Moral equivalence says that I am no better than they; it rejects the concept of right and wrong."

The shrewd Chinese commander outmatched the naïve Englishman. Field Marshal Li distributed £40,000 to the Ever-Victorious Army as victory bonuses, and the British ambassador Sir Frederick Bruce reminded Major Gordon of the need to preserve his force, in order to defend British trade interests in Shanghai. Gordon was forced into a compromise, ending another British–Chinese incident.

From the elevation of his Heavenly Throne a tired king, wrapped in a cloak of the imperial dragon yellow, stared into the darkness of his crumbling empire. He suffered from a recurring nightmare, trying to put out the fire that was consuming the stripped and decomposed corpses. Out there, somewhere in the grey of a dawning day, lurked the dragon. A fire-spitting dragon from a foreign land. His Heavenly Mandate had been withdrawn from him; now there was only one way out of the dilemma. Shortly before midnight on 1 July 1864, he mixed himself a brew of sweet wine and thinly shaved gold leaf and downed it to the last drop. It took him several hours to die. He was buried in an unmarked plot in the palace gardens.

It was also the end for a mercenary force. The British had no more need for it and the Chinese Manchu ruler certainly did not want a foreign army bivouacked in his backyard. Gordon accepted Field Marshal's Li's offer of £100,000 to pay off his men. The British government did it more cheaply: it raised the troublesome Gordon to full colonel and ordered him to the Sudan, where he died in the defence of Khartoum.

"The Ever-Victorious Army" was an unfortunate choice of name. Gordon and his 3,500 men hardly decided the outcome of the war, yet the term showed that there was outside interference in what amounted to an internal Chinese problem. Seventy years later Mao Zedong used it to claim that foreigners, defending mercantile interests, meddled in Chinese affairs and suppressed "a just revolution by peasants and workers". In one aspect Mao was correct: the Chinese did most of the the fighting and all of the dying. Even for a nation nurtured in a tradition of bloodshed, the Taiping Rebellion was a cataclysm of rare proportions. As a result of it, 20–30 million died (surpassing the death tolls of both World Wars). The long-term consequences for China were devastating.

Even so, the Taiping Rebellion must be seen as a political watershed, since it heralded the end of thousands of years of dynastic glory. The Celestial Empire of Middle Earth, which had once conquered the world, sent its vessels across the Seven Seas, and in which emperors and mandarins had grown up in the belief that the fundamentals were safe from change, was shaken to its foundations. From a political perspective the Taiping philosophy of equality for all, aiming for the betterment in the living standard of the suppressed masses, was a precursor to Chinese Communism, and Hung Hsiu-chuan's teachings must be considered a forerunner of the thoughts of Mao Zedong.[2] A Heavenly King left his messianic prophecy, which Mao took to heart a century later: "Beware a foreigner: if you let him into your lands, never will he leave again."

In that sense the Taiping idea lived on. What Hung had started, Mao finished.

# 9

# A LEGION'S STAND

## 24 FEBRUARY 1885, TUYEN-QUANG, VIET BAC PROVINCE, TONKIN

The siege of Tuyen Quang had been going on for 90 days. It was the same for everybody. A continuous battle fell into little bits and pieces, one coming right on top of the other, and no one any longer kept track of which came first. With no end in sight, Captain Moulinay of the French Foreign Legion volunteered to make a sortie to reach a French expeditionary force. His daring feat so surprised the Chinese that they forgot to shoot. Just when his men thought that they had broken through, musket fire erupted all around them. Before the soldiers of Moulinay's 1st Company had time to scramble for cover, three men went down, struck by musket ball. The Chinese knew that the Legionnaires would never abandon their comrades, and had the path targeted accurately. Five volunteers, including their sabre-waving captain, lunged out of their ditch and started sprinting down the trail. They were halfway to the bodies, when the Chinese opened up.

The first to be struck in the chest was the valiant Moulinay. Seeing their captain fall, the company's staff sergeant yelled: "*A moi la Légion!*" and, leading his men, went after the hidden attackers. The battle was brief and extremely bloody. The enraged Legionnaires spared no one who happened to find himself in front of their bayonets, and shot all those who tried to run. Then they picked up their fallen comrades and fought their way back into the fortress. That action took place on 24 February 1885.

Four days later a French relief force arrived.

In the aftermath of its inglorious defeat in the Franco-Prussian War of 1870–1, France cast its eyes abroad and picked on a vast territory in South-East Asia, prepared for them by French Catholic missionaries. Annam, as the Chinese called what today is the central portion of Vietnam, had been overrun by a remnant from the beaten Taiping Rebellion, the ferocious

Black Flag Sect. Under their leader Liu Yongfu (in Vietnamese: Luu Vinh Phuoc) they fled from China and crossed via Guangxi province into Upper Tonkin. There they continued what they had practised during the Taiping rampage in China: wiping out the local population and taking away their land. This added greatly to the historic hatred between Vietnamese and Chinese,[1] and it was only natural that the indigenous population looked to the French as their protectors.

Once the Black Flags began harassing European shipping on the Red River a French naval officer reacted to their challenge without waiting for higher orders. On 25 April 1882 Captain Henri Rivière, part-time poet and correspondent for *La Liberté*, took a handful of sailors and navy commandos and moved on Hanoi. In an extraordinary feat of personal initiative he surprised the Chinese garrison and seized the city. This astounding exploit precipitated the Sino-French War. Rivière's single action gained for France the large territory of Upper Tonkin, and opened the way into China's wealthy Hunan province. China, which had always considered Annam its trust territory, reacted. So did France, dispatching an expeditionary force to lend support to Rivière and his handful of men, still hanging on to Hanoi. Before French reinforcements had time to come to the aid of Rivière in encircled Hanoi, monsoon floods had stopped navigation on the Red River and the jungle paths were impassable mud.

News that relief was on its way never reached Captain Rivière. A local runner, paid by the French to deliver the message, was captured, tortured and strangled. Without news, and his supplies running short, Rivière ordered a breakout. On 19 March 1883 he and his men reached the Pont de Papier, a stone bridge across a Red River tributary at Can Giay. All looked peaceful and quiet. Without taking the precaution to scout the opposite shore, Rivière walked across the bridge, when suddenly musket fire erupted, and he fell down dead. Shortly afterward the rains stopped and a French column marched into Hanoi with the excuse of "recover[ing] the body of the valiant Rivière". On the same occasion they also threw out the Chinese.

The conflict was precipitated when two former enemies, the Black Flag Taiping and the Beijing Imperials, joined forces. The French next landed an army corps of fifty thousand men: not many when compared with the three million Chinese facing them. But the French backed their terrestrial advance with a thrust by a heavy naval squadron, consisting of the battle cruisers *Bayard*, *La Galissonnière* and *Triomphante*, supported by a number of light cruisers and torpedo boats.

Facing this naval might, China opted for a negotiated settlement. Discussions were well on the way, and China had recognized the previous treaties, which called for a withdrawal of Chinese troops from Annam, when a French force showed up before a small town in Upper Tonkin, Bac Le. A palanquin-borne Chinese and a colonel of the French nobility met for a parley on a field outside town. What developed was a *conversation de sourds*, a talk between two deaf men. Perhaps diplomats would have succeeded where aristocrats failed. These two had nothing to offer, and neither would give ground. When the colonel waved his cap, probably because he wanted to fan himself to relieve the June heat, one of his gun crews mistook it as signal and fired a round. Everyone ducked at the whistle of a shell, which splintered through the roof of a house in the town. The explosion came a few seconds later – and soon a full-blown battle was on. It lasted three days and in the end the French had to withdraw with losses. Their setback was heralded by the Chinese as a great victory, and instilled in them the erroneous impression that Chinese mass attacks could defeat the invaders and their big guns.

Under a pretext to defend *l'honneur*, which had been challenged at Bac Le, Admiral Courbet's French naval squadron, which had been lying offshore waiting for orders, sailed north, entering the strait between the island of Taiwan and the Chinese harbour fortress of Foochow. In August 1884 French cruisers annihilated a brand-new Chinese battle fleet, anchored in and around Foochow's Mawei Naval Dockyard in the estuary of the River Minjiang.[2] On their approach to Foochow harbour, the heavy cannon of the battle cruisers *Bayard* (5,915 tons) and *La Galissonnière* (4,585 tons) knocked out the coastal fortifications. The rest of the squadron sailed unhampered into the estuary, where it split into two formations, hammering away at vessels lying at anchor or sitting in docks. The battle cruiser *Triomphante*, supported by the ironclad *Duguay-Trouin*, *D'Estaing* and *Villars*, blew the wooden cruisers *Chen Wei*, *Fei Yuan* and *Chi An* out of the water.

At the same time another battle took place near the Mawei Naval Dockyard in which the cruiser *Volta* fired its guns at the dock installations. Under cover of the cruiser's bombardment, three supporting gunboats, the *Vipère*, *Aspis* and *Lynx* (each 465 tons), ran the gauntlet of artillery fire from shore batteries, making a dash for China's pride, its brand-new flagship the *Yang Wu* (1,600 tons), and its sisters, the *Fu Po* and *Fu Hsing*. Despite the French gunboats' relatively slow speed – they were dragging behind them mines on ropes – they made it through the curtain of fire. Once they reached the side of the Chinese cruisers they pushed their explosive charges against the ships' hulls. In great gouts of flame, the three ships broke apart and sank. Having knocked out the forts, the *Bayard* joined now in the fray by shelling and sinking the *Yu Yuen* (2,630 tons), while the

Chinese captain scuttled the *Teng Ching* (1,300 tons) to avoid capture. The Battle of Foochow was a valid demonstration of surprise and superior naval firepower.

While the French squadron achieved victory at Foochow, a terrestrial force advanced along the Red River Valley and then headed for Lang Son and the China–Annam border. On their rapid advance they left behind a Foreign Legion garrison at the riverside fortress of Tuyen Quang. In the Foreign Legion tradition of shovel and gun, the six hundred men of Captain Dominé sweated to get a defensive position into shape, since they knew of a sizeable force of Black Flags and Imperial forces on their way to recapture Hanoi. And Tuyen Quang lay directly in their path.

The fortress was badly positioned. Its designers expected it to be able to see off a few dozen river pirates, but never an army. Laid out as a perfect square, each side three hundred metres long, it was open to the river on one side and surrounded on the others by heavy overgrowth and low hills which dominated the position. The fortress was in poor condition and French engineers worked day and night to put the walls back into shape; they dug ditches, filled sandbags, chopped down the encroaching jungle to clear a field of fire and on a rise in the centre put a gun in position to swivel in any direction. The Black Flags were known to be brave to the point of suicidal, and that is what turned Tuyen Quang into such a bloody encounter.[3]

On 23 November 1884 twenty thousand drum-beating Black Flags showed up in front of the walls of Tuyen Quang. They were good fighters but, individually, the six hundred men of the Legion were better.[4] The first attack was an all-out assault by thousands of yelling, flag-waving fanatics. From their position on the walls, the French could see the enemy hordes emerging from the dense undergrowth. The Black Flags advanced in serried ranks in a frontal assault, always a fatal tactic if conducted against skilfully constructed defences.

*"Feu à volonté!"* came the command, and along the entire length of the wall stabs of muzzle fire erupted from the new, accurate *chassepot* rifles. The French kept up such heavy fire that it sounded like one of the new *mitraillettes*, or machine-guns. Bullets raked the field and the attackers fell in their dozens. The Chinese were nowhere near the wall when the first wave broke and scurried back, only to be pushed aside by a new wave, also bowled over in a maelstrom of lead. In the narrow killing field in front of the fortress the corpses of hundreds of dead or wounded lay piled upon one another. Those who managed to pass the deadly curtain of bullets and crawl across the moat to the low wall of rock and sandbags found no cover from the grenades that the French rolled down on them.

Normally instinct would have made the Legionnaires crouch down behind the parapets, but they knew that they could not. They were vaguely aware of musket balls smacking into sandbags, but they pretended to ignore them and kept on shooting standing upright. Their comrades dragged those who were hit to a makeshift hospital, where three doctors sawed and bandaged.

The first Black Flag attack crumpled. *"Cessez le feu!"* was heard, and all went quiet except for screams and moans from those lying below the fortress walls. The French did not rejoice in their victory; their own fallen were buried in a ditch while wounded soldiers sat around the hospital and patiently awaited their turn. The lightly wounded were the first to receive medical attention. Patched up and sent back into battle, they squatted behind the wall, thanked the Lord for being still alive and waited for the next attack.

In two weeks of murderous attacks, Liu Yongfu lost thousands. The Black Flag leader's readiness to endlessly sacrifice his men showed his incompetence. But the attacks grew less frequent and for the besieged French it turned into a war of attrition. Every Legionnaire, firing from the relative safety of the three-metre-high earth wall, became a marksman with his *chassepot*, often bringing down the attackers before they had had a chance to form up. The weather also played a role in the combat: low clouds and a misty drizzle made visual contact difficult for the gunners, while the rain also muddied the ground and slowed attacks. Week after endless week the Legion held. The powder intended for the cannon was used to replenish rifle cartridges; bullets were cast from lead buttons and water pipes. With no outside help in sight, without adequate food, only foul water that upset their bowels and inflamed their gums with stinking wounds, the Legion held.

The Chinese tried an attack from the open river front. They strung together a number of small river junks with their superstructures removed so that more men could be piled aboard, but this work made so much noise that the element of surprise was lost. *La Mitrailleuse*, a river gunboat which had arrived just in time, made a meal of the Chinese. As its name suggests, the vessel carried one of the new inventions that were to revolutionize warfare, a deck-mounted machine-gun. As the junks pushed out from shore, the gunboat made full steam ahead at the flotilla. Its machine-gunners began pounding away, demolishing the wooden junks with a stream of bullets that shredded the attackers. Bodies were swept downstream in water stained with their blood. The attack was over before it had really begun.

Day after day the pattern was the same. The Black Flags attacked, but, mercilessly exposed on the open field, they never stood a chance; yet they came on, yelling, firing, falling and stumbling over the bodies of their comrades who had fallen the previous day. Their casualties mounted into the thousands. The Legionnaires, with their rifles steadied on sandbags, shot as fast as they could work their bolts. Some battles lasted 10 minutes, some several hours, and each time the French kept on firing until the last attacker's yell was silenced.

For several weeks both sides were paralysed by heavy monsoon rains. It brought some badly needed respite but no change in the strategic situation. During this time most of the fighting around the fortress consisted of sporadic skirmishes, and the siege became a "soldier-and-corporal" war. One of the notable actions was that of Sergeant Bobillot of the Engineers' platoon. For days French units had been bombarded by a Chinese cannon from somewhere in the jungle, but then they managed to pinpoint the enemy's gun position by the puffs of smoke rising above the trees. Accompanied by a few volunteers, Bobillot sneaked out at night. Finding their way through dense vegetation in darkness was not easy, but suddenly they stepped out on to a clearing and found themselves facing the gun. After bayoneting the gun crew they blew up the cannon. The noise of the explosion was the commando's undoing. On their way back, Bobillot's troop was waylaid and he was killed. The sergeant was one of the 48 fatalities that the 611 Legionnaires suffered in their amazing three-month stand against 40 times as many Chinese.

When the rains subsided the Black Flags tried again, this time from a different side where their approach was obscured by a tangle of undergrowth. When they reached the edge of this, however, they were about to enter a wide-open field of fire, with the French secure behind a wall, though there was no sign of them. Advancing into the open exposed the Chinese to concentrated French fire. A storm of bullets from the Chassepots, supported by an occasional shell, broke over the Chinese. The air hummed.

But for the defenders a crisis quickly developed as their ammunition ran out. More bullets were sent for, but the dash from the dugouts to the ammunition store was hazardous and caused a number of French casualties. Only a handful of attackers reached the outer wall, where they were shot. In the grey light of a rainy day the field outside the fort was a ghastly sight, with Chinese piled up, the wounded hardly distinguishable from the dead. Lances, swords and muskets were strewn everywhere.

After three months of combat the French were exhausted both mentally and physically. Their only desire was to eat and sleep; mostly sleep. Those still standing were said to be "walking the guard". Those who could not walk but could still hold a rifle were propped up against sandbags "standing

·the guard". Day after interminable day their Chassepots provided a hellish chorus. The Black Flags had learned their craft battling Chinese Imperial troops with muskets, not in the fierce crucible of combat against professional French Legionnaires armed with modern repeater rifles. It was a costly lesson and left the Black Flags demoralized and exhausted. Their waves no longer willingly advanced against the flickering stabs of light that flashed from the earth wall. Those who did jerked and twitched and died.

On 29 February 1885 a French relief column reached the fortress, and the Black Flags took to their heels. The siege of Tuyen Quang was over. It had lasted 97 days. The name of the place has gone down in French Foreign Legion lore as one of the key events in its glorious history. Without the stand by "the 611 of Tuyen Quang", Hanoi would have fallen, the French might never again have set foot in Indochina, and who knows what would have been the future of Vietnam. Seventy years later, at another isolated spot in the jungles of Tonkin, the story of Tuyen Quang was told to defenders of another bastion held by the Foreign Legion – Dien Bien Phu.

The attack on Tonkin was the doorway through which France entered South-East Asia. Indochina became France's India, to be conquered and exploited. Two battles, one big, another relatively small, decided the issue. On the sea French naval guns sank the Chinese fleet. On land a fortress was held, and its stand saved France's colonial ambitions. The outcome of the Sino-French conflict gave France undisputed dominion over Indochina,[5] including the island of Hainan.

The loss of Annam was one more step which brought the Celestial Empire closer to the end of its earthly power.

# 10

## THE BIG LAND GRAB

### 17 SEPTEMBER 1894, RIVER YALU, OFF HAYHANG ISLAND, CHINA

The Japanese naval squadron stirred into readiness, its gunners relieved that the tension of waiting was over. The enemy was coming into range of their hungry weapons. A bell jangled and, in the momentary silence that followed, a voice cried out: "Commence firing!"

The turret guns spat out orange flame and recoiled on their mounts. Strident cracks pierced the crew's ears. As the gunners reloaded the turrets were still smoking. The huge, modern cannon swung like oiled rods and fired again; the howling shells caught the Chinese fleet in the midst of executing a turn.

After Taiping, China was riven by tribal and dynastic feuds and found itself open to foreign military intervention. With an administration chronically diseased and a disintegrating moral climate, the intellectual reputation of China had declined. European powers had greatly profited from China's weakness to force its tottering Manchu emperor into signing more Unequal Treaties. In this manner various European colonial powers – the Queen of England, the Tsar of Russia, the Emperor of France, the King of Savoy and the German Kaiser – had brought much of China's coastline under their thrall. From Hong Kong to the Korean border, foreigners ruled by their monarch's licence and the gun. With their Far East battleship armadas they dominated the major river's estuaries. Territorial claims were not restricted to European powers alone; a new force entered the arena: Japan, Empire of the Rising Sun.

At this point a woman of exceptional political skill and great perseverance made her appearance on the scene. In 1861, on the death of Emperor Xianfeng, his succession was bestowed on his five-year-old son Tongzhi under the tutelage of Prince Gong. In reality two women shared the power behind the throne: the Emperor's widow and his favourite concubine, Cixi

(Tzu hsi). Since "concubine" was degrading, she took the title by which she became famous: Empress Dowager. Born on the 10th Day of the 10th Moon in 1835 to a minor court official, Lan Kuei, "The Little Orchid", became at 16 an "imperial concubine", one of several thousand. This slip of a Manchu girl, only five feet tall, with heavy make-up that turned her face into a white mask, proved herself hyperactive in and out of the Emperor Hsien Feng's bed: in the bed chamber in a game known as Jade Girl Playing the Flute, and in his council chamber as the Dragon Empress. Impressed by her astuteness and sharp wit, the Emperor began consulting her on affairs of the state. She sealed her power by bearing him a son, and the day she said to him: "Here is your son," he replied: "He will succeed to the throne." On the Emperor's death she managed a lightning coup d'état.

When Prince Jung Lu arrived with his troops to take up positions around the Forbidden City, one of his first acts was to post a great many men in front of the Dowager's palace to protect her from all designs at the hands of jealous court rivals. This increased her prestige immensely. She was to become the most powerful person at court and under such powerful protection could safely proceed with her plans to usurp control over the Dragon throne. Cixi allowed eight princes of royal blood, appointed by the dying Hsien Feng as the child-emperor's regents, the privilege to hang themselves with silk ropes she provided for them. The widowed real empress passed away after eating biscuits sent to her by Cixi. The official heir to the throne prowled the brothels of the Outer City and was "visited by the heavenly flowers", that is, contracted syphilis. At the age of 19 he died. Now the concubine put her nephew on the throne; when he became too ambitious she had him locked away and eventually poisoned.

The Emperor's countenance, once her ideal, had long since faded from her memory. According to etiquette at the court, unwelcome visitors were told that the Celestial Presence was indisposed. This refusal extended to Western ambassadors. Should a foreigner, whatever his status, question these immutable laws and attempt to argue, she considered him guilty of unseemly behaviour and he was promptly expelled from the country. For days on end Cixi remained invisible and hidden in her pavilion; only early in the morning or late in the evening did she go for a stroll in the palace's gardens. Shut away in her palace, she ordered bizarre corporal punishments which displayed a sexual craving for tough men and bandits, and she showed a growing fascination for a secretive but rapidly growing society of outlaws, the Boxers. She was deceitful, avaricious, greedy for power, loving no one and by no one loved, changeable in her moods, quarrelsome and cruel. Secretive and suspicious, she was contemptuous of her fellow men and their conventions.

Cixi did not let herself be misled by her officials, but was equally unafraid of trusting them to spin her intrigues. She used them to strip the Chinese provinces clean; her personal lifestyle called for a staggering annual £6 million. And all the while foreign powers were nibbling away at China's borders, demanding ever-increasing concessions and long-term leases – if not outright robbing China of large tracts of territory. Russia grabbed Manchuria, Britain took Burma and Malaya, Vietnam became French, and now Japan moved into Korea. If China wished to survive, it had to rearm and create a navy powerful enough to face up to the encroachment of other nations.

In the mid-1880s China embarked on an ambitious rearmament programme. Cannon merchants from Manchester and Essen made their pilgrimage to Beijing to display their wares. A salesman from Germany's Krupp factory came with blueprints for a revolutionary naval cannon which outgunned anything on the high seas, even the big guns of the Royal Navy. Cixi called for a special armament tax, and offered good returns on foreign loans, to pay for the expensive cannon. Money flowed in, lots of it. Cixi siphoned off the funds intended for the purchase of Krupp naval guns to build a summer palace in preparation for the celebration of her sixtieth anniversary. Her country would pay dearly for the queen's indulgence in personal luxury, and this pleasure dome would lead to disaster.

On 17 September 1894, at the height of the Sino-Japanese War, vessels of the Chinese Navy under Admiral Ting ran into the Imperial Japanese Navy. At twelve thousand yards Japanese guns belched fire and brown smoke, followed by a howl, and the air seemed to shiver from the force of the detonations. When two mighty fountains of white water hit the beam of Admiral Ting's command vessel, he ordered the Chinese guns to riposte. The ship lurched with their recoil, but his shells fell short by a mile. The admiral cursed his Empress Dowager. She had given him a fleet of boats that were nice to look at, but they had scrimped on the single most important item: modern artillery. It was an unequal fight. Chinese cannon shot bounced and ricocheted across the water and clanged harmless against the iron plates of the Japanese cruisers, while Japanese shells exploded on Chinese ships' citadels.

"Full steam ahead," ordered Admiral Ting, and a flag was run up the mast. His only option was to outrun the enemy's guns before they pulverized his fleet. His ship gathered speed. But not nearly fast enough. The admiral watched with horrified fascination the next muzzle flash of the enemy's guns; the impact came after what seemed an age of waiting, and then it was muffled, coming from the bowels of his ship. Smoke billowed from below and threw the bridge into impenetrable darkness. He knew that his proud ship was dying, and with it its crew.

The Empress Dowager dispatched her chancellor, Li Hongzhang, to Japan to ask for terms. The war ended on 17 April 1895 with the humiliating Treaty of Shimonoseki. In addition to paying reparations of three hundred million *taels*, China was forced to cede the island of Taiwan (Formosa), the Pescadores islands and the Liaotung Peninsula in southern Manchuria.[1] By now China was so weakened that it could no longer refuse anything. The tide of the disaster mounted; the limbs of an empire were lopped off before the Dowager's despairing eyes. The European powers competed fiercely to acquire further economic advantages which extended way beyond their spheres of influence.

The struggle in East Asia would soon influence the world policies of the European powers. The French were sitting in Annam and on the island of Hainan; Ningbo was an Italian concession; and Germany's Kaiser hoisted his flag over Jiaozhou, Shandong and Zhefu. Russia did not trifle with minor acquisitions; it snatched the main portion of Manchuria, including Harbin, Mukden and Lushun (Port Arthur). Under its expansionist, militaristic leadership, the naval victory was Japan's entrance fee into the club of the Great Powers. Japan took over Xiamen and Fuzhou, on the mainland opposite Taiwan. With Japan a fast-rising Far East power and a threat to Russian territorial ambitions, the Tsar offered China a mutual-defence pact against Japanese aggression. It was too little too late. China was no longer a viable ally. It was nineteenth-century Britain, still the dominant foreign power, which grabbed the crown jewels: Guangzhou, Hong Kong, Shanghai and Nanjing. Only the Americans missed out on the Big China Land Grab.

The colonial scramble left not a single major harbour along the China coast outside a foreign concession annexed by a European power. At the end of the nineteenth and into the twentieth century, the China of the Qing Dynasty was reduced to little more than a despised tax-collecting agency for foreign powers.[2]

A pleasure dome for an ageing queen had been too heavy a price to pay: Imperial China was no longer an independent power.

# 11

# BURN! BURN! BURN!
# KILL! KILL! KILL!

## JUNE 1900, BEIJING, QING DYNASTY, CHINA

"*Shao! Shao! Sha! Sha!*" "Burn! Burn! Kill! Kill!" resounded the cry in Beijing's hovels on that fateful day in 1900. The signal for the coming horror was given by the Empress Dowager on the Dragon throne; the prospect of expelling foreigners excited her: "All we have to decide is whether to use cunning or violence. We must carefully choose the right method." The hard-liners made up their minds to carry out without delay their devious plan.

The morning of 14 June presented a picture of carnage. A pall of smoke lay heavily over a city filled with thousands of corpses, horribly mutilated, hacked to pieces, with ears and noses cut off and eyes gouged out. Although the massacre was the handiwork of the Boxers, the Chinese regular army had passively stood by, stopped by their officers from interfering. Of the Christian population outside the embassies, only some 1,200 escaped the slaughter. They had found refuge inside the palace grounds of Imperial Prince Su. Altogether four thousand foreigners, plus three thousand converted Christians, were now packed into the embassy compound, or hiding in Peitang Cathedral.

Not everyone was as lucky. Han li-yun, a Christian woman, whose husband worked as gardener in the Italian embassy compound, was gang-raped and had to look on as her husband, trying to rescue her, was decapitated and hacked to pieces by the raging mob. Their home, stripped of its possessions, was then set ablaze. The leaders of the Boxers justified this bloodletting: "With every day the Ocean People population increases. When their merchant ships land they drop off many more of their devilish missionaries, to misguide our brothers."

A badly yellowed photograph shows my Great Uncle Karl in a sedan chair carried by two Chinese with pigtails and conical hats. It tells a story from a far-away place, a land of dragons and pagodas, gleaming swords and red sashes, a tale of danger and bloodshed which had taken place several generations before I was born. In 1964, 64 years after those events, I was offered a rare chance to visit China – not an easy task at a time when China was hermetically sealed off from the outside world. In those far-off days, before Mao's Cultural Revolution destroyed most of its ancient treasures, Beijing's interior city wall, which had once separated the Imperial compound from the international embassy quarter, was still intact. I found the gate giving access to the embassy compound in a sad state of repair; part of the worm-eaten door had broken off its rusty hinges and was mired in mud. Bullet marks on blackened walls bore witness to the drama of decades earlier.

I pictured a 26-year-old Austrian guard officer rounding up soldiers from wherever he could find them on that fateful afternoon of 20 June 1900, in order to block the access into the embassy compound and protect the inhabitants of various nationalities. As I climbed the narrow exterior stairs to the top of the rampart, I tried to reconstruct what had happened. At three that afternoon, with a detachment of Austrians and Russians, my great uncle stormed up this same staircase. His detachment was not the only one; gunfights broke out all along the dividing wall. With it began an incredible defence of the embassy compound by a handful of British and Americans, Germans and Japanese, French and Italians, Russians and Austrians. I do not know precisely where my great uncle made his stand on that day.[1] I know only that at this gate, and all around the interior wall, six hundred held back an attack by tens of thousands, and that their stand continued for the 55 days of the Siege of Beijing.

From the mid-nineteenth century onward, foreign occupation and exploitation of China had brought any number of ultra-nationalistic elements to the fore. In sporadic acts of terrorism, villagers and religious zealots murdered missionaries who had penetrated outlying provinces with a cross and the thought that "a million a month are dying in China without God". The wave of anti-missionary agitation, an excuse to combat openly the increasing foreign influence in the country, became ever more frequent. With it a new trend entered: organized terror, fomented underground until it exploded into the open with the rising of a group who called themselves the I Ho Ch'uan, the Society of the Fists of Righteous Harmony, or, as they became known to foreigners, the Boxers. It took a pure man with a pure heart to become member of the sect, which had sprung up in Shandong province in 1896. Once a convert passed the indoctrination ritual, he believed himself invulnerable to sword and musket ball. With its recruiting slogan "Support the Qing – destroy the foreign religion" the sect soon turned from a group of healers into martial fanatics. Christians, both Chinese converts and foreign missionaries, became their prime targets, since the initial task for a missionary was not education or healthcare – that came later – but saving souls, or, as the Boxers called it, stealing souls. This religious conversion process brought Western missionaries into conflict with local customs and the movement's traditional Confucian moral principles.

One and a half million Catholic and two hundred thousand Protestant converts lived in and around the trade concession ports. Missionaries took care of the superfluous members of a community: the poor, the orphans, the women with children who had been kicked from their homes by brutal husbands, all begging for a meal and compassion. These wretched creatures were treated with ridicule and scorn as they wandered the countryside, feeding on whatever they could find; and when the heavy frost and snow of the harsh Chinese winter brought a final, agonizing twist to their situation, they took refuge in caves or ruined temples. Their sufferings came to an end once they found the open door of a Christian charity where a sister or a missionary would feed them rice cakes and put straw on the floor under a roof. This show of compassion increased the Christians' prestige and they were able to establish a considerable number of charitable missions throughout the country.

But it was not only the presence of an alien religion that stirred anti-foreign hatred. Radical elements began to focus on anything foreign as their target, a result of both the tangible injustice of the Unequal Treaties and Europe's policy of the big gun. The first serious incident took place in Nanchang, a provincial town where in March 1862 a mob sacked a Catholic orphanage. This attack was followed in August 1868 by the burning of the China Inland Mission's compound in Yangzhou. The British ambassador, Sir Rutherford Alcock, dispatched four gunboats "to re-establish order", but this only helped to aggravate the ugly mood. The worst incident was yet to come.

The weather was bright and sunny on the morning of 21 June 1870 in Tianjin (Tientsin), an arsenal town on the railway line from Mukden to Beijing. Under the careful scrutiny of the 10 Sisters of Mercy, toddlers were playing inside the Catholic orphanage. The children loved the sisters, who told them nice stories and fed them well, nor were they afraid of the Missionary Father. But agitators had fanned a disturbing rumour about the Mission's practices and by noon a crowd began gathering outside the building. They listened to a harangue about foreign religions overthrowing Chinese morality, and heard that it was the people's sacred mission to exterminate the foreign devils and burn out their evil spirits. Some claimed to have seen the sisters scrubbing the children in a bath and then drying them with towels. "They misuse our children for their sexual pleasure, and then they kill them to make medicine from the children's eyes and hearts."

It takes only a few to incite an angry mob to riot. As the crowd's mood grew angrier, the priest sent for the local magistrate. The official was afraid of intervening, so a sister ran to the French consul in Tianjin for help. The situation sounded urgent and the consul walked alone to the square in front of the Mission, where he was greeted with screaming and fist-shaking. Then someone struck him in the face and he pulled out his pistol and shot his attacker. Chaos erupted: women screamed, men bellowed and the mob killed the consul.

Inside the Mission children were squatting in a corner, staring up at Irish Sister Alice O'Sullivan, when suddenly the door crashed in and a great many people rushed inside. The orphans were scrambling to their feet, confused and terrified, when an unfamiliar voice cut through the commotion like a knife. "Kill all those long-nosed devils!" The faces of the sisters were blank with terror as they clutched the wooden crosses hanging around their necks, knowing that death had come. After murdering the Mission's two priests the mob set fire to the church. The 10 nuns, stripped naked so that the crowd could be sure of their sex, were then multiply raped, cut into pieces and thrown into the flaming church.

When news of the atrocity reached the French embassy in Beijing the reaction was understandably one of outrage. This was an act of open defiance and the Chinese authorities knew that in an age of colonial supremacy and pride, revenge for the indignity suffered by white women was unavoidable. In a public display of breast-beating, Manchu soldiers rounded up 18 men, who may or may not have been present at the lynching, and hacked off their heads. Furthermore, China had to pay a hefty indemnity and was forced into accepting further concessions.

The Tianjin massacre showed up Beijing's weakness and inability to control its provinces. Indeed, China's fragility throughout this post-Taiping period is striking. With the protection of its isolation gone and its way of life turned upside down by two centuries of foreign intrusion, there was growing unrest throughout the country. Safety was no longer assured. Missionaries in outlying provinces saw all too clearly that it would need political backing from Europe to carry on with their work. This was usually achieved by a foreign fleet sailing up one of the main rivers, training its mighty guns on a city and threatening to reduce the town to rubble. Or, as the French writer Diderot had already predicted in the previous century:

"One day they will come with the crucifix in one hand and the dagger in the other, to cut your throat or to force you to accept their customs."

In 1876 a drought struck Shandong province, causing widespread famine and some two million deaths. Into this misery came a German missionary society that preached Christian love while wielding an iron fist. The murder of two missionaries resulted directly in German annexation of Jiaozhou Bay. For once, the culprit was clear. It was a martial society named the Plum Flower Boxers. Pressure was brought upon Beijing, the Governor of Shandong, Li Bingheng, was sacked and the Empress Dowager told his replacement to repress the whole Boxer sect by any means necessary.

"Death by a thousand cuts!" was her command. Shandong province's new Governor, Yu Xian, did not follow the Empress's dictate; on the contrary, he encouraged the anti-foreign movement and was shunted off to Shaanxi province, where the people received him in a blaze of glory. Yu Xian looked on while a gang of fanatic extremists executed 44 Protestant missionaries and their families. "There were ten Ocean People killed, three men, four women, and three little devils. When the foreigners arrived, a gun was fired for a signal, and all the soldiers set to work at once." His description provided further gruesome details: how the cruel swords had slashed the victims, how the clothing had been stripped from their bodies and how the naked, blood-spattered corpses had been flung into a wayside pit. "We knew when the foreigners left yesterday that death awaited them on the road. Not long after they had gone, the Prefect and the Magistrate rode in their chairs to the gate of the mission, took a look inside without entering, and then sealed up the gate."

This vicious act brought on a power struggle between the Empress Dowager and a clique of ferociously xenophobic court officials and Manchu princes who refused to recognize Cixi as the rightful heiress to the Dragon throne. One who realized the danger and tried to warn the Empress Dowager was Prince Jung Lu, once her lover and then her protector and confidant. It came as a surprise to the diplomatic community to learn that Prince Jung Lu would visit the embassy compound. When a prince rode from the Forbidden City, drums were beaten and long horns blown. After the boom of three firecrackers the prince set off in his sedan chair of blue velvet, borne by four carriers and preceded by footmen and cavalry. It was good to have pageantry in order to gain the respect for the highest authority. People hurried out of the way of his caravan, gaping and deeply bowing. Prince Jung Lu realized how important it was to cement a negotiating relationship with the representatives of foreign powers, just as his royal visit meant a good deal to the Western ambassadors, always at the mercy of the slow-grinding palace bureaucracy, except for those that could reach an ear near the Empress. Jung Lu's conversation with the various envoys was courteous and full of mandarin talk; until he turned to Germany's ambassador, Clemens von Ketteler, and said: "If you need help, come straight to me." The prince expected trouble.

In January 1900 the issue came to a head over the aims of the Society of the Fists of Righteous Harmony. Was the sect trying to purify morale – or to annihilate the Manchu dynasty? Lack of decisive action by a court divided over personal interests led to the rapid growth of the murderous sect. Its members killed with impunity, until the foreign delegations at Beijing asked their countries for military intervention. But that was what Prince Jung Lu wanted to prevent.

The court became involved, though not in the way that the Europeans had wished for. The Empress Dowager thought that by using the threat of a killer sect she could strengthen her hold on power, and despite Jung Lu's repeated warnings, she published an official edict which presented a benevolent view of the Boxer movement as being "in support of OUR rightful claim to the throne, as the one and only leader of this great country". She went on to state that secret societies were part of traditional Chinese culture and that such associations were not contrary to law. This document was a masterpiece of misinterpretation of the situation. It settled nothing and sparked turmoil. Although intended to combat foreign influence in Chinese affairs, when published, on 11 January 1900, it set a rebellion in motion. The Boxers began widespread organized depredations in central and northern China, and in one week 73 converted Chinese were killed. Once the Boxer avalanche began to roll, it proved unstoppable; it was only a matter of time before they would reach a major city and commit atrocities on a vast scale.

On 18 May 1900 an international token force of 337 soldiers arrived in Beijing to protect the embassies. The next day the Boxers cut the rail and telegraph links between Tianjin and Beijing. The safety of foreigners in Beijing's embassy compound was of increasing concern to the German ambassador, Clemens von Ketteler; with the railway line cut, von Ketteler dispatched a rider to the Western fleet anchored on the coast with a request for immediate military assistance. The same day a rumour spread in the international section that the railway had been reopened and a foreign relief force was arriving by train at Beijing's Machiapo Station. Families in festive mood with banners and flags rushed to welcome the intervention force at the rail terminus outside the Yung-ting-men Gate. No train arrived; instead a great number of Chinese soldiers turned up, and forced the families to return to the embassy compound inside the city walls.

That same afternoon Japan's consul, Sugiyama, made one more trip to

Machiapo Station. He had just passed through the Yung-ting-men Gate, when a group of armed men pulled him from his sedan chair and cut out his heart. It took the Japanese ambassador two days to recover the consul's body. On 12 June 1900 the German ambassador, von Ketteler, as the official spokesman of the foreign community, sent another rider post-haste to Admiral Sir Edward Seymour in Tianjin. It was to be his last message:

> In a note received today, the Imperial court demands that your dispatch of 1,000 troops must be stopped. The diplomatic representatives have rejected the demand. Telegraphic lines with Tianjin are cut. The foreign-hostile Prince Tuan, father of the crown prince, together with an equally hostile Prince Ching, have taken control of the Tsungli-Yamen [ruling council]. The summer residence of the British ambassador to Beijing, put under Chinese protection, has been burned down on 10 June. Yesterday, the Japanese attaché was decapitated on his way to the railway terminal. There is strong reason to believe that regular soldiers will be let loose against foreign personnel.

Ambassador von Ketteler was correct in his assessment that Chinese regular forces would take part in the rioting. It was established that soldiers of the regular Imperial Chinese Army had murdered the Japanese consul. On 13 June, as he was about to leave the embassy compound, von Ketteler himself was waylaid, jostled and spat on by a banner-waving crowd; he took hold of one of the Boxer leaders and punched him to the ground. The timely intervention by a German guard unit, wading into the knife-wielding mob with planted bayonets, saved the ambassador's life. In the ensuing scuffle, blood flowed, mostly Chinese. In retaliation, gangs of Boxers moved into Beijing's residential areas and began burning down the homes of foreigners and converts to Christianity. By late afternoon, with parts of the city on fire, the embassies had united in a collective measure for their protection: the Italians installed a one-pounder cannon in Embassy Road, facing east; the Austrians placed a Maxim machine-gun in Customs Street to cover the northern approach; a British unit held Canal Street and the North Bridge; the Russians controlled the South Bridge; while Americans with a Colt machine-gun covered Embassy Road toward the West. That still left Peitang Cathedral, packed with three thousand terrified Chinese Christians who had put themselves under the protection of Bishop Favier of France, 40 French and Italian Marines and the Good Lord.

That evening a great number of Christian converts from all over the city followed the call of their Chinese bishop. They gathered in front of Nantang Church to take part in a religious procession calling for peace in the country. A priest carrying a cross was leading the marchers, when suddenly men with red sashes rushed from doors and pounced on the stunned throng of faithful. A massacre of Christian followers began and continued throughout the night, with several thousand dying. The Boxers prolonged the rampage as long as there was still a chance of murdering one more Christian.

Around foreign embassies, guards remained on permanent duty, while riots broke out and dispersed on the other side of the wall. Gutted chariots and trishaws lay about the streets like carcasses after vultures had done with them. Fires crackled all over the city. The people were terrified, and more died violent deaths that day. The screams of the wounded and raped penetrated the foreign compound from far off. Much of the town was obscured by smoke, its nauseating fumes making the eyes smart. For an instant, a gust of hot air blew the black cloud away, giving a glimpse of some of the scenes of horror that lay beyond the wall. Terrible cries came from the Methodist Chapel in Hatamen Street, which had been set ablaze with its doors blocked from the outside. They were roasting Christians alive. Other churches set alight were Tungtang Cathedral, the Orthodox Church, the London Mission and Nantang Church. Only Peitang Cathedral escaped the onslaught, protected on its main approach by a machine-gun which opened fire on the marching, drum-beating demonstrators, killing several hundred of them. The staff of the embassies knew there was nothing they could do to help the Christians. By now the fires were out of control, with occasional bright flashes accelerating the final destruction of the sacred places. The fires spread to nearby houses and soon the whole district was an inferno.

The Imperial court reached a decision to come out in support of the Boxers during a summit meeting on 16 June, held in the Dowager Empress's winter palace. Prince Tuan showed up with a forged ultimatum which, he claimed, had been presented by the foreign powers. In fact, no such ultimatum had ever been drawn up. It launched a tug-of-war between the Empress Cixi, firmly supported by Prince Jung Lu, Commander-in-Chief of the Imperial Army, and eight princes of Prince Tuan's faction. Jung Lu counselled that the Imperial Presence should make concessions and not launch a full-out assault on the embassies, as this risked a reprisal from the alliance of Western powers. He knew that, once Tuan's hard-line plan was accepted, war must involve the Imperial Chinese Army and that this was unprepared and unequipped for such a confrontation, which would doom the Empire.

"To stand up to the superior Allied artillery is sheer suicide," the prince warned.

"To continue under the dictate of the foreign devils is shameful," countered Tuan. His argument found support among a majority of the Imperial council. The result was a standoff that only the Empress Dowager could resolve. This clever woman was prone to listen to hints and eavesdrop on snatches of whispered conversation by courtiers who vented their worst instincts, before she would decide according to the political climate at court. Often she got it right, but this time "the street" took the decision for her: the xenophobic Yu Xian, Governor General of Shaanxi, had just entered the capital at the head of tens of thousands of flag-waving Boxers. With drums and gongs, screams and fire, they went on a rampage and killed more converts, as well as a few British missionaries, all under the noses of the diplomatic representation of the "outer" barbarians (the difference between "inner" and "outer" barbarians being that the latter came from across the ocean). It was already late into the night when the Empress Dowager issued a statement that was surprising given that it came from a shrewd survivor of half a century of court intrigue:

> The present situation is becoming daily more difficult. The various powers cast upon us looks of tiger-like voracity, hustling each other to be first to seize our innermost territories … Should the strong enemies become aggressive and press us to consent to things we can never accept, we have no alternative but to rely upon the justice of our cause … If our hundreds of millions of inhabitants would prove their loyalty to their Empress, and the love of their country, what is there to fear from any barbarian invader?

Then she added the phrase that decided the issue: "Let us not think about making peace."

The Empress Dowager was now 65, a wrinkled old woman with decaying teeth and a face partly paralysed by a stroke. Neither her unsteady nerves nor the blind rages to which she was subject, nor her unusual chastity nor her belief in astrology, are attributes of singular greatness. She was a mixture of weakness and strength, vice and virtue. And yet this diminutive woman ruled with an iron fist over one fourth of the human race. She was unbending when she demanded the immediate presence of the diplomatic representatives of the nine resident Western powers – the United States, France, Great Britain, Germany, Italy, Austria, Belgium, Holland and Japan. While Boxers roamed the streets of Beijing with their battle cry "Burn! Burn! Burn! Kill! Kill! Kill!", Empress Cixi fixed the foreigners with her ill-tempered stare, her mouth agape, showing off her filed, black teeth, like a shark ready to bite. She waved her hand with the overly long fingernails, a sign for her commissioner, Li Hung-chang, to read out what amounted to a declaration of war: "The safety of the diplomatic community can no longer be vouched for."

Prince Jung Lu's appeal for caution had gone unheard. The hard-liners had triumphed over the negotiators. In taking on all the great Western powers by holding their representatives at gunpoint, the fire-spitting dragon had tickled the terrible tiger's tail. What had pushed Cixi to act in this provocative manner? the ambassadors asked themselves, still unaware of the cleverly manipulated incident which had sparked off the crisis. As commander-in-chief of China's Imperial Army, Prince Jung Lu realized the madness of challenging the might of Western guns and sent out strict orders not to commence hostile action. His messenger was intercepted and his written orders replaced by ones from the hard-liner Prince Tuan. In this way the commander of the Dagu Fort at Tianjin, guarding the river access to Beijing, received orders to "bombard the foreign fleet lying at anchor and sink it".

On the morning of 17 June 1900 the commander ordered his gunners to open fire. Despite operating ancient, round-shot cannon, they made a good effort and put one of the Royal Navy's gunboats out of action. But then the big guns of Admiral Seymour's Combined Navy obliterated the fort's parapets, causing most defenders to die amid flying splinters and brick. By early afternoon it was over. The Allied ships had gained one of the easiest and most significant victories of the entire war. A landing party of Allied Marines walked into the smoking ruins and put the fort's surviving defenders to death. Next they captured the town of Tianjin. Now nothing could slow this deliberately brutal riposte to an unprovoked Chinese attack.

News of the capture of Dagu Fort reached the Forbidden City. In the *Yamen*, Prince Tuan asked Empress Cixi to issue orders to the Imperial Army to occupy the diplomatic compound and take all foreigners hostage. As an initial step, and over the head of Prince Jung Lu's army command, Tuan took it upon himself to order Chinese troops into the German-run electricity plant, a move which put the diplomatic compound into darkness and also cut the embassies' electrically operated telegraph system.

On 19 June Ambassador von Ketteler sent his Mandarin-speaking consul, von Cordes, to the palace to demand the instant removal of Chinese troops from the electricity plant, citing the international code of diplomatic immunity. Prince Tuan not only rejected the German demand – formulated in terms that were rather too Prussian – but ordered all foreign diplomatic personnel to quit Beijing within 24 hours, or face the consequences. After considering the masses of raging Boxers, now openly supported by Imperial soldiers, the cut rail link and the possibility of annihilation if they remained in Beijing, the ambassadors saw they had no choice but to bend to Tuan's ultimatum. However, they did ask for the assurance of safe transport for their families on a reopened rail line to Tianjin. Their note received no reply, so von Ketteler asked for a rendezvous with Prince Tuan in a last-minute effort to defuse the precarious situation. The prince accepted the request and the meeting was arranged for the morning of 20 June 1900.

Despite the horror and butchery played out in clear view of the West's representatives for over a week, nothing much had been done to put a stop to it. It was almost as if the Western powers were not concerned about the slaughter of Chinese by Chinese. But then another grave incident occurred and the world was never quite the same – or in the words of Kaiser Wilhelm II to his Chancellor, Bernhard von Bülow: "*Es ist der Kampf Asiens gegen das ganze Europa.*"[2] Indeed, it was Asia's fight against all Europe. War was only a day off.

At 8.30 a.m. on 20 June 1900, Clemens *Freiherr* von Ketteler, a 47-year-old Prussian Junker and the Kaiser's ambassador to the Celestial Court, left the emergency meeting which had taken place at the French embassy in Beijing. For once the various Western ambassadors had put aside their national priorities and formed a united front to discuss the danger to the foreign legations and the resident Europeans. Von Ketteler would tell the *Yamen* of the anxiety among the diplomatic corps over the rapidly deteriorating situation. His consul, von Cordes, who spoke fluent Mandarin and often acted as the ambassador's interpreter, accompanied him.

The appointment with a prince of royal blood had been set for 9 a.m. The ambassador and his interpreter took their places in two palanquins. To ensure their safety, a German military escort of a sergeant and four soldiers was present. With tensions running high – the latest news was that an Allied military force had stormed the Dagu Fort at Tianjin – an armed escort to the palace would be interpreted as an affront and might provoke spontaneous demonstrations along the way. With this in mind the ambassador decided to refuse his military escort to the palace. The Prussian sergeant tried to talk him into accepting his pistol, but the ambassador flatly refused. How could he possibly show up before the Imperial Presence with a gun in his pocket? Since a royal prince expected his visit, von Ketteler was sure that all necessary precautions had been taken to ensure that nothing untoward befell the representative of His Imperial German Majesty. Indeed, someone at court had taken measures, but not those expected by the German ambassador.

The caravan of two palanquins set off with only two uniformed but unarmed *masu* (flag-carrying servants), one in front to clear a path for the important personalities and one behind to shoo away beggars. The column had just crossed the triumphal arch near the Belgian embassy and approached the central police station, when von Cordes, travelling in the second palanquin, saw a cart with Chinese Imperial lancers crossing the road and coming to a stop just three metres in front of the ambassador's palanquin. This was a calculated insult to a foreign ambassador, whose position was clearly indicated by the *masu* carrying Germany's imperial flag, and most unusual in a city known for its courtesy. A sergeant wearing the distinct blue-plumed hat of the Imperial Mandarin guard jumped from the cart and made a dash for von Ketteler's palanquin. He raised his musket, aimed for the ambassador's head and, from one metre off, pulled the trigger. The envoy was thrown back, and lay slumped over. The sedan carriers dropped both palanquins and ran off, as did the two *masu*.

Von Cordes jumped from his chair. "*Halt! Mörderer!*" he yelled when two more shots rang out and he was struck in the lower abdomen. He stumbled across the road and into a narrow street, pursued by two lance-wielding soldiers. Suddenly the lancers stopped, turned around and disappeared into the crowd which had gathered around the bleeding, staggering German diplomat. The consul begged for help but none was offered. A bystander cried out: "No help for a long-nosed devil who got what he deserved." Finally an old man took pity and helped von Cordes to the American compound, where he collapsed near the gate. He was carried inside the embassy.

An hour had passed since the assassination of von Ketteler, when a German troop arrived at the murder site to discover two empty palanquins and much blood, but no body. A reward was offered. The following day a Chinese took a German lieutenant to a nearby mound of fresh earth. The Germans discovered a wooden box with the remains of their ambassador. The coffin proved without doubt that this had been no impromptu robbery, but a planned assassination. Since those in the *Yamen* were aware of the ambassador's scheduled visit, it showed that someone at the Imperial court was directly involved in the deed. Why the assassin had worn an Imperial uniform was at first unclear, and thought of as deliberate provocation, until it became clear that the killer had not expected a second person, in this case von Cordes, who could provide a detailed description of the killer.

The foreign community of Beijing was in uproar. Nobody could be sure whether the assassination of an ambassador was an isolated act or part of a much wider anti-diplomatic conspiracy. In the beginning they discounted the participation of the *Yamen,* as such a deliberate act would bring an immediate reprisal. They were wrong; it was indeed a provocative act, and now the group of hard-line princes forced the Empress Dowager into taking a firm anti-foreign stand. And she did. "Outer barbarians are like fish in the frying pan. For 40 years have I lain on brushwood and eaten bitterness because of them," Cixi snapped at her chief military counsellor, who tried one last time to change her mind about going to war. Rather than searching for a diplomatic solution, the court came out in open support of the Society of the Fists of Righteous Harmony.

The news of the German ambassador's assassination shocked Europe. In fact, the way this news got out is a story in itself. With the electricity cut and the embassy's telegraph out of order, a Chinese employee of the German embassy walked to Beijing's main telegraph office to send off a lengthy telegram, written in clear, and announcing the death of the ambassador. It detailed the circumstances but, most importantly, it was an urgent plea for immediate military assistance. The Chinese telegraph operator read the message, then called his superior, who also read it, and, before he agreed to send it, asked for an extra 18 shillings for an excess number of words. The servant had to walk back to the embassy to fetch the money before the telegram was finally dispatched, in full and uncensored.

It may well be the only case of a call for military assistance, amounting to nothing less than a declaration of war, dispatched over the enemy's telegraph. The message was received by the Combined Western Forces' command in Tianjin, and from there passed on to Berlin and London. The House of Commons and the British press swayed public opinion in support of a punitive expedition. However, the driving force of retribution was the German Kaiser, who sent a thunderous note to Beijing: "If this city is to become the scene of a dreadful experiment by our mighty guns, we declare that we shall not be the reason for the awful consequences." But until such a force could reach China, the embassy guards, some five hundred European soldiers, would have to use whatever was at their disposal to face the might of the Boxers backed up by units of the Imperial Army.

The Beijing of 1900 was built in a near-perfect square and enclosed by a high wall. Outside the walled city lived the poor, a mob easily riled into any sort of villainy. *Intra-muros* Beijing was divided into four distinct sectors. In the south were two residential and shopping areas. A high wall separated this popular quarter from the Forbidden City in the north-west, which again was separated by a wall from the diplomatic compound and the Christian churches in the north-east. Each embassy had its ambassadorial residence with reception rooms, consular section, trade mission, telegraph office, guardrooms, lodgings, storehouses and armouries, all essential to a pleasant life far from home.

For those living inside the embassy compound, "beyond the wall" was another world: a strange land of noise and delight that were infectious to the visitor, with a bustling maze of lanes and market stalls whose owners urged passers-by to choose from their displays. Porters in ragged clothes carried prodigious loads on their bent backs past wives of mandarins and diplomats in their finery, fingering the quality of the silks. For the diplomats and their spouses living shut off in their ghetto, a special occasion to mingle with the local population was during the annual Shangyuan lantern festival, when restrictions were suspended and the gates not closed that night.

The foreign community went to see the exhibition of lanterns which each family had made in a contest for novelty design, an old tradition handed down for a thousand years. That night the young girls wore flowers in their hair, looking their best in the red glow of the lanterns. Ordinary people sat in public tea houses and small eating places among the stalls lining the riverbank. The rich and noble had installed their own booths and sat on luxurious redwood chairs covered with large vermilion cushions and lanterns that cast a gentle glow on their faces as they sipped tea and tasted delicacies. Along the shoreline firecrackers and rockets soared into the sky and came down in showers of sparks.

Inside the diplomatic compound the streets were wide and spacious, lined with leafy trees and bedded with ochre gravel. Individual walls bordered the streets, an important factor in the weeks to come as they made for good gun positions, and the wide, straight streets for perfect lines of fire.

The siege of the embassy compound began late in the afternoon of 20 June 1900. An unruly crowd had gathered along Embassy Row. A compact mass of Boxers in their distinct red turbans and sashes, jeering and shouting that all foreigners must get out of China, advanced crying: "Burn! Burn! Burn! Kill! Kill! Kill!", strong in their belief that barbarian bullets could not harm them.

"Look at those murderous bastards," said a German sergeant of the embassy guard, expressing what everyone in his troop thought. "Enough to roll over us." He commanded 12 rifles and there were at least three hundred Chinese coming at them. The mob carried no guns, or at least none that he could see; just stones and batons of wood. In the middle of them were three men with bronze swords, obviously the leaders. One with a red sash stepped forward and screamed something at the German guards. Stones zipped through the air and broke windows. The man with the red sash started to run toward the Germans. The sergeant fired and his bullet caught the rioter in the face. Then more shots began to fly, smashing into the massed mob. Bullets fractured a water tank on top of a building and the precious water supply of three families cascaded off the roof, washing away the blood on the ground.

Another detachment of two dozen riflemen, under the command of a young lieutenant, took up a defensive position around the wall gate moments before yelling Boxers poured out from many of the nearby alleys and made for the open gate. These fanatics were used to overwhelming their cowering opponents by sheer numbers, but were not equipped to fight a resolute, trained troop. But they came on all the same, armed only with their hatred.

Lieutenant von Hofstetter, with no idea just how much hatered was raging through the mob, yelled: "*Das ist die letzte Warnung!* This is your last warning! *Zurück oder wir feuern.* Get back, or we'll fire!"[3] He did not realize that in his excitement he had yelled in German; but even in Mandarin it would have made no difference. The answer was a roar from the charging mob. For the young lieutenant this was no time for subtlety or discussion; the success of his men's action depended in large part on laying down a curtain of concentrated fire. *"Feuer frei!"* Hofstetter was deafened by the muzzle blast of a dozen Mausers a few feet from his head. Half a heartbeat later, bodies tumbled, including the tall Chinese dressed in black with a red sash and wielding a bronze sword. Rifles cracked, then a machine-gun chattered; the first line of attack collapsed before the merciless fusillade.

Fighting erupted all along the wall enclosing the embassy compound. Now that the European soldiers were committed to killing, it was a matter of their very survival to cut the enemy down quickly, resolutely and utterly. The Boxers had set out in droves to do battle and in droves they died. Spent cartridges were piling up in prodigious quantities on the ground. The unit's commanders knew that all too soon the supply of bullets would give out and that the men could not sustain their effort much longer. Barrels overheated, rifles jammed and cartridge cases had to be pulled from the chambers manually, scalding fingers.

More Boxers arrived and dragged a cannon into an alley, before training it on the grounds of the German embassy. The first round punched a hole in a residential building. Sergeant Hermann Burkhart led out a group of six volunteers to deal with the danger, but they found themselves surrounded by a howling gang of screaming fanatics. One Chinese rushed at the sergeant with his sword, only to plant himself on Burkhart's raised bayonet. But there were too many of them. Burkhart felt himself going down, his breath crushed from his body, when the rattling noise of a Maxim gun rang out. The mob froze. Seeing their supposedly invulnerable brothers being cut down by Ocean Man's magic frightened them more than anything else. They fell back, scrambling over one another to get clear.

In a flash Burkhart was back on his feet and, with his men, ran along the road to the cannon. There were only three gunners left, the rest having fled. Bayonets put the three out of action. The troopers stuffed the barrel with black powder and blocked the muzzle with their bundled-up uniform jackets. Using a long fuse stuck into the firing hole, they set off a distant explosion. The barrel burst into a thousand pieces, the signal for 55 days of horror and hardship.

One of the many bizarre incidents which so clearly convey the confusion of both assailants and defenders took place in late June around the Roman Catholic cathedral, where a great number of Chinese Christians had taken refuge. Among them were 850 schoolgirls. The Boxers ascribed their failure to capture the cathedral to the poisonous influence of the wailing virgins inside the barbarians' house of their heathen deity. To counter the girls' evil magic, the Boxers created a special female unit composed of dedicated women, adorned with red sashes, known as the Red Lantern Shining, who claimed to be able to ride on the clouds and bring down fire and destruction. But since they did not come riding on clouds but ran screaming down the streets, "the fire in their shining red lanterns was snuffed out by a hail of bullets from our cathedral's valiant French and Italian defenders," as one of the schoolgirls wrote in her diary.

On 26 June an expeditionary relief corps of two thousand British Bluejacket and 112 US Marines, under Admiral Seymour, attacked a Boxer army, supported by regular troops, at Tang-tsu. The expeditionary units were ordered into a flank attack. Defied by so paltry an enemy, Seymour's soldiers claimed it was beneath their dignity to go skulking around the back against a bunch of heathens. They marched frontally into the enemy's guns – and suffered three hundred casualties. Seymour had to abandon his attempt to relieve Beijing, and returned with his bedraggled force to Tianjin. The embassies were now on their own; they united their meagre forces under a common International Legation Guard commander, Sir Claude MacDonald.

Europe was seething with rumours. No real news came out of the beleaguered city. This led to a series of fateful, and in some cases tragic, decisions. An erroneous message claiming that all German residents in Beijing had been brutally massacred reached the Kaiser in Berlin shortly before Field

Marshal Alfred Graf von Waldersee, with a relief force of thirty thousand tough Prussian professionals, sailed for China. On 13 July 1900 the Kaiser sent the Expeditionskorps Waldersee on their way with his notorious "*Hunnenrede*",[4] in which he ordered his battalions to kill without mercy.

"*Kommt Ihr vor den Feind so wird derselbe geschlagen! Pardon wird nicht gegeben! Wer Euch in die Hande fällt, sei Euch verfallen!* ... When you come before the enemy, you will defeat him. Pardon will not be granted. Prisoners will not be taken. Whoever falls into your hands must be ruthlessly extinguished. Just like Attila the Hun, a thousand years ago, put down his name in history, so will the name of Germany in China resound for the next thousand years, [and] never again will a Chinaman dare to look sideways at a German."

The real purpose of this expedition was expressed by Prussia's Chief of Staff, General Helmut von Moltke, in a letter to his wife, dated 11 July 1900: "*Auf das eigentlich treibende Motiv der ganzen Expedition* ... No sense discussing the real reason behind this whole expedition, because if we are frank, it is greed for money which has pushed us to slice into the big Chinese cake. We want to make money, build railways, run mines and force on to them our European culture. In one word, we want to make a lot of money."

Screaming headlines in London newspapers helped stir up anti-Chinese sentiment: "1,500 Europeans Are Massacred In Fresh Boxer Outrage":

> July 27. After fierce fighting, Allied forces have stormed Tientsin and managed to hold the city despite determined counter-attacks by 100,000 Boxer rebels and renegade Chinese soldiers. The Allied force, which involved British, American, German and Japanese troops, lost 400 men in the victorious assault.
>
> It is reported that 1,500 foreigners have been brutally massacred, including missionaries, traders and diplomats. A correspondent reports: "It is difficult to overestimate the magnitude of the task the Powers have before them. It is all China against the foreigner."

In the meantime the battle for the embassies continued unabated day and night. There was nothing particularly sophisticated in the concept of the defence plan for the embassies; its virtue lay in the skill with which it was carried out. The Boxers held an overwhelming advantage in the number of assailants. Whenever the Chinese attacked, Western marksmen concealed on balconies and in windows were ready to pour a hail of Mauser or Enfield bullets down on them. As the author's great-uncle, who witnessed the events, recalled:

The Boxers advanced in a solid mass and carried standards of red and white cloth. Their yells were deafening, while the roar of gongs, drums and horns sounded like thunder. They waved their swords and stamped the ground with their feet. They wore red turbans, sashes, and garters over blue cloth. They were only twenty yards from our gate, when three volleys from the rifles of our sailors left more than fifty dead upon the ground.

The antiquated muskets used by the insurgents were not particularly accurate, but still managed to do some damage; the air hummed with ball and bullets. It was mostly ricochets and masonry chips that inflicted serious wounds on the defenders. Throughout the long siege the embassy guards stuck to their duties with admirable coolness. The besieged could not get out and the attackers could not get in. In this standoff a cease-fire was arranged which lasted from 16 July to 4 August; this break in the fighting allowed more Allied reinforcements to gather in Tianjin. For the first – and certainly the last – time in the history of the twentieth century the nations traditionally at war with one another formed a union to save their hard-pressed citizens. The Allied Expedition Army of 18,700 combined Russians with Japanese, Austrians with Italians and Germans with Americans and Britons. There was no overall supreme commander; generals of every national contingent conducted combat. That such an alliance was possible only 14 years before the Guns of August thundered on the battlefields of Europe, and yet could not be sustained, is one of our history's tragedies.

On 4 August 1900 an Allied Relief Army began its march on Beijing. In a brief but decisive encounter at Tang-tsu they pushed back the blocking force that had stopped Seymour 40 days earlier. News had reached the Manchu court that a combined force of Imperial Army units and Boxers had been defeated at Tang-tsu and that protection for the capital no longer existed. The news of the Allied victory did not reach the harried defenders; with no sign of a relief force, morale in the embassy compound sank ever lower. Commander MacDonald perched on his embassy's roof, scanning in growing frustration the horizon beyond the walls. A suggestion was made that they should try to run for the coast, but MacDonald remained firm, knowing they could never make it. "According to the tactics of war, we must wait for reinforcements."

The fighting for control of the embassies reached its zenith. The Boxers launched repeated suicidal attacks on the compound in an attempt to snatch victory before the arrival of the Allied Relief Army. Day and night their tubas screeched and their drums thumped, and their blood-crazed yells split the ears of the compound's civilians and defenders. Shelling and fires had destroyed much of the diplomatic quarter and, with the gate in its wall shattered, there was easy access to the compound. Furniture, carriages and sandbags were piled into barricades. The streets were littered with the unburied bodies of insurgents. Inside the buildings, everyone had lost track of time and all count of the ceaseless charges.

By the beginning of August the food shortage had become critical and now water was running short. The soldiers were almost out of bullets. Medicine was no longer available. Women tore their dresses into strips to be used as bandages. With no outside help in sight, the sheer hopelessness of their situation hardened people; most had reached the point where even the fear of death had gone. By 13 August, with the Russian advance unit only 20 miles from the walls of Beijing, all but the final barrier, which surrounded the German and British embassies, had to be abandoned to the incessant attacks.

"Burn! Burn! Burn! Kill! Kill! Kill!" Qang-xi, a Boxer commander from Shandong, sat motionless in the courtyard of the Beijing town house with red flags jutting from every window and draped around the courtyard. The house served as the Boxer's general headquarters. Finally the time had come to make up for all the years of disgrace. Long ago the foreign fiends had come to China to humiliate its people. To kill these devils would restore centuries of Chinese pride, hope and dignity.

"Burn! Burn! Burn! Kill! Kill! Kill!" Thousands were waiting for the signal; every few hours some court mandarin came into the courtyard to tell them that political considerations were still delaying achievement of their goal. The Celestial Court, hesitant and fearful of foreign reprisals, hesitated to give the order for the final, all-out attack. Qang-xi had to sit around and listen to the bitter complaints of his brothers, consumed by a glorious commitment to fight with their blood to the end.

"Burn! Burn! Burn! Kill! Kill! Kill!" So many had already fallen. It was a great calamity that thousands of the best had died under the bullets of the Great Satan's machine-guns. But now their moment had come. With the enemy's advance elements approaching Beijing, Qang-xi had just been told that he would have the honour of leading the big assault on the foreign legations. The Boxer leader felt his despair fall away. He gathered his forces and they set off – into the burst of gunfire. His men collapsed on top of one another with howls of confusion. The noise, the screams, the explosions of the battle continued for long moments, until it seemed for ever. Qang-xi would not allow his sacred mission to end in failure. He didn't turn around to see if his men followed him, but waved his sword and sprinted toward what must be the final barrier, when a single shot rang out.

Qang-xi clutched his chest and looked up in surprise at the face of the foreign devil on the balcony. Then his body tumbled forward.

François Dufour, a young corporal in the French colonial forces defending Peitang Cathedral, afterward wrote home: "Our men began picking them off at distances of a hundred yards, but on they came, pouring out of the houses into streets leading up to our barricade, which was nothing more than 60 cm of bricks topped by a few sandbags pushed against an iron fence. They came all day long and continued into the night. And we kept mowing them down, our rifles so hot we could hardly work the bolts. By the end they had still not been able to reach the church. They left thousands of their bleeding on the pavement." The Boxers tried one final time: a single shell, fired from the embassy compound, exploded amid the attackers and stopped them. Private Dufour turned to his lieutenant for reassurance. "*C'était notre bonne fortune* ... That was our good fortune. It came from heaven."

His lieutenant smiled wryly. "You may find that not all good fortune comes from heaven; some comes from a cannon's mouth." In front of the last barricade lay the countless dead; no one buried them, and the nauseating stink from the piles of Boxer corpses, mowed down by Mauser, Enfield and *chassepot* bullets and fetid in the summer heat, was near unbearable. The defenders sat behind the walls as if in a daze, exhausted men who had fought on beyond human endurance, on a stage of deafening explosions, thrusting bayonets and blood. They couldn't go on, and yet they knew they must. Relief? They had given up hope. With aching bodies and strain-reddened eyes they kept watch, knowing that thousands were waiting out there in the darkness, gathering for yet another charge.

That night passed with relative calm as if the Boxers had abandoned the siege. After that most terrible of all assaults, the men in the church shut their eyes and dreaded what the morning would bring. When they awoke the city lay below them in a dark mist, amazingly quiet. A single star hung in the west like a stable lamp; soon it would be light. Then suddenly they heard a tremendous crash; it was the explosion of a shell from a great gun. The first bang was soon followed by many others. "They're ours! They're ours!" A yell went around the church and the compound and the embassy buildings. Relief had arrived!

On 14 August the Japanese forces at the Chi-hua Gate were embroiled in combat with regular units holding the wall, while the Russians attacked the Tung Pien Gate, blew the wooden door off its hinges and stormed it. While these battles were going on, pulling more Chinese reinforcements toward the defence of the outer wall, two companies of the US 14th Infantry overcame the defences on the north-east corner of the exterior wall. Bugler Calvin Titus hoisted the Stars and Stripes over the north-eastern tower. Chinese units, abandoned by their officers, realized the hopelessness of their position. Many simply lay down. Boxer leaders were shot on the spot. A British battalion broke through the Water Gate and became the first to reach the British embassy, where most of the diplomatic personnel of various nations had gathered to make their final stand. Russian and French forces reached Peitang Cathedral, where 40 French and Italian Marines, ably supported by some three thousand Christian converts, had managed to hold out for an incredible eight weeks.

The following day US Lieutenant Charles Summerall braved enemy bullets and calmly walked to the Chi-hua Gate, barring the entry into the Forbidden City. He chalked a round target on the oak door and his field gunners took aim. By the time the American soldiers reached the Imperial quarters, the Empress Dowager, having cut her long fingernails, a sure give-away, had fled in peasant's blue pyjamas. The Forbidden City was sacked. The first Americans to storm into the Empress Dowager's bedchamber stared in wonderment at the magnificent surroundings; a bed with blue silk hangings and heavy gold tassels, its frame carved from ivory with a carved relief of the Imperial dragon-phoenix pattern. The walls were covered with bookcases containing rare and ancient Taoist texts and jade statuettes. On the table was a gold-bronzed duck puffing ringlets of incense from its beak, and suspended in the windows were gilded bird cages with many-coloured twittering lovebirds. In the court-yards French soldiers used bayonets to scrape the gold from monster bells and jars. By accident the library, with its irreplaceable scripts and scrolls, went up in flames.

The Siege of Beijing was over. Five hundred and seven men of the International Legation Guard had held out against thousands for an amazing 55 days. The heroic stand by a relatively small number of embassy staff plus a few machine-guns – a cost-effective weapon in terms of the small number of troops needed to kill a maximum of enemy attacking in human waves – was an equation that weighed decisively in the balance.[5] The overall losses were heavy. One hundred and five thousand Chinese Christians had fallen victim to Boxer fury in their homes throughout the north of the country. The embassy guards had lost four officers and 49 men, while nine officers and 139 men were seriously wounded. Foreign civilian casualties were 12 killed and 23 wounded. In the defence of Peitang Cathedral, seven Marines, four priests and four hundred Christian converts died. There was never a count of Boxer casualties. In Beijing it took weeks to clear the corpses from streets and houses.

None of the Boxer commanders had been thinking tactically, following a pattern that had worked for their forebears, the Taiping, against the inefficient Manchu forces. They suffered the same harsh lesson that Gordon's guns had taught the Taiping. In an erroneous belief of invulnerability they tried to force their way past modern machine-guns.

To the utter disappointment of the glory-hungry Kaiser, his Expeditionskorps Waldersee reached China too late to make any difference. It landed on 27 September 1900, with China militarily defeated. This did not prevent the German corps making their presence felt by conducting 48 punitive expeditions, justified by them as acts forced by necessity in an effort to bring relief to outlying missionaries. In the wake of the Kaiser's "Hun speech", this was not really surprising; but the acts, ostensibly committed in the name of civilization, nevertheless seem despicable. *Freiherr* von Waldersee, elevated by his Prussian Majesty to the rank of "World Marshal", became better known as the Kaiser's "Execution Marshal".

There was a bizarre aftermath. On 21 September 1900 a Japanese officer arrested a man trying to sell him a gold watch. It turned out to be the watch of the assassinated German ambassador, Clemens von Ketteler. Transferred into German custody, the man gave his name as En-hai, a sergeant in the Chinese Imperial Army, and said that he had killed the German envoy on specific orders from a royal prince but then refused to reveal the prince's identity. On 23 September En-hai was taken in irons to the spot where he had shot the ambassador. At 3 p.m., in the presence of German Generals von Lessel and Trotha, his sentence was read out in Chinese. En-hai was forced to kneel, and with the stroke of the executioner's sword, his head was separated from his body. China was forced to erect a monument in memory of von Ketteler with the inscription "Defend the Peace".

Not one of the many accounts of the fighting mentions a determining aspect, since it would have diminished the heroic stand of the legations. Why had there never been a full-scale attack by regular Imperial forces, supported by artillery? Why did the Chinese Army fail to overrun the embassy compound? They had the means, and they had the manpower. The Imperial armoury in Beijing had 60 cannon and thirty thousand elite soldiers in its garrison. All comes back to one man, a prince of royal blood, Jung Lu. As Commander-in-Chief of the Imperial forces, he foresaw the political consequences of a massacre of foreign embassy personnel: just as the Romans did to Carthage, or Hulagu Khan to Baghdad, Beijing would have been erased from the face of the earth. That would signal the end of China and its culture. So, and despite great pressures brought on him by the Imperial court, he refused to issue an order for attack – and thereby saved hundreds of foreigners and thousands of converts from certain death. His courageous stand was never appreciated, nor explained.

History should erect an even larger monument for Prince Jung Lu.

# CHRONICLE: 1911:

# THE KING IS DEAD!

The Boxer Rebellion, just like the Opium Wars before it, was at best an excuse for the empires of western Europe, Russia and Japan to take partial control over China in a policy they called "carving up the Chinese melon".

With the Boxer Protocol of 1901, Beijing was forced into signing a dictated peace. This dictate, which could have brought relief after years of violence and disaster, heralded in the 10 that were to come. The brutal and humiliating peace conditions laid down by the victors proved a Pyrrhic victory. By their overbearing treatment of China the European powers stirred up resentments for which the West is still paying today. For a century they had carried on the practice of handing out territory to suit the imperialist powers. The scramble for more and wider concessions caused disputes among the Allies and opened cracks in their future collaboration which showed up only four years later in a bloody war between Russia and Japan over the annexed Manchuria.

The Chinese Empire, which had survived thousands of years of glory and strife, lay mortally wounded. New political currents sprang up. In his interpretation of the Boxer Rebellion half a century later, Mao Zedong declared: "The peasants were the principal force in opposing imperialist aggression and the carving-up of China." Since Mao did not recognize religion, he did have a point. It was not the ruling class, and it was not the army, that had stood up to the foreigners. It was "the people". Their humiliating defeat instilled in the Chinese nation the strength to put an end to a despotic dynastic regime, and rid itself of foreign domination. The Europeans, led by the British lion, had established their supremacy over China and expanded their territory by measures indistinguishable from armed robbery. For a century they had found it easy to impose their will on a weak, crumbling Imperial China. The West did not foresee the future and certainly could not control it. As they stood by and watched, China began to burn.

"Calamities from within and aggression from without have come upon us in relentless succession." On her deathbed the Empress Dowager appointed Prince Jung Lu's two-year-old son Pu-yi as heir to the throne. Empress Cixi, this tough little woman who had ruled over a fourth of the human race, and saw her country forced into the world of a new twentieth century, died on 15 November 1908. It was her reaction to industrialization and intolerance of necessary reforms that pushed China's four hundred million toward change. The death of the Empress Dowager ended the dynastic age that had lasted for 4,760 years.

*Le roi est mort* ... "The Old China is dead – long live the New China!"

# ACT THREE

## 1911–49
## A Crack of Doom

*The epoch of the masses is the epoch of the colossal.*
*We are living under the brutal empire of the masses.*

—José Ortega y Gasset, *The Revolt of the Masses*

# 1

## WATERSHED

### 10 OCTOBER 1911, WUHAN, CHINA

With the Boxer Rebellion the nineteenth century drew to a close. But not its conflicts. Until fundamental economic, military and political inequalities were corrected, there was little hope for peace in that blood-dripping region. It called for new people with new ideas and new aspirations. New political thinking was coming to the fore; things were happening, and happening fast. While major European powers were sharpening their sabres, getting ready to slaughter one another on the poppy fields of Flanders, a bomb went off in Wuhan. It was not a big bomb, and nobody was killed. But its bang was heard across China.

On 9 October 1911 a dozen soldiers and student leaders joined in preparation for a local mutiny against a thoroughly corrupt local governor. For several months they had pilfered grenades and other explosives from the local arsenal in preparation for a show of muscle. While the explosives were being stacked in a harbour shed in Wuhan, a grenade rolled off the shelf, struck the floor and exploded. The bang was loud enough to bring the local police running. To their utter amazement, they discovered a shed stuffed with explosives, primed to start a bigger bang. A soldier caught at the scene revealed under torture the plan for a rebellion in the coming week and exposed the existence of an underground network. Within hours a number of local revolutionaries were rounded up and three leading activists publicly beheaded.

In an uprising filled with ineptness, nothing was more ironic than its timing. The plotters had twice postponed the date because the political brains behind the rising had missed his train! On the evening of 10 October 1911 a dozen non-commissioned officers involved in the planned putsch, fearing imminent arrest after the discovery of their arms cache, seized the Wuhan arsenal and came out shooting. Their initial aim was to eliminate the guard at the Zhonghemen Gate leading from the city and escape. However, by this time a few dozen more soldiers had taken up arms and joined the insurgents. Instead of making good their escape they rushed to Governor Li Yuan-hong's residential palace, burst through the front gate and shot his personal guard while the official ran out by a back door. A minor insurrection brought on by the panic of a dozen had claimed its first victim.

Suddenly provoked uprisings can have consequences, some good, some not so good, unrelated to the original aims of the insurgents. An accidental explosion sounded the death knell to four millennia of Heaven's Mandate.

"Good iron is not used to make nails, and good men are not used to make soldiers." This ancient Chinese proverb got it all wrong about what happened on a night in October 1911, when the much-overlooked ordinary soldier stepped to the fore. Amazingly enough, what had been feared most by the insurgents never took place: the Western powers remained passive since their commercial interests were not endangered. The West could only gain by sitting back and allowing a further weakening of the Manchu monarchy; only this time they badly misjudged the situation. This was not just one of the perennial shoot-'em-ups; this turned into a modern, well-led revolution which could, and in fact did, lead to an upheaval in the political and social set-up of the country, and thus influenced the future course of Asia.

With the "10-10 Revolution" (which started on 10 October), both colonial and imperial control over China dissolved. A desire for self-determination, and waves of passionate nationalism, together produced a dreadful offspring. This new China on the rise was bound to want to rid itself of its old trade concessions, reclaim its abandoned territories and flex its muscle. *Au revoir*, dynastic Empire, and goodbye foreign imperialism. The country emerged from an internal conflict stronger and with a quickened national character. An outburst by a few became the rallying cry of the masses.

China had reached a great watershed.

The story of the outbreak of the 10-10 Revolution, reprinted from the *New York Herald* in a Colorado paper, caught the eye of a young Chinese taking breakfast in a Denver hotel. He thought it most unlikely that a handful of privates would succeed where generals had failed. Sun Yat-sen (Sun Zhongshan), the "Father of China's Revolution", was educated in Hawaii. He became infected with the American example of democracy, went back to his country at the turn of the century and began stirring up an anti-monarchy movement.

Sun Yat-sen based his programme on the Three Principles of the People: "nationalism, democracy and people's livelihood". To achieve that it would take a nationalist rebellion with the goal of expelling the remnants of the hated Manchu dynasty; a democratic movement to set up a truly democratic Chinese Republic based on the American example; and a social revolution to equalize land rights and wealth. He returned to China and formed the *Tongmenhui*, or Revolutionary Alliance. His movement's rallying cry was: "China is the China of the Chinese". With a price on his head, he fled to Japan and from there to Hong Kong. The British authorities had no time for a Chinese firebrand dabbling in popular revolution among the crown colony's locals. He was dispatched to Britain, having given his solemn promise not to engage in political agitation while there. The first thing he did when he arrived in London was to confront Beijing's Imperial representative at the Chinese Diplomatic Mission. The ambassador's bodyguards seized him and locked him in a cupboard until he could be bundled into a suitcase and smuggled aboard a cargo vessel on its return to China, where certain death awaited the revolutionary-on-the-run.

However, Sun Yat-sen had taken a precautionary step: he informed two English law professors of his perilous undertaking. When they failed to hear from him, they contacted London's Metropolitan Police, who refused to interfere in a "diplomatic matter beyond our jurisdiction". The professors did the next best thing; they went with the story to the newspapers. The tabloids feed on the unusual, and the disappearance of "the great Chinese revolutionary" – although Sun Yat-sen was all but unknown outside a Nanjing police station – made headlines: "Prominent Chinese abducted in the centre of London".

The papers stressed that Sun Yat-sen's arrest on British soil without its being ordered by the British authorities was a serious infringement of HM Government's jurisdiction and could not be tolerated. Forced by the press, the British authorities exerted pressure, first on the local level, then via Britain's ambassador in Beijing. After several days of haggling during which the Chinese delegation in London found itself besieged by a news-hungry horde of reporters, Sun Yat-sen stepped from the door, waving his arms in triumph. This feat established him as the foremost Chinese revolutionary.

With the 10-10 Revolution taking root, a new generation was soon to take up important posts. A young man, an ardent supporter of Sun Yat-sen's social programme, learned about it while residing in a military academy in Japan: Chiang Kai-shek (Jiang Jieshi) rushed back to become the chief of staff of the new Republican Army in Hangzhou. And in Changsha a 17-year-old student followed the birth of a popular movement in the local newspaper: Mao Zedong.

If soldiers were the spearhead of the revolution, believing in their special destiny, the shrewd Sun Yat-sen put together a presentation with which he could announce a Chinese Republic. In December 1911 he made his celebrated entry into Nanjing, and on 1 January 1912 he was inaugurated as the first president of the Republic of China. The final act in the drama took place on 12 February that year. The abdication of the last Emperor of China, the child-emperor Pu-yi (Prince Jung Lu's son), took place in a degrading atmosphere for an heir to Celestial Rule. With a simple phrase he was forced to sign the end to his Heavenly Mandate: "The will of providence is clear and the people's wishes are plain". It brought down the curtain on four millennia of Empire. This momentous event was covered by nothing more than a single line in *The Times*: "Feb 15. At noon today the Chinese cruisers in Shanghai fired a 21-gun salute and hoisted the revolutionary flag, formally recognizing the new Republic of China."

But what a republic! China had disintegrated into warlord principalities, run by brutal and corrupt dictators. Sun Yat-sen's dream of a united, democratic China seemed condemned when he died in 1924. A brilliant young general came to the rescue: General Chiang Kai-shek, fanatically devoted to Sun Yat-sen's vision of a united China.

Chiang Kai-shek was born in Xikou on 31 October 1887, which made him six years older than his nemesis, Mao Zedong. His mentor Sun Yat-sen sent Chiang to Moscow to study the Bolsheviks' political and military system. With Sun Yat-sen's health fading, Chiang used the following years to take a leading role in revolutionary activities; he cemented his relationship with the president by marrying Sun's wife's younger sister, Soong May-ling.

When, on 12 March 1925, Sun Yat-sen died, Chiang was the first to know and immediately arranged a palace coup in which he assumed leadership of the Guomindang (Kuomintang), the National People's Party. His initial task was to establish his role as China's leader by unifying a parcelled-out country. He did this with his Guomindang Nationalist Army and in a series of hard-fought battles he crushed the northern warlords. By 1928 Sun's disciple made his tutor's dream come true. Generalissimo Chiang Kai-shek established a United Nationalist Front with its capital in Nanjing. For the first time China was truly a republic.

And then China had two leaders, both brilliant and equally ruthless: the Nationalist Chiang and the Communist Mao. Mao Zedong (Mao Tse-tung) was born on 26 December 1893 in Chao-chan, a small village in Hunan, in the south of China. An old story has it that this region is three-tenths mountains, six-tenths water and one-tenth valleys, a place where peasants harvested their rice barefoot in the fertile mud of the terraced paddies, their heads protected from the burning sun under conical straw hats. Mao Jen-chen, Mao's father, had started out as a soldier and returned after one of the many wars with a small fortune. He was quite severe, but his mother, Wen ki-mei, was as gentle as can be, an illiterate woman of a certain beauty, devoted only to her family. She was treated no better, no worse, than all peasant women, according to the ancient Chinese wisdom: "A married woman is a mare which walks in front of the plough and which should be whipped from time to time."

Mao's youth is embellished with many fables; only one thing is certain: he was born into a period of open rebellion. At school he was made to feel the injustice of the age-old caste system. For a boy of simple background there was no future; mandarins provided from their social group state officials charged with looking after the empire's finances, and they selected judges and war leaders. In fact, with their prejudice and their corruption, they were a race apart. The law was a farce: any rich man could buy a favourable judgement; and as for generals, they used their armies to oppress the population and amass personal wealth by extortion.

Mao co-founded a student militia, the Society of Studies for a New Man, which was to become absorbed into the Chinese Communist Party. In 1918 the 25-year-old Mao gained a degree which qualified him to become a teacher, but instead he went to Beijing and obtained a post as a library assistant. He visited lectures by Professor Li Ta-chao on Russia's October Revolution. These proved to be decisive for the fertile mind of young Mao. Contrary to the Russian example, the seeds of a Marxist Party of China were not rooted in the proletariat, but in the intellectual society, since an urban proletariat did not exist. In 1921 a small group hired a lake boat, pretending to be tourists, and aboard this they founded the Communist Party of China.

By 1927 the Chinese Communist Party (CCP), from its original three hundred members in 1924, had mushroomed to three million adherents; it now counted a considerable representation among the rural population and the nascent urban working class. Chiang Kai-shek recognized this fact, and he entered into an uneasy alliance with the Communists to do away quickly and bloodily with a series of warlords holding Shanghai and Nanjing. But with his allies he had trouble from the outset. Within a few months their co-operation ended. In the early hours of 12 April 1927, under a pretext of suppressing an internal plot, Chiang ordered "the bloodbath of Shanghai" to purge the CCP. Countrywide massacres took place; tens of thousands of party members were rounded up, taken by the truckload into public places and shot; others were dumped into rivers or thrown into the furnaces of locomotives.

In Changcha, Mao raised the masses to march on Shanghai, but his plan was betrayed and his march stopped amid rivers of blood. Mao was captured and condemned to death, but managed to slip away. Having barely escaped death, he was chastised by Communist leaders in hiding over his failure to lead a successful rising, and excluded from the Central Committee of the CCP. He never forgave this humiliation.

Another who escaped the bloodbath was Zhou Enlai, who now joined with Mao to create a hard core of what was to become the power elite of the Party. This opened a new chapter in Mao's political life. He gathered whatever loyal supporters he had left and installed himself in the inaccessible Ching-kang-chan mountain range, where he acted more like a preacher than a political leader. "The holy fire of revolution is not something illusory and unattainable, but is born and takes life in an infant in the womb of his mother."

If Chiang Kai-shek's coup had done away with the Communists in the cities and made him undisputed president, the Communist movement was far from dead. Even so, at this time Mao was more of a nuisance than a danger. The Nationalist Army had Mao and his men encircled. In November 1931, after a heated discussion with Stalin's Comintern envoy and the Soviet agent's blatant attempt to tie the Chinese Communist forces into the Russian orbit and keep them under Moscow's tutelage, Mao proclaimed his independence by forming a Soviet Chinese Republic with himself as its first political commissar. In Jiangxi and Sichuan over 20 million Chinese were now under Communist control.

Despite a number of setbacks, and facing almost impossible odds, Mao strongly believed that his guerrilla warfare would ultimately end in a popular rising and victory. In this he was fully supported by his diplomatic genius, Zhou Enlai, who never looked at the civil war in terms of a series of military successes, but saw it as the political confrontation of two opposing systems. By contrast, Chiang, quite aside from his costly political aberrations, demonstrated his fundamental misunderstanding of irregular warfare and the guerrilla threat at the start of the civil war by sending his troops into Communist-held territory without basic preparation or training for guerrilla warfare. His "scorched earth" policy was a political folly which imposed a severe handicap on his generals.

Close behind his advancing front line followed Chiang's political commissars, who implemented the directives of total repression with inhuman zeal. In areas which had been abandoned by the retreating Communist forces, the armies of their own regime, supposedly liberating the local population, drove off their herds of cattle and burned their villages and wheat fields, and then treated the locals like savages. The peasants were left with just one option: to survive, they took refuge in the swamps and forests until they were given weapons to defend themselves.[1]

By 1933, with the "Red Menace in China" growing and fear spreading of a general Bolshevik takeover in Europe and Asia, the Western powers reacted; their long-term strategy was to combat International Communism. They thought that the Chinese Communists should be confronted and contained, much as the Soviet Union was treated. Chiang's Nationalists were given robust military support. Britain and the USA offered the Guomindang financial aid, and Nazi Germany sent its military instructors.

Chiang Kai-shek went on the offensive; General Hans von Seeckt, his German military adviser, opted for an enemy encirclement over a full-out frontal attack. Chiang assembled one million men, 150 planes and batteries of artillery. An elaborate network of bunkers and wire entanglements encircled the Communist main base in the mountainous region of Jiangxi. Within a year the Communists had lost half of the territory they had controlled, plus sixty thousand of their best fighters. Von Seeckt's strategy worked, and Chiang's Guomindang now had the capacity to eliminate the Communists.

However, by accepting Western aid, Chiang Kai-shek became for ever tainted with the century-old stigma of a Chinese having allied himself with the hated "people from across the sea". This fact was to weigh heavily in the years ahead.

In the summer of 1934 Communist leaders met in Juichin. Mao, who lacked the power to swing the committee's decision, said there was but one option: slip through the tightening noose and march north, toward the border of a "brotherly state", the Soviet Union. Mao was taking a calculated risk; Stalin was notoriously non-supportive of red revolutions abroad, fearful of an interference with his own long-term plans. The decision for the big escape came so suddenly, and left so little time for preparation, that disaster was in the making. Eighty-six thousand armed men, thirty thousand civilians and porters and 24 women set out without plans or preparations. The first news of the Communist breakout to reach the West came from the *Manchester Guardian*'s Nanjing correspondent:

Oct 21. Nanjing, China. Chinese rebel Communist forces, besieged and defeated by the Nationalist armies of General Chiang Kai-shek, are attempting to break out of encirclement. It will not be an easy task, for the Nationalist commander with 700,000 troops has sealed off their Kiangsi stronghold with a network of barbed wire and concrete block-houses.

The Communists, led by a Hunan peasant named Mao Tse-tung and estimated to be 100,000 strong, have begun a desperate attempt to fight their way out ...

Actually it wasn't "the peasant" Mao Zedong but Otto Braun, a Stalin-dispatched Comintern envoy, who started thousands on this gigantic odyssey, celebrated in years to come in poem and legend as the heroic epic of the revolution.

One of the key episodes in the "Long March" was an effort depicted in heroic posters: the storming of the Dadu Gorge Bridge. Mao's advance guard under Lin Biao (later vice president of China) had reached the River Dadu, only to find the only available passage blocked by three Nationalist Army regiments with heavy artillery support. Another crossing had to be found. A local peasant told Lin Biao that some miles to the West was an ancient suspension bridge, the Luding Bridge, strung precariously across a raging river. Nationalist military engineers had removed the wooden planking, but not the bridge's chains spanning the canyon. From his position above the gorge, Lin Biao looked down on to his objective; the road curved down to what was left of the bridge. He stared through his binoculars but could not see any explosive charges attached to the chains. However, the hillside across the bridge was dotted with pillboxes, mortars and machine-guns. Lin Biao had no artillery to silence the menace. Taking the bridge called for a high-wire act, crossing hand over hand along a rusty suspension chain, beneath hundreds of metres of sheer cliffs filled with fissures and caves and pillboxes, and under constant enemy fire. Lin Biao had no choice. "There is no easy way across, and no place for tactical finesse. We've got to do it head-on, that's all. This is the end spurt. You must make it across."

In the hour before dawn on 17 April 1935, the assault was launched. The first units reached the anchored chains. In an instant dozens were hanging on them like ripe fruit, trying to make it hand-over-hand across the river. Why did the enemy not react? A single machine-gun could have stopped the crossing. Suddenly Lin Biao had his answer: a magnesium flare, fired from one of the bunkers, arced out and lit up the chains. In what seemed a single blast, the canyon erupted with mortar and small-arms fire. Where only moments before utter silence prevailed, now hundreds of projectiles, mortar shells and tracer bullets came shrieking down. The rusty chains thudded and swayed under the force of converging tracers. Those already crossing on the chains were lifted off by the impact of many bullets and crashed into the gorge, to be swept off by the raging torrent, while on the approach to the bridge the bodies piled up. An incessant noise of gunfire swept across the gorge and echoed from rock face to rock face, greatly magnified by the gorge's narrow walls and the cliffs spewing rock chips and ricochets.

Ever more men replaced their fallen comrades; dozens scrambled across the chains until some made it across and, in a sacrificial attack carried out with grenades, jumped into the enemy trenches and pillboxes, blowing themselves up together with the Nationalist soldiers. Others, lowered down the sheer cliff on ropes, tossed grenades into the bunkers. Lin Biao's men had squeezed out some breathing space and were now methodically wiping out the mortars and machine-guns. The initial toehold on the high ground rolled up the Nationalists' defence line. Once the crossing was achieved, the firing stopped. The survivors lay down, wrapped themselves in their padded jackets, and shut their eyes, while others were already laying wooden planking beneath the suspension chains. This legendary struggle opened the way toward the north for Mao's Red Army.

Mao, and less than a fifth of those who had set off on the Long March, survived the ordeal. Behind them lay a ravaged countryside of fire-scarred villages and unburied corpses. Eighteen mountain chains, 24 major rivers and seven thousand kilometres later, the remnants of the Red Army, reduced to unwashed, unfed, staggering ghosts, reached a spot near the Great Wall in Shaanxi province. A haggard-looking, 42-year-old schoolteacher, wasted like the rest, had led his Communists into the Promised Land.

"The biggest armed propaganda tour in history", as contemporaries called the Long March, was a military masterpiece, but even more so, a great moral success. It demonstrated Mao's Communists' incredible will to survive in the most arduous conditions. Chiang Kai-shek found out that he had greatly underestimated the military capabilities of his opponent. It should also have told the Western powers something about the stamina of guerrilla fighters and the leadership qualities of Mao Zedong. He had accomplished his two major goals: victory over incredible odds, and both independence and support from Stalin's Soviet Union.

China's civil war confirmed the two opponents' legacy of having created a more bitterly divided country and a more chaotic, fractured world. To suppress Communism, Chiang had accepted Western military support. Mao countered by distancing himself from Moscow's imperialist influence, and proved his charisma to form a solid movement around him. If Mao could achieve this, he would go on to even greater things.

At the end of their Long March the remnants of Mao's Communist forces found themselves once again sealed off in the mountainous region of Shaanxi, encircled and isolated by the Northern Nationalist Army under a brutal Manchurian warlord, Marshal Zhang Xueliang, who was running his private little war under the overall command of Chiang Kai-shek. A turncoat had betrayed Mao's hideout, which could be wiped out with ease. The Generalissimo gave his marshal strict orders to annihilate Mao's Communists, providing him with artillery, munitions and enough men to achieve the task. Yet time and again Zhang Xueliang failed to act, claiming all sorts of problems; he said that the troops at his disposal were too few and ill-trained and the Communists were a far more powerful enemy than he had been led to believe. In fact, the truth was quite different.

This crucial juncture in the civil war saw the entry of one of the all-time great diplomats, Zhou Enlai. He paid Marshal Zhang Xueliang a secret visit and called for a suspension of the fighting. Already in March 1936, Zhou Enlai had proposed to Xueliang the formation of a National Salvation Association to combat the Japanese in Manchuria, which also happened to be Xueliang's family fiefdom. As added enticement, Zhou flattered the vain warlord with an invitation to take charge of the combined military command. A spy on Xueliang's staff informed Chiang Kai-shek of the secret meeting with Zhou Enlai and the Generalissimo decided to put things right. He was preoccupied with the immediate internal Communist peril, not with some distant Japanese threat.

On 7 December 1936 Chiang Kai-shek flew to Xi'an, Marshal Zhang Xueliang's headquarters town. On his arrival the Generalissimo was shocked to find a thousand rifle-wielding soldiers who blamed him for his inaction against the Japanese in Manchuria. This hostile reception bordered on mutiny by troops who were theoretically under his command. From the airport Chiang Kai-shek was whisked in a motorcade to a neighbouring village which had been emptied of its inhabitants to serve as temporary quarters for the "comfort of the Generalissimo" and his personal staff. It was there, on 12 December, that the Xi'an Incident took place.

Early that morning a senior officer of Zhang Xueliang's command – certainly acting on specific orders – surrounded Chiang Kai-shek's villa with his troops. Shooting broke out between the leader's personal guards and Zhang's soldiers. This exchange of fire lasted for two hours, during which time the Generalissimo managed to slip out – some reports claimed that he ran away in his nightshirt, while others spoke of his bravely returning fire. Whatever the truth, Chiang Kai-shek was captured and brought to Xi'an, where his captors locked him up in a secluded part of Zhang Xueliang's compound. Marshal Zhang did not visit his exalted prisoner, but someone else did.

Chiang Kai-shek was stunned when early next morning a delegation from the Communist Party, headed by none other than Zhou Enlai, showed up in Xi'an. For once the roles had been reversed. During the Shanghai massacre of 1927 the man on whose head Chiang the victor had put a price now confronted Chiang the prisoner. If the Generalissimo expected the worst, nothing of the kind happened – just as nothing ever came of what was discussed during their brief encounter. It is likely that Zhou Enlai's astute diplomacy convinced Chiang Kai-shek that, rather than fighting each other, it was more profitable to form an alliance in the face of a much greater menace that had begun to send its dark clouds over China. And so it came about that in the early hours of 23 February 1937 a telegram landed on the desk of Generalissimo Chiang Kai-shek, sent by the Head of the National Revolutionary Guard, Mao Zedong, who proposed a military co-operation to defend Motherland China against a new foreign peril – from the Empire of the Rising Sun.

Had Marshal Zhang Xueliang followed Chiang Kai-shek's instructions, it is doubtful that Mao and his devastated Communist forces could have survived one more onslaught by Chiang's Nationalist forces. After the Xi'an Incident, this was a forlorn hope. Now Mao and the Communists would survive.

# 2

# SATURDAY, BLOODY SATURDAY

## 14 AUGUST 1937, SHANGHAI, CHINA

At midnight on 7 July 1937 the first shot was fired in what was to become the Second World War in the Pacific. Lieutenant Ichiki Kiyono, a company commander in Japan's Imperial Army, acting upon specific orders from his superior commander, General Koichiro Tashiro, stormed across the Lukouchiao railway bridge at the head of his troop. This unprovoked action received worldwide attention as the Marco Polo Bridge Incident.

The "Chinese provocation" happened when a Japanese soldier vanished into the dark, and, according to Japanese militaries, was kidnapped by a Chinese patrol. In fact, the man had left his bivouac to relieve himself without telling anyone. It can be said that a man's taking a pee escalated into the Sino-Japanese War. Not that it took much of an incident to set off what had been long planned, but this soldier's "disappearance" was a perfectly good reason for the militant Japanese. In pursuance of their policy of domination of China, units of the Japanese Imperial Army crossed a bridge leading from their satrap state of Manchukuo on to Chinese soil. Supported by battalions of Renault tanks and a modern bomber force, three hundred thousand Japanese marched against two million Chinese soldiers lacking just about everything, including shells and bullets. The Chinese were good and brave fighters, but their weapons and uniforms were from another age. Even so, this ill-equipped army fought much better than has been reported.

With tension building, China had repeatedly asked for Western support against a threatening aggressor conducting live-fire manoeuvres within a mile of the China–Manchukuo border. China's ambassadors brought the issue before the League of Nations. A blind world refused China support in what it called an "inter-Asian affair".

In 1935 Shanghai was declared a demilitarized zone. The city was divided into a major Chinese sector and a smaller International Concession with its palatial hotels and their famous bars along the waterfront, known as the Bund, which had replaced tattoo parlours and honky-tonk joints known for their spectacular drunkenness and nightly brawls between crews from rival trading nations. Abiding by the Convention for International Concessions, China had no choice but to allow warships of concession nations to lie at anchor in the River Whangpoo, off the Bund. The visitors on 14 August 1937 were two warships, the USS *Augusta* and a three-funnelled heavy cruiser, the Japanese HIJMS *Idzumo*. It was a Saturday morning and all was calm around the various war and merchant vessels in the harbour, though farther downriver Chinese troops were preparing to scuttle several old coastal tramps to prevent more Japanese naval units from approaching Shanghai. If the river was calm, the city was not. Rumours of an all-out Japanese attack on Shanghai had led to a general panic. First hundreds, then hundreds of thousands, tried to flee the city. The North Railway Station was taken by storm. A human tide swamped bus depots and harbour facilities, with people storming trains, buses and ships in a desperate attempt to get out of the city. For days now the quays had been black with people.

In the early hours of that August day, China's military high command launched a military operation. It began when its ground troops moved into the Japanese trade concession and encircled the trade commission's offices and its warehouses. One of the problems in this act was the reaction of the *Idzumo*. It was one thing to take on unarmed Japanese merchants, but another to face up to 14-inch battleship guns. The intervention by a French battle fleet 70 years before lingered on in Shanghai's collective memory.

Father Jacquinot, a French missionary, had gone to tend to his flock of Chinese Catholics, who were trying to find refuge in the city's international settlement. The only other foreigners he met were some members of the European Volunteer Corps and Karl Engelbacher, a Swiss photographer taking pictures of the dense crowd. The priest fought his way through the throng to the broad boulevard with its concrete wall separating city from sea, until he found his parishioners near the Cathay Hotel on the Bund. At mid-morning on this bright and clear Saturday he heard the heavy throb of aircraft engines. Biplanes of the Chinese Air Force appeared high in the sky, heading straight for the port; slung between each plane's landing gear was a big bomb, big enough to sink a battleship. Their target was the *Idzumo*. The crowd looked skyward as the planes passed overhead, then four black objects detached themselves and came tumbling down. There was no warning, just a sudden cataract of sound. A yellow flash, a

clap of thunder, then nothing. Then deep thuds and shattering noises ...
Four bombs had exploded – not on the Japanese battleship, but among the
huge crowd of refugees.

Thrown to the ground by one of the explosions, Father Jacquinot was
momentarily concussed. After a few moments he scrambled to his feet and
staggered around stunned. Blood was running down his body and soaked
his shirt like sweat. He touched himself all over and found he was unhurt.
Then he looked about; the chaos was so great that his mind went blank. It
was a scene of unspeakable carnage: hundreds of dead, and many more
wounded, some terribly; people with bits of their face blown away, limbs
torn from bodies, baskets and shoes mingled with arms and legs in pools
of blood, splintered bones sticking through skin, blood and more blood,
gushing from terrible wounds and flowing everywhere. Some were sitting
around in shock amid the first horrid screams of the suffering. Others were
staggering and stumbling over bodies. A poisonous yellow haze cast an
eerie light over a carpet of corpses as if in the aftermath of some medieval
battle. Then the sulphurous cloud drifted out to sea and the full extent of
the disaster became visible.

The corner of the Bund at the Pootung was on fire. Two bombs had
fallen between the Cathay Hotel and the Palace Hotel. They killed over
four hundred, including a few dozen foreigners. Two more bombs exploded
at Yu-Ya-Ching Road and Edward VII Avenue, and at Race Course Road,
where huge crowds were jammed together in the vain hope of finding
safety in the international settlement. These blasts killed another 1,300.
The first rescue crews on the scene waded though a horror of bleeding
human wreckage, the smell of cordite and blood and vomit, with slices of
hot metal burned into walls and living flesh.

Shocked Western consuls dispatched a flood of cables; pushed into it by
their own panic, they speculated that the bombing run was, as one put it, "a
deliberate attempt by China to provoke the international community into
joining China's fight against the Japanese aggressor". This misinterpretation
of what in fact was a stupid accident was picked up by the sensation-hungry
Western press and caused an outcry in Europe and America.

For a hapless China, those four bombs were a tragedy. But they were
only the beginning. Shortly before the explosions, a call had gone out from
the Japanese consul in Shanghai announcing an incursion by Chinese
troops into its concession. Japan immediately jumped on this as a valid
reason to attack Shanghai. A seaborne force made a landing 30 kilometres
south of the city; with a resounding *"Banzai"*, Japanese Marine units
attacked the fortifications in and around Shanghai. Reuters News Agency
reported:

Aug 29. Shanghai is today experiencing all the horrors of modern war. A pall of smoke hangs over the great port, set afire by waves of Japanese aircraft dropping incendiary bombs. Air power is being used with naked ferocity to clear the way for their advancing army ... as fires spread to the Shanghai international settlement, 2,000 British women and children were evacuated aboard the P & O liner *Rajputana*. A British battalion has arrived to reinforce the settlement garrison which is in a highly exposed position ... The greatest slaughter of the campaign so far came when bombs from Chinese planes attacking Japanese warships fell on an amusement park, killing over 1,000 ... Today the British Government protested strongly after Sir Hugh Knatchbull-Hugessen, the British ambassador to China, was seriously wounded in a Japanese air raid.

The battle for Shanghai lasted three months and cost two hundred and seventy thousand Chinese military casualties. Despite this sacrificial defence, the city fell on 5 November 1937. Japanese soldiers roamed about looting, killing and blowing up buildings. Hospitals were emptied of the wounded, water conduits were dynamited to cut the city's water supply and warehouses set on fire to deprive the population of food. The number of civilian casualties that resulted from the fighting and the famine is unknown.

Four bombs – but four explosions heard around the globe. Nearly two thousand civilians died immediately or of their wounds afterward. Most of them were Chinese. There were also 21 Europeans – and this number made all the difference! Had it not been for the fact that there were relatively few European deaths, the Western nations might have put their support behind China and thereby averted a bigger global holocaust.

Shanghai's "Bloody Saturday" was the grim forerunner of the much greater slaughter to come.

# 3

# THE RAPE OF NANJING

## 13 DECEMBER 1937, NANJING, CAPITAL OF NATIONALIST CHINA

"This is the day of a New Renaissance for Asia. The Imperial Way is shining forth," declared Lieutenant General Iwane Matsui, of the Army of the Empire of the Rising Sun, as he rode into Nanjing, along a street cratered by shellfire, on that December day. "Tens of thousands of bones will become ashes when one general achieves his fame."

The view of death was inescapable. Nowhere could the cruelty of the conflict between Chinese and Japanese be seen more clearly, unless tears blinded one's eyes. Nanjing looked as if it had been smitten by some enraged divinity. Scores of men, stripped bare, their ankles in mud and guarded by soldiers with planted bayonets, carved out gooey scoops of soil for yet one more mass grave; nearby were heaped piles of dark earth, mute monuments to the tens of thousands of bodies that had already been interred. Pushcarts delivered charred or bloated corpses with grim regularity. In districts where shattered buildings blocked roads corpses were simply stacked in piles, doused with diesel oil and set alight; black smoke from the giant funeral pyres pervaded the city with their nause-ating smell of burning flesh. Where bodies lay unburied and rigor mortis made the arms of the dead stretch out beseechingly as if calling for a final assistance, empty-eyed children wandered aimlessly the rubble-strewn streets in search of their mothers. Human tragedy was played out here, as were greed, crime and indifference. In widespread looting, street gangs stripped rings and jewellery from bodies lying among the debris of their homes.

Japanese elite troops blocked off large sections of the city to prevent foreigners from becoming witness to their heinous atrocities. In a land-scape of rubble and ongoing executions, Japanese officers had their pictures taken as they stood in front of their headless victims, brandishing their samurai swords. "A sword lives by its skilful handling."

For five months the Nationalist Army of Chiang Kai-shek had been in full retreat. It had been routed at Beijing, Shanghai, then Soochow, and now its capital, Nanjing, was menaced.

"Nanjing must be held," ordered the President.

"I don't think it is wise to hold the city," General Li Zongren dared to differ. "From a strategic point of view, Nanjing is of little value. We must avoid useless sacrifices; the morale of the troop is already low. I vote for abandoning Nanjing."

General Li was right, and everyone knew it. Yet nobody dared to back him up. The only sound in the room came from the ceiling fan and the heavy breathing of senior officers. Seated at the head of the table, Chiang Kai-shek looked tormented and nervous. "Correct, General. Strategically Nanjing is not important, but Nanjing is a symbol. What better message can we give our 400 million people than by keeping the White Sun banner flying over our nation's capital?"

It was not a military but a political decision. The President's order stood. Liu Fei, his chief of operations, and Bai Chongxi, his chief of the general staff, were told to hold Nanjing at all costs.

"The wish of the President shall be done," promised Tang Shengzhi, nominated commandant of the Nanjing garrison. With one sentence, tragedy was set in motion.

On 2 December Lieutenant General Iwane Matsui, commanding Japan's Central Army, issued the order for an all-out attack: "The divisional commanders of the 10th Imperial Army are instructed to launch a combined offensive against Nanjing on 5 December. Units of the Imperial Navy will support terrestrial units in breaking the Jiangyin defence cordon and opening the Yangtze waterway. In parallel to the main push, a land force will advance along the north bank of the river to cut the enemy's rail communication between Tianjin and Pukow."

The Japanese Army was on its way. On 9 December Lieutenant General Matsui ordered his crack divisions into a frontal assault on Nanjing's outer perimeter. The attack opened with the screams of a thousand shells falling on to a key strongpoint, the Zijin Shan (Purple-Gold Mountain). This demonstration of cannon fire, the Japanese expected, would push the commandant of Nanjing, General Tang Shengzhi, into instant surrender. But, despite enormous casualties, the Chinese stubbornly hung on to the steep slopes and deep caves.

Then the 16th Japanese Corps launched a *tokko* (suicide attack) against the Guanghua Gate, but was repulsed, suffering heavy losses. Planes appeared over the city, loaded not with bombs but propaganda leaflets encouraging the defenders to surrender by promising them immunity. The deadline for the capitulation was set for noon on 10 December. To leave the defending troops in no doubt, General Tang Shengzhi issued an order: "All units must resist resolutely the taking of their position. You are not to relinquish one foot of our territory, as even a single case will prove disastrous to the rest of the troop."

At 11.30 a.m. on 10 December the deputy commander of Japan's Central Army, General Akira Muto, accompanied by his interpreter, Kimidaira, was driven into the vicinity of the Zhongshan Gate to accept the surrender.

At noon the gate remained shut. Muto turned to Kimidaira and said: "Now we shall reduce Nanjing by the sword."

Japanese tanks advanced toward the Sun Yat-sen Monument and the first shells slammed into the city centre, killing many civilians. Some Chinese units, abandoned by their officers and left without ammunition and food, flooded into town in such great numbers that it seemed as if the entire front had collapsed. One of the arteries, Hanzhong Street, leading to the Hanzhong and Caochang Gates, became the cork in the bottle, jammed with horse carts, stalled cars, terrified city dwellers, refugee peasants – hundreds of thousands of men and women. The other exit road, North Zhongshan Street, which passed Jinling University and the imposing Court of Justice, was also dense with people. All were headed for the last open exit: the Gate of Peace.

General Tang Shengzhi contacted the international community to ask for a neutral representative to arrange a cease-fire, which would allow the civilian population to evacuate the city. The German Edward Sperling offered to undertake the mission, and contacted General Matsui, who said: "They should have thought of that when I gave them a chance."

With his refusal, all hope was gone. General Tang Shengzhi called up the commander of the 78th Guomindang Nationalist Army, which was little more than the remnants of one division, the 36th, posted to protect the Xiaguan ferry crossing. "What's your situation? Is your army holding up?" he asked.

"What army?" laughed General Song Xilian. "All I have left are three thousand demoralized recruits, ready to jump into the river and swim across."

"Nobody is allowed across the river," Tang Shengzhi yelled down the line. "Do I make myself clear?"

"Abundantly, General." And with that, Song Xilian issued the ill-fated order that was to condemn thousands to certain death: "Shut all exit gates!"

From the distance came a rumbling noise, echoing down the narrow, canyon-like streets. The ground vibrated to the clatter of steel cleats. "Tanks!" someone yelled, and the crowd surged ahead like a tidal wave. A town was on the run before a mechanized Japanese juggernaut. Mothers' hands reached for their children as the motion of the masses swept them along. A little girl cried out for her mother; nobody took any notice of her. A boy went down, his breath crushed from his body by trampling feet. Men struck out blindly, trying to break through the weaving throng. Everyone fought to get away. Fleeing Nationalist troops, their faces contorted with snarls of rage, used their rifle butts to force their way through the masses; not even the looters stopped to take what was readily available. Like some gigantic battering ram, a river of humans reached the Yijiang and Heping Men Gates to find them barred. Their Chinese brothers were blocking the gates and the Japanese were moving in from the rear. What irony of fate had called this place of hell, already awash with the blood of thousands, trampled, shot and now crushed against barred doors, the Gate of Peace? Its name would stand only for the peace of eternal sleep.

The city was on fire, with thick blacks clouds of choking smoke hanging over the rooftops. The lucky ones died quickly, killed by a falling bomb or exploding shell. They were saved the coming horror. People rushed about in the red glow of the flames. In the streets, corpses lay everywhere. Apartment blocks ignited and petrol tanks exploded.

The situation at the Xiaguan ferry crossing had taken on desperate proportions. Soldiers milled around the river's edge like mad hornets, shooting one another for the slimmest chance to get into a boat. Little did they know that all prospect of reaching refuge on the opposite shore of the Yangtze was gone; the Japanese Kunisaki division was already dug in, lying in wait with machine-guns at the ready. From their positions on the conquered ramparts, Japanese infantry fired heavy machine-guns, whipping the surface of the river into froth. From everywhere came the screams of the wounded. Farther north, at Yanzi ji (Swallow Cliff), Lieutenant Wang Jinmin shot a man in a rowing boat who refused to approach the shore. A soldier jumped into the river and steered the boat toward the shore. Then, struck by a bullet, he disappeared beneath the waves. When the boat drifted ashore, so many jumped on it that it capsized and everyone drowned. General Chen Yiding managed to escape through an underground passage in the Mausoleum of King Wu. By clinging to a piece of driftwood he reached the far shore, to find, of the six thousand men under his command, only eight alive.

It was now 8 a.m. on a bright, sunny 13 December. Lieutenant General Matsui, wearing a starched uniform and polished boots and riding a white charger, entered the city through the Zhongua Gate. He addressed his wildly cheering soldiers: "This is the day of a renaissance for Asia."

Nanjing had fallen. A new sun was rising: the blood-red Sun of the Empire of Japan. The horror was about to begin.

The worst fate, short of instant death by bomb or bullet, was infection. Open wounds, gashed by shrapnel, sliced up by falling tiles, shards of glass or jagged pieces of corrugated tin, were infected by the myriad of flies rising from the many unburied corpses; even the slightest wounds led to gangrene and tetanus. With no medicine and not enough doctors, people were left to die on street corners. While the victorious Japanese hoisted their flag over the martyred city, there were two places still relatively untouched: the International Security Zone of the foreign concessions, and Jinling University, run by a 35-year-old Chinese Christian named Hang Liuw. Here tens of thousands of panicked refugees had jammed into a compound intended to provide residence for a few hundred students, their only defence a flag displaying the Red Cross in a black circle.

In the name of humanity, professors, priests, doctors, foreign trade representatives and remaining diplomats formed the International Committee for the Security Zone of Nanjing. Its president was the German Johann Rabe, the Siemens representative for China, with Father John Magee and 16 others, German, American, British and Danish, managing the two-mile-square zone that would eventually provide shelter for two hundred and ninety thousand civilian refugees. They informed the commandant of the Japanese occupation forces of the existence of this neutral, extra-territorial zone, out of bounds to military personnel according to the international convention of which Japan was a signatory.

For a time the Japanese did not interfere with the 25 hostels in the Security Zone – until the day a Japanese colonel accused the International Committee of hiding armed Nationalist units. Heavily armed Japanese soldiers stormed into the camp, rounded up a thousand men and bayoneted them. That was only the beginning. Over the next days and weeks, many thousands more, all non-combatants, were taken from the Zone and shot, crucified, beheaded or buried alive. The Japanese went on a rampage, carrying out massacres everywhere. At Swallow Cliff, a famous shrine of pilgrimage, they installed a row of machine-guns, then herded masses of prisoners into a wired-off compound and gunned down as many as a hundred thousand. The corpses were left unburied. Thirty thousand captured Chinese soldiers and police were marched to a forest at Long tan (Dragon Pond) and killed. Another fifty thousand died in Straw Sandal

Gorge. And at Purple-Gold Mountain, where many Japanese had lost their lives trying to storm the steep slopes, the victors dragged two thousand prisoners up the mountain, pushed them at the tips of their bayonets into open trenches and buried them alive.

A number of Westerners bore witness to these atrocities. Dr George Fitch, an American born in China, Leslie Smith of Reuters and Archibald Steele of the *Chicago Daily News* managed to drive around Nanjing to get an idea of the destruction; they found their route blocked by thousands of wrist-tied, headless corpses. As independent observers, their reports defy description. On 18 December 1937 the *New York Times* published the first dispatch from its China correspondent, Tillman Durdin, detailing horrors perpetrated by the Japanese and the thousands of bodies piled up along the riverbank. That same day the *Manchester Guardian* published an account by H. J. Timperley of heaps of smouldering corpses. From various independent Western reports it was finally estimated that in the six weeks that followed the fall of the Chinese capital, well over a quarter of a million Chinese, mainly civilians, were massacred, singly or collectively.

One of the most damning documents is the remarkable diary of a gynaecologist at the Nanjing University Hospital, Dr Robert Wilson, who recorded: "Nanjing, China. 18 December 1937. Today marks the sixth day of a remake of Dante's Inferno, one written in capital letters with blood. Collective massacres and rapes by the thousand. There seems to be no limit to the ferocity, and atavism of these brutes …"

With the Rape of Nanjing a city died a hideous death; a shrieking nightmare of images of a horror that the passing of time has in no way dulled.[1] The brutality of these acts evoked the historic terror of Hulagu Khan and Tamerlane. It should have shaken a universal conscience, but the world was not concerned with China, where millions died every year from famine or flood. After many centuries of meddling in China's affairs, this was one time when the West should have interfered but did not. Instead it stood by, made loud noises and did nothing. Europe's politicians were kept busy by the aggressive tantrums of Germany's Chancellor, Adolf Hitler, by the Spanish Civil War and by Mussolini's invasion of Ethiopia. Britain, which had the most extensive interests in China but lacked the strength to defend them, looked to the United States. And the United States, which, with its Philippine possessions and a chain of Pacific islands, should have taken an active part in containing the possible outbreak of a much wider conflict, fired paper bullets at Tokyo. The United States remained uncommitted – until an incident shook its people from their complacency. For now an incident took place that could have changed world history, since it almost plunged Japan into war with the United States and Britain.

It was 10 December 1936. The waters of the mighty Yangtze parted before the USS *Panay*'s sharp bow and slid rapidly under her flat stem. It was only in her wake that the white commotion gave evidence of the power it took to push her against the strong current. The ship's radio operator climbed down from his cabin, a message in his hand.

"Coded message from US Asiatic Fleet, sir."

He stepped through the door and handed the signal to US Navy Lieutenant Arthur Anders, the *Panay*'s Number Two and officer on watch. Anders looked at the message and realized that it was in a code used only for signals of extreme secrecy.

"Take the helm," he ordered the ship's third officer, and descended the stairs to the captain's cabin, where the codebook was kept. He knocked on the door. "Coded message, Captain."

US Navy Lieutenant Commander James J. Hughes, the *Panay*'s captain, was someone who seldom got roused, never excited, and always inspired confidence in his men. Ever since the outbreak of hostilities between the Republic of China and the Empire of the Rising Sun, the most arduous duty that had fallen on the crew was the rigging of a tarpaulin across the deck to protect foreign diplomats and their wives from the sun while sipping drinks during a reception intended to assure the Western diplomatic community of a continued US presence on the Yangtze. Afterward he had considered it a good idea to leave the tarpaulin up, so that now the ship had more the look of a pleasure cruiser than a gun-mounted river patrol boat.

"OK, let's see what they've got for us …"

This time it was serious. The communication ordered the 450-ton *Panay*, carrying a three-inch cannon and several .30-calibre machine-guns, to make full steam for Nanjing and evacuate all remaining US consular personnel, teachers and nurses, along with sundry Europeans stranded there, before the Japanese army rolled over the city. The USS *Panay* steamed upriver – and into destiny.

Most of the Nanjing-based American community, embassy staff, merchants, teachers, journalists and staff working in missionary hospitals had already been evacuated aboard another American vessel. Among them was the US ambassador, who had duly notified the Japanese that a final group of Americans, needed to look after consular affairs (destroying documents), would leave in a few days' time. Late in the afternoon on 11 December 1937 this group was told that a gunboat, the *Panay*, was about to tie up at the river docks. When they all gathered it was already dark, with the sky an evil glow over the city. Flames flickered and columns of smoke rose everywhere.

The Westerners assembled around George Atcheson Jr, Second Secretary of the American Embassy, who, carrying a star-spangled banner, led them to the quayside past the victims of the shelling and aerial bombardment. They reached the final bottleneck, a checkpoint on the canal bridge. Beyond it, darkly outlined against the reddened sky, stood the big Yangtze storage sheds, a red glint reflecting from the glass in their windows. All eyes were concentrated on a ship with twin funnels that poured forth thick clouds of black smoke; anchored next to it were three barges from the Standard Oil Company – a reminder of Rockefeller's "oil for the lamps of China programme".

The *Panay* had docked 30 minutes earlier. No sooner had the gunboat tied up than a tide of humanity poured at it like a stampede of frightened animals. From the bridge came the order to US Marine guards to ready their weapons, and the small detachment braced themselves for the ordeal. People trying to clamber on to the gunboat were pushed overboard. It was cruel, but the Americans could not risk an international incident by taking Chinese aboard. On the heels of the Chinese appeared a small group under an American flag. The harried US Marines guarding the gangplank filtered the newcomers. They did not call for a passport or a special permit; a sentence pronounced in a Chicago or California accent was proof enough of nationality. In all, 13 were allowed to embark, mainly Americans, but also a few European journalists, relieved to leave this hellish place. Behind them was a burning city; ahead of them the road to salvation.

There was no time to lose. In the darkness of that December evening, the *Panay* and its convoy of three flat-bottomed oil barges, the *Mei An*, *Mei Hsia* and *Mei Ping*, pulled away from the quay. They had reached the centre of the river when the four vessels came under sporadic artillery fire from a Japanese battery under the command of Colonel Hashimoto, who openly vaunted his ambition to commit an act which would provoke the United States into a declaration of war that would bring the Japanese military to the fore and eliminate the civilian influence from Tokyo's decision-making. Colonel Hashimoto was not alone in his action. A little earlier the *Panay*'s captain had been informed by wireless that, some miles downstream of Nanjing, the Royal Navy gunboat HMS *Ladybird* had been shelled by Japanese artillery and had taken several hits, including one below the waterline. As an added precaution the *Panay* now hoisted a second, oversized American flag, though some thought this superfluous, since the *Panay*'s barge train was well out of the combat zone, heading upriver for Chungking (Chongqing).

The sun stood high in the sky. Shortly before noon on 12 December, Captain Hughes ordered a temporary halt near Hoshien, 28 miles upriver from Nanjing, keeping the engine at minimum revs to hold the gunboat against the current. After their hectic dash at full power, the turbines were on the point of overheating and needed time to cool down. With his flotilla halfway between midstream and a reed-covered riverbank, Hughes allowed his crew a quick break, not the usual thing to do on a navy vessel in times of war, but the men had been working 24 hours without a break and were exhausted. He felt that they had put enough distance between their anchoring position and the present zone of combat. With two lookouts at their posts, the rest lined up for a quick meal.

At 12.15 p.m., 45 minutes before this lunch break aboard the *Panay*, Imperial Japanese Navy Air Force Commander Masatake Okumiya, leading a flight of Mitsubishi bombers, took off from an airfield east of Nanjing. His assignment was "the interdiction of *all* ship traffic upriver from Nanjing". This measure was to prevent the escape of Nationalist Army units to Chungking. His flight of three planes was following the wide Yangtze, past the smoke column rising over Nanjing, when, at 1.24 p.m., his co-pilot pointed excitedly to a number of ships on the water. From a height of six thousand feet it looked like a mother duck leading a string of ducklings; but this mother duck was the *Panay*, towing the three Standard Oil barges. Even from that altitude there could be no mistaking the *Panay* for a Chinese river craft; she was considerably larger, differently built, with twin funnels and awning-rigged decks, and flying not one but two star-spangled banners.[2]

To the lookouts aboard the *Panay*, a flight of Japanese bombers appeared high in the clear sky, following the river in a neat arrowhead formation. It was nothing special; Japanese aircraft owned the skies over China, and their planes had been spotted many times before. Captain Hughes was talking to Lieutenant Anders when a shout from the lookout interrupted their conversation: "Japanese bombers approaching at six o'clock." Turning their eyes toward the sky, they saw silver specks moving like glittering fragments high above the lazily drifting water. The men on the bridge were sure the planes would pass over and ignore their well-marked ship.

Commander Okumiya, of Japan's Imperial Naval Air Force, having been informed before take-off of the possible presence of vessels flying a foreign flag, demanded verification of his order to attack *all* shipping north of Nanjing. Colonel Hashimoto reconfirmed his order. Okumiya, flying in the lead, tilted his aircraft forward.

"Three aircraft, sir!" called the *Panay*'s lookout. "Dive-bombers!" And then, at the top of his voice: "They're turning on us, they're turning on us!"

The lead aircraft began its dive. It plunged steeply toward them, silhouetted against the sun like a black crucifix. The three bombers were making straight for the American convoy, their engines howling as they dived. Okumiya's plane roared toward the *Panay*. He had planned his approach with great care. He came diving down in a slight curve, aiming for the topmast so that the crew of the *Panay* imagined that the howling plane was going to plunge into the twin funnels. A single bomb detached itself from the plane's belly. During the next agonizing seconds several things happened almost simultaneously.

Aboard the *Panay* Chief Quartermaster John Henry Lang dashed along the deck, jumping over people and around bales, yelling: "Bombs! Bombs! Take cover!"

The first bomb struck the water just off to starboard. A complete change of expression swept over the faces of crew and refugees at the noise of the explosion and the sight of a water fountain rising. The prospect of getting killed momentarily pushed everything else from their racing thoughts. Quartermaster Lang was struck in the elbow and chin by shrapnel.

"Ship at Battle Stations! Increase engine to maximum revs," Captain Hughes called out.

The funnels belched black smoke, the ship shivered with the sudden acceleration as the mounting revolutions transmitted themselves through the wooden floorboards. The gun crew raced for the board-mounted machine-gun; with a loud clack the first shell slammed into the breech. The planes were separating and seemed to be diving in a shallow sweep toward the ship.

"Bogeys at four o'clock!" came the yell from the lookout. "Commence firing!" ordered Lieutenant Anders. The *Panay*'s machine-guns opened fire, flashes of tracers speeding into the sky. The planes came on, their cockpit glass glinting evilly in the sunlight, followed by bright flashes from their wing guns. More bombs shrieked toward the *Panay*, sending up water-spouts on both sides of the gunboat.

"More bogeys at nine o'clock!"

The sailors manning the deck gun stared tensely at a new flight of planes on the horizon. The buzzing objects were still out of range; the gunner tracked them in his cobweb gun sight. He would fire just enough ahead to give the tracers time to catch up with the target. The machine-gun spat out flame and bullets, as two Mitsubishis turned in their direction, screaming down on to the port beam, oblivious to the tracers spat out by the *Panay*'s guns. The planes closed rapidly at masthead height while the ship dodged gamely through a clutch of bombs. The gunboat's radio operator hit the Morse button, sending out a message in clear: "USS *Panay* … USS *Panay* … we're under aerial attack …"

Shrapnel from a bomb blast caught his equipment as he was about to repeat his emergency call. Dazed, he climbed the radio ladder. "The radio's gone," he reported to the captain, who stood rocklike with folded arms. Following naval tradition, Captain Hughes refused to flinch. The next plane came hurtling at them, faster and faster, as if drawn inevitably to the ship's bridge. Raising his eyes instinctively to the sky, Hughes yelled: "Stern all … Stern all …!"

This was the moment on which hung the fate of the *Panay*, and of all those aboard it. Again they heard the unearthly scream of the bat-shaped aircraft as it dived, releasing a big bomb from its belly. The dive-bomber pulled out of its nerve-tearing plunge as the plane seemed to fill the sky itself. For an instant Lieutenant Anders saw the spread of wings with its painted red suns, even the flash of the face with goggles of the man who was trying to kill them. Then his eyes fixed on the bomb, falling … falling … ever so slowly … closer and closer … until it hit the water alongside the ship in a bone-shattering detonation. The *Panay* was flung full astern, with her hull staved in. A geyser of yellow water washed over the deck. And still more plancs followed, as the stricken ship wallowed in the current, trailing a lengthening slick of oil.

Captain Hughes threw one glance at his littered deck and the trapped and helpless figures lying among the damage, before becoming aware of the noise made by an inrush of water. A gong jangled somewhere inside the ship, probably in the engine room. Machine-gun bullets ripped through the vessel's upper works, shredding the American flag. Then came another deafening crash. The explosion threw the captain against the bridge enclosure. A wave of shredded water with a cordite taste swept over the wounded vessel.

The *Panay* shook herself upright and steamed through the falling spray, swinging helplessly first one way and then the other, a death trap floundering on muddied water. Flames ignited in half a dozen places where fuel pipes had been pierced by shrapnel. The gunboat was out of control, its deck covered with blood and men spilling out their insides. On the bridge, a creature of blood and rags fumblingly clawed his way to the steering post. Hughes's leg was a mess of blood and torn muscle, his voice that of a man who had fought too long to hold his breath: "… get the people into the boats."

With the captain down, Anders took command. There was to be no let-up. Those lying flat on deck could hear the whiplash whine of splinters flying over them. A new attack caused another gash in the *Panay*'s side. Most bomb fragments went past harmless, but not all. Some struck the bridge – and Anders. Across his throat a scarlet stain spread with each painful breath. The wound prevented him from calling out further orders, but he managed to scribble on a blood-splattered envelope: "Abandon ship!"

Men formed into first-aid parties, clambering over the buckled metal to put the wounded into lifeboats, while more flights came in to attack the ship and oil barges. Twelve more aircraft had followed the initial bombing run. Two of the barges had already exploded and one of the captains was dead. While people jumped on to life rafts, nine biplanes circled overhead and then swooped down to strafe the rafts with their wing guns. This time the pilots had no excuse that they could not see the American flag, hanging limp and shredded from the mast of the half-submerged *Panay*.

These strafing attacks on the rafts killed two American seamen and the Italian journalist Sandro Sandri, and wounded many more. Somehow the survivors managed to make it to the riverbank and hid in the dense reeds. Chief boatswain Mahlmann and machinist Weimers volunteered to row back to the sinking ship in order to fetch food and medical supplies for the beached party. They loaded up what they could, but then fled when a motor launch with Japanese soldiers approached the sinking *Panay*. The Japanese raked the ship with bullets before they went aboard. They left within a few minutes, after which an explosion shook the vessel.

With a radio recovered from the oil barge which had miraculously survived the strike, a message was sent to Admiral Yarnell at US Asiatic Fleet Command: "All ships in American convoy destroyed. Stop. All were anchored between Kaiyua Wharf and Hohsien in midriver. Stop. Panay attacked by bombers about 1324. Stop. She was hit and sinking bows first …"

The *Panay* was going down. At 3.54 p.m. she rolled over and sank.

Onboard there was a presence that the Japanese had not counted on. In that group of last-minute refugees was Norman Alley, a newsreel cameraman on assignment to cover the Sino-Japanese War for Universal News. He was sitting on deck when the first attack took place. With a newsman's instinct he grabbed his hand-cranked camera and filmed the entire attack: even the aftermath, as Japanese planes circled overhead to assess the results of their bombing runs, then dived down to strafe the survivors in the water. Alley's film was undisputable proof of the deliberate and wanton attack on an American-flagged vessel.

For 48 hours the survivors remained in hiding, until the USS *Oahu* and HMS *Ladybird* picked them up. Casualties were heavy: three men were dead and 43 sailors and five civilian passengers seriously wounded.

On 24 December 1937 the US Department of the Navy released the results of the Court Inquiry into the destruction of the USS *Panay*. It concluded that the attack had been deliberate and ordered by the Japanese High Command:

> ... a group of six single-engine planes attacked from ahead diving singly and appearing to concentrate on the USS *Panay*. A total of about twenty bombs were dropped, many striking close aboard and creating by fragments and concussions great damage to the ship and personnel. These attacks lasted about twenty minutes during which time at least two of the planes attacked also with machine guns, one machine gun attack was directed against a ship's boat bearing wounded ashore causing several further wounds and piercing the boat with bullets ... *from the beginning of an unprecedented and unlooked for attack of great violence* until their final return, the ship's company and passengers of the USS *Panay* were subjected to grave danger and continuous hardship, their action under these conditions was in keeping with the best traditions of the naval service.

When the story of a Japanese attack on a US vessel reached the United States and President Roosevelt was shown proof of this in the form of newsreel images, he was shocked.

"Mr President, we've got ourselves another Maine affair," stated the Chief of US Naval Operations, Admiral William D. Leahy. He referred to the case of the American battleship USS *Maine*, sunk in Havana harbour during a courtesy visit that had led to war with Spain in 1898. Leahy put the US Pacific Fleet on full alert. The Japanese Imperial court realized that it was facing a grim problem and tried to forestall any American hostile reaction. Japan's ambassador to Washington presented his country's apologies for "a sad mistake" and promised full reparations.

International diplomacy went into top gear. A key conference to discuss repressive action against the rampaging Japanese was held in the White House on 16 December 1937, during which Admiral Leahy proposed a plan to join the capital ships of the US Pacific Fleet with major naval units of the Royal Navy in a blockade of Japan's trade lanes, including those for its vitally needed oil from Dutch Indonesia. British Foreign Secretary Anthony Eden, sensing a growing danger to Britain's trading and banking centre of Hong Kong, and a threat to its military presence at Singapore, backed the American proposal "to produce an overwhelming display of naval power". This plan called for main battle units of the Royal Navy based in Singapore to shut off Japan's Eastern Pacific approaches, while America would use its naval might, centred on Pearl Harbor, to cut off Japan's access to the Western Pacific. Eden replied that in such circumstances "Britain might supply as many as nine Royal Navy battleships".

However, the plan came to nothing after Prime Minister Neville Chamberlain declared in the House of Commons: "I cannot imagine anything more suicidal than to pick a quarrel with Japan at the present moment when the European situation has become so serious." Chamberlain cabled Washington, asking President Roosevelt "to hold his hand for a short while". With Britain's mind fully occupied by Nazi Germany, and to assure Tokyo of its non-hostile intentions in Britain's Pacific sphere of interest, the British Navy was ordered to shift its annual naval manoeuvres from the Pacific to the Caribbean.

Meanwhile Roosevelt, having failed to obtain support from both the US Congress and the British, had to act with caution. He was concerned that presenting the filmed sequence of a wanton attack on an American-flagged ship would generate a nationwide clamour for war and tie his hands in dealing with the Japanese. And since he could not "dictate" to a Hollywood mogul, he "requested" the president of Universal Newsreel to "down edit" the incriminating newsreel footage shot of the attack on the *Panay*. When a truncated version of the original film reached American movie houses in late January 1938, its commentary carried as its opening phrase: "A story of high drama gripped the world's attention …" In fact, it did nothing of the sort. In its slashed form it had little impact on the isolationist mood of America.

Was the attack on the *Panay*, as the Japanese claimed, a pilot's error? The answer must be a resounding *no*. A newsreel proved it. With the USS *Panay* and HMS *Ladybird* incidents, the opportunity to show muscle was given. It would have taken political will, something which London and Washington sadly lacked. The deployment of British and American naval power would have certainly deterred Japan from its adventurism in the Pacific basin. Furthermore, it would have saved Chiang Kai-shek's tottering regime and so perhaps prevented a much larger conflict looming over the horizon.

The Western powers did not react, and the Japanese got away with murder.

"I suppose doing nothing is the next best thing to doing something," Roosevelt confided to a friend in late December 1937. This stance encouraged Japan to believe that the United States of America had gone soft, and played a considerable role in Japan's decision to attack Pearl Harbor.

The final line on the *Panay* episode goes to an editorial that appeared in a small-town newspaper in Idaho: "Now we can all sit back without excitement until Japan decides to sink another one of our warships …"

# 4

# "VINEGAR JOE" AND "THE PEANUT"

## 30 APRIL 1942, THE BURMA ROAD

"On the Road to Mandalay, where the flying fishes play..." No fishes played on that afternoon on the last day of April. Shortly after five o'clock the roaring of planes was heard; then came the artillery, and with it approached the tumult of the fighting front, a great, confused din rolling eastward, a noise that would not stop. The retreating soldiers scattered over the tea plantation but it offered little cover. And then there was another attack, more bombs, more earth and dust and flesh whirling upward as hot, black smoke drifted along the line. So many had already been killed that there were now three water bottles for every fighting man.

At the crack of dawn came the sound of trucks rattling along the road, though there was nothing to be seen through the dense layer of fog. An American lieutenant stumbled uphill from the curtain of mist, waving his hands in a most unmilitary manner: "Japs."

When the fog cleared, the small American unit could see on the rock-paved road, a mere hundred yards below, trucks with soldiers, trucks with guns and crates of ammunition ... trucks and more trucks ... trucks without end. That was the moment when "Vinegar Joe's" men knew that the Burma Road was lost.

Its capture by General Ida's 15th Japanese Imperial Army was "a date which will live in infamy [but] with the unbending determination of our people we will gain the inevitable victory. So help us God." A nation listened in stunned disbelief as President Roosevelt addressed his people. The global holocaust had finally reached the heartland of isolationism. With America's forced entry into the War in the Pacific, Chiang Kai-shek's Nationalist forces became its natural ally. War *matériel* began to arrive to bolster the Nationalists, and with the men came an American commander, Major General Joseph Stilwell.

Stilwell knew the country and its people and spoke passable Mandarin, having spent years in China as commander of the US protection force in Tijian. This general was a hard case with an unpredictable streak for making harsh decisions; stern and angular, someone who would seem to outsiders utterly lacking in charm, but with a magnetism that bound his men to him. He possessed a restless, exacting mind, impatient of old methods and forever striving for the new and untried; he drove himself as hard as he drove anyone else, ruining first his digestion and then his temper. A permanently sour look brought him the nickname "Vinegar Joe". He was also beset with a serious handicap: he respected the Chinese people, though not their leaders, and this never qualified him to reconcile divergent interests. So, when Stilwell was nominated joint chief of staff for the China Theatre, the political expediency of the moment forced Roosevelt to put him under the generalship of others.

As a commander of the American forces in China, not very numerous at the time, Stilwell was answerable to Chiang Kai-shek in China, to the British High Command in Burma and to the US Joint Chiefs of Staff in the States. The British interest was concentrated on Burma, while Chiang's main concern was not combating the Japanese but holding down Mao's Communists. Diplomatically speaking, "Old Vinegar" was a bad choice from the start. An outstanding commander in the field, he was used to saying aloud what he thought of his ally, fuming at the corruption and lack of fighting spirit he found among Nationalist generals. Putting Chiang Kai-shek and Stilwell together was the worst possible idea. To say that the two felt mutual disrespect, and from the very outset, is *the* understatement. Stilwell's disdain of politicians in general was well known, but now he outdid himself.

He arrived in Chungking (Chongqing) on 11 March 1942 and set up his headquarters in the Baptist mission at Maymyo. Immediately arguments surfaced between the two senior commanders, the Chinese and the American. Stilwell considered Chiang a corrupt politician and strategic idiot, while the Chinese regarded the American as brash and insubordinate. In private conversations and in his diaries Stilwell referred to Chiang as "the Peanut" and regarded him as a man afraid to take crucial decisions. The Generalissimo repaid his disdain in full; to him the American was an overbearing boor and power-hungry barbarian.

In fact, Stilwell was all that, but he was also a brilliant tactical commander of the modern school, which the Japanese feared and understood and the Chinese did not. While Stilwell proposed a full-force counter-attack, meeting the advancing enemy head-on, Chiang's tactics relied on the well-proven, traditional Chinese style of the "defensive retreat". Victorious survival in retreat had worked for Mao during his Long March, for the Communists had a fighting spirit. But not so Chiang and his clique of elitist generals. Unwisely Stilwell burst out with the opinion that the Communist forces were more efficient than the Nationalists and "with one division of Commies I could perform wonders". To get Stilwell out of his way, Chiang ordered his "subordinate" to take charge of the Burma front. It was a good choice.

The key to the land war in China was the "Burma Road". In 1937 construction began of a trucking road which cut across the five-thousand-metre-high ridge of the "Himalayan Hump". This road linking China and Burma, formerly a foot-wide mule track on the caravan route to India, was chipped from the rock by a hundred thousand coolies with nothing more than hoes, and paved with flat stones, on the principle that a road was anything a lightly loaded truck could drive over in dry weather. Its architects never took into account that six months of the year torrential monsoon rains battered the region, and that in Asia every truck was loaded way beyond its maximum weight.

This crucial supply route from Lashio, a railhead in eastern Burma, to K'un-ming, in Yunnan province, was completed barely in time for the War in the Pacific. With an average width of three metres, allowing only a one-way traffic, it wound in 1,154 kilometres of never-ending curves across the world's most spectacular, but also most rugged and hostile, scenery; on its vertiginous inclines it strained a truck's engine to the limit. Once war broke out, rain or no rain, an average of two thousand heavily laden trucks a day travelled this road, ferrying fuel and bombs, bandages and food to the fighting troops. When a truck broke down it was pushed over the cliff by the one behind to clear the road. The Burma Road was the key to Chiang Kai-shek's survival, yet he did not see it that way. As a result of the ongoing dispute between the two Allied commanders, Chiang withheld the troops necessary to protect his own army's lifeline. With only one division, the 200th Guomindang, Stilwell had to hold the crucial River Sittang position at Toungoo, waiting for the 5th and 6th Chinese Armies, trundling south at a snail's pace.

The Burma Road disaster began on 22 March 1942 with a two-hundred-bomber raid on Allied airfields in central Burma; at the Magwe Aerodrome it surprised the planes sitting on the ground and in one strike wiped out the entire Royal Air Force in the region. From then on US Army Air Corps Colonel Chennault's American Voluntary Group, better known as the "Flying Tigers", provided the only aerial defence. Its aircrews were first-class but their aircraft were much inferior to the modern Japanese Zero. The "Flying Tigers" had one of their glorious moments on 7 May 1942, when two lead divisions of Japan's 15th Army reached the Salween Gorge, the narrow gateway into south-west China. In an effort to stop the Japanese armies, the Chinese had blown up the bridge spanning the gorge. The pilot of a prowling Curtiss P-40E Kittyhawk spotted stationary Japanese units lining the narrow road through the gorge, waiting for their engineers to rebuild the bridge. His single 250-kilogram bomb was not nearly enough to cause major damage if dropped directly on to the line of trucks, so he dropped the bomb on a rock overhang above the road. The explosion started a rock slide, bringing the entire hillside down on the stalled Japanese column.

With the bridge down in front of them and the rockslide blocking the exit from the gorge, the Japanese division found itself bottled up. The pilot directed three more airborne "Flying Tiger" Kittyhawks on to the enemy's position, and radioed them how best to use their bombs. Three more bombs, dropped in rapid succession on the mountainside, brought rocks rumbling down, burying a great number of enemies alive. As the Japanese dug themselves out, and officers lined up the shattered units, four P-40B Tomahawks armed with wing guns arrived on the scene, their strafing run adding to the confusion and slaughter. Eight planes wiped out a Japanese division as a fighting force. This isolated attack did not halt the Japanese drive, but it bought time for Chinese units to make good their withdrawal. While the British Burma Corps under Major General William Slim, assisted by the 66th Chinese Army, had thrown a blocking force across the Irrawaddy Valley, several crack Japanese divisions kept increasing the pressure on Stilwell's single division, which was guarding the approaches to the all-important Burma Road.

The 200th Division found itself in danger of being cut off by a flanking movement of the Japanese 56th Division, and Stilwell led a counter-attack with whatever was available, including cooks and medics. For a while he managed to hang on, but ever more Japanese were coming up. He radioed Chungking for an immediate support by a Chinese reserve force, but instead of troops he received what must be the strangest reply a general ever got in wartime. It came from the Generalissimo and read: "I insist that you must provide our troops with water melons to make them fight better."

Watermelons? Stilwell was flabbergasted. He vented his anger. "Bloody water melons – with hell about to break loose! If we go, Burma goes."

Chiang's failure to speed up the advance of his 5th and 6th Chinese Armies ended any hope of hanging on to the vital road. On the morning of 18 April, Japanese forces struck Stilwell's force with a massive flanking attack. His prediction came true: by noon most parts of the central Burma front had collapsed. "It was the God-damnedest thing I ever saw," he huffed. "Everyone ran."

Before the order was given to withdraw in an orderly manner and save what could be saved, the entire frontline had disintegrated. It forced the British to pull back along the Irrawaddy Valley, while the 200th Chinese Division fell back along the Sittang Valley, having lost half of its men and all of its equipment. Meanwhile the Japanese 15th Army surprised and mauled the plodding 5th Chinese Army. The British Burma Corps made a final stand at Yenangyaung, but was routed, and only a timely counter-charge by General Sun Li-yen's 38th Chinese Division saved it from annihilation. Within days the main body of the 6th Chinese Army, arriving much too late to do any good, was so mangled on the River Salween that those of it who survived simply melted away, abandoning their equipment as well as their allies.

With both his flanks fatally exposed, Stilwell found himself fighting a war all on his own. His road of retreat was lined with broken vehicles and bodies. Rearguard actions were becoming fierce, his shrinking column fighting off constant attacks. Contact between individual units was lost. Taunggyi, the final blocking position before Lashio, western terminal of the Burma Road, fell on 22 April. After its crushing victory over the Chinese 6th Army, there was now nothing to stop Japan's 56th Division from taking Lashio – and cutting the Burma Road.

Stilwell offered the remnants of a battle-hardened 200th Chinese Division a cash reward before personally leading his troops to recapture the hill station of Meiktila, held by units of the 56th Division. The Chinese and American charge was met by fire from Japanese field guns at the entrance to the village. The attackers threw themselves behind tree trunks, then stood up, fired and ran again. Every Japanese had to be dealt with in turn; they didn't put up their hands in surrender; even the seriously wounded lay behind piles of corpses and emptied their rifles at the attackers. In a heroic charge Stilwell's improvised force retook the village.

"It's getting more difficult – I haven't many people left," Stilwell confided to his aide. "The rest of the front may or may not hold, but I am holding this line." It was no use. The Japanese sent two battalions through the jungle-covered mountains and bypassed Stilwell's position; before becoming cut off, the American general called a retreat. He knew that the Japanese had beaten him for "the Road" and that his only option was to set out on foot for India. With 20 mules, 94 soldiers, an American Baptist missionary doctor and 19 Burmese nurses, almost no provisions and water, Stilwell retreated across the most arduous mountain trails in the world.

They slept in abandoned huts and chewed on tea leaves or whatever edible items they could find. At night they were plagued by red ants and snakes, and in the day they slapped at a myriad of biting insects, or burned off that evil purple bag, the leech. Every day held a new challenge, and every morning they were amazed to be still alive. One night they even rafted through enemy-held territory. When they found their first signposts in English, Stilwell was fighting back his tears. They had made it; he had reached Assam without having lost a single person. This epic test of endurance, vividly described in America's papers and magazines, made "Vinegar Joe" a household name at a time when America needed cheering.

On 29 April the Japanese marched into Lashio, severing the land route into China. The Battle of the Burma Road ended on 1 May, when British troops abandoned Mandalay, crossed the Irrawaddy and blew up the massive Ava railway bridge. The central span was lifted up by the giant explosion and then plunged into the water.

In a case of too little too late, the Allied cause had suffered greatly. Of the ninety-five thousand Chinese troops of the 5th, 6th and 66th Armies engaged in April, only one division, the 38th, commanded by Major General Sun Li-jen, withdrew as a fighting unit; it suffered severe losses, cutting westward across the path of the Japanese advance to act as a rearguard for the British units retreating to Imphal in India. Of the two Chinese armies Stilwell had hoped to lead out, fewer than ten thousand men made it to India, and he found himself blamed for the debacle.

But the general refused to admit that he was licked. "I got a hell of a beating in Burma, and it was humiliating as hell. Now I'll find out what caused it and then I'll go back and retake it." Even as he led his beaten troops north-west, with malaria and monsoon rains tormenting them, he was already working on a plan to win back that "darned truck road". The Burma Road became his obsession. He had lost it, and he would win it back! China's war effort now depended on a few squadrons of twin-engine DC-3 Dakotas flying drums of oil over the Himalayan Hump. This feat bears testimony to the sturdiness of the airframes and the courage of the air crews, flying overloaded planes way above their maximum rated height, where wind currents tossed them about like toys. Yet it was the only way to ferry supplies to China.

Chiang Kai-shek seemed indifferent to the loss of the crucial supply route; he was so blinded by internal problems with his arch-foe Mao that he was distracted from battling their common foreign enemy. An unofficial truce settled over the Sino-Japanese front in eastern China; Chiang used the calm to pull 12 crack divisions out of his frontline to throw them against Mao's Communists, who in theory were still his allies. Stilwell was livid; an attack on Mao's stronghold must lead to a civil war fought in parallel with a world war. He informed President Roosevelt of Chiang's dangerous gambit. As a result of Stilwell's report, the United States refused to increase its supplies to Chungking and Chiang would no longer talk to him. Something had to be done.

In November 1943 Roosevelt and Churchill invited Chiang to attend the Allied Cairo Conference, which was called to bring the strategic debate back to the Pacific theatre. The meeting was a disaster; from the moment they met, the Big Three could not agree on a single point. The implacable Generalissimo demanded much more than Churchill and Roosevelt were willing to give. Churchill's view of China was essentially Victorian imperialistic, while America's stance was best expressed by "Vinegar Joe" in a secret memo to his president: "Why should American boys die to recreate the colonial empire of the British?" Roosevelt refused Chiang's request for more American planes, but then reversed himself, insisting that any Allied aid provided must be limited to action against Japan. Priority was given to recapturing the Burma Road. When Roosevelt asked Chiang about his ongoing struggle with Mao, Chiang stated that a Communist-dominated China would threaten Western civilization; in the end he was to be proved right.

The point of contention for a future conflict was contained in one sentence added to the final Cairo communiqué: "The Three Great Powers, mindful of the enslavement of the people of Korea, are determined that in due course Korea shall become free and independent."

By early 1944 the US Joint Chiefs of Staff had abandoned all hope that Chiang's Nationalists could be coaxed into launching an eastern offensive, aimed at reopening the port facilities of Hong Kong or Shanghai for the final assault on Japan. In September 1944 the Japanese launched Operation Ichigo, and struck the Chinese forces in Henan and Hunan provinces. Chiang's armies collapsed, with millions of deserters joining the flow of panicked peasants. The Generalissimo called for Stilwell's assistance; now it was the American who refused his co-commander his help. He was not about to abandon his successful drive for the Burma Road. Stilwell had been informed that Chiang, despite his agreement in Cairo, continued to siphon off troops and material to fight Mao's Communists. When challenged about this by Stilwell, Chiang asked for the "insubordinate" American general's immediate removal. On 2 October 1944 Patrick Hurley, Washington's political representative in China, had to cable Roosevelt: "Reasons given by the Generalissimo for Stilwell's recall: incompetent, non co-operative, lack of respect, unwarranted diversion of munitions and men to Burma. Responsibility for disaster in South China."

Roosevelt, increasingly frustrated with Chiang's stalling tactics, sent Stilwell a personal message in which he insisted that Stilwell "take command of all the Allied forces in China". Stilwell was delighted; this finally solved his problem. He could finally fight the war his way. But then he committed a diplomatic blunder when he walked into Chiang's office, handing the presidential cable to the Generalissimo. Outraged, Chiang shot off an ultimatum to Washington: "Our army will rise in mutiny with an American in command."

Roosevelt discussed the matter on the phone with Patrick Hurley, who told him: "Mr President, you will lose Chiang and you will lose China too."

A difficult decision faced him, but Roosevelt was a pragmatist and looked at it from a political-strategic viewpoint. He promoted "Vinegar Joe" to four-star general, and then took away his command. America's best land fighter was recalled from the Far East. One thing is certain: had this brilliant military leader displayed only a fraction of General Macarthur's diplomatic skill, he would have ended up commanding the Pacific Theatre.

"If a man can say he did not let his country down, and if he can live with himself, there is nothing more he can reasonably ask for." In 1946, a few weeks after he wrote these words, General Joseph W. Stilwell died.

One week in April 1942 would have made all the difference. Had Chiang acted according to a common scenario and not become influenced by his dislike of another commander, and had the Generalissimo pushed the combined manpower of his 5th and 6th Armies in a rapid advance south, Stilwell could have held Burma. In command of the one hundred thousand men, Stilwell could have rolled up the Japanese in Malaya, and then struck into the enemy's vulnerable flank in southern China. Guangzhou, Hong Kong, then Nanjing and Shanghai would have been retaken. With its resources stretched precariously thin in an arc across the wide Pacific, it is doubtful that Tokyo's war machine could have continued after a military debacle in China. It was not to be. While Stilwell saw as his main objective to blunt the Japanese drive and win a world war, Chiang focused on keeping the Communists at bay. Once their characters clashed, Stilwell's operational plan was doomed.

The loss of the Burma Road set the Allied war effort in the Pacific back by two years.

# CHRONICLE: 1945:

# THE DAY THE WEST LOST CHINA

The commander of the Red Army in Manchuria, Marshal Lin Biao, received the order from Mao Zedong to abandon Harbin, the military key to northern China. His Communist forces had been pushed, and pushed hard, and now it was all over for them. They could no longer stem the assault by Chiang Kai-shek's battalions with their overwhelming firepower. With the fall of Harbin, all of Manchuria was lost for the Communists, and the Nationalists would finally emerge victorious from the 25-year-old civil war.

The Sino-Japanese War killed a staggering 15 million Chinese. And still, after the waste of so much life, the two antagonists in their struggle for post-war China had not grasped the essential futility of putting an issue to the judgement of the sword. They had not learned their lesson that war breeds only more war. In the late summer of 1945 Mao Zedong had set the stage by stating: "Political power grows out of the barrel of a gun." Shortly after the Japanese surrender in mid-August, new fighting broke out in China. Chiang, relying on the supplies he had squirrelled away during the World War, pushed with his Nationalist forces into Manchuria. The Communists were outgunned and outmatched. Lin Biao's force made one final, desperate stand at Siping-ji. Mao's marshal threw a hundred thousand Changchon factory workers into the fray – and wasted them. His human-wave assaults were buried under Nationalist shells; when the red wave cracked Chiang's divisions poured over them. The sacrifice of forty thousand dead factory workers could no longer stem a Nationalist tide. Mao appealed to his Russian comrade for military assistance; but Stalin had other plans, and they did not include Mao's rise to power. It left Mao no choice but to evacuate Manchuria and head back to his mountain redoubt.

Then something unexpected took place. On 27 November 1945 US President Harry S. Truman appointed General of the Army George Catlett Marshall as his representative to broker a settlement in the Chinese civil war. A one-line phrase by Zhou Enlai had achieved that: "The presence of the USSR is the future of China." The Soviets were determined to carve out for themselves a Socialist Chinese Dominion, and then run it from Moscow, just as they were doing with their European satraps. That could not be allowed. Why not let the Chinese Reds rule themselves, rather than pushing them into the Soviet orbit? With such afterthought, America's planners erected a barrier to Soviet designs on Asia. Washington defined its incremental gains, its long-term commitment and its willingness to keep the post-war imperatives in perspective. The key, as seen by the State Department, was to set up a separate Communist state in those parts of Manchuria bordering the Soviet Union, so creating a buffer between US-backed Nationalist China and the Russian naval bases in the Far East.

General George C. Marshall, a highly respected soldier and statesman, was miscast and outmatched in the snake pit of Oriental politics. His initial mission was to put Chiang's invasion of Communist-occupied Manchuria on hold. He outlined to the Generalissimo how any attack on the crumbling Communists would drive Mao into the Soviet orbit, with Russia absorbing the Chinese Reds economically and politically, then gaining control over China's north-east and making Soviet hegemony over their new socialist empire in Asia a *fait accompli*.

The Marshall Mission was doomed from the start. The Americans had not taken into account that Chiang Kai-shek was a product of the 1911 revolution, which had found its cause in the many foreign interventions. Chiang's mood was surly. When an aide tried to brief him on the forth-coming talks, the Generalissimo snapped: "Marshall can go to hell." The Nationalist leader resented America's interference in China's internal affairs, just as the Communists were convinced that Marshall had come to uphold his ally, the "Nationalist reactionaries".

General Marshall declared an embargo on delivery of American weapons to China. In fact, this only affected Chiang's Nationalists and forced him to order his troops on to the offensive before his ammunition ran out. The Nationalist armies made good progress. An added sign of America's increasing annoyance with Chiang was an order for the withdrawal of the US Marines stationed in China. Offering deals which were just short of political blackmail, Marshall pressured Chiang to issue a "halt order". Pushed by the United States, his indispensable ally, Chiang took a fatal step. With an overwhelming superiority in the air, at sea and on land, he ordered his Nationalist armies to stop short of attacking the "thin red line" at Harbin, which would have meant the end for Mao's design of a Communist takeover.

If this sounds incredible, it certainly was to the Communists when in June 1946 – at the moment they were ready to abandon their key position at Harbin – a cease-fire was declared. Chiang Kai-shek's failure to act when he had the troops and the air force was to become the decisive hinge factor in the rise of "Red China". His commanders, incredulous at having been deprived of an easy victory, challenged their leader. Chiang defended his position: "You say that taking Harbin will be easy, but if you knew the reason why we cannot take it, then you would understand why not taking it is not easy at all."

General David Barr, commanding the US Army Advisory Group in China, criticized Chiang's hesitation in taking Harbin by describing it as "a task beyond the Nationalists' logistic capabilities".

With Marshall still trying to smooth things over, falling back on the vain hope that further negotiations would provide a lasting settlement, Washington – with its attention deeply focused on a developing crisis along an Iron Curtain in Europe – was largely unconcerned with the stirrings in Asia. Marshall set out on a shuttle diplomacy, meeting with both Chiang and Mao. His negotiation talks stalled, which did nothing for Chiang and much for Mao. The American had finally met his match; he was checkmated by the suave diplomacy of Zhou Enlai over questions such as political unifications and the integration of Nationalist and Communist troops into a national army. Finally Zhou put it squarely on the table: "We will only negotiate *after* the Nationalists evacuate their forces from the portion they occupy in Manchuria."

From that moment the fate of China depended less and less on what was happening at the negotiating table and only on Mao's next moves. Suddenly things began to change; Stalin realized that by putting pressure on America in the Far East he was redirecting its attention away from Europe. The Russians supplied Mao with the guns and munitions recovered from the defeated Japanese. While the Nationalists vacillated, the Red Army dug in. Throughout this crucial period Chiang's policies were confused, inept and risky, and created the ideal condition for Mao's plan to flourish. Chiang's forces weakened, as Mao's grew daily. The root of the Communists' military predominance was found in the country's culture and its legacies, with its brand of rational thought that rejects all foreign alliances. Chiang was severely tainted by his alliance with the Americans; Mao had no such problem. Also, China has a long tradition of "civic militarism", and Mao's ability to mobilize citizen soldiers and then animate them with the discipline of collective endeavour helped his ascendancy.

With Mao's order "Comrades, your goal is China!", the Communists refused Marshall's mediation of a settlement brokered under the auspices of the United States. The Marshall-negotiated cease-fire ground to a halt when Mao's army went on the offensive. Chiang's Nationalists were pushed back, having to abandon one position after another. Any further compromise was now unacceptable to Mao, and talks were indefinitely suspended. With the collapse of even that faint hope, China was condemned to another two years of devastating civil war, and millions more casualties.

The slaughter of soldiers and civilians continued. In November 1948 the Communists put four hundred thousand Nationalists out of action in Manchuria and then used captured American-made weapons and munitions stockpiles to force General Fu Zhoyi's two hundred thousand Nationalists to surrender Beijing. On 10 January 1949 a further three hundred thousand Nationalist troops capitulated on the River Huai. The Communists crossed the Yangtze, and swept over Nanjing, Shanghai and Guangzhou. With a rapidly deteriorating situation, Chiang decided on the step that proved fatal to his position in China: he abandoned his capital of Chungking, and then quit the mainland altogether, taking his government, the country's gold hoard and his remaining troops to the island of Taiwan (Formosa).

After Chiang Kai-shek was pushed into accepting America's dictate to hold off, the tide changed. Pushed from place to place by a guerrilla warfare they could not cope with, Nationalist generals developed a "wall psychology" by trying to hang on to the major cities – and when the wall fell, the Nationalists fell with it. As for General Marshall, he returned empty-handed to the United States. Briefing his president, he used a prophetic phrase: "Mao and his gang are going to enjoy watching us squirm."

The Marshall Mission was a landmark in the split between East and West. Even more important, it marked China's final rejection of the West. The failure of the First Chinese Republic of 1912, and the spectacle of European powers tearing themselves apart on the battlefields of two World Wars, had had a devastating effect on China's opinion of "Western democracy". The Western model of Sun Yat-sen's First Republic was gone, replaced by a New Order of regimented socialism as practised in Russia. China's disillusionment with the West after its dismal experience of centuries of Western imperialism, and the alternative offered to the oppressed masses by a Chinese version of Marxism-Leninism, came together to make Communism a better option than Western democracy. The birth of Red China was the great story following a devastating Second World War. It was also the source of coming difficulties. The "loss" of China to the Communists in 1949 resulted in vicious attacks on the person of George Marshall by America's anti-Communist crusaders. On 14 June 1951 Senator Joseph McCarthy stood up in the US Senate to denounce a great man's unquestionable patriotism:

How can we account for our present situation unless we believe that men high in this Government are concerting to deliver us to disaster? This must be the product of a great conspiracy, a conspiracy on a scale so immense as to dwarf any previous such venture in the history of man. A conspiracy of infamy so black that, when it is finally exposed, its principals shall be forever deserving of the maledictions of all honest men. It was Marshall who created the China policy which, destroying China, robbed us of a great and friendly ally, a buffer against the Soviet imperialism with which we are now at war. It was Marshall who went to China to execute the criminal folly of the disastrous Marshall Mission.

In the end, Senator Joseph McCarthy was shown up as *the* villain. George C. Marshall was awarded the 1951 Nobel Peace Prize for his plan on American assistance to European recovery.

"China cannot remain independent," declared Mao Zedong shortly after he proclaimed the People's Republic of China on 1 October 1949. "We must lean either to the side of imperialism, or side with socialism."

If he had hoped to keep China's independence in order to exert greater influence in foreign relations throughout Asia, the escalating Cold War between the superpowers forced him to pick sides. He had forewarned George Marshall that such would be the case. With the United States openly supporting the Nationalist Chinese regime in Taiwan, while assisting Japan with its reconstruction – a country which China feared as its challenger to the future economic development in the Far East – Mao's choice was made up for him. In December 1949 the Chairman travelled to Moscow to negotiate a Treaty of Alliance and Mutual Assistance between his nascent People's Republic of China and the Soviet Union. It was signed in February 1950.

History is full of ifs. If Chiang Kai-shek had not listened to George Marshall, and instead delivered the knockout blow against his Communist foe, Washington would have had to follow him in any case. Or if Washington had listened to Mao's warning about choosing sides ... Either scenario would have completely altered the Cold War's strategic equation. However, in the post-war era, super-rich with nightmare scenarios, the world's nuclear superpower, the United States of America, was so preoccupied with the growing conflict along Europe's Iron Curtain that it disregarded and neglected China. The Soviet Union did not. It helps to explain the rise of Mao Zedong and his movement.

The failure of the Marshall Mission is a lesson in what happens when Western democracies "diss" a continent and fail to pay attention to the world's most populous nation.

That day China was "lost for the West".

ПУСТЬ ЖИВЁТ И КРЕПНЕТ
НЕРУШИМАЯ ДРУЖБА И СОТРУДНИЧЕСТВО
СОВЕТСКОГО И КИТАЙСКОГО НАРОДОВ!

Left: Before the break: the not-so-eternal handshake.

Below: When they were comrades: Zhou Enlai – with Mao and Stalin looking on – signs an alliance including a Sino-Soviet defence treaty, Moscow, 15 February 1950.

Above and below: On the march and on the road – China's invasion of Tibet on 10 November 1950.

Two faces of the Korean War: POW Chinese "Volunteers" (right) and Americans (below), December 1950.

Left: Glorification and reality: a benignly smiling Chairman, while millions perish in the greatest famine in recorded history.

万 物 生 长 靠 太 阳

Below: A nation of wooden ploughs.

Right: Taiwan tension rising:
China rattles the sabre.

響應毛主席號召：建設強大的
國防軍和強大的經濟力量！

Below: Showdown on the Ussuri:
a deadly confrontation that led
to the threat of a Soviet nuclear
strike, 2 March 1969.

The opening – Kissinger's great diplomatic coup, Beijing, 21 February 1971. *Left to right:* Zhou Enlai, interpreter, Mao Zedong, Richard Nixon, Henry Kissinger.

Beijing's Tiananmen Square, 3 June 1989: (above) a whiff of freedom crushed under the cleats of tanks, and (below) the unsung hero.

Above: A farewell to British rule: Chris Patten recovers the last Union Flag, Hong Kong, 1 July 1997.

Above: A Chinese fighter jet in a deadly game of bumper cars with an American observation aircraft, 24 January 2001.

Right: China enters the space age: astronaut Yang Liwei pilots the nation's first manned space flight, October 2003.

# ACT FOUR

## 1949–1997
## The East Is Red

*Every Communist must grasp the truth: "Political power
grows out of the barrel of a gun."*
—Mao Zedong, *Quotations*

*Arise! Ye who refuse to be slaves*
*With our very flesh and blood*
*Let us build our New Great Wall*
*March on!*
*Brave the enemy's gunfire*
*March on! March on!*

—National Anthem of the People's Republic of China

# 1

## CAUGHT ON THE
## TREACHEROUS TIDE

### 25 OCTOBER 1949, JINMEN (QUEMOY) ISLAND,
### REPUBLIC OF CHINA (TAIWAN)

In the euphoria of their triumph over the Nationalists, the Chinese Communists – ChiComs in Washington jargon – hastily prepared a plan to strike a knockout blow to Chiang Kai-shek's refuge on Taiwan. Any such operation called initially for the elimination of a ROC-held (Republic of China)[1] archipelago just 10 kilometres off the coast of China's mainland. This chain of small islands captured the world's attention under its collective name of Quemoy (Jinmen in Mandarin).

Mao considered the "offshore islands" as being of great moral significance, but also necessary for his onward thrust toward the Nationalist stronghold of Taiwan. However, he committed a major error when he thought that an amphibious landing on a small island is the same as battling it out on a large landmass. His Communist forces had no combat experience in amphibious operations, and certainly had never studied America's disastrous amphibious assaults on Tarawa and Iwo Jima in 1943, islands where its targeted landing beaches merge with a coral reef submerged only at high tide. Planning and timing of amphibious operations take months; they must be designed to deceive the enemy as to the site of debarkation, but also crucial is the selection of a beach which is suitable in terms of wave height and sufficient water depth at low tide. Tidal information about the Quemoy island group was either unavailable or hundreds of years old. Furthermore, the defences of the islands were formidable, bristling with heavy weapons; aerial photographs, essential for an assault of its kind, were not available and the Communists had no intelligence on the true strength of the garrison.

Mao's military plan called for a surprise move by forces of the PLA

(People's Liberation Army of Beijing) across the narrows of the Inland Sea, to catch the local ROC garrison by surprise, take the islands and use these as a base for launching a massive amphibious assault on Taiwan. Beijing could not risk this invasion failing, for humiliation would result from defeat by an already beaten foe. In fact, there was little chance of that; according to the Communists' reports, following their flight from the mainland the Nationalists were "disorganized and practically inoperative".

But the Chinese Communist Party's Central Committee was guilty of wishful thinking, a dangerous thing for any military planning. From a minor, guerrilla-style incursion, their plan had developed into a full-scale amphibious operation. For that, the entire operation depended on the one thing they did not have: ships and experienced crews to man them. In their withdrawal to Taiwan only three weeks before (1 October 1949) the Nationalists had requisitioned anything that could float, and their crews with it; and what they did not take with them, they sank. The best the Communists could come up with were a hundred fishing vessels and trawlers of different sizes and speeds, handled by conscript recruits, not sea-wise captains.

Moreover, the PLA commanders had no precise idea of where to land on the islands, because they had not tried to find out. They were convinced that even an inexperienced crew on a slow fishing boat could manage 10 kilometres of sea. They did not plan on any more complicated manoeuvres than running the ships up on to the sandy shore. They had no tide charts and never gave a thought to the possible presence of submerged coral reefs. And yet the surprise almost worked. It is remarkable that neither the Nationalists, with their spy connections to the mainland, nor the Americans, with their daily aerial reconnaissance, discovered the presence of a major invasion force opposite the islands.

Shortly before the start of the invasion the commander of the strike force dispatched a report to Beijing which was as reassuring as it was misleading. His troops were ready and the local population was ready to welcome them, and "having inflicted a crushing defeat on the enemy, our men will be cheered as liberators". In fact, there were almost no civilians on Quemoy to cheer; the locals had been evacuated, and the islands' fishing grounds were turned into an off-limits military zone.[2]

The invaders gave little or no consideration to the strength of the ROC force holding the islands. Yet it was substantial. Under the command of General Li Liangwang, the ROC 22nd Army Group was made up of four divisions – the 11th and 44th at one end of the islands, and the 14th and 118th at the other – equipped with the modern American M5A1 battle tank, tenderly called the "Jinmen Bear". The approach waters were heavily mined, and another seven thousand landmines protected possible invasion beaches.

The attack was to be carried out by the PLA 28th Assault Group, under the command of General Xiao Fang and the political commissar Li Mancun. They had assembled six regiments, equipped with light assault weapons, but no heavy mobile back-up and no air cover. At their assembly points the first group of men scheduled to land were told that a great army was ready to take over as soon as they had established a beachhead. Had there really been a back-up army, they would have had to swim across, because no ships were available to transport them.

On the first day of the operation, 25 October, it was realized that there was not enough space for six full regiments aboard a hundred fishing craft, so a decision was taken to embark only nine thousand men as the first assault group, with the rest to follow in two consecutive waves in a shuttle service provided by trawlers. To preserve the element of surprise, the assault was launched without preparatory artillery support from bases on the mainland, the emphasis being to get the troops ashore before the defenders had time to react. Shortly after midnight, the first wave, made up of elements of the 244th and 251st PLA Regiments, struck out from their assembly places on the mainland. In the dark of the night, the inexperienced sailors quickly lost contact, or rammed into one another. Six boats were lost before the sky lit up with a blinding flash. Mines ripped two vessels apart; an ensuing panic spread the invasion fleet to the four winds.

Parts of the 244th Regiment were the first to make it to Quemoy at a point unsuitable for approaching the shore. Embarked on a multitude of vessels of various speeds, the lead elements had drifted off course and found themselves on a part of the island with offshore reefs. Because of the high tide the flat-bottomed riverboats scraped over the outer barrier without grinding themselves to bits on the razor-sharp coral heads. Troops began jumping into the knee-deep water and then stumbled across the rocky shore. On another beach, where the coral was only a few inches below the surface, half a dozen vessels had their bottoms ripped out. The men were pitched into the water and their heavy equipment pulled them down. The various landing parties were so spread out that the three battalions of the 244th could not find one another in the darkness. Their commanders had failed to warn them that the beaches were heavily mined; as explosions rattled along the north shore, PLA units were blown to pieces wading ashore.

One of the first to come into contact with the initial wave of attackers was ROC Sergeant Tang Shih Liu, who commanded a heavy M3 battle tank. The tank's engine had broken down on a coastal road, and the sergeant and his crew were working on it, when out of the darkness emerged a dozen boats. Tang jumped into his tank, slammed the hatch shut – and waited. He let them come close. Their captains realized the situation too late. Tang fired two rounds with his main armament, and two boats sank. His third shot burst on the bridge of a larger vessel stuck on a submerged reef, flaying its crew with shrapnel. He loaded and fired, loaded and fired again. His rounds slammed into landing boats, disgorging soldiers, whose uniform clearly showed they were not ROC.

Tang began firing bursts with his turret-mounted machine-gun; his bullets scythed through the attacking wave struggling for shore in the shallow water. Tang's weapon kept spitting out bullets and empty brass cartridges like confetti; the attackers were shot to pieces to a man. Meanwhile his driver got on to his radio and alerted the company command post. Within moments all radio frequencies were jammed with Chinese voices; ChiComs or Nationalists, the radio operator could not tell. Rifle bullets struck the tank and pinged harmlessly off the steel. Tang was still pouring bullets into the attackers, when the first ROC tank relief column came roaring in like fire-spitting dragons. Tang took a break. In front of his tank lay heaps of dead and wounded invaders.

The attack by the men of the 251st PLA fared no better. Alerted by the sea-mine explosions, a ROC shore battery was waiting for them. Searchlights stabbed out to sea and caught the approaching flotilla in their beams. Two shells straddled a vessel bigger than the rest. The shore gunner dropped his range by two hundred metres, and his next shell punctured the hull. The ship staggered, belching smoke, before it blew up in a white-hot flame. It had been the invasion's ammunition ship; gone were mortars and heavy machine-guns. Its accompanying troop-carrying vessels, manned by inexperienced crews, ground to a halt on the jagged coral. The PLA units, dumped off in chest-high water, began an agonizing struggle toward the shore, lashed by a storm of shellfire and subjected to a murderous machine-gun fire from every angle as bullets whipped inches above the water. Soon a carpet of corpses floated on the sea. The wounded had no hope of rescue; they were simply left to drown. One in every two became a casualty. Only a few reached the shore.

By first light only one beachhead, about two hundred metres wide and 30 metres deep, was established on barren sand, in plain view of the defenders' guns. No more reserves or heavy *matériel* could be expected. The vessels that had escaped the terrible opening barrage and made it inshore turned around to head back, only to discover to their horror that the tide had gone out and they were locked in by a coral barrier. Confusion reigned, then disaster struck when ROC tanks lined up on shore used the marooned ships for target practice. Tank shells reduced the vessels to matchwood. The large ship which carried the communications centre for the entire operation was destroyed. From the moment co-ordination was gone the invasion was doomed. The PLA units that had made it through bullets and mines were left stranded in their shallow beachhead, armed with nothing more lethal than rifles, and with no prospect of back-up. Some units tried their luck in suicide attacks. The "Jinmen Bears" wiped them out.

Only one part of one battalion managed to break out; it reached the village of Peishan, where its commander established his headquarters in a one-storey brick building. All hope of conquering the small island had vanished. The PLA dug in and went on the defensive, and the trap snapped shut. Hammered into submission by heavy shells, they slackened off their fire. When all was lost, and surrender the only sensible solution, the men's political commissar forced them to make a stand to the last bullet. Almost none survived. With the arrival of more ROC reinforcements, including a battalion of heavy battle tanks, it was over. It had taken 56 hours. Thousands of PLA troops were dead, the rest taken prisoner. The six regimental commanders either died fighting or committed suicide.

The ChiCom leaders were guilty of several serious mistakes. The initial error was the inadequate size of the amphibious force. But the decisive factor was tide and the limited access to the channel, which made Quemoy into one of the worst places for an invasion; it was the Communists' failure to understand the geographical features that hastened their defeat. If the capricious tide had played havoc with the aggressors, even more fatal was their belief in their own propaganda, which portrayed the ROC as finished as a fighting force. Tactically the terrible setback established the future pattern of warfare between Mainland China and Taiwan, determining the success or failure of any further assaults on the Nationalist fortress. It showed that the New China needed both a navy and an airborne attack force of planes or rockets to succeed in taking on Taiwan.

Ultimately the abortive invasion had a contrary effect to the one Mao expected. Chiang Kai-shek recognized its psychological benefit by inviting the world's press to inspect the invasion beaches and see for themselves the full impact of the Red disaster. The Nationalists' stand on Quemoy was inspiring, and the world press reported it so. Reports of the "Great Communist Defeat" were flashed around the world. Quemoy was a first victory after a long series of setbacks. The outcome of the battle was of great propaganda value for the Taiwan regime, just as it was a grave blow to Beijing. If the Communist leaders had thought that it was enough to storm ashore carrying red flags, they were taught a severe lesson. Their hope of conquering Taiwan was dead. The Battle of Kuningtou put a halt to the tide of Communism spreading out into the Pacific, and it secured the survival of Nationalist Taiwan and the Pescadores.

It had a much more wide-ranging political effect. Though the battle itself was relatively minor, it upturned the American president's non-interference stance. If President Truman had previously announced that "the United States will not interfere in a conflict between the People's Republic of China (PRC) and the Republic of China (ROC)", he now reversed his decision. Taiwan and its chain of islands suddenly became a vital element in America's Red containment policy for the Pacific basin, and Truman ordered the might of the US 7th Fleet into the Formosa Strait. Its presence became the rampart that once had been the Great Wall.

On the Chinese mainland there was a pervasive air of frustration, rivalling in intensity the elation following the victory over the Nationalists only a few weeks earlier. Then crowds were called out to wave their red banners and now they had to put them away. In the aftermath of Quemoy, Communist Party high officials said many problems had arisen: military forces did not penetrate the beaches in sufficient numbers; they lacked effective co-ordination; the local population wanted to co-operate but were afraid the invasion would not last and they would be left to suffer for their sympathies when the Nationalists returned.

Mao was not satisfied with the answers he was given. The lack of popular support, the heavy casualties and the failure to make greater gains raised grave doubts about his movement and its future. Internal rebellions that challenged Party authority were springing up all over the country, especially in the southern provinces. The most pressing problem following the Quemoy setback was orders to PLA forces to repress these growing internal troubles by any means. Mao realized that the surest way to redirect the country's attention away from home and unite the people behind the patriotic Red Flag was to achieve a resounding victory over "a new foreign intervention" that presented a danger to China's integrity. "We need to motivate large and powerful forces against an external threat ..." he recorded.

Chairman Mao began to re-evaluate his own convictions, as did the Americans and the West, but all looked in the wrong direction. They failed to see Korea coming.

# 2

# REHEARSAL FOR A BIGGER SHOW

## 10 NOVEMBER 1950, LHASA, TIBET

One event, widely ignored at the time, served as Mao Zedong's rehearsal for a much bigger show. For endless generations, Tibet had been a kind of vassal Holy See, enjoying a peaceful bishop-to-monarch relationship with China. The Chinese had no true pattern of colonization. Instead, if their vassal behaved, sent his tribute to Beijing and accepted being pulled into Chinese culture, he could expect to be treated as a lesser brother. This was about to change.

On 24 November 1949, in a radio message transmitted from Beijing, the Panchen Lama, a Chinese puppet and refugee rival to the nominal ruler of Tibet, called for the "liberation of our homeland from the oppressive rule of the Dalai Lama". The Chinese Communists quickly responded favourably to the Panchen Lama's appeal, which they themselves had written. By mid-October 1950 masses of Chinese troops had gathered along the border between China and Tibet. Without an army or weapons to defend his country, the Dalai Lama turned to the United Nations, asking for assistance by diplomatic intervention. His request did not even receive the courtesy of a reply.

Winter had settled in over the Tibetan high plateau; temperatures dropped way below zero in this wind-swept wasteland leading up to the High Himalayas. With the world's attention focused on the war in Korea,[1] Beijing's brutal might invaded hapless Tibet. In October 1950 strong PLA units overran the minor Tibetan army post holding at Chamdo, capital of Kham province, and its governor, Ngawang Jigme Ngabo, was taken prisoner. Until now the Chinese leaders were most careful not to alert international interest by engaging in major military action. This changed when a Chinese division, under the cover name of "Tibetan Volunteers", moved on the capital, Lhasa, and occupied it on 9 September 1951. Shortly before their arrival, the 15-year-old Dalai Lama, his entourage and select government officials evacuated the capital to set up a provisional administration near the Indian border at Yatung.

In Lhasa opposition to the Chinese occupation grew; in the beginning it was relatively passive, with wall posters denouncing the oppression and dried yak dung hurled from rooftops at Chinese military parades. During these protests it was not the poorest class who set the tone; these, dazed by shock and hunger, kept silent. It was the non-violent resistance sect Mimang Tsongdu, made up of the middle classes and small landholders. Its demonstrators marched into the centre of Lhasa to find it sealed off by Chinese military with armoured cars and machine-guns. Things turned violent when the occupying troops charged the marchers using percussion grenades and rifle butts, and then dragged away the stunned protesters. Most of the arrested were never heard of again.

Within three years the PLA occupation force numbered two hundred and twenty-two thousand. This large new population fed themselves off the land, which led to widespread famine among the local people in a barren country noted for its delicate subsistence agriculture. The Khampas of the High Plateau formed into guerrilla bands to resist the aggressor; the PLA responded by arresting Tibetan nobles and senior monks, some of whom were publicly tortured and executed to discourage an outbreak of large-scale resistance in the outlying countryside. It didn't calm the situation. Kham and Amdo guerrilla groups engaged in reprisals against the invaders.

Chinese units went on the rampage, bombing monasteries and burning villages, with a grim determination to destroy all resistance before the world had time to react. They killed thousands. To pacify timid Third World protests, such as those of India's charismatic leader Pandit Nehru, the brutal masters of Tibet permitted the Dalai Lama to return to Lhasa, then kept him as a figurehead in a residence which was closely watched. To run the country, the Chinese installed a rubber-stamp Preparatory Committee for the Autonomous Region of Tibet (PCART).

To secure an all-weather passage for their military convoys, the Chinese used forced labour to hack out a highway from Lhasa to Chungking. And to strengthen its territorial claim, China set out on a gigantic resettlement project and implanted five million Chinese in Tibet. Confiscation of land and fiercely repressive measures drove the native population into the outlying mountainous regions, from where they conducted guerrilla warfare. The Chinese replied with wholesale executions and deportations. Sixty-five thousand Tibetans were killed and ten thousand children deported to China to become "assimilated" into Chinese culture, and then produced as proof for a policy of "two brothers – one nation".

A few years passed with the situation in Tibet going from bad to worse.

In the early hours of 10 March 1959 a minor flag-waving demonstration by religious students galvanized the people of Lhasa into a spontaneous rising. Later that morning Brigadier General Fu, commanding the Chinese occupation forces, informed the Dalai Lama's Tibetan guard commander that he expected to see the high priest immediately in his military camp, and that this visit was to be kept secret. Rumours that the Chinese were forcing the Dalai Lama to appear before their General Assembly spread rapidly through the city. By early afternoon three hundred thousand loyal Tibetans surrounded the Dalai Lama's residence in the Norbu Linka palace and prevented His Holiness from attending the forced appointment. The crowd stayed there all that night, chanting and praying. The following day a procession of five thousand Tibetan women marched through Lhasa carrying banners and shouting: "From this day Tibet is independent." When a women's delegation called on the Indian consul general for help, he gave them to understand that help could not be expected *on this side of the border*. The meaning of his words was clear.

While the women's demonstration was in progress, members of Mimang Tsongdu, anxious to safeguard their religious leader, began to erect barricades across Lhasa's narrow streets. The situation became critical when armed Khampa rebels moved into strategic positions around the city. The Chinese riposte wasn't long in coming: at 4 p.m. on 17 March Chinese guns fired two warning shots at the Norbu Linka palace. With the situation quickly approaching a critical point, it was decided that the Dalai Lama had to be ferried to safety on *the other side of the border*.

The Fourteenth Dalai Lama describes the critical hours in his autobiography:[2]

> … when the Chinese guns sounded that warning of death, the first thought in the mind of every official within the Palace, and every humble member of the vast concourse around it, was that my life must be saved and I must leave the Palace and leave the city at once. Everything was uncertain, except the compelling anxiety of all my people to get me away before the orgy of Chinese destruction and massacre began.

In darkness, and wearing a palace guard's uniform with a gun slung over his shoulder, the Dalai Lama set out on his perilous trek to India. His escape came just in time. By 2 a.m. that night Chinese heavy artillery and mortars began shelling the Dalai Lama's residence. Tracers flew like silvery birds over the palace grounds. Glass shattered, orange flame flickered, and stabs of light filled the crowded courtyard. Shells, bombs and grenades burst as people spun away, their cries echoing against the brute beat of guns. Over the following hours thousands of men, women and children who had camped around the palace walls to protect their living God were torn to pieces. The Chinese stormed the palace; the Dalai Lama's body-guards, who had remained behind to cover his escape, were disarmed and shot. Open rebellion erupted throughout Lhasa. People had learned in the most practical of schools, that of daily repression, the technique of street fighting. It caught the Chinese by surprise. But the surprise did not last. By midday the PLA units had moved into the city with tanks, heavy artil-lery and machine-guns. The Tibetans stood their ground and fought bravely. The narrow streets of the city became a fierce battleground.

The following morning the Chinese launched a heavy bombardment and renewed their assault. Crack units of the PLA moved into the city under orders to advance at all costs. Their tanks trundled forward, mud flying round the tracks. Shell after shell found its target. Behind a rolling barrage of shells the Chinese charged forward. The battle became a series of horrendous group actions: self-propelled guns blasted holes into build-ings and flamethrowers spewed burning oil through windows. Soon the city was filled with nauseating smoke from burning houses. The fright-ening roar of firefights was continuous.

Many inhabitants had come out in support of the rebels and took a stand. They were hard to kill; houses had to be blasted again and again before the men barricaded inside were silenced. Shattered walls lurched grotesquely. Women and children hid in cellars or were cut down as they raced for shelter. The wounded continued to struggle among the ruins. No place was safe from shellfire; whole streets disappeared. One by one the defenders were annihilated. Tanks overran the last barricade and crushed its defenders under their caterpillar tracks. The Tibetans died a courageous death, but they died as free men. By night, as machine-guns barked and took more lives, women and children escaped from the shattered city. For weeks the wretched wandered aimlessly around the countryside until fatigue, hunger, gales and bitter frost cut them down.

In a grim echo of Genghis Khan's merciless horde, rampaging Chinese troops smashed the final resistance on the high plateau. In monasteries, holy scriptures were burned and monks were gunned down, or disappeared into slave-labour camps. For those who did manage to find refuge among the crags and valleys, a slow death by famine was in store. The temperature dropped and a piercing wind swept the high plateau. The frozen dead lay in snowdrifts, pitifully small, like wax figures that had once been alive. Between eighty and ninety thousand Tibetans died in those months.

For the Dalai Lama, hunted by the Chinese, the ordeal was far from over. On foot and yak's back his column snaked its way across fields of ice and snow to the high passes across the Himalayas. "… our party had increased to 100, and we were escorted by about 350 Tibetan soldiers, and at least 50 guerrillas. From Ra-me, a detachment of about 100 men was sent to the south-west, to protect us in case the Chinese approached from the direction of the main road into India …"[3] On 31 March 1959 the Most Holy Man of Tibet crossed into India by the Khenzimane Pass. On 3 April, Prime Minister Pandit Nehru stood by his promise when he announced in the Indian Parliament that the Government of India had granted asylum to the Dalai Lama.

For years uncertainty had existed about the situation inside Tibet, hermetically sealed off from the outside world by the world's highest mountains on one side and a cordon of army garrisons on the other. Little news about the continuing destruction of a nation filtered out, until the Dalai Lama's party reached India and the faithful accompanying him on this perilous journey brought with them pictorial proof. The Dalai Lama went on a world tour to speak out against the genocide and suppression of human rights committed by the Chinese Communists. The world refused to listen. While Tibetans died, from bullet or famine, the world slept, and went on with business as usual. The bickering and manoeuvring in the stately halls of the United Nations revealed the depth of the division between Western powers and Asia. The West showed little will, and its grasp of Asian realities was badly out of date. Its myopic view of a new and dynamic China, together with a volatile Cold War climate in the United States and Europe and an almost pathological concern about matters along Europe's Iron Curtain, discouraged it from taking a firm stand on far-off Tibet.

And yet Mao's calculations did not quite work out the way he had intended. On one international front the suppression of Tibet badly backfired. In the spring of 1959, after the escape of the Dalai Lama, the Soviet Union began to shift its full support to India. It was an important step toward China's isolation, and one of several factors that led to the schism between China and the Soviet Union.

Was the 1950 invasion of Tibet a political test of the West's will? It took place shortly before Mao's intervention in Korea. It is likely that the West's non-reaction to Tibet's plea for assistance served Beijing as a trial case for a much bigger event. Mao saw in it a weakness to be fully exploited, which he did when he unleashed his hordes in Korea.

On the hard-packed road across the Tibetan Plateau, headlights weaved and bobbed. A ribbon of lights in a snowy wasteland. A PLA division moved on to a new battle.

"From this day Tibet is independent" was a call that belonged to history.

# 3

# A Cold *Nyet*

On 2 October 1950 Chairman Mao Zedong forwarded a secret dispatch to Marshal Joseph Stalin. If put into action, it would be sure to shake up not only the United States of America, but the world:

1. We have decided to send a portion of our troops, under the name of the Chinese Volunteers, to Korea, assisting the Korean comrades to fight the troops of the United States and its running dog Syngman Rhee. We regarded the mission as necessary. If Korea were completely occupied by the Americans and the Korean revolutionary force were fundamentally destroyed, the American invaders would be more rampant, and such a situation would be very unfavourable to the whole East.
2. We realize that since we have decided to send Chinese troops to Korea to fight the Americans, we must first be able to solve the problem, that is, we are prepared to wipe out the invaders from the United States and from other countries, and thus drive them out of Korea; second, since Chinese troops will fight American troops in Korea –although we will use the name of the Chinese Volunteers – *we must be prepared for an American declaration of war on China*. We must be prepared for the possible bombardments by American air forces of many Chinese cities and industrial bases, and for attacks by American naval forces on China's coastal areas.

Soviet sources have always denied the existence of this secret telegram, stressing that Mao never sent it. This sounds far-fetched. In a different version, the Russians stated that China never wanted to enter into the Korean conflict, but needed to be convinced in a strongly worded message by Comrade Stalin that "in the interests of the world proletarian revolution it was necessary that China sent its troops into Korea".

In fact, Stalin had been shocked by the quick and unyielding American response to North Korea's invasion of the South, and worried that a bold approach by Moscow could well lead to a direct confrontation between the United States and the USSR. Should the United States succeed in reversing the situation following General MacArthur's successful Inchon landing in September 1950, which crippled the North Koreans, the balance of power in North-East Asia would change radically in Washington's favour. This could lead to a direct confrontation between the two superpowers, since the Soviet Union could not allow America to become master over the Korean peninsula. On the other hand, should Soviet units, ground or airborne, appear in Korea, the world order established at the end of the Second World War would be overturned. Stalin's patent solution was to get the Chinese involved on the ground. He even introduced a thesis that sounded very much like a Communist version of the domino theory, warning Mao and his comrades that "failure to send Chinese troops to Korea could result in grave consequences, first for China's north-east, then for all of China, and finally for the entire socialist world revolution".

China's active entry into the Korean War, fought until then between the regiments of the autocratic North Korean leader Kim il-Sung and an alliance of United Nations forces, had been discussed during a session of the Chinese Communist Party's Central Committee, and a decision was taken only hours before the cable to Stalin went out. To strengthen the Communists' still uncertain hold over China, and to promote international prestige and recognition abroad of the Era of a New Socialist China, called for a daring act. Glorious victory was its outward target; silencing dissident voices and strengthening Mao's stranglehold on China its principal aim. Everything was in place; only one thing was missing: China's protective air cover. Without a viable air force, the country would leave itself wide open to US retaliatory air strikes.

The issue of air cover had been discussed and settled on 15 February 1950, the day Russia and China formed a common, progressive front against the "conservative portion of the world". After three months of difficult negotiations Stalin and Mao had signed an alliance that included a mutual defence treaty. For Stalin it was a strategic coup; at the height of the Cold War he acquired a massive ally, to whom he would give the role of protecting Russia's immense land border in Asia, thus freeing himself to concentrate his military resources in Europe. Specifically included in the treaty was a Soviet air umbrella for China. When the test finally came, Stalin did not keep to his part of the bargain. In Korea, Chinese soldiers did all the fighting and all the dying, while the Soviet Union sat back and looked on while their comrades were buried under a deluge of American napalm and bombs – a betrayal Mao Zedong was never to forget.

The Korean War resulted from a series of unsuccessful efforts to solve the problems of a Cold War confrontation in a world divided into two camps. Both in its origins and in the way it was fought, the war for supremacy over Korea was an outgrowth of a worldwide conflict that raged from 1939 to 1945 but had already begun in 1932 with Japan's invasion of Manchuria. It was set in motion by the collapse of China's Nationalist forces and the astoundingly easy Communist victory in 1949, which caught the Western world by surprise. Once the USA failed to prop up the tottering Guomindang regime, America became a paper tiger in Chinese eyes.

With its victory over Chiang Kai-shek's Nationalists, Communist China had become an emerging power to be taken seriously. The crucial elements in its foreign policy were the Party's perception of the outside world and China's position in it, and Mao's central role in the policy-making structure. Beijing's decision to enter the war was based on the belief that the outcome of the Korean crisis was closely related to a New China's vital domestic and international interests. There was little possibility that China's entry into the Korean War could have been averted while the conflict between the Chinese Communist Party and the United States escalated, and, at the same time, a strategic co-operation developed between Beijing and Moscow. Beijing perceived Washington as the barrier to its Asian ambitions, and that set the stage for Sino-American confrontation. In the beginning was the "Ward Affair", and it goes to show how a small, bizarre incident can lead to dramatic consequences.

On 2 November 1948 forces of the People's Liberation Army battling the retreating Nationalists stormed into the city of Shenyang, which had been evacuated by its foreign diplomatic corps, leaving representatives of only the USSR, the UK and the USA. The American consul general, Angus Ward, acted on specific instructions from Washington to remain behind as a neutral observer. The new Communist boss of Shenyang, Commissar Zhu Qiwen, who also happened to be the head of the Party's North-Eastern Bureau, summoned the remaining three members of the diplomatic community to a meeting in his office, during which he promised to protect the American, British and Soviet envoys with his PLA troops. This courtesy came from Zhou Enlai, who had ordered Qiwen to deal softly with foreign diplomats, foreign investment firms and foreign banks.

Two weeks passed and then America's consul was ordered to hand over his radio transmitter. The Soviet envoy, I. V. Kovalev, had advised Commissar Qiwen to confiscate the radio transmitter in order to prevent military espionage in aid of the Nationalists, and Qiwen ordered this drastic step without referring for instructions to Beijing. When Mao and Zhou were informed, both were upset; it was too soon to confront America head-on. But it was also too late to rescind the order without losing face. Challenged by a harshly worded telegram from the US State Department, the Chinese dug in. Mao told Qiwen to go ahead and seize the American diplomat's radio. To justify his move, Mao stressed: "As American military attachés have been involved in direct support of the Guomindang's civil war efforts, we should dispatch our soldiers to supervise them and allow them no freedom of movement."

Insisting on his diplomatic immunity, US Consul Ward barred his door and refused to hand over US government property installed in the American compound, which, according to international law, was extra-territorial. On 18 November 1948 the Communists showed just what they understood by "extra-territorial". They did not storm the consulate, but surrounded it with troops. Angus Ward, plus 20 consular personnel – vice consuls, radio technicians, mechanics and "one stateless woman" (a Chinese national who had taken refuge inside the consulate) – were put under house arrest which lasted until the end of 1949, when Ward and his staff were expelled. A minor incident that could have been easily settled was not, and with it was lost any chance of further diplomatic dialogue. So when, on the morning of 25 June 1950, the world woke up to the stunning news that North Korean army units had crossed the 38th Parallel into South Korea, China, the only mediator who might be able to stop the aggression, was already linked to the aggressor.

Seven North Korean infantry divisions under Marshal Choe Yong Gun scored an initial success and overran the southern capital, Seoul, before General Douglas MacArthur, Supreme Commander US Forces Far East, in one of the most daring tactical strokes in the history of modern warfare in both conception and result, landed the US X Corps at Inchon. A high-tide variance of only six hours was sufficient for American troop transports to unload soldiers on a rocky shore. The "Inchon Gamble" of 15 September 1950 was a total success and crushed the North Korean invasion force.

For weeks Beijing had been threatening an intervention should "United Nations troops cross the 38th Parallel and approach Chinese territory". General MacArthur ignored the warning. He showed that he was prepared to overturn US State Department policy and march beyond the 38th Parallel. President Harry S. Truman did not instruct him to the contrary. On 9 October 1950, with what he thought to be a clear presidential mandate to destroy North Korea's armed forces, MacArthur pushed his United Nations 8th Army across the disputed line of the 38th Parallel. Never once did he consider that China would make good on its threat to intervene – unless he crossed the River Yalu and entered Chinese Manchuria. In any case, MacArthur did not believe in the ChiComs' staying power since they had not long ago emerged shaken from a devastating civil war with its great human and material losses. An American general, not thinking like a politician, was wrong in both of his assumptions.

In fact, Chairman Mao had more pressing reason to shift his nation's attention to a threat coming from the outside. South of the Yangtze, communities had banded into secret societies to resist the harsh Communist land reforms. What had worked throughout history, Mao would now use to work for him: he would enforce his internal power by creating a diversion in the form of an external crisis. By drawing attention "to an external peril" he would have a free hand in solving his problems at home. The signs of imminent trouble were clear and should have alerted the leaders of the Free World. They did not. Just as the Chinese thought of Americans as paper tigers, Washington was sure that the Chinese would never try anything as foolish as challenging American air and naval might. There was an even bigger reason for China to desist: America had "the Big One". It had not dawned on Washington that the bomb could never be used without starting a global holocaust, yet that was what the Chinese counted on. There is no indication that Mao even considered the possibility of the United States reverting to the use of nuclear arms. Or, to paraphrase a famous quote by Mao from 1946: "The atom bomb is a paper tiger which the United States reactionaries use to scare people."

Shortly after China took the decision to enter the conflict, Zhou Enlai asked India's ambassador to Beijing, K. M. Panikkar, to meet him, and requested: "Please convey via diplomatic channels a message of the highest importance. Should the American forces cross the 38th Parallel and expand the war, we will not sit still. China will be forced to intervene."

An empty warning? Or the justification for what had already been decided? Mao was certain of victory. In February, Stalin had promised him complete air cover against America's bomber squadrons, along with a plentiful supply of weapons that the Soviet Union had recovered from the Japanese. This meant that China could count on a vast numerical superiority in conventional artillery weapons. With France and Britain eliminated as military powers in the Second World War, and the Cold War confrontation along Europe's Iron Curtain, America was fully committed to the defence of western Europe. But America had only limited human resources to throw into the war, whereas China had Genghis Khan-sized hordes at its call: five million men under arms. To lead a portion of this human arsenal into Korea, Mao picked Marshal Peng Dehuai.

The decision to enter the war was taken on 2 October; the only question was the appropriate date to do so. Mao decided on 15 October 1950.

Peng Dehuai, in overall military command, assembled huge forces: the 4th Field Army Group, consisting of four armies, three artillery divisions and three anti-aircraft regiments; a total of 40 divisions of three hundred and eighty thousand front-line troops, with back-up from over a million more. Marshal Peng was ready. All it took to fire the first shot was a green light.

Then, three days before the action was due to start, Peng received an urgent order from Mao: "Stay where you are. Do not, repeat, do not begin hostile operations!"

If Mao had relied on the strategic Russian–Chinese agreement, he suddenly found Stalin unreliable and untrustworthy. He had to deal with the cold fact that the Soviet leader had reneged on his original promise. And all in the space of one short week in October 1950.

On 8 October 1950, the date Mao had designated for the first Chinese reconnaissance units to cross on to Korean soil, an Ilyushin jet carrying a Chinese delegation, led by Zhou Enlai, Lin Biao (who was already in Russia for medical treatment), Wang Xiaxiang (China's ambassador to the Soviet Union), Kang Yimin (Zhou Enlai's secretary) and Shi Zhe (an interpreter), landed on an airfield near the Black Sea, to see to the final arrangements as covered in the Soviet–Chinese defence pact. Presenting the Soviet side were Stalin, his deputy Malenkov, KGB chief Beria, Kaganovich, Bulganin, Mikoyan, Foreign Minister Molotov and Fedorenko (a Russian interpreter).[1]

A man wearing a uniform cut from simple cloth walked into the room. There was no need to introduce him, his picture hung in every Russian village assembly hall just as the image of Christ filled every church in the West. Attention focused on this man. In an atmosphere of extreme suspicion and high tension, since nobody quite knew anybody else's position, the discussion opened between the two leaders.

Stalin asked Zhou Enlai: "The situation of our Korean comrades is preoccupying and urgent. What do our Chinese comrades make of it?"

Zhou tried out the mined territory: "Marshal Stalin, after years of civil war, China is faced by serious difficulties. It might be better for us *not to enter into another conflict.*"

Stalin: "Without outside help, our Korean brother will not survive. Consider the American menace to the security of your North-Eastern border if their forces reach the Yalu. Also, an American occupation of all of Korea would completely alter the situation of both China and the Soviet Union in East Asia."

Zhou: "That we fully realize and it is a subject of great concern to our Party leadership. But may we expect your assistance? Our direct involvement may not be feasible, given our shortage of war material."

Stalin needed to sweeten the offer to make the Chinese accept: "We shall supply the Chinese Army with much of the artillery it requires. In our stockpile is an amount of war material from our Great Patriotic War which we can put at our Chinese comrades' disposal."

With this, the bargaining began. Zhou wanted more, much more, and Stalin knew it.

Zhou: "We shall require direct and active assistance. Can we count on it?"

Stalin cleverly dodged his Chinese counterpart's question about Soviet active involvement. Here began the laying down of cards in what turned out to become a gigantic poker hand. Stalin wanted to push the Chinese into having a go at the Americans, in order to relieve US pressure on his area of principal concern, Europe's Iron Curtain and his plans for a Communist Europe. It was a pleasant enough thought to watch the US traipsing off into the icy wastes of far-off Manchuria. Stalin hoped for shades of Napoleon in Russia, yet he held off giving Mao active military support since the Americans would see it as direct interference, and this again could lead to a fatal clash between the Soviet Union and the United States.

Interpreter: "Comrade Stalin says that Chairman Mao has the very difficult task of leading a nation to war, and the Soviet Union will do all it can to help their socialist brothers in their struggle." When the interpreter, Fedorenko, had delivered this, he looked at his boss, who sat in silence smoking his cigarette. Then he finished Stalin's sentence, the key to the meeting: "However, in certain aspects our hands are tied."

There followed a moment of shocked silence across the table, before Stalin, through Fedorenko, continued: "The Soviet Union cannot supply ground troops; for that our common border with Korea is too narrow." It certainly was not, but it gave Stalin a valid excuse to stay out of Korea. "Also, we have committed ourselves at the United Nations to a total withdrawal from Korean territory. Should we reverse this situation, *it might lead to a direct confrontation between the Soviet Union and the United States.*"

Stalin was not about to test the Americans in Asia, neither on the ground, nor in the air. While the meeting was in progress he was told that two US fighter aircraft (probably a case of mistaken target identification) had attacked a Soviet airbase a hundred kilometres from the Korean border. Intentionally or not, it clearly pointed to the danger of a widening conflict. Stalin was told of the incident, but then withheld this information from Zhou Enlai.

Zhou: "In the matter of an air umbrella?"

Stalin switched to a more conciliatory tone: "Our air force will cover Chinese troop movements *along the Yalu*, and, if needed, we will defend China's North-Eastern coastal regions."

The moment had finally come. Zhou asked the key question: "Will the Soviet Air Force cover a Chinese advance on to Korean territory?"

"That will take some time to prepare. *We cannot do that at this time.*"

Stalin had spelled it out – a clear and harsh *nyet!* You go into Korea, you risk getting smashed by the US Air Force, but we will do nothing to protect you.

This was not the reply Zhou had expected, and he was visibly taken aback.

Stalin: "So, what is your date? When are your troops launching the attack?"

"Marshal Stalin, I am in no position to give you a reply before I confer with Beijing."

It was now 5 a.m., still dark, with no stars in the sky, when the Chinese delegates were escorted to their limousines. The 10-hour meeting had been a disaster. Within minutes, Zhou informed Mao that they could not count on the previously agreed Soviet air cover. It was Zhou's message from the Black Sea that delayed China's entry into the Korean War. Mao dispatched his last-minute "stop" message and put his troops on hold. As a decisive turning point for quick victory the Chinese had staked their strategy on a bold move through an unsuspecting enemy. After all, luck in war is mostly on the side willing to take chances. Now Mao was suddenly made to realize that his ambitious plan to annihilate the Americans in Asia stood a vastly diminished chance of success. PLA Marshal Peng Dehuai was so angered by Stalin's refusal to supply the vital air cover that he asked to be relieved of his command of the Chinese People's Volunteers (CPV), and only a personal intervention by Mao prevented it.

One enigma remains. There is no mention in Shi Zhe's account of this fateful Black Sea meeting of why Zhou Enlai – with three hundred and eighty thousand Chinese ready to cross the border into Korea – told Stalin that China was reluctant and that "it would be better for us not to enter into another conflict".

There exists another account that contradicts Shi Zhe's explanation of China's reluctance to enter the conflict. Kang Yimin, Zhou's personal secretary, states: "We arrived to inform the Soviet leaders that China had *already decided and was ready* to send troops to resist America and assist

Korea, and to ask the Soviet Union to provide China with military support and send Soviet air forces to the North-East." And that it was only *after* Stalin's *nyet* that Zhou gave his vague reply as to a date.

In a later discussion between Mao and North Korea's Kim il-Sung (in 1970), the Chairman revealed that during that decisive Black Sea conference Zhou Enlai had presented Stalin with two options, and Stalin left both without a reply. "We were ready to send our troops into Korea," Mao told Kim, "and we needed to make certain that the Soviets would give us air cover. Molotov had agreed, but then Stalin called to say that their air forces could not fly beyond the Yalu. Finally we took the decision and cabled him that – whether the Soviets would dispatch its air forces to Korea or not – we would go ahead." Mao's remark referred to the famous telegram that the Russians claimed had never been sent.

Without Russian support, China would now have to depend on Mao's principle of self-reliance. And it was up to the CCP's Central Committee to come to a decision. On 13 October Mao dispatched a secret cable to Zhou Enlai: "… In short, we believe that we should enter the war and that we must enter the war. Entering the war can be most rewarding; failing to do so may cause great harm …"[2]

At the same moment as the Stalin–Zhou conference, another meeting took place on Wake Island, where US President Harry S. Truman met with General Douglas MacArthur. At a politically trying moment in a steadily heating Cold War which would lead to the McCarthy witch-hunt period, Truman was harried by America's hard right over his supposed softness toward Communism. Out of political necessity, and by associating himself with the "military conqueror of Japan", he ensured that he scored massively at home. As Truman put it: "I thought that a general ought to know his Commander-in-Chief and that I ought to know my senior field commander in the Far East." Already on 29 June, Truman had authorized MacArthur to use naval and air resources of the US Far East Command in support of South Korean troops.

Preoccupied with his role in post-war Japan, MacArthur had all but ignored the land fighting of 1948 in China, since he expected to learn nothing from the lethargic performance of Chiang Kai-shek's disheartened Nationalist Army, just as the planning, tactics and operations of the Communists were so patently amateurish that he dismissed them as unworthy of study. So when he took command in Korea he never even considered the risk of a huge Chinese horde storming across the Yalu to dislocate his lines of communication. He was obsessed by the idea that Korea would carry him to yet another glorious victory, and this long before the Chinese had a chance to react. And should the Chinese carry out their threat, the ageing general was quick to assure his president, not more than sixty thousand Chinese troops could be expected across the Yalu, "and these will be mangled by our air force before they will have a chance to get started". It goes to show how unreliable MacArthur's intelligence was: nearly half a million Chinese were poised to pounce on his armies.

On 20 October 1950 MacArthur issued his controversial order for the rapid advance into North Korea. The troops under his command crossed the 38th Parallel. Neither the US President nor the US Joint Chiefs of Staff countermanded the general's decision,[3] not even after MacArthur entered the political arena with a rash statement: "To give up any portion of North Korea to the aggression of the Chinese Communists would be the greatest defeat of the Free World in recent times. Indeed, to yield to so immoral a proposition would bankrupt our leadership, and influence in Asia, and render untenable our position both politically and morally."

For the moment a general rather than a political leader became the final arbiter of the fate not only of Korea, but also of his country and its fighting men. A military opportunity had become the engine of war at the expense of a political afterthought. In this matter MacArthur was anything but a prudent commander; all he saw was another summit of personal glory in the predictable outcome of this war. It was not to be. The Chinese had given a warning that their threat should be taken seriously.

Then it happened. With MacArthur's forces battling for the northern capital of Pyongyang, and a ROK (Republic of Korea, or South Korea; as opposed to the Democratic People's Republic of Korea, or North Korea) division pushing toward the Yalu, Mao Zedong issued his order for attack: "It has been decided that the four armies and three artillery divisions will follow our original plan to enter northern Korea for war operations. These troops will start to cross the River Yalu from the Andong-Ji'an section tomorrow – 19 October evening. In order to maintain strict secrecy, the troops should start to cross the river after dusk ..."

It was 9 p.m. on 18 October 1950. The "big war" was on.

*Alea jacta est.* Nothing could stop another bloody confrontation between East and West.

The first major war in the nuclear age became a conflict of two opposing ideologies – not only East versus West, and Capitalism versus Communism, but the ideological struggle between Chinese Communism and Soviet Communism. On 15 February 1950 China had signed its Treaty of Friendship and Alliance with the Soviet Union. On 12 October of the same year Stalin broke it. It demonstrated clearly the ideological differences and conflicting power ambitions which helped to widen the crack in the "monolithic" structure of World Communism. The Red Tsar had handed his socialist brothers a cold *nyet*. The duplicity of Stalin over support for its Korean venture redefined China's future policy, and altered its security strategy. Never again would Mao allow his country's national security to be put into an ally's hand.

Mao decided on a collision course against a coalition of virtually all the Western industrial powers. Beijing propped up the tottering regime of Kim il-Sung, but at a price of burying all hopes for a Sino-American accommodation. The victor's price was hegemony over Asia. Was Mao's motive simply to create a new empire – not Ming but Marxist – and become Communism's undisputed global champion? Perhaps.

However, there was a much more pressing reason: Korea happened at a time when Mao's dictatorship drummed up nationalist sentiments to divert attention from his, and the Party's, failings at home. With a rise in patriotic feeling, and the support of flag-waving masses as a sign of "the people's will", the Communists cracked down on dissidents and cemented their power. As a direct result of the Korean War no more dissenting voices were raised in China for the next 30 years.

In this defining time following a devastating world war, an important aspect of the entry by the United Nations into the Korean War has been greatly ignored: the true role played by Stalin. Over all his strategic manoeuvring lingers more than just a whiff of Soviet duplicity. On the eve of the vote by the United Nations on entering the Korean conflict, the Soviet Union's representative quit the UN Security Council in protest at the UN's failure "to provide brotherly China with a permanent seat on the Security Council". Yet a refusal to accept China as a full-time member was precisely what Stalin had in mind.[4] A "fraternal rivalry" within that decisive world body the Security Council was the last thing the Red dictator could wish for. So it happened that, on the day the resolution to dispatch a coalition of United Nations troops to Korea was put to a vote in the UN Security Council, the delegate of the Soviet Union was absent from the council chamber.

No Soviet *nyet* – and no Security Council *veto*! The vote was passed.

For the first time in its brief history, the United Nations marched to war.

Three things combined to lead to great suffering: an American general's belief in the soundness of his plan, a Chinese chairman's need to silence opposition at home and a Soviet dictator reneging on a treaty for mutual assistance.

# 4

# THE EAST WIND PREVAILS OVER THE WEST WIND[1]

## 6 DECEMBER 1950, CHOSIN RESERVOIR, NORTH KOREA

"We are at the Yalu!" – the commander of an advance unit was proud to report. A stunned voice came back from UN 8th Army headquarters: "You cannot be on the Yalu. It's absolutely out of the question. I have the latest aerial images right in front of me. You must have made a mistake."

"No mistake, General. We are at the Yalu."

A long silence, then a voice came on line. It was US Lieutenant General Walton Walker. "Well, if you're there, then stay where you are."

It was 26 October 1950. The commanding general of the UN 8th Army stared at the big wall map. Incredible! A battalion from South Korea's 6th ROK Division had reached the Yalu – the river border separating Korea from China!

While an American general got ready to push on with the rest of his forces and then hold them on the south bank of the river, a Chinese marshal dictated a string of orders. His huge force was also on the Yalu; only they had not held to their side of the border. They were already across!

For weeks UN commanders had been driving the remnants of a near-annihilated North Korean army in front of their guns; they were blind to the presence of two Chinese Army Groups in the area. How was it possible that half a million men of a potential enemy – who by the way wasn't an enemy as yet – along with trucks, artillery and stores, could have assembled along the Yalu without their presence being discovered?[2] How could two hundred thousand men plus columns of vehicles cross a mighty river on the only two available bridges, even in the dark of night? Despite the extent of sophistication that Western military intelligence had achieved by the waning days of the Second World War, when they could read Frau Göring's daily shopping list, this time the West's intelligence service broke down so completely that their fighting men were caught completely unawares. When the crunch finally happened the United Nations Alliance was left gasping.

In one of history's classic examples of surprise, following Mao's "go order" as many as a hundred and eighty thousand CPV troops crossed the Yalu and marched stealthily to encounter an advancing enemy. By the end of October 1950 the 13th Army Group of Marshal Lin Biao's 4th Field Army – 38th, 39th, 40th, 42nd, 50th and 66th Armies, altogether 18 divisions – waited in hiding in forward areas north of the River Chongchon, from Chongju in the west to the Chosin reservoir in the east, ready to engage General Walker's UN 8th Army. The 13th Army Group was reinforced by the 9th Army Group of General Chen Yi's 3rd Field Army – 20th, 26th and 27th Armies, comprising another 12 divisions – ready to strike at the flank of Major General Edward M. Almond's US X Corps near the reservoir. Counting on 30 divisions of Chinese People's Volunteers – with another half a million men in reserve on the north bank of the Yalu – Marshal Peng Dehuai's plan was a tactical masterpiece: to strike into the gap that had opened in the rapidly advancing UN forces between the Fusen and Chosin reservoirs, as well as the junction of the rivers Kuryong and Chongchon, split the United Nations forces in two and roll them up from the flank.

In late October an American patrol took some prisoners who were arguably not Koreans. Under interrogation by an American lieutenant and his young South Korean interpreter, they told the lieutenant that they were part of an ethnic group living in the northern region of Korea. The prisoners were sent back under guard, and nobody thought to check if such an ethnic group really did exist. This happened in the hectic days of "let's get to the Yalu before others do". The 6th ROK Division had finally won the race. In a symbolic gesture, their first act was to fill a bottle with "water from the Yalu" and present it to their country's president, Syngman Rhee.

Back on 27 October, near Ongjon, the same 6th ROK Division had been surprised by a great number of enemies, jumping at them out of nowhere. The 6th ROK was mauled; nothing before had pointed to the presence of a large number of Chinese troops *south* of the Yalu. On 1 November a similar incident took place between an "unidentified enemy force" in uniforms that were definitely not North Korean, and a unit of the US 8th Cavalry near Ansung in North Korea. It was one of the many warnings that went unheeded by American Intelligence. On 6 November aerial reconnaissance informed General MacArthur of a massive troop movement crossing the Yalu, and he ordered the immediate destruction of the main bridge between Antung (China) and Sinuiju (North Korea). The US Joint Chiefs countermanded his order and limited aerial operations to five miles south of the river border. MacArthur fired off a furious message: "Men and material in large force are pouring across the two bridges over the Yalu from Manchuria. The movement not only jeopardizes but threatens the ultimate destruction of the forces under my command ... every hour that this is postponed will be paid dearly in American and other United Nations' blood."

Not everyone ignored the danger of a Chinese intervention. In Washington retired General Omar Bradley advocated the instant bombing of the Yalu bridges. The reaction to this suggestion by American allies was "highly unfavourable, as such an act might incite China to react". Washington decided that China, despite its voiced threats, was making a face-saving gesture and was quite unwilling to face the United Nations over Korea. Washington and its military were prepared to call "the Chairman's bluff". That undue delay, brought about by a political and not a strategic decision, proved to be one of the key factors in America's subsequent losses and the continuation of the war. Those who had previously dealt with Mao should have known that he was trading space for time. He would attack when the enemy was beyond his major supply bases in rugged terrain. For this, the hilly border region of North Korea was ideally suited.

On 24 November 1950 – Thanksgiving Day, when the good folks back in the States dug into their family turkey and gave little thought to a far-off war that, so the newspaper kept telling them, was already won – the UN 8th Army was driving north in what had turned into a road race for the Yalu. For the fighting troops a special treat was in store. US planes had delivered turkeys to its forward units, when out of the blue the 8th Army was struck a massive blow by "non-existent forces".

"The hell – what is this?" demanded General Walker.

"ChiComs, General."

"What?"

"The Chinese are coming!"

Minute after minute more engagement reports were coming in. Little red flags popped up in disconcerting numbers on Walker's frontline map. Confusion reigned in the UN 8th Army. Contradictory orders went out to divisions, battalions, companies and platoons: "Hold the breach!" "Get your unit into defensive posture!" "Don't retreat!" "Reinforcements on the way!" "Pull back!" "Pull out!"

That night Marshal Peng unleashed the full force of his hidden might. Six armies of the 13th CPV Army Group, at the time the single most powerful formation in Asia, struck the sector between Sanju and Kunu-ri, while his 42nd CPV Army turned sharply west to prepare an ambush on the only road open for a UN retreat, through a defile that was to gain notoriety as "the Pass".

"We face an entirely new war," declared a stunned MacArthur. Indeed, he did. Hour after hour the dazzling opportunity to destroy the North Korean aggressor grew fainter and then vanished altogether. The first to suffer the Chinese crusher was the 8th ROK Division, then the 1st ROK Division. While Walker had to yield to the pressure from overwhelming numbers, and pulled his UN 8th Army back to the River Chongchon, MacArthur finally ordered the planes of the US Air Force to smash the Sinuiju Bridge across the Yalu – a fortnight after two entire Chinese Army Groups had crossed into North Korea! The ROK II Corps disintegrated, opening a wide gap between the two advancing UN prongs and exposing the flanks of both the UN 8th Army and the US X Corps.

On 26 November, in Walker's 8th Army sector, Peng's armies broke out of hiding and raced across a thinly defended countryside for Kunu-ri. Walker's men could do nothing to stop the onslaught. Peng's unleashed hordes smashed the American and South Korean line of resistance and reached the north bank of the Chongchon with three armies, where they hammered the UN forces with concentrated artillery fire. Divisions were cut to pieces; battalions or companies tried to hold a crossroads here, a bridge there; detachments were cut off from the rest and annihilated. Figures, ragged and shell-shocked, came panting along narrow farm roads, dragging their wounded.

"This is now the frontline," they were told, and put into newly constituted units. That was before the entire UN front collapsed.

The 30th November 1950 was a day the men of General Keiser's 2nd US Division would never forget. Struck by two Chinese armies, the 9th from the east and the 13th from the north, Keiser had ordered a withdrawal to the south bank of the Chongchon. With confusing reports coming in from all forward elements, I Corps commander Milburn called Keiser. "How do things stand in your sector?"

"Lousy. I'm hit from all sides. Right now they're shelling my command post."

Before a new defence line could be established, the Chinese had crossed the river and the forward units of the 2nd Division were cut to pieces by mortar bombs. Then came a massive onslaught which left the Americans almost helpless. The men of the 2nd Division were falling back in disarray; their strung-out column was retreating along the Kunu-ri–Sunchon road, when great numbers of Chinese fell on them from both sides of the highway. Small-arms fire poured down on the Americans. They kept their heads close to the ground; all they could do was pray. "Dear God, please take care of my family when I'm no longer around."

Bullets poured in, kicking up dirt next to the men as they huddled in ditches and behind rocks.

"I'm hit, I'm hit," voices cried out; "I'm hit!", as more rounds hammered into bodies.

"Get me out!" groaned one, writhing in pain. When the firing let up momentarily, a medic crawled to a wounded man, lying with his head turned to the side, his mouth open, with thick red spittle easing over his lips and down his chin. "I'm hit in the chest," he mumbled. That moment the medic was hit in the leg. He crawled back on hands and knees, dragging the wounded soldier with him into the roadside ditch. The redeeming feature was the courage of those who kept their discipline and fought their way through the tangle of wreckage that blocked the road, and the buddy system whereby those still able to walk helped thousands of the wounded make it along the blood-splattered ribbon of death. One of the retreating units was the 23rd US Infantry Regiment of Colonel Paul "Great White Father" Freeman, who managed to bring out most of his regiment in fairly good shape.

"The power of Western civilization, as God has permitted it to flower in our own beloved lands, shall defy and defeat Communism," declared a defiant UN 8th Army's commander. "Whether the rule of men who shoot their prisoners, enslave their citizens, and deride the dignity of man, shall displace the rule of those to whom the individual and his individual rights are sacred; whether we are to survive with God's hand to guide and lead us, or to perish in the dead existence of a Godless world."

General Walker had every reason to feel concerned. East of his UN 8th Army, the US Marine divisions of General Almond's X Corps were spread paper-thin across miles of barren mountainsides. The first of December was a cold, steely winter evening along the Chosin reservoir; it promised to be an even colder night where General Oliver P. Smith's 1st US Marine Division was dug in near Yudam-ri. Next to him was David Barr's 7th US Army Division. Nothing moved in the yellow sky and nothing moved on the ground. During the day the Marines had dug in. The ground was frozen and so were their fingers. Two men per foxhole, one on watch and one to sleep, both rolled up in blankets. Suddenly and ghostlike out of an icy fog appeared hordes of Chinese. Three Chinese divisions (79th, 89th and 59th) struck advance positions of the US Marines. Everything happened so fast that "Ollie" Smith was unable to reach most of his units with orders. Those who escaped the surprise artillery barrage formed defensive lines around their platoon sergeants or lieutenants. Men from dispersed units joined others to make their stand.

The enemy advanced over open country, running toward the Americans' positions, not in open order but in tightly packed formations. Those without rifles came with explosives strapped to their backs to blow up the American guns. The American field guns opened up. Fountains of earth shot into the sky. Hundreds of attackers fell, but hundreds more came behind them. An American artillery commander, staring through his binoculars in disbelief, saw ranks tumbling like bowling pins, before the follow-up wave climbed over their bodies. With the human wave dangerously close to the perimeter he shortened his guns' range, firing almost point-blank. The noise of battle rose, the guns roared without let-up, with their tubes overheating and ammunition running short.

Reports of new encounters came by the minute into General Smith's headquarters. At the same time as three divisions attacked his front at Yudam-ri, another four enemy division (58th, 60th, 76th and 77th) attacked his crucial supply route between Hagaru and Koto-ri. In 24 hours enough companies had been shot out from under Ollie Smith for him to know the dimensions of the disaster. He commanded a division in name only and now faced a mission of crushing proportion. His order came down to his units: "Withdraw, and save what can be saved." Mainly lives. Ten thousand US Marines retreated along the Chosin reservoir to a defence perimeter that had been thrown up around the village of Hagaru. Even that could not be held, and on 6 December 1950 it too was evacuated; guns which could not be taken along were blown up. But there was one thing they would never leave behind: their fallen comrades.

Colonel Lewis B. "Chesty" Puller of the 1st US Marines Division was a colourful character. Just before they set out to run the gauntlet, he climbed on top of his jeep to cheer up his boys. "Hell, I don't give a goddam how many Chinese laundrymen there are between us and Hungnam. There aren't enough in the world to stop a US Marines regiment going where it wants to go! Christ in His Mercy will see us through!"

All who could walk or crawl began their move from Hagaru toward distant Koto-ri. Those who could not walk were carried, strapped across the hoods of jeeps, or hunkering on the running boards of trucks. So began the US Marines' famous "attack backward".

Marshal Peng Dehuai had brought up four full-strength CPV divisions to strike the flanks of the retreating Americans. His 58th and 60th Divisions were in an ambush position west of the defile, and the 76th and 77th Divisions to the east of the 78-kilometre, single-lane road snaking along "Hellfire Valley". Without adequate winter clothing in mountains where the thermometer dropped way below zero, the retreating Americans slugged past the positions they had stormed only a few weeks before. General Smith was aware that his division could not expect help. They had to fight their own way out. The snow-covered landscape was covered with shell holes; new black patches appeared beside old grey ones, already covered with snow. The pursuing Chinese suffered horrendous losses whenever engaged in bloody rearguard actions. Frequently a point section engaged in hand-to-hand combat. The men were tired, and many walked with their eyes shut; but even with closed eyes the nightmare would not go away.

Night came like a wall of darkness; magnesium flares cast ghastly shadows of yet another horde coming at them. Tracer bullets found easy targets. After each firefight the men squatted by the side of the frozen road, worn out by their never-ending combat. Dysentery, hunger, shellfire and cold – how far would they go, or rather: how far could they go? They stumbled on doggedly, with feet moving according to their elementary laws. An icy storm blew in their faces, their lungs were on fire from the cold air they inhaled, and this reduced them to a state of exhaustion and raggedness. An American division dragged their wounded through that cursed defile, surrounded on all sides by the enemy. They sucked on tubes of sweet condensed milk; wells could not be used as the enemy had poisoned them by dumping corpses down the shafts.

In a small temple next to the road was a first-aid station caring for the wounded. Some were so badly hurt that the medic could do little beyond easing their pain with morphine. Others sat sullenly on the ground, holding a blood-soaked rag over their wounds, patiently waiting their turn. Trucks with tarpaulins were emptied of crates to make room for the dead. "The speed of our withdrawal is governed by the dispatch of our wounded," said their general, who would not leave a single wounded or dead Marine behind.

The 1st Marines fought on – backward! – blasting their way through roadblocks, seizing hills which their enemy could have used as gun positions in order to zero in on the retreating column. Oil froze in recoil mechanisms; much of the contact with the enemy was at such close quarters that a man's best weapon was his hand grenade. Mortar rounds rained down on the column, scattering shrapnel into the ribs and limbs of the US Marines. An unfailing will not to give in kept them going. "Onward backward! Farther south!" How far was farther south? They knew that somewhere through the next gorge, over the next pass, waited shelter and hot food. They must reach it before they froze to death or were struck down by a sniper bullet from one of the many hills to either side of that cursed gauntlet. Continuous air strikes by fighters and bombers of Carrier Task Force 77 supported them. Throughout 38 hours of sheer hell they clawed their way to safety and put seven enemy divisions out of action.

At the village of Koto-ri a group of war correspondents, hungry for the latest news, waited for details of the torturous retreat. From their dispatches America could follow the tale of the heroic struggle of the 1st US Marines. A mass of tired Marines were jammed into a small perimeter; transport planes airdropped supplies; some of the parcels contained – condoms!

"And what the fuck are we supposed to do with these? There ain't no women anywhere near," cursed a sergeant. The sergeant was wrong; there was at least one woman present: Marguerite Higgins, a highly respected reporter for the *Herald Tribune*; once she had filed her story, and despite cries of sexual discrimination, she was put on to a plane and flown out. That led to a controversy between the divisional commander, Ollie Smith, and his superior, the commander of US X Corps; at stake was Lieutenant General Edward M. Almond's share of glory. A Marine told his own story about this general: "Two weeks before, we're sitting fuckin' freezing in our holes, so this Almond shows up in Hagaru. 'Bloody cold out here,' says he. 'This morning when I got up, the water in my toothbrush glass was frozen.'"

"'Ain' that just too fucking bad, General,' says Charlie, my platoon sarge."[3]

Major General Oliver P. Smith of the 1st US Marines Division, slim and unpretentious, earned his place in US military history. There is nothing more difficult than disengaging a large body of men in the face of a vastly superior enemy. Few are the historic examples where this operation has been conducted with similar success. Ollie Smith did it, and he put it in a sound bite that made headlines: "Retreat, hell! We're only advancing in another direction!"

A Chinese marshal had failed to destroy the Americans. What had seemed an assured victory turned into virtual defeat. Not only had the enemy managed to slip away close to the coast, where he could be resupplied; in doing so, the Americans had severely mauled his central column, intended as a pincer movement to cut into the rear of the enemy's 8th Army. His artillery commanders had emptied their precious ammunition stores and very little of his first strike human reserve was left. What remained of his central prong was all mixed together into one mangled lot.

Nobody came out blameless. America's politicians had greatly underestimated the danger of getting embroiled with "a real enemy" – not North Korea, but China. And when it happened, their military masterminds blundered by disregarding the climate and nature of the land where they would have to do battle. The UN troops were ill equipped to fight a winter war. An American supreme commander's plan to annihilate the North

Koreans had come to a grinding halt in the snows of North Korea, when out of the cold winter fog appeared ghostly hordes.

Despite the military setback, the retreat from the Chosin reservoir was strategically crucial to the final outcome of the war. Marshal Peng had engaged half of his overall resources in the central sector, which allowed the UN 8th Army to the west to withdraw in relatively good order. Peng's strategy, to push the American divisions into a pocket, had failed. Leaving the Americans and their United Nations allies as fighting units, the Chinese lost the chance to win the war. For a time, however, they had succeeded in halting the United Nations' offensive.

The only certainty in war is that a battle never develops exactly as foreseen by commanders. Circumstances which seem possible at the onset turn out to be quite unrealistic and dictate new, significant changes. If the objective is achieved, it is held to have been capably executed. If something goes wrong, lack of initiative is suspected. Or, in Beijing's political jargon: battles are won by generals and lost by soldiers ...

One thing was certain. The political face of war had changed.

Korea was no longer the issue. China was.

# 5

# "Keep 'em dying!"

## 1 March 1951, all across the Isthmus of Korea

It happens in war that a military situation can be judged better from afar than by using tunnel vision along the frontline. Beijing noticed it before its forward commander, Marshal Peng Dehuai: the encirclement and destruction of the enemy force had failed. Victory was slipping from their grasp. Peng had promised quick victory, but it was not as easy as his planners had thought. What was discussed during strategy meetings in Beijing as a war plan had become a harsh reality in the forward command centre, once theory was translated into action. Peng had experienced anxiety before implementing the attack, exhilaration at the initial successes and apprehension as his drive began to stall. Mao remained inflexible in his demand: total victory over the paper tigers.

Peng had ordered his division commanders to penetrate the enemy's lines, and this they had done; but their losses were great, and they had failed to encircle the Americans and destroy them. Peng stared at the flags on the wall map and his frown deepened; the flag positions had not changed in days, in weeks. His unease came from the knowledge that he could never match the West's logistics, supplies and firepower. He was provided with intelligence of the numbers of cannon and piles of ammunition his enemy received daily by the shipload, while he stood by unable to act. He could not bomb their harbours and their ammunition piles since he had no bomber force. Waving flags and stirring speeches did not win a war. His gun tubes were worn out; his trucks broke down or ran out of petrol; whatever ammunition stockpiles were still at his disposal were in the wrong locations; and he had no transport to shift troops. Divisions had to walk, and that took time. American spotter planes reported on their moves; the element of surprise was gone, and by the time a division got into its jump-off position, the Americans had fortified their line with guns of every calibre, while their air force knocked out his bridges and supply lines. The mighty US 7th Fleet, with its carrier group, had shifted into attack formation. Its aerial strike force was overwhelming, and the Chinese lacked a protective air umbrella. While they had the men, the Americans had the trucks and jeeps, artillery and aircraft. Comrade Marshal Peng knew that the countdown was under way, and a counter-offensive could take place any time. His troops would be facing battle-hardened veterans who had learned their trade in Normandy and Okinawa.

"When victory?" came the peremptory call from up high.

"No one could be more concerned than I, Comrade Chairman." One more drive and he would push the Americans into the sea. It had to work. The latest version of the Korean War was fought exclusively by the Chinese! Mao and the Communist Party of China had mobilized a whole family of peoples and races against the United Nations forces. The human reserves of a continent faced the dug-in Western alliance. The Americans were holding their line with a string of fortified places. Deadly porcupines, bristling with guns.

"They're all around us, but this is where we fight it out," seemed a daring statement by Colonel Paul Freeman, commander of the 23rd US Infantry Regiment, holding his part of the line at Chipyong-ni.[1] Five thousand four hundred Yanks were facing seventy thousand ChiComs. Private Seymour Harris had arrived in time for the big battle. "Jesus, I am praying. Not for my life, but for the guts it will take to see me through this. I pray that I will not let anybody down. I pray that I will be able to do what I came here to do. And if I get killed, it won't be without a fight. I won't lie down like a whipped dog. If the Chinks get me I promise they are going to have to work at it ..." Within hours he was able to prove his boast.

The moment the first wave of Chinese rose from the ground a smoke grenade arced into the sky and was instantly followed by a single, valley-wide blast. The whole countryside erupted with gun, mortar and machine-gun fire. Radios crackled with messages. Colonel Freeman gained control of the battle, directing the defences, issuing firing directions. The field shook and spewed earth and rocks and shrapnel for what seemed for ever. The 3rd Platoon, Alpha Company, had a heavy machine-gun set down on its swivel. "Aim at their guts!" the platoon sergeant shouted, and young Private Seymour braced himself for the coming mêlée. The machine-gun opened up and fired several long bursts, spitting out hot bullets. The Chinese lurched, spun and collapsed, thrashing in agony. "Keep 'em Reds dying!" the sergeant yelled. A bugle blew and the attack stopped. Wiping the sweat from his face,

Private Harris glanced up, shook his fist at the dead enemy and said: "I told you, you slant-eyed fuckers: you have to work at it."

"Give me a break with your heroic stuff," said a veteran who had seen it all before. "Look at yourself, you're bleeding like a pig." Harris touched his scalp. It was matted with blood. "Looks like someone's put a hole in your head," his sergeant said grimly. "Better call on the girls." "The girls" was an unshaven medic with a bag full of bandages and aspirin. A tank sergeant tried to cheer up his men. "Those fuckers don't know they've just started to dig their own graves." Twenty-four hours later the same sergeant was dead, blown up by a Chinese who had thrown himself against his tank with a satchel charge.

Every day was a repeat of the one before it, with the valley floor covered by running men, while a deluge of shells rained down among them. Detonations sent red-hot metal fanning out like a scythe, tearing men apart or tossing them into the air. Machine-gun bullets zinged at breast height, slicing into the closely packed enemy, and sending their sundered body fragments flying among the follow-up line. A continuous bellowing thunder rang out. The smoke of the bombardment reared up to blot out the sunlight and cast a shadow on the Korean hills. It seemed impossible that such a noise could be made by the will of men. And always the same: "Keep 'em dying!"

The Chinese fell back, leaving their dead, only to close ranks once more and come forward. The men of Freeman's 23rd US Infantry Regiment counted eight consecutive charges. Together with French Lieutenant Colonel Ralph Montclar's Bataillon de Corée they held the perimeter around the village of Chipyong-ni. The Chinese didn't give up; failure only seemed to increase the Chinese general's determination to succeed. The point had come when so much had been done that it seemed folly not to do that little extra which might turn the scale; the madness went on for hours, then days. The UN forces' morale was high. The Chinese threw five fresh divisions against the 23rd's perimeter. From the ground rose groups of Chinese, struggling forward, over the shattered corpses of the many fallen. The shells that had killed the last wave had also punched holes into the frozen ground, and helped the soldiers to find shelter in the craters. The attack broke down. A formless mob streamed away from the mounded dead and began their retreat.

But next morning they came on again. For three consecutive days and nights the Chinese commander threw his masses against Montclar and Freeman's thin line, and for three days and three nights all his attacks were repulsed with horrendous loss. Daylight revealed scenes of carnage in front of every sector of the perimeter wire.

During a moment of calm Lieutenant McGee and a few men from the 3rd Platoon left their foxholes to conduct a patrol forward of their position. They found a great number of Chinese corpses as well as wounded soldiers. Suddenly McGee saw a company-sized group of Chinese leave the dry creek bed to launch a frontal attack on his right squad. The Americans dived into their foxholes. The Chinese began lobbing grenades toward the squad leader's three-man dugout. Two men were wounded. McGee arranged for their evacuation under fire. At some point during the firefight, Private Inmon, who until now had been sharing his foxhole with the lieutenant, was also hit. McGee reassured him while at the same time desperately fighting off further attacks on his position. When his automatic rifle jammed he took the rifle of the wounded Inmon and lined up the few grenades he had left on the edge of his dugout. He sent a runner to find Lieutenant Heath on the bottom of the knoll, telling him he needed men, ammunition and litter teams.

Heath quickly rounded up 15 men. As McGee's runner led them up the hill and they came to the crest, enemy fire hit them, killing one man and wounding another. McGee watched helplessly as the rest ran back down the hill. At the bottom, Heath humiliated them. "Godammit, get back up on that fuckin' hill! You'll die here anyway. You might as well go up on the hill and die there." Murderous gunfire continued to pour from muzzles on both sides. During the next hour, the hill fell to the Chinese assault. McGee and his platoon sergeant flung their last grenades and, with the five men who were all that was left of his section, he slid down the hill.

At first light the US Air Force executed a number of napalm drops and strafing runs. The sight of American jets coming down for a run on the Chinese caused an eruption of cheers, but they could not be heard over the din. After three days the Chinese had enough. A captured English-speaking Chinese officer was brought before Major Perry Sager. "It has only taken 15 minutes for your men to kill every single one of my company," said the prisoner.

"Hell, it shouldn't have taken that long," replied Sager.

With their supplies at an end, and so many casualties that could no longer be replaced, the Chinese offensive bogged down. On an inspection tour of his forward units, Marshal Peng found a lethargic, starving frontline, hanging on by nothing more than the order not to give way and certainly in no shape to stand up to an enemy counter-attack. Many Chinese in their light uniforms, with basketball shoes designed for summer war, with sweat from exertion freezing on their drenched shirts and blood freezing on their wounds, fell down dead and lay stiff as boards.

Peng issued an order to halt offensive operations and consolidate their positions, and informed Chairman Mao of this in a cable on 10 January 1951. Peng's halt order frustrated Mao and angered the original aggressor, North Korea's Kim il-Sung, who had counted on the Chinese to drive the Americans from the Korean peninsula. Mao pushed Peng into developing another offensive "to end the war with glorious victory". Before Peng could execute the order, there happened what he had feared all along: in mid-January 1951 UN forces launched their counter-offensive. Within a week they had Peng's army on the run.

On 27 January 1951 Peng, his troops exhausted and short of everything – men, ammunition and food – proposed to exercise a tactical retreat. Mao decided otherwise, unwilling to consider anything short of a total victory, and ordered an all-out counter-offensive. The attack was conducted with merciless disregard for its soldiers. As soon as the CPV left their cover, machine-guns chattered and men pitched backward, rolling down the slope, dead or dying. Under the cover of machine-guns and flamethrowers, the UN troops held, burning and blasting everything that came at them until the entire frontline sounded with cries of agony and frustration. Jets roared overhead, the destruction of the enemy manpower their principal aim. Peng's last wave ran into a driving bank of smoke and death after American, British and French field gunners screwed their fuses to the shortest range.

The Chinese marshal's dense ranks were thinned out, before they slowed, like the sea's wave sliding up a sandy beach. His shattered ranks had moved back beyond the edge of the enemy's artillery fire and were once more regrouping, screwing up their courage for the next and final assault, when suddenly there was a great rushing sound in the air. In the midst of the squatting ranks tall columns of flame and smoke and earth sprang into the air, and the bodies of men with it. The heavy battleship guns had found their target. Peng's co-ordination broke down: his individual commanders knew nothing of the overall situation; their units were fighting with their flanks exposed and hammered.

All across the isthmus of Korea great waves of sound were beating, advance and retreat were taking place, sometimes because someone had ordered it, and sometimes on a sudden impulse of the soldiers doing the fighting and the dying. Mao's expectation for an all-out victory died. The best that could be achieved was a stalemate.

In late February Marshal Peng was called to Beijing, where he conveyed his concern to Chairman Mao and filled him in on the seriousness of the strategic situation. Peng stressed that the only way to limit damage was to go on the defensive. Mao promised that new troops would be sent to Korea to replace those units that had suffered maximum casualties and had been eliminated as fighting units. Mao continued in his belief that Americans lacked the heart to sustain heavy casualties and that this would make him victorious in a war of attrition. He called up 12 new armies to feed into the meat grinder. Peng had to advance without air cover, and with a supply line that was continuously cut; the Chinese repaired the bombed bridges by night and the Americans blew them up the next morning. Chinese massed-wave attacks gave the Allied machine-gunners targets easier than those on a shooting range. With plentiful ammunition, it had become a "kill-the-enemy ground".

The mood in all the United Nations units was definitely upbeat. The new UN 8th Army commander, Lieutenant General Matthew B. Ridgway,[2] made it quite plain: "I'm out to punish the NKPA [North Korean People's Army] and their Chinese CPV allies with paralysing losses." For that he had the artillery and the fighter-bombers. Mao's spring offensive was about to start – only this time the American knew all about it. Thousands of CPV fighters were stretched out in the wet grass; during the previous night they had stealthily made their way through ploughed land and swamp and the ashes from previous bombardments, waded waist-deep through water and climbed ashore on the marshy south bank of the River Han. Their clothes had dried on their bodies and became soaked again with their sweat and fear. Now they lay and waited for the bugle call that would send them forward. An hour passed and the sun had climbed over the edge of the hills in front of them, when the earth under them began to tremble. At first it was like a train rumbling along in the distance, then it became a roar that filled earth and sky.

Wherever the Chinese lay, stretched out in a long line, yellow mushrooms of smoke rose among the huddled soldiers, tearing them apart by the hundreds. Everywhere it was the same picture, as fountains of earth rose and dropped back. Adding to the mayhem were one-ton shells, fired from the mighty US battleships lying offshore. The explosions of these monster shells addled the Chinese troops' brains: thick, oily smoke, fiery showers spurting into the air. Across the waist of Korea was one long wall of fire, the noise of the guns and the echo blending together. A gigantic, eardrum-breaking sound. The crack of doom. General Ridgway had launched his own Operation Ripper. In Chinese staging areas, the only tomorrow was the certainty of death.

At the height of this successful UN counter-offensive came a political hiccup. General MacArthur was defying presidential authority and influencing national policy. He had openly vented his criticism of the restrictions placed on him by Washington when he advocated first the bombing of the Yalu bridges and then the destruction of Chinese supply depots and troop assembly bases in Manchuria by conventional aerial carpet bombing – but not with nuclear weapons, as he was misquoted in the press. The general also let it be known that American air and naval attacks against the Chinese mainland could be a follow-up option. This threat was political dynamite and anathema to Truman. The US President shocked the nation with his radio announcement: "In the simplest terms, what we are doing in Korea is this: We are trying to prevent a third world war, not start one … The Communists in the Kremlin are engaged in a monstrous conspiracy to stamp out freedom all over the world. If they were to succeed, the United States would be numbered among their principal victims …"

This was a clear indication that Truman wasn't referring to China, but worried about Stalin's reaction to a bombing of Mainland China. "So far, by fighting a limited war in Korea, we have prevented aggression from succeeding and bringing on a general war. A number of events have made it evident that General MacArthur did not agree with that policy. I have therefore considered it essential to relieve General MacArthur so that there would be no doubt or confusion as to the real purpose and aim of our policy …" On 11 April 1951 President Truman exercised his legal prerogative and fired General Douglas MacArthur, who was, in the words of the official announcement, "relieved of his command".

From late April to the middle of May 1951 the CPV gave it yet one more try. The outcome was the same – with the loss of another quarter of a million Chinese. The sky thundered to the sound of jets and squadrons of American planes as they blasted another depot, another bridge, or sprayed death by napalm on green recruits cowering in shell craters. A wind of death moved over the tortured earth. There they were lying, slashed and smashed by the thousands. Mongolian faces, ash-grey in death. Thick smoke, with a stench of burned flesh, rose like a shroud.

Mao's last hurrah fizzled out. His blunder was like that of MacArthur before him: overwhelmed by his initial success in November 1950, the Chairman had proceeded beyond his original objective, which was originally limited to pushing the Americans back from China's Manchurian frontier. If Mao had expected a weakness similar to that of Chiang Kai-shek's tottering Nationalist Army in the autumn of 1949, the Americans and their allies, with superior strategy, technology, material and an air force that could supply the Big Hammer, had taught him a lesson. Once the Allies brought to bear a sufficient supply of heavy weapons and fighter aircraft, they buried their enemy under a rain of fire.

Time and again Mao threw his battalions against barbed wire and machine-guns with no apparent effect, while the West used its mobile and aerial forces with devastating results. The cardinal defect of Mao's strategy on entering this war was to rely on his vast superiority in troop numbers, instead of concentrating on the material available to both sides and the use of specific arms best suited to the situation, as his enemy did.

Mao was a pragmatist; once it became clear that this was one war that would not be won, he was forced to think seriously about proposing a cease-fire. On 10 July 1951 an initial contact was made between a group of Chinese and North Koreans and a UN delegation. They met at Kaesong, but neither side would trust the other until they could act from a position of strength. This would take another two long years.

The remainder of the war was a series of senseless battles that changed nothing while causing only more losses. Casualties sustained by the Americans and their allies were 118,515 killed and 264,591 wounded. Of the ninety-two thousand UN prisoners of war in Communist hands, only 12,700 returned home; the rest died of mistreatment or starvation. The Communists scorned all ethical standards of civilization; the crimes perpetrated on prisoners of war by their Chinese captors, the daily beatings and shootings and the attempts at brainwashing, became known only after the exchange of POWs. This cruel and inhuman treatment encouraged by the country's political commissars recalled memories of the brutal hordes of Genghis and Hulagu Khan, and stigmatized China as a rogue nation in the years to come.

Perhaps the single most important issue that stalled talks and prolonged the war for two more years after the summer of 1951 was the issue of "forcible repatriation". The United Nations did not want Chinese or North Korean POWs forced to return home as the USSR had insisted after the Second World War, which sent millions of Russian POWs to the gulag.

Chinese and North Korean military losses on the battlefield were more than 10 times those of the UN forces. However hopeless their human-wave attacks, Chinese political commissars were butchers; with utter contempt for their men, they squandered millions of lives. An army was foolishly and wantonly sacrificed. When the war finally ended in a cease-fire, Chinese battle casualties were in excess of a staggering 1.6 million soldiers, while civilian casualties were at least double that figure. Chinese warfare was a return to the nineteenth century's human-wave-versus-heavy-cannon syndrome. Mao Zedong had failed to take a lesson from the past, when British naval guns had devastated human pile-ups. In a historic parallel, Allied gun and air power were enough to inflict such tremendous losses on the enemy that the continuation of a war without gains no longer made strategic sense, even for a People's Emperor used to mega-death figures. But then what are a few million lives, if, according to the "Little Red Book" of their Great Helmsman: "For the sake of the achievement of a specific political goal, it is possible to sacrifice half mankind"?

The Korean War is notorious for the degree to which politics affected strategy. Pushed into it by Stalin, then abandoned by the same Stalin, Mao still went ahead, knowing the odds. After all, Mao had achieved a victory of sorts. With the world's attention drawn away from China, he had attained his principal goal: with a brutality reminiscent of Stalin's Great Terror, he had solidified his political hold over the country. In the period shortly before and during its Korean involvement, the Chinese Communist regime ordered the elimination of over 2.5 million "counter-reactionaries", of whom at least seven hundred and ten thousand were officially executed. Mao's "Red Terror" was committed in the name of "Suppressing Reactionary Activities, and in support of the Great Movement of Resisting America and Assisting our Korean Comrades". With it he could blame the massacres on the evil influence of the Americans. In fact, he was trading his losses in Korea against gaining a stranglehold on China. The blood-purges made him into the undisputed leader of China.

Stalin was also right: he could not interfere in Korea without risking a Third World War. It is questionable whether the Red Tsar, who considered a million lives a mere statistic, would have been willing to exchange Washington for Moscow by helping Beijing. Fortunately, it never came to the test. And though it sometimes seemed that the war would race out of control, it certainly added immeasurably to the "long peace by necessity" between the USSR and the USA. With Stalin's death in 1953, the new men in the Kremlin pushed Mao for a settlement in the Korean conflict. This, with the losses already suffered, made Mao's plan for victory a lost cause. Nor did the United Nations emerge from the conflict with an enhanced reputation. In the beginning, America used the UN as an instrument for its national policy, whereas toward the end other nations used the same organization to restrain America, and this added to the determination of many Third World neutrals to avoid committing to either side.

As for America, it was seen as a superpower at war, with all its confusion, indecision and deception, a country flawed by a collective impulse for action. It was caught unprepared by the sheer speed of modern warfare, the mutual fear and crushing burden of possessing nuclear arms, and uncertainty about the extent of an enemy's threat. General MacArthur, in his publicized statement that "in war there is no substitute for victory",[3] never once referred to the use of the atomic bomb or to launching a land invasion of Chinese territory. He estimated that the Soviet Union could not afford to risk war by coming to the aid of Red China, but – should Russia make such a mistake – there would be no better time for America to face a showdown with the Kremlin. The political stink over the A-bomb issue came from a directive by President Truman which said that he would leave any military decision to his commander in the field.

Among the principal domestic results of the Korean War were the McCarthy witch-hunts and the fear of an unknown nuclear tomorrow. Military thinking moved toward "more bang for a buck", in which nuclear-tipped ballistic missiles would replace marching divisions on the ground. It never worked. In this, Chairman Mao was proven right: the Big Bang was *not* the solution. The nuclear threat was a paper tiger, not a weapon that could be used: "… the initial nuclear bombardment and counter-bombardment would end any war in days, if not hours …"[4] Or, in General MacArthur's frightening prediction: "If you have another war, only those will be happy that are already dead!"

The war ended officially on 27 July 1953. The final outcome of the Korean War was that many died, nothing was resolved and nobody emerged as clear-cut winner – except perhaps morally the Chinese, who could no longer be treated with contempt.

When the fighting ended after three years of slaughter, each side held exactly the same positions as they had on the day the war started.

# 6

# THE NUKE OPTION

## 23 AUGUST 1958, OFFSHORE ISLANDS JINMEN (QUEMOY) AND MATSU, REPUBLIC OF CHINA

Shortly after the end of the Korean War the US Joint Chiefs of Staff (JCS) had proposed *the use of nuclear weapons against Mainland China*, in the event of a repeated attack on the disputed offshore islands. That memo went out on 12 September 1954. In midsummer of 1958 this option was reiterated in a secret memorandum from Gerard C. Smith, Director of Policy Planning in the US State Department, to Christian Herter, US Undersecretary of State:

TOP SECRET 13 August 1958
Memo for Mr Herter
Subject: August 14 Discussion on Taiwan Strait

1. It is our understanding that current JCS war plans call for the defence of Quemoy and Matsu by nuclear strikes deep into Communist China, including military targets in the Shanghai-Hangchow-Nanking and Canton complexes where population density is extremely high ...

3. While nuclear strikes would be with "low yield" weapons, this would include weapons having a yield comparable to 20 KT weapons dropped on Hiroshima and Nagasaki. It is my judgment that before such hostilities are over there would be millions of non-combatant casualties ...

5. ... If our present military planning was carried out Peiping and its Soviet ally would probably feel compelled to react with nuclear attacks at least on Taiwan and on the Seventh Fleet. *Under our present strategic concept this would be the signal for general nuclear war between the US and the USSR.*

Gerard C. Smith

The Soviet intelligence network managed "to lift" this secret document. It shook the Russians. First Secretary Nikita Khrushchev took careful note of the nuclear rumble.[1]

Beijing's leadership continued to issue warlike threats. Their military intelligence kept telling them that the United States would never risk a major war over Taiwan, and certainly not over a few square miles of offshore coral. From the perspective of the secret US memorandum, Beijing was quite wrong. But then, of course, the Soviets had not made their brothers in China party to the purloined secret document of a possible American nuclear response. That "oversight" almost precipitated another war.

Beijing, willing to adopt a hard line on the Taiwan question, was ready to put America's will to the test. With tension mounting, the US Joint Chiefs of Staff developed detailed plans to launch nuclear strikes on major Chinese population centres. They knew that it would result in mega-death. President Dwight D. Eisenhower made it perfectly clear that the United States would lend its full support to Nationalist China in defence of its offshore islands. Secretary of State John Foster Dulles spelled it out: "The United States will take *timely and effective action* to defend Taiwan."

On Eisenhower's orders the US military began with the deployment of nuclear-tipped missiles in Taiwan[2] – and then let China know, because the nuclear threat is valid only if an enemy knows about the risk of being wiped out. Suddenly the nuke option became a definite choice.

Beijing would not listen. At 5.30 a.m. on 23 August 1958, hundreds of guns placed on the mainland around Xiamen (Amoy) opened up. Thousands of shells flew across the 10-kilometre strait and struck the ROC (Nationalist) garrisons on Little Quemoy. This onslaught caused four hundred casualties and signalled the beginning of a renewed bombardment of the offshore island group that lasted for 44 days. In the course of nine weeks, four hundred and fifty thousand shells of all calibres were fired. After the initial surprise their explosions made a lot of noise in the political arena, but did no further damage on the ground.

If Beijing's attack stunned China's enemies, it shocked even more China's ally, the Soviet Union. The "Bombardment of Jinmen" was the lead-up to the final Sino-Soviet split. Following Stalin's death in 1953, relations between the Soviet Union and China had somewhat improved, to a point where the Soviet Union agreed to supply China with a nuclear test reactor and a planeload of specialists to run it. With the uncertainty over China's intention and future actions, Nikita Khrushchev became worried about nuclear noises made by leading Republicans in the US Congress. In November 1957, during a summit meeting between Khrushchev and Mao

Zedong, the Chairman disagreed with the First Secretary's assertion that no one could come out winner in a nuclear contest. Mao claimed that at least half of the world's population would survive. By that obviously he had in mind his vast human pool of seven hundred million.

In this climate of high anxiety over China's next move, with America waving the nuclear stick, Khrushchev dispatched his Foreign Minister, Andrei Gromyko, to Beijing to meet with his homologue, Zhou Enlai, in order to defuse the Quemoy question.

"Our strikes may be heavy, moderate, or light," Zhou tried to soft-talk his Russian counterpart. "We do not want to beat them to death in one go. Our intention is to make them desperate. The longer it takes, the greater will be the difficulties for the United States."

Gromyko did not buy this explanation, saying: "A bombardment will create difficulties for the USSR." He did not specify what kind of difficulties the Soviet Union expected, but the writing was clearly on the wall: "Comply with us, or we drop you." Mistrust of China's intention soured relations between the two countries. As the Sino-Soviet crisis deepened, no attempt was made to find a solution. It showed up the unbridgeable divergence in their ideology and national interests.

After Chinese guns roared, the harsh threat contained in Eisenhower's address shocked Khrushchev. Moscow was not looking for a nuclear confrontation with America. The Russian leader tried to soothe the situation with a reassuring statement that the Soviet nuclear umbrella "will only apply to aggression against China's mainland, but not include Chinese military actions beyond its national boundaries". This statement showed Beijing its dependence on Big Brother Russia, and demonstrated an urgent need to create its own nuclear deterrent.

The Second Bombardment of Jinmen (Quemoy) was the ground marker to the rapid deterioration in Sino-Soviet relations. No single factor explains this complex dispute. One thing was certain: the halcyon days of Sino-Soviet friendship were over. It opened with a barrage of verbal mudslinging, acrimonious notes and vicious articles, in which Mao accused Khrushchev of betraying their socialist goal, and openly condemned the Russians' "cowardly behaviour" toward the United States.[3] It went much further. China's doubtful military plans led to the unilateral abrogation by the Soviets of the agreement of 15 October 1957, by which the USSR promised to supply China with technical assistance in the production of nuclear weapons. The final break came on 20 June 1959 when Khrushchev ordered the return of all Soviet technicians and advisers. From that moment China had to continue its nuclear programme without the assistance of the Soviet Union.

In January 1961, shortly after his inauguration, the new American president was briefed in the Oval Office of the White House. On the agenda
was national defence.

"... what else?" asked John F. Kennedy.

"China – and plutonium, Mr President. *The Chinese are building the
bomb.*"

Assistant Secretary of Defense Paul Nitze demanded that the US Joint
Chiefs of Staff prepare a study to "persuade or compel" China to accept a
test ban treaty. The US military provided a chilling solution:

"... The United States has the military forces and capabilities to quickly
counter any military action which may be initiated by the Chinese
Communists ... *This would probably include the use of tactical nuclear
weapons...*"[4]

Tactical – not strategic! Limit the damage. Confine the destruction.
Prevent mega-death.

At 7 a.m. on 16 October 1964 China became the world's fifth
nuclear power when it exploded an atomic bomb.[5] The bang, heard
around the world, caused a political shock wave. In one of the stories
of secretive actions in an uncertain world, both atomic superpowers
began work on a scenario to take out China's nuclear menace. No one
could foresee the consequences at home and abroad should the United
States or the Soviet Union sacrifice peace in the interests of a strategic
ambition. The world as we know it today would be greatly diminished
by the experience.

The world, dulled by living under the balance of terror of the Cold War,
knew how deadly the bomb was, but failed to understand how helpless it
was in the face of the mechanism of war. Leaders of nations and military
thinkers never seemed to have the slightest comprehension of the message
of Hiroshima. If they thought that the bomb meant devastation, in fact
modern nuclear war meant life being replaced by a black void, with civilizations evaporated in milliseconds. The moral issue of such terror was
almost beyond contemplation. America and Russia understood that. Not
so China. Chairman Mao's verbal sabre-rattling was anything but reassuring. During China's pre-nuclear period, and even at its entry into the
nuclear club, its position was ambiguous. America – just like the Soviet
Union – was worried. Despite the certainty that his country would be
wiped out in a retaliatory attack, the leader of a rogue nation might act,
undeterred by a calculation of self-preservation, when in his mind only size
counts. He might be willing to believe that by unleashing nuclear hell
upon his foe he would advance his cause – and that afterward his nation
would crawl out of their basements, push away the rubble and rebuild

society brick by brick. He forgets that *afterward* society no longer exists.[6] Only dark night at high noon.

"I believe we must adjourn this meeting to some other place," said one of America's founding fathers on his deathbed (Adam Smith, in 1790). He was a prophet. Mao inherited a nation of wooden ploughs, and left it with the atomic bomb.

# 7

# AND *NOT* SO QUIET FLOWS
# THE USSURI

## 2 MARCH 1969, RIVER USSURI, USSR–CHINA BORDER

While Moscow's citizens slept peacefully, lights burned late in the Kremlin. But also in Paris, London, Washington and Beijing. The situation was preoccupying, to say the least. China was no longer some vague future problem. The Soviet Union's military were pushing for a solution, and pushing hard, and its Politburo was considering the nuclear option. It all started over an incident on the outer frontier of the Soviet Empire.

As that March day dawned the sky gleamed with flashing needles of ice. The wind blew thick snow clouds over the desolate land, swept great stretches of river ice bare and drove billows of snow particles before it. There were no landmarks under this howling, freezing sky. No river, no land, only drifts, belly-deep, soft snow, which allowed no distinction between what was solid ground and what frozen water. Out of this white nightmare appeared soldiers clad in white camouflage. At the sight of these ghostly shapes the hearts of the men of Lieutenant Strelnikov, commanding a Soviet Army platoon in a forward observation post on Damanski Island, beat faster.

"*КИТАЕЦ* – Chinese!" Their worst fears were coming true. A horde of Chinese, shouting Mao slogans, moved toward the Soviet island in the middle of a frozen river. "Platoon with me!" Sixty men, including an army photographer, jumped on trucks and raced to the island's southern bank. There they took up their positions.

"Shoulder your weapons and link arms," ordered Lieutenant Strelnikov. The Soviet soldiers strapped their automatic rifles to their chests and linked arms to prevent the Chinese from passing. Forty Russians against two companies. Three hundred Chinese! The first rank of Chinese had almost reached the Russians. "Do not use your weapons!" ordered Strelnikov. It was to be the last order he ever gave. On a barked command, the first row of seemingly unarmed Chinese dropped to the ground; behind them stood a second row, who pulled machine pistols from beneath their quilted jackets and opened fire. The Russians, still with their arms linked, stumbled and fell. Strelnikov and six of his men died instantly. Before the remnants of the platoon got over their shock, the Chinese came storming at them. A number of Russians were beaten to death with rifle butts, strangled or smothered in the snow.

Lieutenant Bubenin, commanding another Soviet platoon, had heard the shots and rushed to his comrades' assistance. He was giving orders to his men when the snow puffed up at his side. The next bullet got him, and he fell wounded. His men dragged him to safety. As suddenly as it had started, the firing stopped, and once again winter held sway. Nineteen Russian corpses lay in the powdered snow, frozen and contorted.

Ever since Korea, and especially since the Second Quemoy Crisis, relations between China and the USSR had varied from frosty to outright non-existent. Taiwan was China's continuous bone of contention, but Taiwan was not Korea. This time the United States had made it perfectly clear: the Nationalist stronghold existed under America's nuclear umbrella. The Chinese knew it, and so did the Russians. This situation had already led to serious problems between the Communists during the second attack on the offshore islands.

In addition there was internal trouble throughout China, brought on by the failure of Mao's "Great Leap Forward". Under the slogan "Go all out and continue the Great Leap Forward and defeat rightism", peasants all over China were marshalled into massive, labour-intensive projects. As its direct consequence, millions died from starvation – estimates vary between 45 and 55 million deaths from the terrible nationwide famine in the four years of the disastrous Great Leap Forward. In Sichuan province alone over nine million people starved to death in a province famous for its agricultural surpluses. Unrest continued until the internal problems were laid to rest during Mao's "Cultural Revolution", which killed many more and also destroyed priceless treasures in order "to build new on the old". All this handicapped Beijing in forming a coherent foreign policy.

In October 1962, using the Twenty-Second Soviet Communist Party Congress as his platform, Chairman Nikita Khrushchev exploded a verbal bomb when he touched on the existence of a Soviet–Sino ideological rift. Shortly afterward Mao Zedong stated in a meeting with a group of visiting Japanese Socialists that in the days after the Second World War the Soviet Union "occupied too many places in North-East Asia". To improve relations after Stalin's death, Russia's new strongman Khrushchev had visited Beijing in 1954; during their initial meeting, Mao raised the question of Outer Mongolia. Khrushchev wouldn't even discuss it. Mao was furious. "China has not yet called the Soviet Union to account over Vladivostok, Khabarovsk, Kamchatka and other towns and regions east of Lake Baikal which became Russian territory only a hundred years ago." To this Khrushchev replied with a stern warning: "The borders of the Soviet Union are sacred, and he who dares to violate them will meet with a most decisive rebuff on the part of the people of the Soviet Union."

In May 1964 Marshal Chen-yi declared to a Canadian television team (of which I was a member, and he repeated it later to a group of Scandinavian journalists) that the Russians were thieves who had annexed 1.5 million square kilometres of Chinese territory. The situation almost got out of hand in October 1966 when a whipped-up throng congregated outside the Soviet embassy in Beijing after Moscow charged that Chinese guns had fired on Russian merchant vessels sailing on the River Amur. China organized "spontaneous people manifestations" demanding the return of "lost territories". In fact, not one of the disputed territories was previously inhabited by Chinese. Russian fur trappers had reached the Amur in 1643 and built Fort Albazin in 1665. The border with China was fixed by the Treaty of Nerchinsk in 1689, and reconfirmed by the Treaty of Kiakhta in 1727. In the summer of 1859 Count Nikolai Pavlovich Ignatiev arrived in Beijing with a letter from the Tsar, astutely playing the Chinese against the British and French. The count secured the Ussuri region for Russia in the Treaty of Beijing (1860). The Russians laid a single-track spur of the Trans-Siberian railway to the regional capital, Khabarovsk, in 1897. For a century the border problem was put on hold. On 14 October 1964 Nikita Khrushchev was deposed and replaced by the Sinophobe Leonid Brezhnev.

When it finally came to a *clash*, it was over Damanski (Zhenbao in Mandarin), an obscure island in the River Ussuri (Wusuli). China's newspapers headlined it the "just fight of our revolutionary military forces to regain what is China's land". Which land? An uninhabited island, most of the year buried under a solid layer of ice, and the rest of the time submerged under the waters of the Ussuri. Possession of such a piece of worthless real estate was never a valid reason to start a war. However, Comrade Brezhnev had put down a hard line: "Not an inch of Soviet territory to be lost!"

In March 1969 the verbal sparring turned bloody, when an advance party of China's People's Liberation Army soldiers crossed the frozen Ussuri at night to capture Damanski Island. The next morning they made their presence known by waving flags and shouting pro-Maoist and anti-Soviet slogans in defiance of the Soviet border guards. That day 19 Russians died.

Two days later another 34 Russians were killed. Such provocative actions could not have been taken on the authority of a local unit commander. The River Ussuri battle was no simple rift involving two sovereign states over a frozen island, but the fierce competition for the support and allegiance of the multifaceted components that made up the international Communist movement. Both countries were only too aware that he who controlled the movement also controlled Socialist history. There is no doubt that the Ussuri Incident was initiated with the direct connivance of Beijing to provoke a Russian response. That muscular response was not long in coming.

The situation became extraordinarily confused, with small Chinese units infiltrating the thinly held Soviet border along the Ussuri. On 15 March 1969 the Russians conducted a fake withdrawal from the sector, with a great number of Soviet guns and armoured helicopters ready to pounce on the Chinese. A Russian forward observer stared across the white expanse. On the Chinese shore of the Ussuri rose a stretch of open country bordered by a high forest. Under cover of darkness eight hundred men of Lieutenant Colonel Zhai-tong's PLA Rifle Battalion had moved into position to strike. Zhai-tong had received specific directives from his political superior. Radio silence prevailed. The Chinese commander could not call up aerial support and he had no real intelligence on the enemy's strength; he relied on a report from a foot patrol, which had found the Soviet dugouts on Damanski Island abandoned. His plan of attack called for moving into the deserted Soviet positions, and, from there, fanning out. A cold mist hung over everything. It was time ... A bugle blew. There was no doubt about what his battalion had to do. The troops were told the importance of their mission.

"*КИТАЕЦ* – Chinese!" yelled a hidden Soviet forward observer into his radiophone. Out of the woods came tightly packed formations of Chinese, running toward the river ... the Russian guard instantly fired a signal flare, which was followed by the sharp bark of a Russian 130-mm gun. One gun became three, then quickly a dozen, until there were so many guns that they could no longer be counted, and the opposite riverbank erupted in a confusion of white-yellow flashes. Salvoes of 132-mm Katyusha rockets howled in and ripped the massed Chinese to shreds. Within minutes the blinding whiteness of the ice was streaked with blood. Despite their heavy losses, more PLA soldiers were advancing from the forest on to the ice, when a swarm of armoured helicopters came swooping low over the ice. Rockets streaked from the sky. The Chinese tumbled in droves, as shells and bullets ricocheted off the hard, white surface. They were pushed back, and as they fled they provided clear targets for more strafing runs on the glaring white of the river's ice.

A Chinese colonel had gone into an almost predictable calamity hoping for a miracle. It had not happened. All the guns and helicopters in the world seemed pointed at his pitiful attempt to take an uninhabited island in the middle of nowhere, as he had been ordered by some bumbling fool of a political commissar. Lieutenant Colonel Zhai-tong fought on until his own cruel and heroic death. He and his soldiers lay in the snow, smashed like flies. A PLA battalion had ceased to exist. Irreparable errors had been made in Beijing.

The following day brought a snowstorm, sweeping horizontally over land and frozen river, building drifts as high as trees. Soon there were no more fields, no frozen stream – and no more frozen corpses. A white shroud covered the scene of slaughter. The Chinese had been denied.

Mao and Defence Minister Lin Biao had initiated the opening round of the Ussuri Incident by trying to occupy an island where nothing grew and nobody lived, but which was symbolically Russian. With tension mounting, both sides built up their military presence in the region. Along a frozen frontier the death toll rose quickly and dramatically; it escalated from 19 to 34 to eight hundred, and on it went. Following the Zhai-tong debacle, Lin Biao, a hard-liner, went on a tour of inspection to the Damanski sector. A sullen quiet had descended over the land, broken only by sporadic artillery duels. By continuing with their "Twilight War", the Russians and the Chinese were inviting disaster. Charges and countercharges were thrown back and forth. China's *Liberation Army Daily* reported: "Soviet troops have penetrated Zhenbao [Damanski] Island and the region west of that island [i.e. China]. The Soviet government must bear the entire responsibility for the grave consequences which could result from this."

Moscow shot back: "The Soviet government declares that if any new attempts are made to violate the integrity of Soviet territory, the Soviet Union and all its peoples will defend it resolutely and will answer with *a crushing riposte* any further such violations."

The USSR and China showed no willingness to lower the temperature. A week after the initial clash the Soviet government presented a note to the Chinese embassy in Moscow. This fell short of a declaration of war but Moscow was ready to teach Beijing a lesson. They failed, however, to spell out what they called "a crushing riposte".

On the day of the Zhai-tong attack, a young Russian lieutenant had glanced impassively at the scene of carnage. "Green recruits."

"Yes," said his battalion commander, "but they will learn. *And then what?*"

The *what* had already been decided by Moscow. In fact, the Soviet Union was ready to go nuclear.

# 8

# THE DAVYDOV QUERY

## 18 AUGUST 1969, WASHINGTON DC, USA

The clashes along the Sino-Soviet border left the world puzzled. Not the combat with guns and bullets, but the turmoil it caused in the political arena. Military actions conducted without analysis of their political effectiveness are at best ineffective and at worst assist the enemy. All military strategy is a compromise between what generals want and what politicians will permit.

But not so in China. A notable consequence of Mao's Cultural Revolution was an increased interference by PLA generals in political decisions. Chairman Mao, 75 years old and worn out by a life of struggle, betrayal and intrigue, was losing his grip; this shrewd and ruthless politician had never intended to turn China into a military dictatorship. But the situation had slipped out of his control. A power struggle erupted at the top. In April 1969 the Ninth CCP Congress picked Lin Biao as Mao's future successor. Were the events on the Ussuri once again the political means to draw attention away from the power struggle? Did Lin Biao mastermind the military aggression to discredit Mao, or was it the Chairman who had launched the "Ussuri Gamble" to revive his fading image? Because a dangerous gamble it had turned into: if Mao had been willing to accept one million casualties in Korea, this time he risked much more. There were questions the ageing Chairman had to ask himself. Were the political conditions favourable for such a perilous venture? What were the risks of Russian retaliation? Would the reprobation evoked by a sudden invasion seriously set back the ideological cause of the war-maker? Quick victory had failed in Korea; could it be achieved on the Ussuri?

During the wars of the past, even as late as Korea, extended times were given for bringing troops to a state of readiness. That changed with the speed of rockets. It was now readiness in a few minutes. The use of thermonuclear missiles was the most devastating and rapid form of instant attack.

This option was open to a nuclear power, with a retaliatory strike in kind as its only defence. Tactical, or theatre, nuclear devices were closely linked to both the training and operational plans of the armed forces confronting one another along this explosive Asian frontier. The possibility that their use would quickly escalate into a major nuclear exchange made such weapons a dubious asset in the inception of hostilities. And especially since in the nuclear field the Soviet Union had so great a quantitative preponderance that it would be insane for its neighbour not to be prepared for a pre-emptive *blitzkrieg*, or, in modern terms, a nuclear wipe-out.

It all started in the heyday of a revived socialist honeymoon, when the Soviet Union had provided its Chinese brothers with a nuclear reactor. This had worried the United States. A top-secret document from the Department of the US Air Force stated on 8 February 1961: "… if the Russians provide the Chinese with nuclear weapons, they most certainly will do everything to ensure that the weapons remain under Russian control …"

This was no longer the case: their brotherly friendship had come to a grinding halt, and China had its own bomb; a hydrogen bomb, a hundred times more powerful than the Hiroshima device.

On 8 July 1963 Sherman Kent, assistant director of US Central Intelligence, warned in a memo: "The Soviets must also realize that when the Chinese have such a capability, it might be directed westward against the USSR as well as eastward against the United States."

Six days later President Kennedy dispatched special envoy Averill Harriman to Moscow in order to emphasize to Nikita Khrushchev that "a nuclear-armed China could be very dangerous to us all". Harriman then asked Khrushchev straight out if he agreed to "limiting or preventing Chinese nuclear development and his willingness either to take Soviet action or to accept US action aimed in this direction".[1]

At the time the Russian strongman remained vague. A special committee of US military experts and scientists was constituted to study the issue. By the time Robert H. Johnson, China expert on the US Policy Planning Council, finished his investigation, President Kennedy was dead. The expert's findings and suggestions were passed on to Special Security Adviser Walt W. Rostow for presentation to the new US President, Lyndon B. Johnson:

Eyes Only. From Special Security Adviser Walt W. Rostow, to US President Lyndon B. Johnson.[2]

SECRET MEMORANDUM FOR THE PRESIDENT          April 17, 1964
(prepared by R. H. Johnson,[3] April 16, 1964)
SUBJECT: The implications of a Chinese Communist Nuclear Capability

1. <u>The Threat.</u> The great disproportion between US and Chinese Communist nuclear capabilities makes Chinese first-use of nuclear weapons highly unlikely …
2. … the Chinese Communists would eventually be able to do significant, but hardly crippling, damage to the United States by attacking US forces and installations in Asia, but *the US will have the ability to destroy Communist China as a modern governmental and war-making entity* …

Six months later, on 16 October 1964, China became a nuclear power when it exploded an atom bomb equivalent in force to the Hiroshima bomb. The People's Republic had its own "paper tiger". Mao had been right to call it this. Innumerable non-nuclear conflicts have exploded since the birth of the bomb between nuclear-armed nations. America's Vietnam, Israel's Middle East, Russia's Afghanistan – responsible governments which have shown restraint, and helped to dispose of a mistaken illusion that the bomb would solve all.

On 14 December 1964, two months after the Chinese test, G. W. Rathjens of the US Arms Control and Disarmament Agency outlined his conclusion in a secret report under the heading "Destruction of Chinese Nuclear Weapons Capabilities": "… further consideration of direct action against Chinese nuclear facilities, or at least consideration of exploration of that possibility with the Soviet Union, may be warranted." In the same report Rathjens answered his question: which way the Russians?: "Soviet co-operation or acquiescence would be improbable, the degree of improbability depending on the circumstances of the attack, i.e. whether or not ostensibly in response to aggression in South East Asia."

Thus for a long time one aspect remained unclear: Russia's reaction to China's bomb. For the Soviet Union the threat was real, but the Russians kept silent. Until the Ussuri. US government officials had long watched with growing stupefaction the extent of the political break between the Soviet Union and the People's Republic of China, until it escalated into artillery battles along the Sino-Soviet border. Suddenly the tension was such that it led to one of the most extraordinary episodes in Cold War history – a conversation between a high Soviet Intelligence agent and his American counterpart in which the US official was asked to pass on an amazing piece of information.[4]

Boris Davydov, a grey man who seemed to blend in with the wallpaper, was in fact a high-ranking GRU[5] operative in the Soviet Embassy in Washington. A senior US Intelligence official, William Stearman, had accepted a surprise lunch invitation by his counterpart Davydov to the Beef and Bird Restaurant in Washington's Hotel America; during the meal

Stearman expressed concern that the Ussuri clashes might escalate, especially if "some junior lieutenant took a wrong step". Davydov had the American with his mouth agape when he asked *how the United States would react if the Soviets solved one nuclear proliferation problem by attacking China's nuclear weapons facilities.*[6]

On 18 August 1969 a secret "Memorandum of Conversation" by William Stearman landed on the desk of the US President's National Security Adviser, Dr Henry Kissinger.

> Davydov asked point-blank *what the US would do if the Soviet Union attacked and destroyed China's nuclear installations.* I replied by asking him if he really meant this to be a serious question. He assured me that he was completely serious and went on to elaborate. He said, in essence, that two objectives would be served by destroying China's nuclear capability. First the Chinese nuclear threat would be eliminated for decades. Second, such a blow would so weaken and discredit the "Mao clique" that dissident senior officers and Party cadres could gain ascendancy in Peking …
>
> … he then rephrased his original question by asking: "*What would the US do if Peking called for US assistance in the event Chinese nuclear installations were attacked by us?* Wouldn't the US try to take advantage of this situation?" …

The initial reaction by America's intelligence community was one of "the Russkies are having us on, they're trying to use us to pass on their bluff".

"They have enough trouble inside their own Red Empire," a deputy director of the CIA said off-handedly, "they know fully well what disaster another war would bring to them. They'll make noises; they'll rattle their sabres, but war? When push comes to shove, the Russian bear will pull in its tail."

In fact, Soviet behaviour had been notoriously opportunistic, and frequently involved the use, or the threat of use, of military force. This did not dispel the doubts. Nothing did. The Stearman Memorandum was fed into a Cray computer that was very clever; it knew all about every human being on earth, including an individual's hair colour and the date of birth of his grandmother; its mainframe swallowed a colossal quantity of data, took in millions of newspaper cuttings and accessed vast quantities of secret documents. The Cray dissected that amazing slip of information about a Soviet nuclear threat and came up with a fat zero. Nothing the computer spat out helped in solving the mystery. In the corridors of the CIA in Langley, Virginia, and at the Pentagon it was openly suggested that the Davydov leak was a product of the Soviet disinformation service, which was far from idle.

Downplaying the significance of the "Davydov Query", the CIA called it a "50/50 option". Presidential adviser Henry Kissinger did not go along with this opinion. Should a local conflict go beyond the nuclear threshold, this would lead to the destruction of civilization. China was not yet a serious enemy of a superpower such as the Soviet Union. But, with its immense human reservoir, China would certainly be a survivor in the event of a generalized nuclear conflagration. As the situation was heading toward a climax, a US National Intelligence Estimate on Sino-Soviet relations referred to the nuclear menace as "at least some chance that Moscow may be preparing to take action to prevent Chinese nuclear forces from threatening the Soviet Union".

Kissinger believed the Davydov Query to be genuine. Though he did not know it then, he had every reason to be apprehensive. The Russians were not bluffing.[7] William Hyland of the National Security Council suggested that a limited Sino-Soviet war was "by no means a disaster for the US" and Soviet strikes to destroy Chinese nuclear facilities might be "*the* solution" to the China nuclear problem. On Dr Kissinger's direct intervention, things began to happen. The Republic of China (Taiwan) received delivery of the sophisticated American U-2 spy plane; flown by Chinese Nationalist pilots, it took photographs in the disputed Ussuri region. The photos were computer-enhanced and scrutinized. Nothing untoward was discovered; no sign of a movement by millions; only the kind of reinforcements that might be expected in a clearly defined, localized conflict.

Dead end: the Americans were stymied. Especially since the man who started it all, Boris Davydov, had disappeared – "evacuated", as they called it in the Soviet Union. Evacuation of an operative was ordered if someone was ineffective (which Davydov certainly was not) or suspected of preparing to defect. Was that his motive? Had he put out feelers to get in with the Americans? No! His revealing query was too big for a simple intelligence operative in a state where a man's position meant nothing. No, this had originated within the secret, unseen world of the Kremlin.

An exchange of messages between the US Secret Service and the State Department followed the Davydov–Stearman luncheon; it not only gives a measure of the seriousness, but also reads like a blueprint for a nuclear nightmare. China expert William Hyland provided for Henry Kissinger a follow-up assessment in a National Security Council memorandum:

> Even if all the specific problems could be miraculously sorted out, the world at large and domestic opinion is going to scrutinize our position and conclude that we favour one side. One way out of this dilemma could be to adopt an avowed position of impartiality but one of enlightened self-interest ... a Sino-Soviet war, for a limited period and

if limited in scope, is by no means a disaster for the US. It might just
be the way to an early Vietnam settlement. It might also be a "solution"
to the China nuclear problem … the Soviets are not going to attack
China in some quixotic mood. If they take this drastic step, they will
be fully and totally committed to pursue it to the end …

Another indication of Soviet intent came in an Ultra Secret Airgram
from the US Embassy in Tehran. On 30 August 1969, during a reception
at the Turkish embassy, the Soviet Military Attaché, Major General Sergei
Krakhmalov, cornered his American counterpart, US Military Attaché
Colonel Duvall, who passed on the Russian's message: "The Russians will
not hesitate to use nuclear weapons against Chinese if they attack with
major forces. The Russians would permit the Chinese to penetrate Russian
territory to a sufficient depth, and then employ tactical nuclear weapons
against the Chinese, but on Russian soil." This shocking revelation was
substantiated by yet another cable from the US embassy in Moscow, which
said that the Soviets saw in the Maoists a "universal threat". Should border
fighting escalate further it could not be ruled out that Moscow would take
military action. The expression used by the CIA's Moscow informant was:
"to teach Beijing an exemplary lesson".

Yet the final statement must go to Arkady Shevchenko, a Soviet official
at the United Nations (who soon thereafter defected to the West). In a
conversation with US diplomat Michael Newlin, Shevchenko confirmed
in no uncertain terms that the Chinese were badly mistaken to think that
Moscow would "compromise in any way" – or that Russia would not
"*employ larger-than-tactical nuclear weapons*".

Contrary to Chinese thinking, Russia could not bear the thought of 30
or 40 million casualties. Therefore it was vital to develop a wipe-out strike
scenario. And while US spy satellites and Nationalist Chinese U-2s could
detect no major troop movements on the Chinese side, the Russians
stealthily moved rocket batteries deep into the woods of eastern Siberia. A
lethal armada on movable transporter-erector-launchers, SCUD SS1
missiles and SS-4 medium ballistic missiles, with a range of two thousand
kilometres and a nuclear warhead of either one or two megatons – should
the need arise – could provide the Big Soviet Hammer. Already, before final
confirmation of Soviet intent had come from their US military attaché in
Tehran, even the most sceptical of security chiefs in Washington had caught
on that something major was up. Generals huddled in the map room of the
Pentagon, discussing options; secure phone lines rang constantly. As viewed
from the State Department and the CIA, there was something unreal and
yet frightfully tangible to this blasted Davydov Query. If the Russians

should go nuclear, what about China's nuclear stockpile ready to be used? If Mao was willing to go down in flames and take the world with him, the unimaginable was only a rocket's flight off. To defuse the situation called for a prime example of international crisis management.

It was raining in Washington; an angry sky enveloped the city. People hurried through puddles, yelling for taxis; the Great American Multitude was blissfully unaware of the acute crisis. The President's National Security Adviser, Henry Kissinger, worked the phones in one of his secret "telecons" with his direct contact into the Kremlin, Soviet Ambassador Anatoly Dobrynin. A Kissinger–Dobrynin "back channel meeting" was arranged. It took place in the Map Room of the White House, a place that easily escaped the attention of the news-hungry White House press corps. The *Washington Post* had become aware of something unusual taking place at top level and put its best tracker dogs on the scent, yet silence prevailed. In a notoriously gabby Washington, that in itself pointed to the seriousness of the situation.

It was also raining on the outskirts of Moscow. Incoming calls jammed the main switchboard in the "Aquarium" located in the "Red Zone" of Khodynka Airfield. This Main Intelligence Directorate or GRU, Soviet Military Intelligence, was a more powerful organization than even the notorious KGB. While the secret police's priorities were keeping a lid on the population, the general staff had a more pressing concern. It was the border with China. Or rather, the Russian hinterland of the border with China. A cunning plan was being developed, and for once the interests of the KGB and the GRU coincided. On the map it looked like a relatively easy exercise, yet the inflexibility of Soviet organizational structures was to create difficulties.

In Beijing the sun rose brilliantly. But none of the sunrise was seen by the members of the Communist Party's Central Committee, cocooned in an emergency session behind guarded walls. Present at the political meeting were high military commanders. Until recently even a top rank commanded little respect within the political decision-taking of the Party. However, that situation had drastically changed with the arrival of Lin Biao and his clique of military hard-liners. The news, transmitted from Moscow by their spies, was worrying. The Ussuri Venture had tickled a tiger's tail, and the beast was showing its fangs. The ageing Politburo members had all experienced land warfare during the Great Civil War, but none had ever faced a nuclear threat, and no one doubted Russia's retaliatory capability. Despite the Chairman's bellicose statements, China was not ready for a nuclear exchange with neighbouring Russia. China had entered into a situation that called for instant damage control – but without losing face!

"There will be enough warrior knights for many more Kulikovos," Yevgeny Yevtushenko was to write in his epic poem *Ussuri*, referring to Prince

Dmitri's final defeat of a Mongol horde at Kulikovo in 1380. Was that build-up of a nation's morale necessary? Were nuclear arms really needed to contain Chinese expansion? In sparking the build-up, not to mention the tremendous destruction it threatened in human lives, both countries took a frightful gamble. But there is also reason to believe that it played a stabilizing role in international politics; that without the Ussuri clashes and the international (Western) response to them, a tragedy of far greater magnitude might have occurred. Suddenly the crisis was played down, as neither the Soviets nor the Chinese were looking for a full-scale holocaust.

In this climate of maximum tension Soviet Prime Minister Alexei Kosygin, using as a pretext his trip to Hanoi for the funeral of "our much regretted Comrade Ho Chi-minh", made a significant stopover in Beijing on his way home. In an atmosphere of strict secrecy, Kosygin met with Zhou Enlai in an outlying building at Beijing Airport. Nothing came out of what was discussed, except a brief mutual communiqué: "The people of the Soviet Union invite the government of the Chinese People's Republic to abstain from all action along the frontier that would risk bringing about complications. Let our two brotherly socialist nations resolve any differences in calm and by means of negotiations."

Words could no longer hide the truth. For two enemy brothers it was all over. With the Ussuri clashes the Sino-Soviet rift had become irreparable. All their past efforts to form a united front against Satan America had come to naught. In a contest for socialist dominion, the Soviet Union still held sway because of its much superior military technology. China was forced to bide its time, knowing its day would come. On 12 May 1969 Beijing accepted a Soviet proposal for the resumption of borderline discussions, but not without demonstrating that there was no question of a Chinese surrender; Beijing continued to accuse Moscow of naval expansion on the Amur. Even while discussions to solve this problem were under way, the USSR and China continued to exchange artillery duels across the Amur and Ussuri. Finally, on 7 October 1969, Beijing issued an official statement that it saw no reason for two socialist countries to go on fighting over a simple boundary question: "The Chinese government has never demanded the return of territory annexed by Tsarist Russia, and has always stood for the settlement of existing boundary questions in earnest all-round negotiations."

But it was not so; following weeks of fruitless discussions, and seeing the hopelessness of their attempts to find a way out of the impasse, the Chinese delegation returned home.

There is an epilogue to this story. The man who masterminded the Ussuri Gamble was blamed for the disaster and did not survive. Lin Biao, Mao's "closest comrade-in-arms" and heir apparent, who authored much of Mao's "Little Red Book" promoting Mao's cult of personality, and who was raised to the position of vice chairman of the Chinese Communist Party, fell foul of the Chairman. Mao's wrath dispatched Lin Biao and his family to their deaths.

On the evening of 12 September 1971, while Lin Biao's family were celebrating the engagement of their daughter in Beidaihe, a sea resort in China, his son, Lin Liguo, returned from Beijing and told him that Mao had told the Central Committee that Lin Biao had betrayed him and no longer followed unconditionally his instructions. Such a remark was equal to a death sentence. That night Lin Biao and his family boarded a plane. Beijing later claimed that the traitor was trying to flee to the Soviet Union. The aircraft exploded. Accident or sabotage?[8] Lin Biao's death triggered one of the most ruthless episodes of political cleansing, with fabled show-trial confessions and massive "suicides". And like Stalin's Great Terror of the 1930s, Mao's Terror culminated with the crushing of Lin Biao's army command, whereby the Great Helmsman purged over a thousand senior officials at or above the rank of army commander.[9] In ordering the terror Mao only reaffirmed Engels's dictum, "Terror consists mostly of useless cruelties perpetrated by frightened people in order to reassure themselves."

The Ussuri Gamble was a conflict fraught with paradox. By threatening to escalate out of control, it accentuated bipolarity by increasing tensions, and split China and Russia apart more rapidly than otherwise would have been the case. The era following the Ussuri episode led to an assessment of new political alliances.

The capabilities of an enemy can be measured – not so his intentions. The West had played a significant role by sitting firmly on the lid of Pandora's box. There is an ancient Chinese proverb: "Caution is the mother of wisdom." An ageing potentate overlooked this piece of wisdom; his insane gamble led the world to the brink of a nuclear war.

A severe storm had blown across North-East Asia; its icy breath touched not only the Siberian tundra and the wastelands along the Ussuri, but also Moscow, Beijing and Washington. Then the storm died. A rush to war became a rush out of war. Along the Ussuri, winter held sway. A young Ukrainian soldier stared at the endless whiteness. *"Chrystos Vokres! Voyistyno Vokres!* Christ has risen! The Truth has risen!"

Beneath the snow lay dead Chinese and dead Russians, their bodies frozen and contorted.

# 9

# BREAKING THE IMPASSE

## 16 APRIL 1971, TSINGHUA UNIVERSITY, BEIJING,
## PEOPLE'S REPUBLIC OF CHINA

In the early 1970s increased unrest in the Middle East pointed to a strong possibility of yet another Israeli–Arab conflict. Plans were made. Egypt's President Sadat had outlined the relative tank strength of Israel and the Arab countries, when Libya's revolutionary strongman Muammar Gaddafi burst out: "We must go to an all-out war and liquidate Israel!" Several months later Gaddafi dispatched Major Abdel Salam Jalloud on a secret mission to Beijing.[1] Jalloud travelled on a forged Egyptian passport, changing planes in Karachi, and then again in Calcutta. But, as for his mission being kept a secret, the Russians knew all about it and had him followed, as did the Americans and certainly the Israelis. And of course Zhou Enlai was perfectly informed about the purpose of the Libyan's pilgrimage to Beijing. Major Jalloud had come with a purse of unlimited funds for a special purchase.

Zhou Enlai courteously received the Libyan Number Two. Following talks about future oil delivery terms – discussions conducted through an interpreter – Jalloud came to the point. "China is the pride of all Asian countries. You have done a great deal to help the developing countries, and have given proof to the world that you are as strong as the West. So we from Libya have come to you for help. We have no wish to be a burden to you, and we know that these things cost a lot of money. We wish to buy an atomic bomb."[2]

Zhou Enlai heard him out; always the perfect diplomat, reflecting on the practice the great master Machiavelli had stressed: "One of the great prudences men use is to abstain from menacing or injuring anyone with words." Statesmen might benefit from maintaining a discreet silence and avoiding offence unless absolutely necessary. This was one such necessity. Zhou also knew how to turn a bad thing to profit, and for this the Libyan was playing perfectly into his hands. US President Lyndon B. Johnson's administration had spelled it out in its secret Kilpatrick Report of 21 January 1965, of which Chinese Intelligence had obtained a copy:

"<u>China</u>: We believe that it will prove difficult over the long term to halt nuclear proliferation … until China has joined the society of nations and is willing to participate responsibly in arms control measures …"

That was the key phrase – and now Zhou Enlai reacted to it. "Of course we are willing to help our friends with technical assistance in many domains," Zhou replied to the Libyan's request with perfect politeness, "but on this issue, every nation must practise self-reliance." There followed a long pause, before Zhou added, this time not in Chinese but in French: *"La bombe n'est pas à vendre.* The bomb is not for sale." His refusal to sell the Chinese bomb was a political masterstroke. One little phrase – "not for sale" – removed China's rogue-nation status. It proved China's will to exercise moral restraint and it opened the way for discussions with the world's economic superpower, the United States of America. The US as well as China looked at the world from a position of realistic politics. Here was the first real chance of a rapprochement.

Imagine the surprise of Graham Steenhoven, a supervisor of personnel for a Detroit car manufacturer, and his gang of housewives, students, computer programmers and chemists, on that 14 April 1971, as they stepped off the plane in Hong Kong to find a senior official from the People's Republic of China waiting to shake their hands. Who was this American red-carpet delegation? They were the first group of US citizens permitted entry into China since the Communist takeover in 1949, and certainly the first American delegation since the Korean War. At China's invitation, they had been able to surmount a US State Department travel embargo and cross from the New Territories of Britain's Crown Colony of Hong Kong into the People's Republic of China. They were certainly the most improbable bunch of diplomats ever assembled – but behind their visit lay a genial coup, engineered by a master of diplomacy, Zhou Enlai. His opening moves on the international chessboard overshadowed Washington's steps toward some kind of normalization. The day that Zhou declared the beginning of a new chapter in Sino-American relations, in a gambit that went down in the annals as "ping-pong diplomacy", Washington had a rude awakening to the fact that a smart Chinaman had stolen their show.

The American table-tennis team, because that's what it was, 15 players and three journalists, engaged in friendly competition with their Chinese opponents in the festively decorated stadium of Tsinghua University. The Chinese won, of course – after all, they are by far the best at the game – but they also made sure to win by a score that would not embarrass their guests. After the competition the teams exchanged flags and gifts and walked hand in hand off the stage, to the wild acclamation of a selected cheering gallery of eighteen thousand – and the television cameras of the world. The next day their hosts took the US ping-pongers on a visit to the Great Wall.

On their return to Beijing, the overawed Americans were received by Premier Zhou Enlai. Their perfect host had taken a page from America's PR specialists. "You have opened a new chapter in the friendly relations between American and Chinese people," he told the ping-pong diplomats. "I am confident that this is the beginning of mutual friendship that will meet the approval of our two great nations." And to the journalists: "Why don't you ask more of your colleagues to come and have a look at our country?" before he added, smiling: "But please, not all at the same time." It came as a surprise to no one that while Zhou Enlai was entertaining the ping-pong team, the US announced plans to remove a 20-year-old trade embargo on China.

It was a truly triumphant table-tennis tour. Wherever the ping-pongers went, people stared at them with open curiosity, while local and provincial authorities put on a great show to make it obvious that the "People of China welcome the People of America". The most important message the good-will ambassadors brought back with them was what their hosts managed to get across in a subtle manner: China was a rational society, business-minded and trying to open its doors to the world – and especially to the capitalist United States of America. The message was passed on, and America listened. Never since the Olympics in ancient Greece had a sport been used so ingeniously as a tool for international diplomacy.

One not overly surprised by the invitation of a ping-pong team to China was this author. I can wake up in London, Tokyo or Vancouver and think I am still in Paris. But when I woke up in Beijing – in the spring of 1964 it was then still called Peking or Peiping – that instinct of half-awake orientation did not readily surrender itself. A peculiar contribution of most Communist regimes is to organize the din of the street to occur at the most unnatural hours. What had awakened me was the sound of the street cleaners outside my window – two women, one on each side of the street, shouting to each other. That was before the trucks went by, creaking and clanking as though about to fall apart. Our hotel – a two-storey affair which at that time was the only sleeping place for foreigners in Beijing – was located between the imposing entrance gate into the Forbidden City and the ancient city wall. Our hotel was guarded around the clock, so that no ordinary Chinese would disturb our tranquillity – or perhaps to prevent us from strolling forth on unguided forays and – God forbid – meeting Beijing's citizenry. The three months I travelled all across China became an omnipresent Big Brother affair. Few foreigners had been allowed access behind the Bamboo Curtain since Mao's revolutionaries marched triumphantly into Beijing, and certainly no Western media.

We had been invited to China to film a documentary for Canadian television. I did not see how it could be done in a country hysterical about internal security. China was not a human landscape easy for any Westerner to fade into. We were tall and blond and did not wear padded, uni-colour jackets. In fact, we looked very much like Russians, the only Westerners this generation of Chinese had ever been exposed to. In 1964 – before Mao's Cultural Revolution – travelling around China was like visiting another planet. The China we saw 40 years ago no longer exists. In those days the glory of the Celestial Empire of the Middle was all but a distant memory. There were no bright colours and no laughter. Beijing was a dark and forbidding place; in Nanjing's streets there were no cars; and in the harbour of Shanghai no big ships.

The result of our stay in China in April–June 1964 was a television documentary, *The Seven Hundred Million*. Imagine: seven hundred million. Today China's population is double that. Our film provided the outside world with a candid peek behind Mao's Bamboo Curtain. At the time we had no explanation for our surprise invitation. Wherever we went throughout the country, officials received us with extreme courtesy, though the ordinary man in the street fled on seeing us. The socialist brotherhood of China and Russia had taken a turn for the worse – and to the average Chinese we were tall and white – well, to them we were Russians. And Russians were no longer their dearly beloved comrades.

We must not claim the credit for having furthered – even in a minor way – the thaw between China and the West, even if millions viewed our film. Years later we were to discover how Zhou Enlai had planned our visit from the very beginning, and how one of us had been steered into asking permission during an initial contact with a Chinese diplomat over steamed crab in a Hong Kong restaurant. With the Soviet Union out of play, and China's industrialization stalling, Mao's man for all seasons, Zhou Enlai, put out feelers to test the mood in "hostile territory". Canada is also America without being the United States … and by 1964 China was already looking for an opening in the West!

In the footsteps of an American table-tennis squad came Henry Kissinger, another man for all seasons. He left on an "Asian fact-finding tour", his announced destination Karachi, only he never showed up in Pakistan. His press secretary informed the media that Dr Kissinger had come down with a severe case of flu – a diplomatic disease, since his plane had landed on a military airfield outside Beijing where he met with Premier Zhou Enlai to discuss a possible US presidential trip to Beijing at Chairman Mao's personal invitation. Kissinger emphasized the great need for more friendly Sino-American relations. He backed up his argument with an intelligence run-down of Soviet forces along China's borders, with special attention to nuclear weapons. Only on the sticky Taiwan issue did Old Henry remain vague, but then went on to assure Zhou Enlai that he would give neither encouragement nor support to the Taiwan Secessionist Movement.

As they shook hands, Zhou said: "These talks may now proceed."

Dr Kissinger replied: "They will."

That was in July 1971. That this meeting between the two highest officials of both China and the United States was kept a secret for six months shows how important it was to both parties. Nobody found out – certainly not the Russians! It was agreed that, shortly before the forthcoming presidential trip, China's Xinhua News Agency would release an announcement that US President Richard M. Nixon was scheduled to visit China. "My goal is to pull China back into the world community," he had previously declared.[3] On 21 February 1972 Nixon became the first US President to visit the People's Republic of China. While two nations symbolically shook hands, an American president stood next to a Chinese chairman and said to the world's cameras: "Our two peoples tonight hold the future of the world in our hands, and if we think of that future, we are dedicated to the principle that we can build a new world."

The world woke up to a *fait accompli*.

A ping-pong team's visit was the first sign of a major power shift in world politics. It stunned the world – and shocked the Kremlin. There was nothing the Soviets could do. With one brilliant stroke, two true masters in the Game of Nations, Zhou Enlai and Henry Kissinger, had deftly outmanoeuvred the Soviet leadership. For Dr Kissinger the China trip of President Nixon became his mandate's greatest triumph. In a devilishly clever manoeuvre, he had driven a solid wedge between Red China and the Soviet Union, and with it, changed the course of the Cold War.

From that moment the centre of political gravity began to shift to the Pacific basin.

# CHRONICLE: 1997:
# A DETAIL OF HISTORY

## 1 JULY 1997, BRITISH CROWN COLONY OF HONG KONG

The band was playing "Land of Hope and Glory". At the stroke of midnight huge crowds all across China stared fixedly at giant television screens, put up for the occasion in town squares, and roared their approval as the Union Flag was lowered. For once there was no particular incident, no riot and no hinge factor that set it off. Everything had been programmed and planned down to the smallest detail.

"This is a momentous and historic day. Hong Kong and China are one again," pronounced Tung Chee-hwa, the new governor-mayor of Hong Kong, as he, and countless millions, proudly watched the red flag with five yellow stars climb the flagpole.

Charles, Prince of Wales, as the personal representative of Her Majesty Queen Elizabeth II, accompanied by the last British Governor of Britain's Crown Colony, Chris Patten, boarded the Royal Yacht *Britannia* and waved a final farewell to the strains of "Rule Britannia". But Britannia no longer ruled Hong Kong. China did.

And the band played on – only now it played a different tune.

"You cannot fight against the future; time is on our side," declared W. E. Gladstone before the House of Commons in 1866. That was then, and this is now. The handover of the last colonial enclave in China signalled an end to the period of "foreign occupation". In terms of human history, it had not been all that long: a century and a bit. China was once again unified.

In Chinese terms, the *brief colonial interlude* was a thing of the past.

# ACT FIVE

## TODAY AND TOMORROW
# Young Dragon Rising

*Grief has its limits, whereas apprehension has none.*
*For we grieve only for what we know has happened,*
*But we fear all that possibly may happen.*

—Pliny the Younger (AD 62–114)

*The strength of a nation derives from its integrity at home.*

—Kung fu-tse (Confucius) (551–479 BC)

# 1

## CRUSHING LIBERTY'S CRY

### 3 JUNE 1989, TIANANMEN SQUARE, BEIJING, PEOPLE'S REPUBLIC OF CHINA

How do people remember history? And how does a totalitarian government create believable history based on facts that have, in the view of those who actually experienced that particular event, been distorted? Ask the youngsters who were in Tiananmen Square that June night in 1989.

The students' outcry against nepotism and corruption in the Chinese Communist Party had found an echo. By the early afternoon of 3 June, Tiananmen Square was packed with people. The student demonstrators were joined by tens of thousands of passers-by, and the human mass had grown steadily for several hours. A striking feature were the intense discussions between strangers, an explosion of talk by people who had been saving up for years what they had to say. They had gathered in a form of group therapy and listened to endless diatribes delivered from the makeshift podium in the square – a truly remarkable occurrence. Everyone agreed that the system was wrong: it forced a nation to stand to attention before a few whose vision of a socialist heaven was not the people's paradise. The students, the onlookers, in fact the entire country, felt that the younger generation was marching toward some sort of bloodless victory. Everyone was eager to hear the news – the good news that Deng Xiaoping would offer a positive response to their demand for democratic reform.

The jubilant mood of the demonstrators was not fully shared by all of the organizers. They had a valid reason for concern: high-ranking Party hard-liners had been intriguing against Deng Xiaoping, claiming that he was acting "too soft". Show weakness, they argued, and the masses will take over, as the historian Alexis de Tocqueville had theorized back in the nineteenth century: "It is not always by going from bad to worse that a nation is driven to revolution. It often happens that a nation which has suffered without complaint, almost as if it were insensible to the most oppressive laws, will suddenly reject them with violence at the first sign of alleviation ..."

The hard-liners forced Deng Xiaoping into action; when it came it was done with tanks. The exact number of deaths will never be known, but it was heavy, once steel cleats met up with human flesh. On the morning after that fateful night, a radio communiqué was beamed at the country: "The People's Liberation Army, together with the State Security Authority and armed workers' guards, have liquidated an attempted counter-revolutionary coup d'état during the night of 3–4 June ..."

Rebellious mass movements are mainly a violent shift to alter the daily life and potential for development of the individual citizen. This sudden emergence of public opinion – the students' demand for democratization – both angered and frightened China's Communist leaders. An already divided Party leadership was caught off guard by this extraordinary militant phenomenon that endangered the dictatorship exercised by their central apparatus. Turmoil within the Communist Party Politburo Standing Committee had paralysed decision-making for weeks. The reformists allied with General Secretary Zhao Ziyang pushed for greater openness and economic liberalization, while Deng Xiaoping had decided to allow the students enough rope to hang themselves, knowing from experience that brutal repression breeds more violence rather than stills it. The immediate effect of a crude display of strength would only unite the uncommitted behind the rebels.

The execution of Deng's policy required nerve; he hoped that the students' verbal violence and anarchistic excesses would win him back that measure of public support required to strike them down in a political but relatively bloodless act. The Party supported Deng; the military did not. Once it became clear that talks with the student leaders would not lead to any result, the orthodox faction within the Party finally triumphed. In the last days of May 1989 armoured divisions of the People's Liberation Army massed around Beijing.

For Deng, 3 June 1989 was a turning point in the mounting crisis; in the final, tense hours leading up to the climactic horror, he must have doubted if his policy of appeasing the students had been a wise one. That crucial afternoon Deng's role as China's leader faced challenges from the students and their growing following of workers, as well as from the military hard-liners who were insisting on ruthless suppression. And all that in the midst of ongoing diplomatic negotiations aimed at achieving worldwide recognition as a peace-loving member of the international community, and after the Chinese government had opened its borders to global television; and now their cameras were all pointed at Tiananmen Square.

That critical afternoon Deng Xiaoping held a council of war with members of his political apparatus in the presence of the military. He argued that it was essential to split the revolutionary student leaders from their mass following by keeping students and workers apart. The hard-liners would not hear of it; they had already decided to drown the student revolt in blood. Deng could no longer check the headlong flight of events. It was too late for a peaceful settlement of the crisis. By late afternoon it had become clear that something terrible was about to happen. Tension mounted. Reports of armoured units moving into the outskirts of Beijing sharply increased the anxiety in Tiananmen Square. Ever more workers joined the students gathered in the square and everyone was listening to speakers addressing the huge crowd from the makeshift podium next to a plaster statue of the "Goddess of Democracy".[1]

Shortly after darkness, foreigners looking out from the diplomatic compound at Jianguomenwai noticed tanks and armoured personnel carriers (APCs) advancing toward the city centre. The vehicles' markings were those of the PLA's 27th Army, commanded by the nephew of the People's Revolutionary Council President, Yang Shangkun. An urgent cable reached Washington from the US Embassy in Beijing: "The Force Option is real."

Crowds began erecting barricades by overturning buses; the first incidents took place, verbally to begin with, then with fists. To assist their hard-pressed comrades, a truck with a dozen PLA soldiers sped toward a line of people strung out across the road. Some saw it coming, others did not. The truck did not stop and two demonstrators disappeared under its wheels; another was tossed into the air and slammed against the wall of a building. A girl screamed, her face hidden in her hands in an effort to block out the horror. When she opened her eyes, a man's body sat propped up against the foot of a wall, his neck twisted and his open eyes staring after the truck that had inflicted his sudden death.

The crowd's roar rose to a hysterical pitch. The truck's windscreen was shattered, then the mob pulled out its driver and the soldiers and stamped them to death in an incident which sparked off the shooting. Demonstrators formed human barricades and attacked army trucks with sticks and stones. It was a sudden release of aggression on both sides, but only one side had the bullets. Shooting erupted on most of the arteries leading toward Tiananmen Square.

Armed units waded into the hysterical crowd, using rifle butts as truncheons to club down demonstrators, pushing bleeding victims into APCs, including some foreign journalists. Soldiers fired into the crowd with automatic weapons and truck-mounted machine-guns. "They're firing real bullets!" The students had been told that the army would use rubber bullets, but sparks flew as bullets ricocheted off cobblestones. And then came the tanks; the first pushed straight ahead, moving over the crowd and crushing 11 demonstrators under its steel cleats. Blood covered the streets as people screamed in pain, fury and terror. Teams formed on the spot, carrying the wounded off on makeshift litters or on bicycles. Others were put into rickshaws and taken to a children's hospital, where many died shortly afterward of their terrible wounds. Some had been shot in the back while trying to escape the massacre. Many wounded demonstrators were taken from first-aid stations by armed PLA units.

The morning of 4 June revealed scenes from hell. The silence of death covered Beijing like an evil-smelling blanket. Men and women moved like shadows through the streets and across the square, staring at the debris after a night of horror. The world's press was there to record it all. Streets were lined with the carcasses of burned-out trucks and buses; empty shell cases were ground into the tarmac by the tracks of tanks; blood, bandages and sandals littered the ground. Corpses of students and workers overflowed the corridors of hospitals. To cover up the growing casualty count, bodies were dumped on to army helicopters and ferried to the outlying Tongxian airfield.

It was the worst rioting Beijing had known since the civil war of 1948–9. The People's Liberation Army had shown what it understood by liberation, and demonstrated its willingness to interfere in political decisions. The Army's brutal assault paralysed the student movement and left the public traumatized and confused. For a few days in spring, the call for personal liberties had been heard by the people and misled many into believing that their moment for reformist ambitions had finally come; for a brief moment the crisis had released a torrent of energy that had almost stripped a Red Emperor of his clothes. Then the cry for freedom was snuffed out. The Communist Party's hard-liners had achieved their aim – but at a steep price.

The West was mistaken in believing that it could stand by as an uninvolved observer. A diplomatic incident was in the making. From a global perspective it was minor, but it led to grave international consequences with the "Fang Lizhi Incident". The 53-year-old astrophysicist Fang Lizhi, theologian of the student revolt, openly challenged Communist ideology by pointing clearly to the shortcoming in its dictatorial system. In the opening stage of the revolt neither Fang Lizhi nor his wife was directly involved; however, his theories, calling for democratization, served as the movement's bible. Called upon to justify his remarks, he denounced the blindness of the Communist leadership with a prophetic warning: "You must listen to the young before it is too late."

Fang Lizhi was dismissed as deputy director of China's Scientific and Technical University, and expelled from the Party. In early 1989 he addressed a letter to Deng Xiaoping in an attempt to secure the release of a political dissident called Wei Shengjing. His letter, mimeographed and circulated among university students and intellectuals, sparked off a wave of protests that quickly spread throughout China's universities. Fang Lizhi's name was put at the top of China's "most-wanted" list, with his wife's immediately below it. The "Chinese Sakharov couple" managed to slip the police dragnet and were granted political asylum inside the US Embassy, when a cowboy act by a junior PLA commander sparked off a diplomatic incident which blew up out of all proportion – and in plain view of the international press corps.

A PLA Special Forces unit screeched to a halt outside the US Embassy gate and an armoured car pointed its gun at the US Marine guards at the gate. An officer issued them with an ultimatum: hand over "the criminal couple" immediately, or face the consequences. The Americans refused the demand. When Deng Xiaoping was informed he realized the diplomatic implications, but it was already too late to put out the fire. Within minutes the story had gone out over the international press corps' satellite. Deng's only option was to issue an official warrant for Fang's arrest as an "instigator of vile propaganda", a charge that was extended to read "in the pay of a foreign power which now hides him from justice".

The US Embassy was surrounded in a move that recalled the Boxer siege of 1900. Cables flew back and forth between the US ambassador to China and the US State Department. A strongly worded message from the White House announced a package of economic and diplomatic sanctions against China, to take immediate effect – just what Deng had tried to prevent. This challenge shocked the wiser politicians, just as it hardened the posture of the military. Foreign interference in "a strictly internal affair" – even referred to as a return to the imperialism of the nineteenth century – infuriated Party hard-liners and whipped up hatred within the military. A tank unit from the 27th Army drove past the diplomatic compound and fired over the embassy's roof, causing legation personnel to dive for cover. This act raised further tensions. Together with instructions from Washington to protect the dissident couple and grant them political asylum inside the extra-territorial embassy, the Fang Lizhi Incident put a severe strain on Sino-American relationships.

With a "Chinese Sakharov" the American media had found its ace-in-the-hole story, which in turn led to anti-American outpourings in the Chinese government press.[2] A lead editorial in *Red Flag* accused "a handful of people in the United States, the meddling US media, and the US Embassy in Beijing" of telling lies and stirring up trouble. On 30 June the US President dispatched National Security Adviser Brent Scowcroft and Deputy Secretary of State Lawrence S. Eagleburger on a secret mission to "keep open the lines of communication" between the United States and China. A document published after their visit referred to the riots as "an internal affair" and stated that the US President "wants to manage short-term events in a way that will best assure a healthy relationship over time". The break was avoided.

At the inquest into the Tiananmen Square massacre, the troopers who killed the "state's enemies" were regarded as brave men who had carried out their duty. Not one of them was tried for gunning down the young men and women of their country. The Chinese press buried the truth in silence, or gave distorted accounts of arbitrary arrests, confessions and sometimes executions. The students were described as stooges of capitalism, unruly hooligans, disaffiliated vagrants and wall-taggers. Newscasts by foreign networks showed the behaviour of young Chinese who were exemplary in their courage; the young protesters had stepped through the boundaries of their self-imposed prudence only when provoked in the extreme. Testimony to this was a front-page-grabbing photograph of a young man in a white shirt with a shopping bag, bravely blocking a line of advancing tanks.

It was a Brave New World standing up to brute force. The party hacks, all in their seventies, refused to listen to the voice of a new generation. Lenin had stated that the working-class members of a revolutionary vanguard are unable to recognize and pursue their own long-term interests once they ignore the generation gap. The young had shaken the old cadres from their complacency. That this radical transformation of a country's youth was not exclusive to China was demonstrated beyond any doubt five months later, when other young men and women brought the Berlin Wall crashing down.

In one night of horror the outside world got its first glimpse of a young, awakening dragon: China's generation of tomorrow.

# 2

# "WILD AND ARROGANT PLANES"

## 1 APRIL 2001, CHINA SEA NEAR HAINAN ISLAND

"The wild and arrogant planes often jumped up and down and suddenly turned steep left and right to provoke the pilots of our side again and again with extremely dangerous actions."

Editorial in China's *Liberation Army Daily*, 24 April 2001

1 April 2001. It is 8.45 a.m. on Lingsui air base, Hainan Island, in the People's Republic of China. Pilot Lieutenant Commander Wang Wei, in flight suit, is sitting in the ready room, reading the morning's edition of *Red Flag*, when the alarm bell rings. Together with his wingman, Zhao Yu, Wang Wei sprints to his *Shenyang* F-8-II interceptor-fighter,[1] equipped with the latest (Israeli-made) Python air-to-air missiles. Moments later two sleek jets fire their afterburners and streak for the sky. Their mission: to intercept an American spy plane 110 kilometres off China's coast.

Out to sea, inside a big American turboprop, 23 electronics warfare officers sit in their compartments, oblivious to the crackle of sound in their headsets, their eyes fixed on the 12-inch-square cathode-ray tube which displays the information from an array of electronic eavesdropping equipment in the radar cones of the aircraft.

Wang Wei, 33, a squadron leader in the 8th PLA (People's Liberation Army) Naval Air Force Wing's 22nd Regiment, was a flashy jet-jockey, and no stranger to a bit of "jet hot-dogging". Only three months before, in another aerial intercept of a US observation aircraft on 24 January 2001, he flew so close to the aircraft that the American pilot could read Wang Wei's email address, which the Chinese had written on a piece of paper. A videotape showed clearly Wang Wei's F-8-II encroaching to within 20 feet of the American plane at a speed that made it difficult for the sleek jet to fly alongside the much slower US EP-3E.

Pilot Wang Wei's flight on 1 April 2001 was to be his last, for it was to spark an international incident of a kind which in former days could have ended in a shooting war.

"The struggle against hegemonism and power politics will be a prolonged and complicated struggle. It requires powerful political and national defence strength and national unity to safeguard state sovereignty and national dignity," reported the *Liberation Army Daily*.

One hundred and ten kilometres off Hainan Island, an aircraft of the "World Watchers", America's aerial eavesdropping unit, lumbered along at a leisurely 180 knots. It was a US Navy EP-3E Aries II surveillance plane from the US Fleet Air Reconnaissance Squadron #1. The EP-3E was an improvement on the venerable radar aircraft of the Cold War period (its initial version flew in 1969), but whatever modifications the airframe had gone through, the plane was still a "flying pig" to US aircrews. The only reminders of a glorious past were the coffee-cup holders; everything else was computerized. The digital readouts glowed in a multi-function display and were locked into a constellation of several Tracking and Data Relay Satellites. The big turboprop carried the latest ultra-secret anti-jam UHF communication system, ARC-187; its two radar pods could take high-resolution images 30 miles in every direction, then digitalize them and dispatch them by high-speed data links via satellite to the United States for instant analysis. Perhaps the plane's most astounding system was "spoofing" – a communication interceptor which picks up a radio transmission, alters its meaning and retransmits a changed wording in the original operator's voice.

This particular mission was under the command of US Navy Lieutenant Shane Osborne, carrying out a routine "electronic eavesdrop" of China's Coastal Defence Command. The plane's flight path was clearly in international airspace; informally China controlled the skies over the China Sea by its sheer presence of force. It was a calm flight on a calm day, and the noise of alarm bells going off would have been heard all the way to California.

Since the collapse of the Soviet Union, and despite efforts by Muslim fanatics to upset the universe, peace had broken out all over the world. There wasn't a threat on the horizon that could possible justify action by the might of the US Air Force. For Lieutenant Shane Osborne that was just as well. To him, and his crew of 23, checking consoles, automated status board monitors and all the rest of the dazzling electronic gadgets, this was just another routine mission. So all he had to do was sit back, put the ship on autopilot and slurp thin Air Force coffee.

A little over a hundred kilometres away, Pilot Wang Wei, ensconced in his sleek jet, stared straight ahead. He and his wingman were travelling close to the sea to remain out of sight of the enemy's radar. Inside Wang throbbed with the knowledge that the American plane was out there in front of him. He felt deep loathing about spies threatening his homeland, and as far as he was concerned his feelings were always right. He did not need his unit's political commissar to tell him that. As an intensely practical pilot, he laughed at the notion of some spiritual guidance. His life held two certainties: he would emulate the feats of great heroes before him, and he would die performing his duty.

The permanent readiness for something that repeatedly refused to happen never dulled the concentration of an American crew. The Chinese were known to vector fighters from their Hainan base against American observation aircraft. The American radar operator was staring at his green tube, when two red triangles appeared on the edge of his radar screen. The central processing unit computed instantly their altitude, heading, airspeed and closure rate. A bright line indicated their projected flight path. There was no doubt, the two bogeys were barrelling straight for their aircraft.

"Two unidentified aircraft at nine o'clock, 80 miles, heading this way," came his message loud and clear over the interphone.

"Verify vector," Lieutenant Osborne demanded. By now his head-up display had also locked on to the target. As he looked through the Perspex, the ocean was black and the sky above it slate-grey. Osborne searched the sky in a 90-degree scan, then traversed it again, eyes alert for visual contact.

The radar operator confirmed the contact. "Two non-identified aircraft, on interceptor course, accelerating and closing."

Pilot Wang Wei's target popped up live on his radar display; the computer gave him data to set his flight path on an interception course with his target. As the flight leader, Wang Wei put his Shenyang inter-ceptor in "attack mode". He leaned forward and lifted the Polaroid visor on his helmet for a glimpse of the American aircraft. Soon his eyes picked out a dark speck against the shimmering water; he made a slight adjust-ment at his controls to approach the US plane from its blind back. The distant speck swelled in size as he headed for it at 450 knots. Several miles behind the American plane, Wang Wei reduced power to conform in speed to his big, lumbering target. Every second decreased the distance between the planes. Three aircraft were heading for a fateful encounter.

Pilot Osborne checked his visual readout on his multi-function display. A stream of tracking figures appeared on the screen, red triangles closing fast, not trying to manoeuvre, burning up the fuel. For a moment the triangle on the screen slid back, but then he turned on power and came steadily toward the big turboprop until he flew literally in Osborne's shadow. Osborne had developed an instinct as he watched the lead F-8-II inch higher. The red triangles were almost on top of him, everything was happening fast. Osborne was still on autopilot when, behind and to the left side of the big aircraft, there appeared two silvery-white interceptors with red stars on their tail fins. The sleek lead interceptor dropped like a dart, dived down just behind the tail plane, rapidly overhauling the huge multi-engine plane, to pull up steeply in front of the spy plane's nose.

This man was playing the "Red Baron" von Richthofen, First World War dog-fighting ace, banking off, then coming around in a tight turn, until he was once again level with the EP-3E, this time flying close to the American's wing – much too close for the speed it was going. Or in the words of old, wise pilots: once is a coincidence, twice is something else. If some jet-jockey was doing aerobatics a mile high over the China Sea, Osborne didn't want to know about it; he kept his plane flying straight. There was no sense trying to test how strong this joker's nerves were. Mid-air harassment had not been uncommon during previous electronic surveillance missions, but the behaviour of this plane, playing hare-and-turtle at five hundred kilometres per hour, was plain stupid, if not lethal. The chances of two aircraft colliding were very high.

According to pilot Osborne: "We were obviously being intercepted, and one of the aircraft was approaching much closer than normal, about three to five feet off our wing. So, I was just guarding the autopilot, listening to the reports from the back end and from my other pilot, Lieutenant Patrick Honeck, who was glued to his side of the Perspex watching the aircraft's movements. One Chinese jet came out a little bit in front and its pilot was making gestures; we could all see him. He had his oxygen mask off and was waving us away and mouthing some words, but I couldn't make out what these were. His aircraft made two close approaches, with the pilot making gestures."

Still, with danger clearly at hand, the pilot of the US aircraft continued his straight flight path on autopilot, which would later serve to rebut accusations that he had veered off manually and thereby deliberately caused a mid-air collision. "His two prior join-ups were within three to five feet," said Osborne. "Lieutenant Honeck was looking out the window giving me updates as best as he could, and we knew that this was an unusual type of intercept."

Farther back in the aircraft, Lieutenant John Comerford, who was out of his seat and staring through a porthole on the left side, got the best view of the crucial moments. "I was kind of down on my haunches, looking out to the port side, the left side over-wing exit window, at the fighter as it approached, and I was closely observing the approaches he made for our plane. Suddenly I was thrown backward by the collision."

Later Osborne spoke of the encounter: "I could see him right out of our cockpit. I'm looking right in his face. 'This ain't good.' You know, we were nervous. We had autopilot. I'm just guarding the autopilot, making sure we don't make any movements into him because it was that close – you know, a couple feet from hitting us ... he'd dropped away once, then came back. The second time, I was, like, 'OK, he's going home for sure.' And then when I heard him come the third time, I had an eerie feeling. I was, like, I knew, you know, you just knew he was going to hit us because he wasn't stable. He was all over. His plane's mushy, flying that slow. You heard screams coming from the back as he came and he pitched up into us. He was flying right off our wing and got too slow and nosed up and went right into my number-one prop ..."[2]

Everything happened in milliseconds. The Chinese pilot must have realized in the last fraction of a second what was happening. He was too late. On impact the Chinese interceptor jerked forward, then spun violently to the side and out of sight. His plane fell out of the sky. "Then he shot off to the side, and we were, you know, upside down, looking up at the ocean." Inside the US aircraft the shock and vibration were felt as if they had hit the ground without the wheels down. Osborne grabbed the stick controls; they shook violently and were unresponsive. The plane was shaking violently and he could hear the wind screaming through it. The big turbo-prop's left wing dipped lower, and, though both pilots pulled with all their strength on the manual controls, nothing they did would stop the slide. The plane was going down, almost flipped on its back, going down ... down ... down ...

"Get the wing up!" What seemed an eternity later, and imperceptibly slowly, the nose began to rise and the plane righted itself. One engine was howling out of control. "Fuel cut-off, number one engine, pull!" yelled Osborne. Co-pilot Honeck reached for the black-and-yellow emergency cut-off handle, but nothing would halt the wild blades. It was hard to believe that only seconds had passed since the collision. To the crew, jammed into their seats by the accelerating G-forces, it seemed an eternity. Osborne scanned the flight instruments. Most were gone, but the airspeed seemed enough to hold the plane in the air. They still had a chance, but not for much longer.

Osborne: "It happened on his third approach; his closure rate was much too high, joining up on us at too high a closing rate, and instead of going low, he went up – and then impacted our #1 propeller, which caused a violent shaking in the aircraft. Then his nose impacted our nose, and our radar nosecone flew off. Our aircraft snap-rolled to about 130 degrees and became uncontrollable. We were going down."

Osborne went immediately to manual. "All I could think of on the impact was that he just killed us."

Lieutenant Richard Vignery added: "We all thought we weren't going to make it."

A "slowed-up" fighter jet is still considerably faster than a lumbering turboprop. Wang Wei's initial two passes went without a hitch. It was on his third approach that the drama occurred. His much faster jet entered the air turbulence created by the EP-3E's broad-bladed propeller, a phenomenon known as the Venturi effect.[3]

The Chinese pilot was no novice, so he must have been fully aware of the disabling airflow created by the broad-bladed propellers of a big turboprop. One thing is certain: he came too close. Wang Wei entered into a partial vacuum, which destabilizes anything entering into it; the triangular wing of his jet was pulled into the twisting air stream and his aircraft slewed. The propeller-wash suddenly sucked up the fighter jet's wing. Wang Wei attempted to correct the abrupt lift, without being able to correct his higher speed. Impact was now unavoidable. The sleek jet slid ahead. His vertical tailfin went straight though the high-speed propeller and was shredded. This sent the MiG spinning away to its death. In doing so, a part of his lifted wing bumped into the EP-3E's nose radar, which was ripped off and parts of it flew into the turbojet's number-three propeller.

With one propeller out of control and another damaged, the big aircraft vibrated violently and immediately rolled over at 130 degrees, turning on its back, plummeting toward the ocean. Down it plunged: one thousand … two thousand … three thousand metres, steadily increasing its falling speed, with both pilots pulling hard on their manual controls. At four thousand metres above the sea, Osborne and Honeck succeeded in levelling out the stricken plane. This violent manoeuvre, coming on top of the collision, caused severe structural damage to the airframe. A first, quick check showed that some blades of number-one propeller were torn or warped when they ripped through the vertical stabilizer of the Chinese interceptor, and that the madly spinning propeller risked shearing off at any moment and tearing a hole in the wing, which would prove fatal. All attempts to shut down the crazily spinning blades of the damaged engine failed. Increasing vibration shook the plane and made it highly unstable.

Osborne realized that they could not stay in the air much longer. Even in perfect conditions, the EP-3E was difficult to control, and this "flying pig" was nowhere near perfect flying condition. With a structurally damaged plane, one propeller out of control, another damaged and the nearest friendly airfield six hundred miles away, they were in a Mayday condition. It was decision time. They couldn't go on and they couldn't go back. They had to divert, and there was only one option: China.

"Navigator, I need a vector for the nearest airfield."

At 9.15 a.m. US Navy Lieutenant Shane Osborne put out a Mayday call, which, according to international law, allows any aircraft in peril to make an emergency landing at the nearest available airfield. Osborne ordered his navigator, LTJG Regina Kauffman, to set a course for the closest landing strip, which happened to be the airbase from where the two interceptors had taken off, Lingsui Field on Hainan Island. Only Lingsui Field was highly military and reeked of radar and secret installations of all kinds. If he put down anywhere near Hainan without permission, they would put them inside first and ask questions afterward. Short of dumping the highly sophisticated aircraft in the water and risking the lives of his crew, he had no better option.

"We have a critical situation..." Osborne really had to use his head to think of multiple ways out. In a routine flight, nobody had ever predicted this type of incident. Now he had it, and along with it, right at the top of his list of priorities, was to prevent the electronic secrets his plane carried from becoming a prize of war. It was time to shut down and take hold – and time was not what they had.

Osborne ordered: "Destroy the equipment."

The plane had just undergone an upgrade to the latest in technical sophistication, the SSI (Sensor System Improvement). The crew had less than 20 minutes in which to achieve the complete destruction of all sensitive material. Each member was assigned a specific task to wipe programs and destroy software, use high-power magnets to wipe tapes, rip out hard disks and drop them into lead-weighted bags, which were jettisoned overboard. As a last safety measure, they stashed secret codes in special containers and then blew them up with incendiary grenades. Over the next 20 minutes, while two pilots tried to keep the wounded plane in the air, 23 technicians ripped out its innards. They worked efficiently and with speed; in an emergency the feeling of helplessness often becomes so overwhelming that it threatens to shut down a person. Not this professional crew. Their many hours of drill, training and simulator sessions pulled them through the emergency.

While this hectic activity was in progress, Osborne fought the plane on to a heading for Hainan Island. An EP-3E has all the inherent gliding capacity of a brick. With power failure on two engines, and almost no way of keeping the nose up, the pilot fought the vibrating aircraft to give his people more precious transition time before he needed to accelerate to keep the airframe from stalling. Throughout the decisive moments, Lieutenant

Osborne showed a high degree of maturity, experience and skill. With the control gauges gone, he was flying the wounded plane visually. His eyes were fixed straight ahead; the aircraft appeared to be wings-level. He asked for a final report on ongoing destruction proceedings, before shutting down all but the equipment required for a crash landing. He counted on his reflexes to help him get everyone safely down. The trouble lay in the imponderables.

He had no illusion what was in store. The Chinese must be aware of what had happened in the skies over the China Sea, and expecting him. The crew strapped themselves into their seats and steeled themselves for the moment of contact – first with the ground by landing in a half-disabled aircraft, and then with the Chinese who had just lost their ace pilot. With his flap controls gone, and no airspeed indicator to check his landing speed, Osborne dropped the plane's tail and thereby increased the wings' angle of attack of the airflow, getting the speed down. Over-correcting would be as fatal as making no correction; the aircraft was in the worst possible trim for a touchdown. Osborne's eyes were glued to the view ahead; was the plane level, the nose up? Instinct had to be fought because instinct always demanded correction and instinct was wrong. And then the approach path was straight ahead, coming up quickly toward him. Flaps, throttle, landing gear, the airframe shook and rattled. Flying on two and a half coughing engines, Osborne did an excellent job in getting the shaking plane down. Those aboard heaved a massive sight of relief. As he taxied toward the buildings, US Navy Lieutenant Shane Osborne knew that his fortunate landing was only the beginning.

In an incident of this kind there are always two sides, and it was obvious that the Chinese would tell a very different story. They began by deifying their heroic pilot (inasmuch as deification was permissible in that Communist country, given the apotheosis of the defunct Chairman); they even claimed that sharks had eaten him as he plunged into the sea.

"You dedicated your body to defend our national integrity, proved yourself to be a good son of the Chinese nation and you are the pride of all Chinese people," was the official eulogy for pilot Wang Wei. A monument was erected in his honour. An account by his wingman, pilot Zhao Yu, was published in the *Liberation Army Daily*:

> I saw how the head and left wing of the US plane bumped into Wang Wei's plane. At the same time, the outside propeller of the US plane's left wing smashed his vertical tail wing into pieces. I reminded Wang Wei, "Your plane's vertical tail has been struck off. Pay attention to remain in condition, pay attention to remain in condition." Wang Wei

replied, "Roger." About 30 seconds later, I found Wang Wei's plane was rolling to the right side and plunging. The plane was out of control. Wang Wei requested to parachute. I replied, "Permission granted." Afterward, I lost contact with Wang Wei.

Chinese Air Force Lieutenant Commander Wang Wei's foreknowledge of death in action had been accurate. In dying he would become his nation's celebrated hero. As the American spy plane was plunging down, his interceptor fighter was already sinking to the ocean floor. In a shallow dive, Wingman Zhao Yu flew to within 2,500 metres of the sea and spotted parts of the wreckage, and claimed to have seen a rescue parachute "floating in the air". This report set off a huge rescue and recovery expedition in which fifty-five thousand sailors and soldiers took part, and which received full national television coverage. Wang Wei's body was never found.

The *Liberation Army Daily*:

… Wang Wei, the Chinese pilot who died in a mid-air collision by a US spy plane with Wang's fighter jet on 1 April, was posthumously awarded with the title of Guardian of Territorial Airspace and Waters.

During his mission of tracking and monitoring the US spy plane, Wang kept calm and firm to fulfil his task of safeguarding national sovereignty and dignity. Wang's relatives and comrades in arms and other people embarked on a warship, holding his portrait, and steered to the sea area off Hainan Island, where his fighter jet was crashed by the US plane. To the funeral music, Wang's wife Ruan Guoqin offered up flowers Wang himself planted during his lifetime. "Wang Wei, you may rest in peace. I will take more care of our son and educate him to become a useful person to serve the country," Ruan said.

Navy soldiers of Wang's unit expressed the will to follow Wang's heroic deeds to safeguard the country's airspace and waters.

China had its hero, while America found itself with a sophisticated spy plane, and a crew of 23, grounded in China. An aerial mishap revealed a fault line in American–Chinese relations. Something extremely serious had occurred on the other side of the globe. A "hot-dogging" jet jockey had made a zig where he should have made a zag, and the world held its breath. A hundred years before, guns had thundered over much less.

"We have legitimate complaints," was China's immediate reaction. "You have exacerbated the situation with your adventurism out there – adventurism which brought this situation on us!" Zhu Bangzao from the Chinese Foreign Ministry added: "A US surveillance plane entered Chinese airspace and landed on a Chinese air field. This is an illegal action. It is an invasion of Chinese sovereignty and Chinese airspace." America's ambassador to China, Joseph Prueher, snapped back: "The United States will not take a bunch of accusations. We were in international airspace. We were obeying the law."

Mrs Zhang Qiyue, the official Chinese Foreign Ministry spokesperson, showed reporters video footage that documented "dangerous and aggressive" flying by US pilots the year before. In a reverse of the videotapes taken by US pilots, these pictures showed US planes flying within sight of Chinese jets, at times coming within a few wingspans of one another. At one stage an American pilot was seen taking a picture from the plane's cockpit. Zhang said the tape was shot the previous year off the Chinese coast. To prove her point, the Chinese spokeswoman showed the foreign press a computer simulation of the US EP-3E spy plane turning into the path of the Chinese fighter jet, ending with double impacts. An analysis of paint scrapes and antennae breakage suffered by the US plane, she stated, "proved that the spy plane caused the collision. This evidence is just the tip of the iceberg. From this evidence, we can see clearly that the collision was caused by the US side."[4]

The "Hainan Incident" was the dreaded head-on collision after a series of near misses. It culminated in 1996, when Beijing began once more to exert military pressures on Taiwan, a client state of the USA. Washington told Beijing in no uncertain terms that they would not allow a "normalization of Taiwan by force". The chief of the Chinese military staff, General Xiong Gungkai, launched a phrase which led to a rapid cooling of relations between the two powers: "Our strategic armament has been considerably improved. Instead of protecting Taiwan, the United States should worry about Los Angeles."

In 1998, after the "liberal" Zhu Rongji had replaced Li Peng, US President Bill Clinton made his highly publicized trip to China. "Let us stop pointing nuclear missiles at each other," the leader of the Free World proposed to the leader of the Communist World. What a switch from 1992, when Clinton, during his presidential campaign, derided the red regime as "the butchers of Beijing"; now he was standing on a platform, hugging and kissing their president, Jiang Zemin. Both countries were trying for a diplomatic breakthrough. Clinton had much to lose by an empty-handed return to Washington, and Jiang Zemin was facing a similar problem from his hard-line generals. This was then, and now the situation had suddenly worsened.

"How bad is it?" asked President George W. Bush that weekend in April 2001.

"We really don't know yet," Condoleezza Rice, his National Security Adviser, told him, after working the phones to US Secretary of State Colin Powell and Joseph Prueher, America's ambassador to China. With an international incident at hand, the first diplomatic step was to put ice on the affair and try to play it down, before it turned into a crisis. It was in the interests of both nations to tone down the rhetoric. Powell had spent frustrating hours trying to reach someone senior in Beijing; it took a Central Committee decision before any Chinese official was ready to speak.

The aerial mishap was the kind of incident that the Chinese and Americans had always dreaded. For many years US and Chinese war vessels and planes had been shadowing one another, and sometimes just managed to avoid a major incident, until a day in April 2001 when the thawing relations between the two countries suffered a severe cold. From a military debacle the ball was bounced into the court of the diplomats. The timing was awful; nothing could have been more unwanted for China at a time when it was negotiating for international recognition. Was President Jiang Zemin willing to sacrifice his country's lucrative export trade with the United States, an annual dividend in the billions? Should US President Bush consider China a strategic competitor, and not a partner in trade, only two weeks after he had extended a warm welcome to Qian Qichen, China's Vice President and Foreign Minister, an act which had given a tremendous boost to the two countries' relations? This step forward was now trampled underfoot by a silly jet-cowboy act.

"It is not normal practice to play bumper cars in the air," stated the head of US Pacific Command, Admiral Dennis Blair. With two planes down, the military part in the drama was over; it was time for the diplomats to enter the arena. In Washington a tug of war began between Secretary of Defense Donald Rumsfeld and Secretary of State Colin Powell, who said: "If you think of a military solution to this, that's not the way ahead. The only way ahead is a diplomatic one."

Donald Rumsfeld favoured the hard line: "It's our air crew, they're military people."

President Bush followed Rumsfeld; he went on the air, firm but not threatening: "Our priorities are the prompt and safe return of the crew, and the return of the aircraft without further damaging or tampering."

Ever since the end of the Cold War, Sino-US strategic relations had tried to resolve their sharp differences over Taiwan, the export of nuclear and missile technologies, and human rights issues. And now there was this unfortunate plane incident which neither side could possibly wish for in an era of a possible bilateral agenda, one in which China aspired to become an alternative centre of the global power structure. Damage had been done, yet it was still possible to limit further harm. If Chinese international behaviour had long been full of mystery and fear, now, in its desire to become a potential alternative pole in any international system, it was up to Beijing to show a genuine desire to resolve this incident and put the issue behind them in the interests of stable long-term relations with the United States. President Jiang Zemin could not afford to upset Washington, just as he could ill afford to lose face over the incident with the hard-liners of Party and Army. Internally it strengthened the position of Chinese military figures, hostile toward their president's soft policy of seeking a diplomatic way out; one of Jiang's principal counter-arguments was his anxiety that America might pressure its allies to vote against Beijing's bid for the 2008 Olympics.

In both camps, dissident voices were raised; some tried to save the China–US relationship, while the hard-liners were intent on blowing it up, reverting to a Cold War syndrome. The Chinese stand became clearer in the first statements released in Beijing by its Foreign Ministry spokesman, Zhu Bangzao: "A plane of a foreign nationality has violated China's airspace, and landed without prior permission on one of our airfields. Thereby it lost its sovereign immunity. It is the right of the Chinese state to board the aircraft and discover the reason for this intrusion of our national territory." That made it plain: the Chinese were stripping the plane to its tiniest technical detail, to gain information on which of their systems was vulnerable to interception.

While discussions were going on, a call came through from Brigadier General Neal Sealock, America's military attaché to China; he had been allowed a 40-minute meeting with the captured aircrew, and although they were not allowed to discuss technical details, in spite of the watchful eyes and ears of his captors, Lieutenant Osborne had managed to slide across the fact that most of the sensitive equipment had been wiped or destroyed in time. This important news was now relayed to the President. "The plane no longer matters, it's wiped clean." This again changed the situation. With the sensitive equipment destroyed, the plane could no longer be used as a weapon for diplomatic blackmail. Bush followed up with another statement, in which one sentence in particular was calculated to make Beijing listen: "We have allowed the Chinese government time to do the right thing, but now it is time for our servicemen and women to return home." And then he applied the hammer: "This accident has the potential of undermining our hopes for a fruitful and productive relationship between our two countries."

Two opposing teams were quickly put in place. Leading the "Blue Team" (US) was Secretary of State Colin Powell, accompanied by Richard

Armitage (Powell's deputy), Joseph Prueher (US ambassador to China) and the President's security adviser, Condoleezza Rice. The "Red Team" was made up of Zhu Rongji, responsible for China's economy, Qian Qichen, Vice Premier, General Zhang Wannian, Central Military Commission member, and Zeng Qichong, the President's man behind the scenes. And of course, making decisions at every step of the negotiations: George W. Bush, President of the United States, and Jiang Zemin, President of the People's Republic of China. At stake was the ancient Chinese game of Saving Face. This fact was illustrated by a single phrase from Vice Premier Qian Qichen: "The United States must apologize to the Chinese people. This is the key to solving the problem."

China had to react strongly. In an article in its official Party newspaper, China put the blame squarely on the United States:

> Today, China produced evidence pointing to the fact that the US spy plane was the culprit in the mid-air collision, and that it was the US plane that rammed into the Chinese fighter jet and caused the crash of the Chinese jet and the loss of the Chinese pilot.
>
> Chinese Foreign Ministry Spokesperson Zhang Qiyue's accusation was based on a *computer simulation* of the US EP-3E spy plane turning into the path of the Chinese fighter jet, ending with double impacts between the two. "From this evidence, we can see clearly that the collision was caused by the US side," said the spokesperson. "US explanations that the Chinese pilot caused the crash are totally baseless and riddled with holes."

With articles like these, negotiations got off to a bad start. In the game of diplomatic Monopoly that now developed by ambassadorial representation, the question became one of what mattered more: an American crew or a sophisticated aircraft? Bush had to take a tough stand, if only to follow his hard-line policy that had won him the election, while at the same time he needed to protect the lives of American servicemen. Similarly, the ageing President Jiang had to hang in tough or it would reveal his weakening power at home, his party line challenged by an ever-hardening senior officer corps, and thereby jeopardize his own and his faction's position. The Chinese military accused him of having become too friendly with the devil himself. According to a US security adviser on Chinese affairs: "A military likes to have an enemy. And for a Chinese military, America makes for an ideal *feindbild*."

President Jiang's mind was already made up. He would allow the American crew to return, for which in any case he had no use; in return, he would hold back the aircraft, allow it to be stripped and play up to his military.

Jiang was not the only one with a problem. In America militant voices were raised. "Let's get our people home and then bomb that damn plane on the tarmac." President Bush looked for a way out, and for this he took advice. In a series of White House emergency meetings it was decided to apply diplomatic pressure, which would include the cancellation of Bush's scheduled visit to China, put into question China's status as a trading partner and, last but not least, block Beijing's bid for the 2008 Olympics.

Any measure is only valid if your opponent has been advised of the threat. It was up to America's ambassador to make this clear to Beijing. They understood. It now came down to the "time cycle". China is used to waiting a century for things to change, while America reacts to a 24-hour news beat. Someone had to come up with an acceptable solution, and that someone was Colin Powell.

"Let's send them a letter which shows regret without actually apologizing," Powell suggested to President Bush.

"I'll go along with that, but if I don't like what the letter says, it's not going out."

Powell had a note drafted, which was cleared during a meeting with Bush and Condoleezza Rice. This diplomatic note was signed not by the US President, nor by his Secretary of State, but by the US ambassador to China. Just like the signature, its text was left open to interpretation. The US government had sent a clear message to Beijing: let's get this thing over with and go on with "business as usual". The next day President Bush declared before national news editors: "China is a competitor, but that doesn't mean that we can't find areas in which we can partner. Economy is the place where we can partner." An argument that counted big: in the previous year China had shown an export surplus of $83 billion with its number-one trade partner, the USA.

On 12 April 2001 the 24 crew members of the ill-fated flight were released, and flown from Hainan aboard a chartered Continental Airlines commercial plane. One of the conditions was that the pick-up plane was not to arrive on Chinese territory before 6 a.m., since the exchange would be filmed to allow for maximum propaganda value, and for that, the Chinese needed daylight. There was a minor incident which nearly jeopardized the mission: the general flight declaration (international flight plan) was incorrectly filed as "Haikou, ROC". ROC (Republic of China) is the name for Taiwan. Everything was straightened out, and the American crew boarded the charter jet, which flew them to a hero's welcome at Hickam Airforce Base in Hawaii.

To get the damaged aircraft released took further negotiation and more delays. The Chinese used this period to conduct a thorough autopsy on the spy plane. They dismantled it, studied its secrets and then slapped it back together again. On 3 July 2001 a chartered Russian Antonov AN124, loaded with the fuselage and other salvageable parts of the stripped surveillance plane, left Hainan on its way to the EP-3E's final destination, Dobbins Airforce Base in Georgia.

In an official statement, Foreign Ministry spokeswoman Zhang Qiyue put China's position in these terms: "We have enough evidence to prove that it was the US plane that violated flight rules by suddenly veering in a wide angle at the Chinese plane in normal flight, rammed into and damaged it, resulting in the loss of the Chinese pilot." Ignoring international conventions, which clearly stipulate that a smaller, faster aircraft must stay clear of larger slower planes, Zhang continued:

> After the collision, the US spy plane intruded into China's airspace and landed at a Chinese airport without permission from the Chinese authorities. These facts are manifest and we have irrefutable evidence the US side cannot deny. The US side should realize that the release of the 24 crew members of the US reconnaissance plane by China out of humanitarian considerations does not mean the end of the case. The Chinese government and people demand that the US side bear full responsibility for the incident, give acceptable explanations to the Chinese people, stop sending spy planes on frequent reconnaissance flights off China's coast and take concrete measures to prevent the recurrence of such incident. The US side shall be held fully responsible for all consequences if it sticks to its mistake and causes further damages to Sino-US relations.

The aerial collision was never the issue. Saving face was. In the end, China ended up with a worthless apology in the form of a carefully drafted expression of regret signed by an ambassador. The regret was for a minor technical violation – having landed in China without permission – which was just short of a diplomatic equivalent of being involved in a head-on car crash and expressing regret for having had a faulty tail light. But just as in a car crash when people get hurt, it never helps to point an accusing finger.

It was on the question of national airspace that the two parties disagreed, and on which China placed emphasis. While a nation's airspace is internationally recognized, China had unilaterally extended it to 320 kilometres, a political move, as it automatically absorbed Taiwan into its national territory! However, it is also unlikely that the United States would look kindly on foreign spy planes cruising 116 kilometres off Los Angeles or New York, without taking adequate counter-measures. It was the ongoing American control of the Taiwan Strait that caused the incident. Damage had been done, but it had been limited – and that only a few months before another aerial incident brought the tallest buildings in New York crashing down, and demonstrated the dire need to protect a country's national airspace from aggression.

Nobody wanted the Hainan Incident, least of all the Chinese, and though it involved the military, there was no military solution, only a diplomatic one. Encouraged by the Republicans and fearful of appearing soft to the New Religious Right, President Bush had to take a hard stand. Internal politicking in China forced President Jiang to do the same. The incident was put to rest with a "we are sorry" note. The Americans were smiling: even in the midst of a great crisis, there is more than one way to skin a cat. On the strategic issue – a continuation of American spy flights around China – America gave nothing.

Both sides came out a head shorter. In the end, China let go of an imprisoned American aircrew – and in exchange got the vote for the 2008 Olympic Games.

# CHRONICLE: 2008:

# A GOLD MEDAL FOR GLOBAL GOODWILL

## 8 AUGUST 2008, BEIJING, PEOPLE'S REPUBLIC OF CHINA

The next battle between China and the rest of the world will take place on a groomed lawn, surrounded by many thousands in the stands, in plain view of billions around the globe. Chinese will cheer, roar, weep; they will wave flags, sing and send white doves into the blue. And when everything is over and the curtain comes down, they will hold hands with their sisters and brothers from two hundred nations, participants in this glorious, unique festival of youth.

Bigger, taller, stronger: the Beijing Olympics of 2008 are planned as a showcase for the Chinese economic miracle. Nothing is spared to ensure that national pride reaches the level of China's overtly ambitious expectations. Its window on the world will be the 2008 Beijing Olympics, certain to provide a surfeit of drama. The appeal of sports is worldwide; it is a time when the greatest stumble and fall in full view of television cameras, and provide millions of viewers with a welcome break from their daily lives. People around the globe cheer when records are broken, though in this chemically enhanced chase for Olympic gold, it is often difficult to determine a clear-cut winner.

The Olympic Games are much more than sport. They have as much to do with politics as they have with sports, and that is nothing new. Awarding the Games by a not-so-impartial International Olympic Committee is an intricate game of power politics. It has more to do with bestowing a label of prestige on a country which the committee members believe deserves it – or are lobbied into voting for by political pressure, and, sometimes, financial reward – than it has to do with the running of the Hundred Metres. And, contrary to the event in the sports arena, it is not always the fastest who wins. That is also nothing new. The Olympic vote does not award the seal of approval to a regime's political system, but to a player on the global scene. A country permitted to hoist the five-ring flag of international goodwill for an event in which the world's youth gathers in a display of universal togetherness is sure to receive a tremendous boost to its national pride.

If an arms truce and the silencing of recriminations are at the very heart of the Olympic ideal, the Chinese leaders are benefiting from it. The Beijing leadership puts everything to work to ensure that the Olympic Games will become an unprecedented success, and that nothing will spoil what they consider to be China's well-deserved international recognition. Beijing has promised that the Games will be the cleanest in Olympic history. In order to achieve that, Beijing will have to reduce its smog count, or athletes will choke in the sulphurous soup which hangs daily over the most polluted city in the world.

China will make a gargantuan effort to ensure that the world no longer looks at it as the land of panda bears and dragon pagodas, but as a nation achieving immense economic progress. For China the Games herald a Giant Leap Forward as they did for Germany 70 years ago. The Chinese leader will be well advised not to repeat Hitler's error of 1936 by showing his iron fist with a display of party flags (it can be assumed that wall posters of Chairman Mao in glorious sunrise will be pasted over with the latest model from Shanghai's booming motor industry). Yet the global legitimization that the Games bring is the same for Communist Beijing as it was for Nazi Berlin. It is the crowning benediction for a government better known for its human rights abuses than its advance toward an open, modern, democratic society. Beijing's rulers fully realize that they face a serious image problem. Until now, neither the question of human rights and religious repression nor China's inflexible stand on Tibet and Taiwan seems to have thrown the slightest shadow on what still is the greatest totalitarian dictatorship on this planet.

The 2008 Beijing Olympic Games are certain to open with a display of pyrotechnics to dazzle the billions glued to their TV screen to see the world's youth unite, hold hands and sing. That is not all the world will be watching. The experience of finding itself in the Olympian limelight will call for a rapid change in China's internal policies. The country has to temper its political tantrums and military threats. It will be forced into showing an openness it is unused to, by putting its land, its people and its political mandarins on public display. A China openly observed – and that means more than the feats in the sports arena – is better than one that cannot be watched. Everything will be exposed by a modern media-blitz, with its thousands of cameras peeking into every nook of this vast land: the whole world will listen and look on, including the people of China. The 2008 Beijing Olympics will be the biggest international spectacle ever staged on Chinese soil, the showpiece of a technological revolution on a cosmic scale. It will be a surge of implacable nationalism to replace America – not only on the medal table, but also as *the* new world power in Asia.

A nation's pride is at stake. A country has been mobilized into producing tomorrow's laurel-wreathed heroes. For this China has even created an "Olympic Glory Winning Plan", in which athletes are required to present a "patriotic front". With a long-term plan recalling that of the Soviets and their satraps, sport scouts comb the lands for suitable youngsters to be trained in one of the hundreds of specialized sports academies, where, in order to gain recognition on the international stage through winning gold at the Olympics, China has modelled its sports system on that of the country it is determined to dethrone. Nation will challenge nation, if only to confirm a country's greatness on the world's biggest stage; such a challenge will be deeply satisfying to a nation on the rise. There will be many more medals added to China's gold harvest.

Beijing, and with it all of China, will be a place under the glare of klieg lights; with the presence of the world's media it will be a test to the limit of China's ability to accept critical scrutiny. The world will be watching. Yes, the 2008 Beijing Olympics will be a revelation. The countdown has begun.

The final gold medal might well be awarded for the best demonstration of a new political openness.

# EPILOGUE

# THE DRAGON FACTOR

"We don't hope for foreign intervention – but we're not afraid of it." Prime Minister Wen Jiabao, a pragmatic and practical politician, has spelled it out: tomorrow's China aspires to become the alternative centre of the world power structure. Its newly acquired international status may significantly change the dynamics of international security and development. *"For us Chinese, the nineteenth century was one of humiliation, the twentieth century one of restoration and the twenty-first century will be that of domination."*

True enough. The China of the past is dead and buried.

In 1973 US President Richard Nixon asked the CIA to give him an idea of what China's Red Empire would look like in the future. He needed the information for talks with his Soviet guest, Leonid Brezhnev, who was visiting him at his weekend home at San Clemente, California.

"In 25 years we are really going to have trouble with the Chinese," said Nixon.

"No," replied Brezhnev, "in 10!"

Both were right. Russia had to worry in 10 years and America in 25. Henry Kissinger, architect of a Sino-American détente in the years before the demise of the Soviet Union, added prophetic words, which today belong to history. "China is our best ally! They're obsessed by a fear of a Soviet attack. But don't misunderstand me about the Chinese; they would kill us if they got the chance, and they would pick up Japan if they thought they could get away with it. But right now they are so concerned with the Russians that they'll co-operate."

The refusal by the two post-Second World War superpowers to wage total war was not due to a lack of arms. The New World Order brought about by the nuclear bombing of Japan was one in which fear was mingled with hope. As the military historian Clausewitz wrote: "Danger dominates the leader. Who could resolve on a great battle without feeling paralysed by the danger and responsibility which such a great act of decision carries in itself?" Mao shared no such fears when he said that for his political goal he was willing to *sacrifice half of mankind.* Genghis Khan is a ghost, perhaps a glorious ghost for some, but for the rest, a frightening ghost. His memory lingers on.

The twenty-first century is that of the New China, one where massive rider hordes no longer count. The formula "one man – one plane – one bomb", or, in its latest version, "one rocket – multiple warheads", has solved the problem of confronting the million-man horde. "The atom bomb is a paper tiger which the United States reactionaries use to scare people," declared Chairman Mao in August 1946. Then America had a monopoly on the decisive weapon, and with it, ultimate power. Half a century later this power is also with China. Three thousands years ago China's greatest military strategist, Sun Tse, defined the principle of attack and defence: "gather enough arms to never have to use them".

Over the past five "peaceful post-bomb decades" it has become clear that the atomic bomb is a potent deterrent, but not an arm for attack. It is a weapon with which to move beyond revolutionary rhetoric and exert political pressure. Nuclear weapons have deterred the use of other nuclear weapons; fear of the consequences is the accepted rationale: "Nobody will employ them – it's simply too horrid to imagine!" But, like the spear and the cannon, which ensured compliance with the wishes of those who had them, every deterrent was at one time wielded in rage. Beijing's ambitious military modernization programme and a burgeoning emphasis on nation-alism will create unease among peripheral countries, causing instability throughout the region. China is pursuing its goals through a complex web of initiatives aimed at expanding its international influence, especially in relation to the United States. It strives to become the dominant power in the Pacific by displacing the US, which still considers the Pacific an American lake.

China's move has implications for global governance by applying its own ground rules, like playing tic-tac-toe with a six-year-old. Under these weird circumstances, the nuclear disarmament talks between regional rogue regimes and China are a collusive cover; while proclaiming its concern for nuclear proliferation and instability in Asia, Beijing is providing advance technology to its neighbours[1] and then applying nuclear blackmail to establish a "Pacific Nuclear Crescent" with a single aim: to remove the United States – and with it, Japan – from its own sphere of political and economic influence.

For the moment, Beijing is divided into two camps: those who advocate strategic restraint and those clamouring for a maximalist option. A series of variables could tilt the balance. Party and military hard-liners believe that political pressure will eventually lead to the end of America's protection of Nationalist China (Taiwan). In July 2005, in an example of psychological warfare, General Zhu Chenghu, the head of China's National Defence Academy, made the provocative statement that "in case of an open conflict over Taiwan, any American intervention would be met with a nuclear strike by long-range ICBMs on to the landmass of the United States".[2] China's verbal sabre-rattling is not only aimed at eliminating the United States as a Pacific superpower, but also intended to intimidate Japan and send a loaded warning to Asia's other rising giant, India (China fully co-operates with Pakistan).

China is not worried about external attack. Throughout the ages China was sometimes shaken, but never ruined, by a foreign invasion. For that it is too vast. And today, as a responsible member of the existing nuclear club, it knows that the weapon of ultimate terror is "a paper tiger to frighten children", to paraphrase Chairman Mao. Its leaders are too sophisticated to resort to the weapon of ultimate terror – Zhou Enlai provided proof of this when he refused to sell a bomb to the trigger-happy Libyans. As for China's paranoid North Korean neighbour, Beijing holds the key. It will not allow a potential nuclear threat on its doorstep. Unlike some irresponsible emerging powers, trying to establish a nuclear arsenal and willing to use it in order to obtain their dubious aims, be it regional hegemony or religious supremacy, China realizes that a nuclear attack would lead to immediate retaliation, and a disastrous push of a button would result in mutually assured destruction – from which China would not emerge as winner, but certainly as a survivor, perhaps the only one, given its landmass and huge population.

There is a paradox to Beijing's atomic equation: China does not need a nuclear threat to achieve superpower status. While the United States must rely on its military arsenal to maintain its position, China will bludgeon today's industrial nations with its low-wage economy. For this to happen, it needs to grab an ever-bigger slice of the natural resource pie in cutthroat competitiveness. By 2040 the wealth produced by China will be double that of a basket of industrialized nations: America, Germany, Britain, France and Italy. It is hard to imagine that America, Russia or Japan will greet this development with equanimity. Someone will stand up and say no. And that is where the peril lies. China and the West have different attitudes toward power, military force and sovereignty – and the divide is widening.

Supremacy comes in many shapes. Some countries reach the summit of power with their military might, others by their technological advance. Yet there is a supremacy that cannot be denied: that of a land with the biggest population. The might of the masses. It is these masses that might become China's greatest problem. To escape impoverished rural communities, agricultural labour floods the mega-cities, which can no longer absorb the millions looking for work; those who do find work are pressured to work harder for less by those with power. It has turned China into one of the world's least egalitarian countries. "The worker will become an ever-cheaper commodity the more commodities he creates." Marx's *Lumpenproletariat* is daily experiencing his prophecy in China.

China's bitter chill comes from within. From Genghis Khan to the Taiping, from Chiang Kai-shek to Mao, the country was shaken to its foundation by internal civil strife. This was so a thousand years ago, as it is today. Beijing's leaders wish to prove that a breath of economic relaxation does not entail political liberalization, and that capitalism can thrive in the bosom of authoritarianism; even a non-Maoist tyranny is still a tyranny in China. The Communist regime was never designed to cope with the internal problems that it now faces – it is starting to lack ideological legitimacy and survives mainly on its bureaucratic power, backed up by guns and tanks. The Party's resistance to any kind of democratization process, its fight against "bourgeois ideology", has led to the dialectics of the "marry-me-or-I'll-kill-you" policy. Allegations of executions and disappearances, and torture to extract confessions, are rife; human-rights violations on a massive scale and state terror are still the order of the day.

But violence has its own logic; violence breeds a backlash. Any crackdown only helps to produce a new generation of dissidents. By decrying the use of state violence, young people are challenging Beijing to confront hard truths. Tiananmen Square was a valiant attempt which failed. Next time will be different. Society will respond. Some counterweight will emerge, be it in the shape of a new and powerful dissident movement, or in other guises we do not yet discern. China's Communist leaders will inevitably seek to suppress this movement brutally. But suppression will only promote its growth, all the fears notwithstanding.

Beijing must listen to an ancient Chinese proverb: "The sea carries the ship, just as easily as the sea can turn it upside down." In bygone days, whenever a dynasty became corrupt the peasants revolted and stripped their emperor of his "celestial mandate".

*Gaige kaifang.* Reform and opening! There is little doubt that reform must come because China has no feasible alternative. And although reform destabilizes, in the long run the failure to reform is even more destabilizing. Undoubtedly the Party cadres would prefer to muddle through if only they could. The slogan-shouting dinosaurs of a discredited political direction are dying out. Muddling through is not sustainable, as a young elite is coming to recognize. The former student rebels of Tiananmen Square are, or will soon be, in influential positions, working to replace the rigid political structures of the past. Young people do not like being told what to do. The individuals who succeed will be those who have the courage to take difficult decisions. Their "second revolution" has become one of the most transfixing spectacles of modern times, bursting into the light of a new century. In this situation almost nothing that has been handed down is still valid. Only one thing is certain: it is impossible to maintain a totalitarian one-party system when the economy becomes as pluralistic as China's.

A young generation is clamouring for the good things in life. For the moment the young Chinese are too preoccupied with their rush toward a form of capitalism, but a time will soon come when the call goes out for respect of human rights and basic freedoms and for the rule of law under a democratic system. They want to watch whatever there is to watch on television, they want to read a newspaper they like. Most of all, they want a society in which they have the right to play a full part, and to choose the people they want to be governed by. With world peace and the world economy directly concerned, the West cannot afford internal trouble in China. Let us hope that long before that, Beijing's leaders will help bridge the divide and create new liberties, based on the people's confidence and trust.

A New China is set to make the twenty-first century its own. To achieve its goal, the country must find its way back to the road that history, geography and manpower have dictated. China has entered the exclusive nuclear club and has sent a man into orbit. China's final aims are partly a cultural, but mostly an economic hegemony – or, in the maxim of the late Deng Xiaoping: "To get rich is glorious!" But the country's growing wealth has also brought corruption at the highest level, increased crime and a fraying social safety net with a mounting social protest. China is facing a daunting challenge from within that could easily derail its present phenomenal rise and deliver a stunning shock to the global economy.

To its domestic social problems has been added a serious health crisis (galloping AIDS and SARS epidemics being only two aspects of this): China's population suffers pulmonary ills from a steadily worsening environmental degradation. This country, with its ambition for juggernaut-like economic progress, keeps vomiting greenhouse gases into the atmosphere, fouling the air of its industrial centres and contributing to global warming. The writing is on the wall: Mother Nature does not negotiate.

Like any country in the past, if it is to complete the transition to a capitalist economy on which it has now embarked, China faces a tough choice between benefit and cost of modernity. It is a road beset with difficulties and dangers – but nothing, given time, which a dynamic New China, given democratic liberties, cannot overcome. China is rapidly emerging as *the* new supernation. So, after a thousand years of chaos and carnage, of war and rivers of blood, the age-old quest of emperors and khans may finally come true: China's undisputed domination over Asia, the Pacific and, who knows, the world.

China's view of international relations is one in which peace is, at best, a temporary state. It remains to be seen which match will ignite the powder keg. It could come from a regional conflict, most likely between China and Japan.[3] One thing is certain: the fate of future generations will be decided along the Pacific Rim, where four economic superpowers collide. One of them is the New China, a China that is no longer exactly Communist, but not non-Communist either.

The effects of China's economic expansion, leading to a direct impact on our lifestyle, are beginning to be visible (and breathable). This is bound to bring it in conflict with the present industrial powers, possibly resulting in a trade war of unimaginable proportions. Trade wars can easily lead to shooting wars – with China they always have.

A Thousand Years of Bloodshed. A legend comes to us from the dark depths of the ages; it is the story of a mystic "Kingdom of the Middle" with immense power; of societies that created, discovered, conquered and suffered, and where millions of soldiers and peasants paid with their lives. History looks back, never forward. We glance at the conflicts of the past to retrace their essential features. We must ask of the present what it is preparing for the future. China will have the power to cause instability and pain, just as it is itself prone to the same instability and pain.

The Chinese sign for "crisis" combines the characters of "danger" and "opportunity". So it has been throughout the ages: a dangerous and opportune dragon. When the monster was asleep, the world was at peace. But when it rose from its sleep, worlds collided.

"Beware the dragon! When it wakes, the world trembles."

The historic tale of a wakening dragon is not all in the past, as it is not yet in the future. The story of a New China commences today. The world has accepted the fact of uncertainty; it fears China's capabilities but not, apparently, its intentions. Yet China is a nation on which the jury is still out. We do not know the final outcome, but we shall live it each and every coming day. More than ever before, the sun rises in the East.

This story is not yet finished – nor can it ever be.

# NOTES

## Prologue: Heaven's Choice

1. Chinese proverb.
2. On 18 November 1957, while addressing a Communist audience in Moscow's Great Hall of the People.
3. Two thousand four hundred and fifty kilometres long, built by General Meng Tian between 221 and 210 BC on the orders of Emperor Chin Huang-ti.

## Act One

## 1218–1348: Thunder from the East

### 1. A Wolf's Rage

1. The name means "Ruler over the Oceans". Its origin is unknown, but it may refer to Lake Baikal.
2. East to West: Khanate of the Great Khan (China, Mongolia and East Asia), Khanate of Chaghdai (Afghanistan and Samarkand), Khanate of Il-khan (Iran, the Caliphate and Mesopotamia) and Khanate of Kipchak (Russia, Siberia and Ukraine).
3. Genghis Khan's conquests: Xia Xing Empire 1206, Northern Jin Empire 1215, Western Liao (Qidan) Empire 1221, rest of Xia Xing Empire 1226, rest of Jin Empire 1234.
4. Ibn Sina (980–1037), the great Islamic philosopher known in the West as Avicenna, was from Otrar.
5. Today's Ukraine and large parts of Byelorussia.
6. Kalka, also Kal'chik, near Berdjansk, Ukraine.

### 2. The Savage Chevauchée

1. The Second Lateran Council (1139) forbade the use of the crossbow except against infidels. As infidels inhabited the Holy Land, few crossbows were available in the European theatre of war.
2. Recent tests have shown that a Mongol arrow could penetrate a five-inch oak board at 250 yards.

3. Juvaini, a Sunni Muslim and personal chronicler of Hulagu Khan.

4. *The Annals of Friar Jan Dlugosz*, written around 1247, a few years after the events described.

5. At Waterloo, Napoleon had no idea of the whereabouts of Marshal Grouchy's army, whereas Wellington was informed hourly of the approach of his ally Marshal Blücher.

### 3. The Battle of Nations at Liegnitz

1. Contrary to film versions of knight attacks, a quick canter was about the fastest a big, heavily laden knight's steed could manage in a charge-by lance attack, while Mongol ponies performed best at full gallop.

2. *Fürst* Heinrich's mother, Queen Hedwig, ordered a Benedictine abbey to be built on the site of the battle.

3. *The Annals of Friar Jan Dlugosz*, c. 1247. Although it is easy to exaggerate manpower losses, the numbers given as per bag in Mongol campaigns are set throughout at a constant 2,500 ears. This suggests between twenty and twenty-five thousand enemy dead.

4. Napoleon's *attaque à l'outrance*: a solid, massed bayonet charge, but backed up by artillery.

5. The French never learned the lesson of Liegnitz: bad planning; and Welsh archers played the decisive role at Crécy (1356) and again at Agincourt (1415).

### 4. Last Exit to Hell

1. Common Prayers, *Litany*.
2. Today near Miscolc.

### 5. The Divine Miracle

1. A play on the Latin word *Tartarus*, meaning Hell. The word gave the name by which the Mongols became known.

2. *Viennese Pictorial Chronicle*, a fourteenth-century text which describes an attack by the Mongol horde in 1241–2.

3. *Carmen miserabile super destructionis regni Hungariae per Tartaros*, written by Roger, canon of Varad.

### 6. The Cult of Blind Terror

1. It is unclear if "beyond the Sea of Sand" meant the Gobi Desert or the Arabian Sands.
2. Juvaini.

## 8. The Turn of the Tide

1. Baibars would murder Sultan Kotuz and declare himself Sultan. At the head of a Mameluke army he rode north and began the destruction of Hulagu's khanate. In doing so, he expelled almost all the Crusaders from the Holy Land, leaving only a few coastal fortresses in their possession. With the demise of the Caliphate and the elimination of the Crusaders, Baibars the Mameluke, an agnostic by birth, became ruler of the World of Islam.
2. The Mongol yoke over Russia was still in place when King Edward III tried out his new military machine against the French at Crécy in 1346; for the English monarch there had been ample time to study and digest the lesson of the "lethal hail of arrows" used at Liegnitz, so he deployed his Welsh longbows, the impact of which was comparable to that of the Mongols' laminated bow. By contrast, the French *chevalerie* were never much interested with learning all they could from mistakes made by a knights' army in that historic battle. Crécy proved much more relevant than anything which had happened under vastly different circumstances on the battlefields of Europe in the days of the Mongol threat.
3. The story of the Divine Wind is told in the author's *The Weather Factor*, London, 2000.

### Chronicle: 1348: The Yellow Scourge
1. G. Boccaccio, *Decameron*.

## Act Two

## 1554–1911: Gunboat Diplomacy

### 1. A Fleet of Monstrous Dragons
1. Today Cheng-ho has again found his place as folk hero and is indeed deified.

### 2. Devils Knocking at the Door
1. Xiang-gang island, a settlement of a few fishermen's huts, eventually became Hong Kong.
2. Albuquerque, an incredibly successful admiral, was ill rewarded by his king. In 1515 he was recalled on a trumped-up charge of treason and died during his journey home.
3. Tomé Pires wrote *Suma Oriental* (Eastern Account).
4. The population of China was 150 million, compared with England's 5–6 million.

### 3. The Lin Zexu Memorandum

1. Malwa is a province of the Indian state of Madhya Pradesh. A derivative of opium, morphine, invented by the German chemist Sertürner, led to an even more potent drug, developed in 1898 by Bayer & Co.: heroin.
2. Ssuyu Teng and John Fairbank, *China's Response to the West*, Cambridge, Mass., 1954.
3. P. C. Kuo, *A Critical Study of the First Anglo-Chinese War*, Shanghai, 1935.

### 4. The Pearl River Grouse Shoot

1. A distant cousin of Commissioner Charles Elliot.
2. Throughout the Chinese campaigns British units were mainly armed with the 0.69-calibre smooth-bore musket of 1837 vintage; this had, under the hammer, a percussion cap which was susceptible to humidity.

### 5. Tiger Day, Tiger Hour

1. Ningbo is the twin city of Shanghai, located across the Hangzhou Bay. Construction of the longest ocean-crossing cable bridge to link the two cities is now under way.

### 6. The House of a Thousand Blossoms

1. E. Cook, *Delane of The Times*, London, 1916.

### 7. The Taiping Madness

1. The horror was repeated 80 years, almost to the day, later.

### 8. The Ever-Victorious Army

1. A. Nutting, *Gordon of Khartoum*, New York, 1966.
2. In 1940 Mao wrote: "… down to the Taiping Heavenly Kingdom, there have been many uprisings, all peasant movements of resistance, that is, peasant revolutionary wars".

### 9. A Legion's Stand

1. In the 1950s, during a meeting between US Secretary of State John Foster Dulles and Viet Minh leader Ho Chi Minh, the Secretary of State asked if Ho wanted the US to put pressure on their French allies to withdraw, and Ho reportedly replied: "You get rid of the Chinese for us, the French we take care of ourselves."
2. In today's military jargon such an attack is called a "pre-emptive strike";

its purpose is the elimination of a fighting force before it has even been tested.

3. Outdone only by the siege of Dien Bien Phu, 80 years later.
4. Engaged were: 1st Company (Moulinay), 2nd Company (de Borelli), both under Commander Cattelin (8 officers and 380 men); one company of Tirailleurs Tonkinois (2 officers and 160 men); one gunnery section (1 officer and 31 gunners); one platoon of Engineers (Sergeant Bobillot); and the river gunboat *La Mitrailleuse*; in total 611 men.
5. Today Laos, Cambodia and Vietnam.

### 10. The Big Land Grab

1. Japan would come into conflict with Russia over the Manchurian annexation less than 10 years later.
2. M. Elwin and G. W. Skinner, *The Chinese City Between Two Worlds*, Stanford, 1974.

### 11. Burn! Burn! Burn! Kill! Kill! Kill!

1. My Great Uncle Karl was killed during another war, 14 years later, while leading his regiment against the Russians who had been his country's allies during the Siege of Beijing.
2. Handwritten note from Kaiser Wilhelm II to Germany's Chancellor, Bernhard von Bülow, 21 June 1900.
3. Much of this account of the siege was told to me by my father, Lieutenant Hofstetter's nephew.
4. The Kaiser's "Hun Speech" has been quoted many times since, especially during the First World War.
5. Though proof was there, at the start of the First World War this fact was greatly overlooked.

## Act Three

## 1911–1949: A Crack of Doom

### 1. Watershed

1. Much of the following description comes from personal interviews with Long March survivors conducted by the author during his stay in China in April–June 1964.

### 3. The Rape of Nanjing

1. Even today the controversy between China and Japan over the Nanjing massacre has lost none of its intensity.

2. Statement by George Atcheson, Second Secretary at the US Embassy in Nanjing and a passsenger aboard USS *Panay*, during naval inquiries aboard USS *Augusta*, 23 December 1937.

## Act Four

## 1949–1997: The East Is Red

### 1. Caught on the Treacherous Tide

1. There was now a ROC – Republic of China (under Chiang Kai-shek), based in Taiwan – and a PRC – People's Republic of China (under Mao Zedong) with Beijing as its capital.
2. In 1958, at the height of the shelling, I was allowed on to Little Quemoy as a television correspondent, and, with the noted exception of an old missionary, I was the only non-military presence on the island.

### 2. Rehearsal for a Bigger Show

1. At the time China was only peripherally involved in Korea.
2. Dalai Lama, *My Land and My People*, New York, 1962.
3. Ibid.

### 3. A Cold *Nyet*

1. Two versions exist of what occurred at the historic meeting. The most believable is that of Shi Zhe, who took copious notes. This is his version.
2. Cited in *Mao Zedong's Manuscripts*, Beijing, 1987.
3. In MacArthur's defence it must be stated that the advance was approved by the UN – just not all the way to the Yalu.
4. See Robert Simmons, *Strained Alliance*, New York, 1975.

### 4. The East Wind Prevails over the West Wind

1. Pronouncement by Mao Zedong.
2. In June 1941 Stalin also ignored the presence of Hitler's forces along the USSR border.
3. Almond's command of X Corps ended in July 1951.

### 5. "Keep 'em dying!"

1. The account of the 23rd US Infantry Regiment's stand is from Colonel Kenneth E. Hamburger, *Leadership in the Crucible*, Texas A&M University, 2003, and interviews conducted by the author.

2. Lieutenant General Walker had been killed in a car crash.
3. In a letter to Republican Congressman Joseph Martin (Mass.), which, when made public, caused a public outcry.
4. *Outline of Future Policy on Defense*, New York, 1957.

## 6. The Nuke Option

1. It was to play a significant role in Khrushchev's pullback of the Soviet Union's missiles in Cuba. If the United States was willing to drop a bomb to defend Taiwan, how would it react about an island only 90 miles off its coast?
2. Matador missiles, carrying conventional or nuclear warheads to a distance of six hundred miles.
3. Communist China's aggression against Quemoy turned into a major issue in the debates leading up to the 1960 presidential elections between the candidates Richard M. Nixon and John F. Kennedy, in which Nixon berated Kennedy on both his soft stand on the China issue and his statement that he would refuse to use nuclear weapons.
4. Ultra Secret: Memorandum by the Joint-Chiefs of Staff to Secretary of Defense Robert McNamara, 29 April 1963.
5. At the Lop Nur salt flats, a tower-mounted fission device (U 235) of twenty thousand tons of TNT, codename "569". Contrary to intelligence, no plutonium 239 was available, and it was a uranium bomb of 1,550 kilograms.
6. Today some radical and totalitarian countries aim to obtain nuclear arms since they have no similarly effective weapon; their conventional arsenal would prove useless in the event of open conflict with a modern superpower. Should they find themselves up against the wall, or steered into action by a suicidal fanatic of a leader, they might start a surprise war. The result would be MAD: mutually assured destruction of both sides.

## 8. The Davydov Query

1. G. Chang, "JFK, China, and the Bomb", *Journals of American History*, March 1988.
2. US Department of State, Central Foreign Policy Files, 1964–1966, US National Archives.
3. From 1962 to 1964 the Policy Planning Council's Robert H. Johnson conducted studies on China's nuclear capability.
4. According to a report by William Burr, analyst at the National Security Archive, in "Sino-American Relations, 1969: Sino-Soviet Border Conflict and Steps Toward Rapprochement".

5. GRU: *Glavnoye Razvedovatel'noye Upravlenie*, or Military Intelligence.
6. Ultra Secret: US State Department Memorandum of Conversation, "US Reaction to Soviet Destruction of CPR Nuclear Capability; Significance of Latest Sino-Soviet Border Clash", 18 August 1969, National Archives, SN 67-69, Def.12 ChiCom.
7. Such a take-out operation was tactically feasible, as the Israeli Air Force demonstrated when its planes destroyed Iraq's nuclear facilities in a single raid in 1981.
8. All memory of Lin Biao was erased from the collective memory, and a once-famous poster of him waving Mao's "Little Red Book" toward a rising sun has now become an item of great rarity in China.
9. Very much like Stalin's Tuchachevski purge.

### 9. Breaking the Impasse

1. Mohamed Heikal, in *The Road to Ramadan*, New York, 1975, confirms · Jalloud's trip to Beijing.
2. Ibid.
3. In an article published in 1967 in the influential journal *Foreign Affairs*.

### Act Five

### Today and Tomorrow: Young Dragon Rising

### 1. Crushing Liberty's Cry

1. A bronze copy of this goddess has been sponsored by the big Chinese community of Vancouver, Canada, and stands in the grounds of the University of British Columbia.
2. In June 1990 Fang Lizhi was given official permission to leave China. Today the couple live in the United States.

### 2. "Wild and arrogant planes"

1. NATO designation: the "Finback"; a Chinese copy of the old Soviet MiG-21.
2. Public Broadcasting System (PBS), 18 October 2001.
3. Giovanni Battista Venturi (1746–1822), Italian physicist, demonstrated the effect of turbulence when a liquid is forced through a narrowing passage, best visually observed in the wake created by a ship's propeller. It produces a partial vacuum, which destabilizes anything entering into it. The same effect happens in the air, but much amplified owing to the speed of a fast-rotating propeller. This leads to sudden changes in air

velocity, where "pitting" occurs, which collapses the straight airflow into a tubular cone. Carburettors use the Venturi effect to suck gasoline into an engine's intake air stream, and it demonstrates how a wing generates lift to allow an airplane to fly.

4. *China Daily*, Hong Kong edition.

## Epilogue: The Dragon Factor

1. Much trade is done on a triangular basis: China to Pakistan and Pakistan to North Korea.
2. China has a missile capacity both conventional and nuclear. At present it produces annually 75–100 nuclear warheads. For its short-range target (Taiwan), China has both conventional and nuclear-tipped DF 11 (700 km) and DF 15 (1,200 km) short-range missiles. Medium-range cruise missiles (GLCM and LACM) and ship-borne SS-N-27B missiles are aimed mainly at the US 7th Fleet. China has considerably increased its submarine fleet and currently deploys the Han-class 404 SSN, a nuclear attack submarine of 5,500 tons; the Xia-class nuclear missile submarine of 6,500 tons, armed with several CSS-NX-4 missiles, with three or four MIRV at 90 kilotons each (8,000 km); a new type of Kilo-class attack submarines of 3,730 tons; and the new Song class of 2,250 tons. Kilo and Song are torpedo-armed. China will increase its submarine fleet to 85 units by 2010. (The US has 35 Pacific submarines of the most modern type, able to outgun any that China deploys at present.) These submarines, together with a sophisticated network of satellites (Shezhou), surveillance and submarine-killer aircraft, will make China by 2020 the Pacific's superior naval power. Under construction are a number of destroyers similar to those of the Russian Navy's Sovremenny class, capable of firing nuclear-tipped SS-N-22 cruise missiles.

China trains and equips a large force of rapid intervention and invasion troops, based on the US Marines of the Second World War. Annual invasion manoeuvres are held on the island of Jiaodong. China develops electronic viruses to inject into the enemy's intelligence and information network. It is working on a laser gun to blind an enemy's spy satellites, and microwave ray-gun technology. At present it could harm America's satellites only with nuclear missiles, which would certainly pose incalculable risks. Many of the four thousand planes of China's Air Force (PLAAF) are obsolete and soon to be phased out. With the exception of some fourth-generation Russian fighter aircraft, 150 SU-27, 50 SU-30 and its own J-10 advance fighter, it cannot keep up with the West's modern fighter technology. In technical co-operation with Israel, China has developed its F-10 fighter, plus a sophisticated airborne missile system. Russia has provided it with a number of Airborne Early Warning planes (IL-76). The United States is directly concerned about China's new rocket arm, the long-range DF 31 (7,250 km), and its latest version, the DF 31 A (11,270 km) rocket, which could prove invulnerable to the US space defence system. In space rocketry China has launched a dozen military spy satellites. But then, of course, "Beware of a fire-breathing dragon with a bite." For that China might fall back on its ancient, magic wonder-weapon, the *shashojian.*

3. Japan is in a phase of a historic revisionism which recalls that of the European great powers in 1914.

# ACKNOWLEDGEMENTS

An author describing real events does not work in a vacuum. His analysis of events that have led to great drama builds on works that have come before him, describing the incident, sometimes vague or distorted (to please a king), but often in great detail. Therefore I am grateful to the ancient scribes whose efforts provided a valuable foundation and inspiration.

My fascination with China goes back to 1959, when I was allowed to report from one of the shelled "offshore islands", Little Quemoy, and then was granted an interview with Generalissimo Chiang Kai-shek. My interest was furthered by a surprise invitation to visit the People's Republic in 1964 – at the height of the Soviet–Chinese split, and before Mao's Cultural Revolution. During my 10 years in the Vietnam War I was exposed to Chinese literature and history. In 1985 I was invited to the "Kingdom in Isolation", North Korea, where I received a guided tour and spoke with former army commanders who had served in the Korean War. My research for this book has led me around the world, from Warsaw and Vienna to Baghdad, from Tokyo to Seoul and Pyongyang, from Moscow to Beijing and Washington. I walked battlefields to get a feeling of hooves thundering from the East and guns from the West.

It would take a book in itself to list all those who helped provide me with information and generously offered their time. Publishers granted me permission to use excerpts from my previous works and archival researchers pointed me to the right page in the right book. Some of the more recent information on the future of nuclear response came from my "old boys' network". I thank them all. Special thanks go to Colonel Kenneth Hamburger, US Army (ret.), commander of artillery along the Demilitarized Zone in Korea, and Professor of History at the US Military Academy, West Point, whose assistance was invaluable.

As the result of all the advice and help offered, the manuscript was much improved, but I am entirely responsible for omissions and errors that remain.

E. D., Domaine de Valensole, France, autumn 2007

# BIBLIOGRAPHY

From the many works consulted, some selected reading, arranged by subject headings:

## Mongols

Much of this part comes from a Chinese manuscript, *Yüan chao pi-shi*, written around 1240 and translated by the German explorer Erich Haenisch (Leipzig 1937) as *Die Geheime Geschichte der Mongolen* (The Secret History of the Mongols).

An important Chinese source is Yüan-shi, *Die Geschichte der Yüan*, chapter "Cingis Han", trans. F. E. A. Krause (Heidelberg 1922); also important is Sheng-wu Quizeng-lu, *Die Aufzeichnungen der von den weisen und kriegerischen Kaiser persönlich geführten Kriegszuge*, written by the stepson of Genghis Khan partly during the latter's lifetime.

Ala ad-Din Ata Malik Juvaini (Muslim/Hebrew source), 1260; trans. J. A. Boyle as *The History of the World Conqueror* (Manchester 1958)

Rachid ad-Din, a Hebrew-Iranian scholar; trans. Franz von Erdmann as *Temudschin der Unerschütterliche* (Leipzig 1862)

*Viennese Pictorial Chronicle*, fourteenth century.

*Carmen miserabile super destructionis regni Hungariae per Tartaros*, Roger, canon of Varad

Archives of Chinese and Japanese Cultural Institutes, Paris

Ballard, G. A., *Influence of the Sea on the Political History of Japan*, London, 1921

Barthold, W., *Turkestan down to the Mongol Invasion*, London, 1928

Burman, E., *The Assassins – Holy Killers of Islam*

Carpini, Giovanni DiPlano, *Geschichte der Mongolen und Reiseberichte 1245–1247*; trans. Friedrich Risch, Leipzig, 1930

Donat, Richard von, *Militärische Aspekte der Schlacht von Wahlstatt: Schlesisches und mongolisches Heer im Vergleich*, in *Wahlstatt 1241*, Würzburg, 1991

Dupuy & Dupuy, *Encyclopedia of Military History* (2nd edn.), New York, 1985

Göckenjahn und Sweeney, *Der Mongolensturm: Berichte von Augenzeugen und Zeitgenossen, 1235–1250*, in *Ungarns Geschichtsschreiber 3*, Graz, 1985

Grousset, R., *L'Empire Mongol*, Paris, 1941

Grousset, R., *L'Empire des Steppes*, Paris, 1948

Jahn, K., *Die Chinageschichte des Rasid ad-Din*, Vienna, 1971

Julianus, *Drei Texte zur Geschichte der Ungarn und Mongolen: Die Missionsreisen des fr. Julian OP ins Uralgebiet (1234/5) und nach Rußland (1237) und der Bericht des Erzbischofs Peter über die Tartaren*, ed. Heinrich Dörrie, in *Nachrichten der Gesellschaft der Wissenschaften Göttingen*, 6, Göttingen, 1956

Kodanasha Encyclopedia, *The Mongol Invasion*, Tokyo, 1983

Lamb, Harold, *Genghis Khan, The Emperor of All Men*, McBride and Co., 1927

Lewis, B., *The Assassins*, 1967

Moule, A., and Pelliot, P., *Marco Polo, Description of the World*, London, 1938

Neumann, J., *The Mongol Invasion of Japan*, American Meteorological Society, 1975

Ratchevsky, P., *Un code des Yüan*, Paris, 1937

Rogers, Greg S., "An Examination of Historians' Explanations for the Mongol Withdrawal from East Central Europe", in *East European Quarterly* 30 (1996).

Rubruk, W., *Der Bericht des Franziskaners Wilhelm von Rubruk über seine Reise in das Innere Asiens in den Jahren 1253–1255.* trans. Hermann Herbst, Leipzig, 1925 (also available in English: Rockhill, William Woodville, *The journey of William of Rubruck to the eastern parts of the world, 1253–55, as narrated by himself, with two accounts of the earlier journey of John of Pian de Carpine*, trans. London, 1900)

Schmilewski, Ulrich, *Wahlstatt 1241: Beiträge zur Mongolenschlacht bei Liegnitz und zu ihren Nachwirkungen*, Würzburg, 1991

Schmieder, Felicitas, *Der Einfall der Mongolen nach Polen und Schlesien – Schreckensmeldungen, Hilferufe und die Reaktionen des Westens*, Sigmaringen, 1997

Spuler, B., *Die Mongolen in Iran. Politik, Verwaltung und Kultur der Ilchanzeit 1220–1350*, Berlin, 1968

Strakosch-Grassmann, Gustav, *Der Einfall der Mongolen in Mitteleuropa in den Jahren 1241 und 1242*, Innsbruck, 1893

Wladimirzow, B., *The Life of Jinghiz Khan*, London, 1930

Yamada Nakaba, *Ghenko – The Mongol Invasion of Japan*

Yule, H., *Cathay and the Way Thither*, London, 1913

## Great Plague

Boccaccio, G., *Decameron*
Bryant, A., *The Age of Chivalry*, London, 1969
Coulton, G. G., *The Black Death*, London, 1929
Hedin, Sven, *Transhimalaja*, Leipzig, 1909

## Dragon Fleet

Duyvendak, J., *China's Discovery of Africa*, London, 1949
Levathes, Louise, *When China Ruled the Seas*, New York, 1994
Wang Xiaoqiu, Professor of Chinese History, Beijing University
Wiethoff, B., *Die Chinesische Seeverbotspolitik (1368–1567) ...*, Hamburg, 1963

## Opium Wars

Chang, Hsin-pao, *Commissioner Lin and the Opium War*, Cambridge, Mass., 1964
Clowes, W. L., *The Royal Navy: a History from the Earliest Times to the Death of Queen Victoria*, 1903
Cook, E., *Delane of The Times*, London, 1916
Fairbank, J. K., *Synarchy under the Treaties*, Chicago, 1957
Greenberg, M., *British Trade and the Opening of China 1800–42*, Cambridge, 1951
Kuo, P. C., *A Critical Study of the First Anglo-Chinese War*, first pub. Shanghai 1935; reprint 1970
Polachek, J. M., *The Inner Opium War*, Cambridge, Mass., 1992
Ssuyu Teng, and Fairbank, John, *China's Response to the West*, Cambridge, Mass., 1954
Torr, D., *Marx on China 1853–1860*, London, 1968

## Taiping

Michael, F., and Chang, Chung-li, *The Taiping Rebellion: History and Documents*, Seattle, 1971
Morse, H. B., *International Relations of the Chinese Empire*, London, 1910
Nutting, A., *Gordon of Khartoum*, New York, 1966
Shih, V. Y., *The Taiping Ideology*, Seattle, 1967
Waley, A., *Opium War through Chinese Eyes*, London, 1958

## The French in Asia

Archives of the Museum of the Foreign Legion, Aubagne, France
Kim, Kei-huk, *The Last Phase of the East Asian World Order, 1860–1882*, Berkeley, 1980
Lee, R., *France and the Exploitation of China*, Oxford, 1989

## Boxers

Buck, D. D., *Recent Chinese Studies of the Boxer Movement*, New York, 1987

Elwin, Mark, and Skinner, G. William, *The Chinese City Between Two Worlds*, Stanford, 1974

Esherick, J. W., *The Origins of the Boxer Uprising*, Berkeley, 1987

Feuerwerker, A., *China's Early Industrialization*, Cambridge, Mass., 1958

Harrison, J. P., *The Communists and Chinese Peasant Rebellions*, London, 1970

Lutz, J., *Christian Mission in China*, Boston, 1965

Miner, L., *Two Heroes of Cathay*, New York, 1907

Murphy, R., *The Treaty Ports and China's Modernization: What Went Wrong?*, Ann Arbor, 1970

Penzler, J., *Die Reden Kaiser Wilhelms II*, Leipzig, 1896–1900

## Revolution

Esherick, J. W., *Reform and Revolution in China*, Berkeley, 1976

Fung, E., *The Military Dimensions of the Chinese Revolution*, Canberra, 1980

Schiffrin, H., *Sun Yat-sen and the Origins of the Chinese Revolution*, Berkeley, 1970

Wright, M. C., *China in Revolution: The First Phase 1910–1913*, New Haven, 1973

## Civil War

Barlow, M., *Mao Tse Tung*, Paris, 1975

Han Suyin, *Le Siècle de Zhou Enlai*, Paris, 1993

Kennedy, M. D, *A Short History of Communism in Asia*, London, 1957

Lötveit, T., *Chinese Communism 1931–1934*, Copenhagen, 1978

Sheridan, J. E., *China in Disintegration, 1912–1949*, New York, 1975

Snow, E., *Red Star over China*, London, 1937

Wilson, D., *The Long March*, New York, 1971

## Nanjing and USS *Panay*

Boyle, J. H., *China and Japan at War, 1937–1945*, Stanford, 1972

Jones F. C., *Japan's New Order in Asia: Its Rise and Fall, 1937–1945*, London, 1954

Morison, S. E., "History of US Naval Operations in World War II"

Okumiya, Commander, *How the Panay Was Sunk*, US Naval Institute, June 1953

Wilson, Dr Robert, *Diary*, Yale University Library

Xu Zhigeng, *Le Massacre de Nankin*, Ed. Littérature Chinoise, Beijing, 1995

Contemporary articles: *Chicago Daily News, New York Times* (Hallet Abend), *Manchester Guardian* etc.

Excerpts from the Military Tribunal, statements by Professor M. S. Bates and Lewis Smythe

USS *Panay* Court of Inquiry report, printed in *Foreign Relations, Japan 1931–1941*

**Second World War**

Arnold, H. A. P., *Report to the Secretary of War*, Washington DC, 1945

Belden, J., *Retreat with Stilwell*, New York, 1943

Feis, H., *The Road to Pearl Harbor*, Princeton, 1950

Liu, F. F., *A Military History of Modern China, 1924–1949*, Princeton, 1956

White, T. H., *The Stilwell Papers*, New York, 1948

Romanus, C. F., and Sunderland, R., *Stilwell's Command Problems*, Washington DC, 1956

Romanus, C. F., and Sunderland, R., *Time Runs out in CBI*, Washington DC, 1959

Russell, Edward Frederick Langley (Lord Russell of Liverpool), *The Knights of Bushido*, New York, 1958

**Manchuria**

Record of Marshall's Mission to China, Wilmington, 1987

Beal, J. R., *Marshall in China*, New York, 1970

**Tibet**

Dalai Lama, *My Land and My People*, New York, 1962

**Korea**

Interviews with war veterans during the author's trips to South and North Korea and China

Chen Jian, *China's Road to the Korean War*, New York, 1994

Fehrenbach, F. G., *This Kind of War: A Study in Unpreparedness*, New York, 1963

Gitting, J., *The Role of the Chinese Army*, New York, 1967

Gray, G., *The Warriors: Reflections of Men in Battle*, New York, 1967

Hamburger, Colonel K. E, *Leadership in the Crucible*, Texas A&M University, 2003

Han Suyin, *Le Siècle de Zhou Enlai*, Paris, 1993

Hastings, M., *The Korean War*, London, 1987

Mao Zedong, *Manuscripts since the Founding of the People's Republic*, Beijing, 1987

Schram, Stuart, *Mao Tse-tung Unrehearsed: Talks and Letters*, Harmondsworth, 1974

Simmons, R., *Strained Alliance*, New York, 1975

Stueck, W., *The Korean War*, Princeton, 1995

Wingrove, P., *Mao's Conversations with the Soviet Ambassador, 1953–55*, Washington DC, 2002

Xue Litai, *Uncertain Partners: Stalin, Mao, and the Korean War*, Stanford, 1993

### Ussuri

Burr, W., in "Sino-American Relations, 1969: Sino-Soviet Border Conflict and Steps Toward Rapprochement", National Security Archive

Gitting, J., *Survey of the Sino-Soviet Dispute*, London, 1968

Han Suyin, *Le Siècle de Zhou Enlai*, Paris, 1993

Whiting, A., "The Sino-Soviet Split", in Roderick MacFarquhar and John K. Fairbank (eds.), *The Cambridge History of China*, vol. 14, New York, 1987

Ultra Secret: US State Department Memorandum of Conversation, "US Reaction to Soviet Destruction of CPR Nuclear Capability; Significance of Latest Sino-Soviet Border Clash," 18 August 1969

US National Archives, Nixon Presidential Material project

US State Department, Bureau of Intelligence and Research, "USSR/China"

Central Intelligence Agency, Direction of Intelligence, Top Secret Umbra

### Bomb Sale

The author's interviews with Mohamed Heikal, Golda Meir and General Pierre Gallois.

Heikal, Mohamed, *The Road to Ramadan*, New York, 1975

### Tiananmen Square Massacre

Contemporary articles in *China Morning News, Hong Kong Standard, New York Times*. Strategic Studies Institute. The author's interviews with survivors shortly after the events.

Scobell, A., and Wortzel, L., *Decisionmaking under Stress*, SSI 2005

### Final Chapters

Much of the material used here comes from the author's one-on-one interviews with sources involved in the affairs, or from eyewitness accounts.

Contemporary magazines and periodicals (*Politique Internationale*). Access to US National Archives and declassified National Intelligence Estimates. The US National Security Archive.

Becker, J., *Hungry Ghosts: China's Secret Famine*, London, 1996

Fairbank, J. K., *The Great Chinese Revolution: 1800–1985*, New York, 1986

Friedman, E., Pickowitz, P. G., Selden, M., and Johnson, K. A., *Chinese Village, Socialist State*, New Haven, 1991

Gallois, P. M., *L'Heure Fatale de l'Occident*, Lausanne, 2004

Garthoff, R., *Detente and Confrontation: American–Soviet Relations from Nixon to Reagan*, Washington DC, 1994

Han Suyin, *Le Siècle de Zhou Enlai*, Paris, 1993

Kissinger, H. A., *Years of Decision*, Boston, 1982

Zumwalt, E. R., *On Watch*, New York, 1976

Historical dates from Dupuy & Dupuy, *The Encyclopedia of Military History*, New York, 1986

# INDEX